THE QUOTABLE
FOUNDING FATHERS

*A Treasury of 2,500 Wise and Witty
Quotations from the Men and Women
Who Created America*

Also by Buckner F. Melton, Jr.:

Aaron Burr: The Rise and Fall of an American Politician

A Hanging Offense: The Strange Affair of the Warship Somers

Aaron Burr: Conspiracy to Treason

The First Impeachment: The Constitution's Framers and the Case of Senator William Blount

THE QUOTABLE
FOUNDING FATHERS

*A Treasury of 2,500 Wise and Witty
Quotations from the Men and Women
Who Created America*

Edited by
Buckner F. Melton, Jr.

Research Assistant
Jane Garry

POTOMAC BOOKS, INC.
Washington, D.C.

Editorial Administration and Design by Ron Formica

Library of Congress Cataloging-in-Publication Data

The quotable founding fathers: a treasury of 2,500 wise and witty
quotations from the men and women who created America / edited by Buckner F. Melton, Jr.
    p.   cm.
    Includes index.
    ISBN 1-57488-609-6 (cloth)
    1. Statesmen—United States—Quotations.   2. Presidents—United States—Quotations.
    3. United States—Politics and government—Philosophy—Quotations, maxims, etc.
    4. United States—Politics and government—1775–1783—Quotations, maxims, etc.
    5. United States—Politics and government—1783–1865—Quotations, maxims, etc.
    6. National characteristics, American—Quotations, maxims, etc.
    7. Social values—United States—Quotations, maxims, etc.
    8. Quotations, American.
    I Melton, Buckner F.   II Title.

E302.5.Q68   2004
973.3'092'2—dc22   2003021720

ISBN 1–57488–829–3 (paper)
Printed in the United States of America on acid-free paper that meets the
American National Standards Institute Z39–48 Standard.

Potomac Books, Inc.
22841 Quicksilver Drive
Dulles, Virginia 20166

First Edition

10   9   8   7   6   5   4   3   2   1

CONTENTS

INTRODUCTION

A book of quotations is a distillation of some of the most powerful words and ideas from the sea of language that rises with each passing year. If those quotations are from an age of particularly eloquent words and fertile thoughts, such as the time of America's founding, then the book is all the more potent. *The Quotable Founding Fathers* is just such a book.

It was in 1818 that John Adams, one of the greatest of the American Founders, made one of the greatest of his many observations on the creation of the United States. "The Revolution was effected before the War commenced," he wrote of the 1760s and 1770s. "The Revolution was in the minds and hearts of the people; a change in their religious sentiments of their duties and obligations. ... This radical change in the principles, opinions, sentiments, and affections of the people, was the real American Revolution."[1]

Adams was well-read in history, law, political philosophy, and the writings of the moderns and the classical world. He sensed that the essence of what it means to be human lay not in action but in idea. Thought and will gave meaning to acts, setting persons apart from the rest of creation, for better or worse. An individual is most truly revealed, then, in the telltales of his thought—that is, in his written and spoken words. By the same token, the words of a generation are how we best know the history of an era.

Adams, of course, was not alone in his outlook. Many philosophers since classical times have held the same idea of human nature; for the ancients of Cicero's day, the better a person's rhetoric and command of language, the more human he was. And a century after Adams, a very different sort of revolutionary would twist the concept to his own purposes. "Ideas," V. I. Lenin is supposed to have declared in 1920, "are much more fatal things than guns."[2]

But the rebellion of Lenin was vastly different from the one in which John Adams joined. More than one scholar, in fact, has asked whether the American Revolution was a revolution at all. It was led by lawyers, merchants, and property-owners—groups that tend to have a stake in social and political stability—and those Americans who held power before the Revolution were, by and large, still in power afterwards. The new state and federal governments the Founders established, moreover, enshrined traditional English liberties, some of which dated back to the time of the Magna Carta. In these respects, the Founders seem to have been acting to preserve a way of life against new, imperialistic British encroachments on old colonial freedoms, rather than establishing a new political or social order.[3]

Yet Adams was certain that a revolution had happened. And the changes that took place in the "minds and hearts of the people" did give rise to new and different economic and political systems. Even while waging the Revolution and the war that secured it, the founding generation began to build a society that departed from what had gone before. What Thomas Jefferson wrote in the Declaration of Independence about human rights and equality and the purpose of government was nothing new; he was, after all, borrowing from English thinkers such as John Locke.[4] The Declaration's novelty was that it ensconced these values as a more or less official cornerstone of a nation's way of life, a basic creed of a secular American religion.

There were other novelties as well. New state constitutions came into being, each of which, unlike the British constitution, was a document written down at a set place and time. These American constitutions established experimental new systems, including, in one instance, a fourth branch of government—a council of censors—to serve as a people's watchdog over the other three branches.[5] The federal Constitution, too, held innovations. Among other things, it required states to respect the obligation of contracts, a new concept better suited to Adam Smith's age than to that of feudal England where land, not commerce, was the basis of wealth. The upper house of Congress, in a break with English tradition and with a bow to the ancient Roman Republic, was named the Senate. Even well-established concepts inherited from the English system, ideas such as impeachment and treason, now had new and sometimes fundamentally different characters than they had had in the British Constitution.[6]

The changes, the building of the new order, did not stop with the end of the War of Independence or with the writing of the new constitutions. In the decades after Yorktown and the Philadelphia Convention, the founding generation did a great deal of work and faced many problems. The challenges were not merely constitutional, but political, military, economic, diplomatic, cultural, and social. What should be the relationship of the newly emergent political parties of the 1790s to American constitutional government? How should the American national debt be handled? Did a standing army have a proper place in a peacetime republic? Did that republic need a navy to engage in overseas commerce with far more powerful nations? What side should the country take if those nations went to war against each other? Should it take sides at all? By what means could it remain neutral if it desired to do so? Whose interests were paramount at home—merchants or farmers, Easterners or Westerners? If the Jeffersonian manifesto was true and not mere rhetoric—if all men really are created equal—then how could those words be reconciled with the existence of slavery and other forms of gross inequality within the new nation? If legal slavery was a moral evil, did that mean the law itself was immoral? Did that, in turn, mean that morality should have a role in the making of laws and in public discourse? If so, what was the source of moral tenets—revealed religion, human reason, or both?

At times the issues must have seemed endless, yet again and again the remarkable generation of the late eighteenth century rose to meet the challenges. The Founders were aware that they were indeed in the process of creating something new, even as they borrowed heavily from tradition and history. The borrowings, of course, were consciously selective and deliberate, but they were also deliberative. They usually came after intense debate and reflection, carried out in private correspondence, speeches in legislative assemblies and even courtrooms, and, of course, in the pages of hundreds of newspapers and pamphlets. The influence of the latter was truly profound: writings such as Thomas Paine's *Common Sense* and George Washington's Farewell Address had massive impacts in shaping public opinion and America's understanding of itself and its destiny. And the words that the Founders used to express themselves, whether in public pamphlet or private diary, contained the essence of what lay in their "minds and hearts." Because of this crucial fact, in reading their words today, we can see into the very core of the Revolution and the nation-building that followed.

The Founders drew heavily on two separate traditions. One was the Protestant culture established on American shores by various sects, especially the Puritans; the other was the Enlightenment, the new faith in human reason that Europe spawned during the age of American colonization.[7] While the two heritages were at odds with each other in some ways, they were in agreement in others, as was the case when it came to literacy. The Protestant ideas of *sola scriptora* and the priesthood of all believers made a reading knowledge of sacred scripture essential for each Christian, while the virtue of reason required an ability to read and reflect on the writings of thinkers ranging from the ancients to the latest *philosophes*.[8]

America, as a result, was a land of readers and writers. "Americans were literate," observe two noted historians. "A greater percentage of citizens could read and write than was true of any other nation on earth. ... Nearly four times as many newspapers were published in the United States as were published in France, though France had six times as many people and was possibly the most literate nation on the European Continent."[9]

And the literacy encompassed more than English. In 1786 Isaiah Thomas, printer of a weekly newspaper in Worcester, Massachusetts, called the *Massachusetts Spy*, was seeking ways to amuse his readers in the absence of pressing news. (There had been some controversy over Alexander Pope's translation of the *Iliad*— Samuel Johnson is said to have quipped, "It is beautiful, sir, but is it Homer?"— and Thomas gave his readers the opportunity to decide for themselves by printing Pope's translation and the original Greek in parallel columns.[10])

Oratory, too, was important. Legislatures were places for persuasion as well as for the considered exchange of ideas, and the arts of rhetoric were very much in vogue. And when the Founders were separated by distance, still the dialogue flowed in torrents of letters. The Great Awakening of the mid-eighteenth century with its itinerant ministers, along with the growing interest in science spurred by the investigations of Benjamin Franklin and others, had done much to disseminate ideas and to show colonists that a larger world lay beyond each province's borders. Jefferson was not the first American to speak in Lockean terms; in 1744 the Reverend Elisha Williams declared that "Reason tells us, all are born thus naturally equal, [possessing] an equal Right to their Persons [liberty]; so also with an equal Right to their Preservation [life]; and therefore to such Things as Nature affords for their Subsistence [property]."[11] By the time of the Revolution, inter-colonial correspondence was a vigorous channel of communication, and as resistance to parliamentary authority united the colonists further, they put this channel to good use. After the Revolution the discussions continued as citizens of different regions explained themselves to fellow Americans hundreds of miles distant who were products of different economies and cultures, from the fisheries of New England to the coastal rice and sea island cotton plantations of the South.[12]

These differences had many causes, ranging from geography to individual temperament. The broad plateau that made for a wide continental shelf off the New England coast, and that also brought the mountains there close to the sea, produced excellent fisheries adjacent to a land of rocky soil ill-fitted for large-scale farming. Below New England the reverse was true, especially in the subtropical South, where plantations began to flourish on the fertile coastal plains.[13] Settlement by different nationalities at different times and places created a cultural patchwork, with highland Scots and Scots-Irish inhabiting different regions from settlers of more Teutonic blood, including English, lowland Scots, and Germans.[14] Congregationalism came to New England, Quakerism to Pennsylvania, and Catholicism to Maryland, while Anglicanism predominated in the South.[15] With all of these elements shaping colonial society, differences of opinion and outlook could be sharp and divisive.

Arguments could be especially strong given that the stakes were high; the question, after all, could be one of whether to secede from the British Empire or the legality of scrapping one state (or even national) constitution in favor of another. The Founders had a wealth of learning upon which to draw, but no one in history had ever faced the particular circumstances of late eighteenth century America. The questions of the founding era rarely had easy answers. As a result, the Founders often disagreed with each other even on some of the basics. The 1770s gave rise to the learned Scottish attorney James Wilson, who feared and warned of the dangers of Revolution but who also pointed out that loyalty to the Crown was quite different from obedience to Parliament;[16] it also spawned the firebrand Thomas Paine, who, unlike Wilson, had nothing at all good to say about England. ("Even brutes do not devour their young," he retorted when reminded that England was the "mother country".[17]) In the 1780s, Thomas Jefferson and James Madison could debate with each other whether a national bill of rights was necessary or even desirable, and by the 1790s a decades-long melee arose with the coming of political parties, with adherents of each fearing that members of the other were out to destroy the country.[18]

With the strength of feeling involved, it is no surprise that the differences could be personal as well as philosophical. In the early 1790s Adams and Jefferson, two longtime friends and the greatest of the Founders, ended their friendship over political differences, their reconciliation delayed for nearly twenty years by the swirl of domestic and foreign disputes. In 1798 there was a brawl on the floor of the House of Representatives between a Federalist and a Republican, armed with a heavy stick and a pair of fire tongs, and throughout the whole of the revolutionary and early constitutional eras, leading figures were never at a loss for invective, as well as outright hatred.[19] John Marshall, one of the most affable of the Founders, could not stand his cousin Thomas Jefferson and despised his political views. Alexander Hamilton was a vain charmer as well as a brilliant financier and theorist, but he was hated by both Adams and Jefferson. While the fatal duel that Hamilton fought with Aaron Burr was largely born of a personality conflict leading to an exchange of insults, the fact that Hamilton loathed Burr's chameleon-like politics no doubt played a role in the battle.

Given the Founders' depth of learning, all of these personal and philosophical differences meant that when it came to debate, discussion, and diatribe, they had an ancient and well-equipped arsenal of thoughts and words upon which to draw. A paragraph, even a single sentence, could simultaneously sound of deep wisdom and barbed attack. Any speech, any writing, could be aimed at a personal or political enemy as well as at a more or less neutral audience, including the court of posterity, that demanded persuasion on some important issue.[20] The Founders' greatest words were thus jewels of many facets. Jefferson's comment about John Marshall, for instance, both hints of his dislike of his cousin and provides a commentary on Marshall's analytical and rhetorical power. "When conversing with Marshall," declared Jefferson,

I never admit anything. So sure as you admit any position to be good, no matter how remote from the conclusion he seeks to establish, you are gone. So great is his sophistry you must never give him an affirmative answer or you will be forced to grant his conclusion. Why, if he were to ask me if it were daylight or not, I'd reply "Sir, I don't know, I can't tell."[21]

But for all the Founders' differences, these speeches and writings were in a lingua franca. Polybius, Cicero, Locke, Blackstone, Montesquieu, and others, not to mention the Bible and Shakespeare, were constantly quoted and cited. It was a time when the most learned of men could nearly master—or at least have a passing knowledge of—all Western scholarship and fields of endeavor. The Founders spoke and wrote a rich language, mining a treasure trove of thousands of years history and experience. If it was selective, it still eclipses by far the superficial expressions of modern public figures bred to a volatile e-mail and sound-bite world, a world of information overload in which few scholars and next to no public servants ever learn Latin, much less Greek or Hebrew. Society has become too specialized and busy for today's political and intellectual leaders to ground themselves in the history, philosophy, and literature that the Founders regarded as essential and common knowledge among those aspiring to lead.

This volume makes the treasure trove available to many types of reader. Students will find it a useful introduction to the key words and thoughts of many great Americans. Those in political life may refer to it not only for speeches and public statements, but also to help them reflect more deeply on current issues they and their communities face. Attorneys can tap it for briefs and oral arguments, and historians, both amateur and professional, will find it an invaluable guide when researching the early decades of the American nation. These quotations are of great practical value to today's citizens; they allow us to be, as Bernard of Chartres said in the Middle Ages, like "dwarves on the shoulders of giants, by whose grace we see farther then they.

Users of this work will find that reading the Founders' words is in itself an education in the classics and Enlightenment thought. A glance at the subject headings of this volume will reveal the many things with which the Founders were concerned. Personal qualities such as "pride" and "humility," "thrift" and "sloth"; the emotions of "anger" and "fear"; fields of human endeavor as diverse as "banking," "science," and "war"; and relevant interests ranging from "nature and wildlife" to "manners" and "solitude." But while late eighteenth century leaders had nearly countless interests, and they often wrote in partisan and adversarial fashion, they nevertheless were nearly always wrestling, in their writing and speaking, with some of the most fundamental of human questions, questions that never lose their relevance. What is the nature of humanity? What is the source of human knowledge? What is the basis of society? What is the purpose of government?

While many thinkers continue today to make a life's work of studying such issues, the Founders, for all of their erudition, were no idle scholars. The questions were not academic for them. More than any other generation of Americans, and arguably as much as any group in history, they had the opportunity and responsibility to act upon their theories, the power to create a new order. In their writings and their speeches, in their most biting wit or in their most theatrical orations, in their partisan diatribes, in their more detached reflections, and in their earnest, often private, unveiling of their thoughts to one another, they wove a verbal web that no American generation before or since has come close to matching for insight and eloquence. Those words, many of which are collected in this volume, are still priceless today, as they will continue to be for as long as we wrestle with the basic issues of life, society, and government.

Notes:
[1] John Adams to Hezekiah Niles, Feb. 13, 1818, in *The Works of John Adams*, vol. 10 (Boston: Little, Brown and Company, Charles Francis Adams, ed., 1856), p. 282.
[2] Lance Marrow, "A Holocaust of Words," *Time*, May 2, 1988, p. 96.
[3] See, e.g., Daniel Boorstin, *The Genius of American Politics* (Chicago: University of Chicago Press, 1953).
[4] Carl L. Becker, *The Declaration of Independence: A Study in the History of Political Ideas* (New York: Alfred A. Knopf, 1942), pp. 27-28; Henry Steele Commager, *Jefferson, Nationalism, and the Enlightenment* (New York: G. Braziller, 1975), p. 84; *cf.* John Locke, *Second Treatise on Civil Government* (1690).
[5] Willi Paul Adams, *The First American Constitutions: Republican Ideology and the Making of State Constitutions in the Revolutionary Era* (Chapel Hill: Published for the Institute of Early

American History and Culture, Williamsburg, Virginia, by the University of North Carolina Press, 1980), *passim*.

[6] U.S. Const. art.1, § 10, cl. 1; ibid., art. 1, § 1; ibid., art. 1, § 3, cl. 7; ibid., art. 3, § 3, cl. 2.

[7] Henry F. May, *The Enlightenment in America* (New York: Oxford University Press, 1976), pp. xi-xii.

[8] Ibid.; Paul A. Rahe, *Republics Ancient and Modern: Classical Republicanism and the American Revolution* (Chapel Hill: University of North Carolina Press, 1992), *passim*.

[9] Forrest McDonald, *Novus Ordo Seclorum: The Intellectual Origins of the Constitution* (Lawrence: University Press of Kansas, 1985), pp. 3-4.

[10] Ibid., p. 5. Actually, the words attributed to Johnson were probably Richard Bentley's. "'It is a pretty poem, Mr. Pope,'" said Bentley, "'but you must not call it Homer.'" Samuel Johnson, *The Works of Samuel Johnson*, vol. 4 (London: John Hawkins ed., 1787), p. 126 n.*.

[11] Elisha Williams, *A Seasonable Plea for the Liberty of Conscience* 2-8 (1744).

[12] Lawrence Henry Gipson, *The Coming of the Revolution* (New York: Harper & Row, 1962), pp. 7-13.

[13] Ellen Churchill Semple, *American History and its Geographic Conditions* (Boston: Houghton, Mifflin and Company, 1903), pp. 31-35, 42-44; D.W. Meinig, *The Shaping of America: A Geographical Perspective on 500 Years of History*, vol. 1 (New Haven: Yale University Press, 1986), *passim*.

[14] Kevin Phillips, *The Cousins' Wars: Religion, Politics, and the Triumph of Anglo-America* (New York: Basic Books, 1999), pp. 181, 203, 225; Grady McWhiney, *Cracker Culture: Celtic Ways in the Old South* (University, Alabama: University of Alabama Press, 1988).

[15] Phillips, *The Cousins' Wars*, pp. 94-100.

[16] James Wilson, *Considerations on the Nature and the Extent of the Legislative Authority of the British Parliament* (Philadelphia: William and Thomas Bradford, 1774), *passim*.

[17] Thomas Paine, *Common Sense*, in *Thomas Paine: Collected Writings*, ed. by Eric Foner (New York: The Library of America, 1995), pp. 22-23.

[18] See generally Stanley Elkins and Eric McKitrick, *The Age of Federalism* (New York: Oxford University Press, 1993).

[19] Ibid., pp. 710, 900 n. 47; Aleine Austin, *Matthew Lyon: New Man of the Democratic Revolution, 1749-1822* (University Park: The Pennsylvania State University Press, 1981), pp. 93-100.

[20] Joseph J. Ellis, *Founding Brothers: The Revolutionary Generation* (New York: Alfred A. Knopf, 2000), *passim*.

[21] Charles R. Williams, *Life of Rutherford Birchard Hayes* (Columbus, Ohio: F.J. Hear, 1928), p. 33.

$\mathcal{A}$

JOHN ADAMS

This illustrious patriot has not his superior, scarcely his equal for abilities and virtue on the whole of the continent of America.
—*BENJAMIN RUSH* (1745–1813)
Rush to a friend,
September 1776

He can't dance, drink, game, flatter, promise, dress, swear with the gentlemen, and small talk and flirt with the ladies—in short, he has none of the essential arts or ornaments which make up a courtier—there are thousands who with a tenth part of his understanding, and without a spark of his honesty, would distance him infinitely in any court in Europe.
—*JONATHAN SEWALL* (1728–1796)
1787

Popularity was never my mistress, nor was I ever, or shall I ever be a popular man.
—*JOHN ADAMS* (1735–1826)
Letter to James Warren,
1787

He is vain, irritable, and a bad calculator of the force and probable effect of the motives which govern men. This is all the ill which can possibly be said of

him. He is as disinterested as the Being who made him.
—*THOMAS JEFFERSON* (1743–1826)
Letter to James Madison,
1787

I hate speeches, messages, addresses, proclamations and such affected, constrained things. I hate levees and drawing rooms. I hate to speak to 1,000 people to whom I have nothing to say. Yet all this I can do.
—*JOHN ADAMS*
Letter to Abigail Adams on the prospect of becoming President of the United States,
February 1796

The answers of Mr. Adams to his addressors form the most grotesque scene in the tragi-comedy acting by the Government . ... He is verifying completely the last feature in the character drawn of him by Dr. F[ranklin] however his title may stand to the two first. "Always an honest man, often a wise one, but sometimes wholly out of his senses."
—*JAMES MADISON* (1751–1836)
To Thomas Jefferson,
June 10, 1798

Bred in the old school of politics, his principles are founded on the experi-

1

ence of ages, and bid defiance to French flippancies and modern crudities. ... Always great, and though sometimes alone, all weak and personal motives were forgotten in public energy and the security of the sacred liberties of his country. ... Deeply versed in legal lore, profoundly skilled in political science; joined to the advantage of forty years' unceasing engagement in turbulent and triumphant scenes, both at home and in Europe, which have marked our history; learned in the language and arts of diplomacy; more conversant with views, jealousies, resources, and intrigues of Great Britain, France, and Holland than any other American; alike aloof to flattery and vulgar ambition, as above all undue control [he has as] ... his sole object ... the present freedom and independence of his country and its future glory. On this solid basis he has attempted to raise a monument of his honest fame.

—UNKNOWN
Editorial in the *Washington Federalist*
October 7, 1800

It has been the political career of this man to begin with hypocrisy, proceed with arrogance, and finish with contempt.

—THOMAS PAINE (1737–1809)
"Open Letter to the Citizens of the United States"
November 22, 1802

I consider you and him [Thomas Jefferson] as the North and South Poles of the American Revolution. Some talked, some wrote, and some fought to promote and establish it, but you and Mr. Jefferson *thought* for us all. I never take a retrospect of the years 1775 and 1776 without associating your opinions and speeches and conversations with all the great political, moral, and intellectual achievements of the Congresses of those memorable years.

—BENJAMIN RUSH
To John Adams,
February 17, 1812

JOHN QUINCY ADAMS

I am a man of reserved, cold, austere, and forbidding manners; my political adversaries say, a gloomy misanthropist, and my personal enemies, an unsocial savage.

—JOHN QUINCY ADAMS (1767–1848)
Diary entry,
June 4, 1819

His disposition is as perverse and mulish as that of his father.

—JAMES BUCHANAN, (1791–1868)
Letter to Hugh Hamilton,
March 22, 1822

SAMUEL ADAMS

No man contributed more towards our revolution, & no man left behind him less, distinctly to mark his resolutions, his peculiar genius & communications. He was feared by his enemies, but too secret to be loved by his friends. He did not put confidence in them, while he was of importance to them. He was not known till he acted & how far he was to act was unknown.

—REV. WILLIAM BENTLEY (1759–1819)
Diary entry,
October 3, 1803

He possessed a quick understanding, a cool head, stern manners, a smooth

address, and Roman-like firmness, united with that sagacity and penetration that would have made a figure in a conclave. He was at the same time liberal in opinion and uniformly devout; social with men of all denominations, grave in deportment, placid, yet sober and indefatigable; calm in seasons of difficulty, tranquil and unruffled in the vortex of political altercation; too firm to be intimidated, too haughty for condescension, his mind was replete with resources that dissipated fear, and extricated in the greatest emergencies. Thus qualified, he stood forth early and continued firm through the great struggle.
—*MERCY OTIS WARREN* (1728–1814)
1805

ADVICE & ADVISORS

You desired ... I would at least give my Advice. I think it is Ariosto who says, that all things lost on Earth are to be found in the Moon; on which somebody remarked, that there must be a great deal of good Advice in the Moon.
—*BENJAMIN FRANKLIN* (1706–1790)
To James Hutton,
February 1, 1778
(Franklin is alluding to Italian poet Ludovico Ariosto's epic poem "Orlando Furioso".)

That advice should be taken where example has failed, or precept be regarded where warning is ridiculed, is like a picture of hope resting on despair.
—*THOMAS PAINE* (1737–1809)
The Crisis
1780

In a multitude of counselors there is

the best chance for honesty, if not of wisdom.
—*JAMES MADISON* (1751–1836)
To Edmund Randolph,
May 1, 1782

It is infinitely better to have a *few* good men than *many* indifferent ones.
—*GEORGE WASHINGTON* (1732–1799)
To James McHenry,
August 10, 1798

AGE & AGING

Youth is the time of getting, middle age of improving, and old age of spending.
—*ANNE BRADSTREET* (c. 1612–1672)
Meditations Divine and Moral
1644

Wish not so much to live long as to live well.
—*BENJAMIN FRANKLIN* (1706–1790)
Poor Richard's Almanack
1746

Many foxes grow gray, but few grow good.
—*BENJAMIN FRANKLIN*
Poor Richard's Almanack
1749

Life is sufficiently short without shaking the sand that measures it.
—*THOMAS PAINE* (1737–1809)
The Crisis
1778

In the moment of our separation upon the road as I traveled, and every hour since, I felt all that love, respect and attachment for you, with which length of years, close connexion and your merits have inspired me. I often asked

3

myself, as our carriages distended, whether that was the last sight I ever should have of you? And tho' I wished to say no, my fears answered yes. I called to mind the days of my youth, and found they had long since fled to return no more; that I was now descending the hill I had been 52 years climbing, and that tho' I was blessed with a good constitution, I was of a short lived family, and might soon expect to be entombed in the dreary mansions of my father's. These things darkened the shades and gave a gloom to the picture, consequently to my prospects of seeing you again: but I will not repine, I have had my day.
—GEORGE WASHINGTON (1732–1799)
To Marquis de Lafayette,
December 8, 1784

I find as I grow older, that I love those most whom I loved first.
—THOMAS JEFFERSON (1743–1826)
To Mary Jefferson Bolling,
July 23, 1787

The older I grow, the more apt I am to doubt my own judgment, and to pay more respect to the judgment of others.
—BENJAMIN FRANKLIN
Speech to Constitutional Convention,
September 17, 1787

To be happy in old age, it is necessary that we accustom ourselves to objects that can accompany the mind all the way through life, and that we take the rest as good in their day. The man of pleasure is miserable in old age, and the mere drudge in business is but little better: whereas natural philosophy, mathematical, and mechanical science, are a continual source of tranquil plea-

sure. ... Those who knew Benjamin Franklin will recollect that his mind was ever young; his temper ever serene. Science, that never grows grey, was always his mistress. He was never without an object; for when we cease to have an object, we become like an invalid in an hospital waiting for death.
—THOMAS PAINE
Age of Reason, II
1795

Tranquility is the old man's milk. I go to enjoy it in a few days, and to exchange the roar and tumult of bulls and bears for the prattle of my grandchildren and senile rest.
—THOMAS JEFFERSON
Letter to Edward Rutledge,
June 24, 1797

By my rambling digressions I perceive myself to be growing older.
—BENJAMIN FRANKLIN
Autobiography
1798

My one fear is that I may live too long. This would be a subject of dread to me.
—THOMAS JEFFERSON
Letter to Philip Mazzai,
March, 1801

Being very sensible of bodily decays from advancing years, I ought not to doubt their effect on the mental faculties. To do so would evince either great self-love or little observation of what passes under our eyes: and I shall be fortunate if I am the first to perceive and to obey this admonition of nature.
—THOMAS JEFFERSON
To Mr. Weaver,
June 7, 1807

It is wonderful to me that old men should not be sensible that their minds keep pace with their bodies in the progress of decay. ... Nothing betrays imbecility so much as the being insensible of it.
—*THOMAS JEFFERSON*
To Benjamin Rush,
August 17, 1811

Of all the faculties of the human mind that of Memory is the first which suffers decay from age.
—*THOMAS JEFFERSON*
To Benjamin Henry Latrobe,
July 12, 1812

The hand of age is upon me. The decay of bodily faculties apprises me that those of the mind cannot be unimpaired, had I not still better proofs. Every year counts by increased debility, and departing faculties keep the score. The last year it was the sight, this it is the hearing, the next something else will be going, until all is gone. ... As a compensation for faculties departed, nature gives me good health, & a perfect resignation to the laws of decay which she has prescribed to all the forms & combinations of matter.
—*THOMAS JEFFERSON*
To William Duane,
October 1, 1812

Our machines have now been running seventy or eighty years, and we must expect that, worn as they are, here a pivot, there a wheel, now a pinion, next a spring, will be giving way; and however we may tinker the up for a while, all will at length surcease motion.
—*THOMAS JEFFERSON*
Letter to John Adams,
July 15, 1814

Nothing is more incumbent on the old, than to know when they should get out of the way, and relinquish to younger successors the honors they can no longer earn, and the duties they can no longer perform.
—*THOMAS JEFFERSON*
To John Vaughan,
February 5, 1815

I have lived in this old and frail tenement a great many years; it is very much dilapidated; and, from all that I can learn, my landlord doesn't intend to repair it.
—*JOHN ADAMS* (1735–1826)
Letter to Daniel Webster,
circa 1820s

That happy age when a man can be idle with impunity.
—*WASHINGTON IRVING* (1783–1859)
Rip Van Winkle in *The Sketchbook*
1820

Whenever a man's friends begin to compliment him about looking young, he may be sure that they think he is growing old.
—*WASHINGTON IRVING*
Bachelors in Bracebridge Hall
1822

The solitude in which we are left by the death of our friends is one of the great evils of protracted life. When I look back to the days of my youth, it is like looking over a field of battle. All, all dead! and ourselves left alone amidst a new generation whom we know not, and who know not us.
—*THOMAS JEFFERSON*
To Francis A. Van Der Kemp,
January 11, 1825

AGGRESSION

Complaints ill become those who are found to be the first aggressors.
—*GEORGE WASHINGTON* (1732–1799)
To James Madison,
March 21, 1787

AGRICULTURE & FARMING

The first useful class of citizens are the farmers and cultivators. These may be called citizens of the first necessity, because every thing comes originally from the earth.
—*THOMAS PAINE* (1737–1809)
To Henry Laurens,
Spring 1778

Cultivators of the earth are the most valuable citizens. They are the most vigorous, the most independent, the most virtuous, and they are ties to their country and wedded to its liberty and interests by the most lasting bands. As long therefore as they can find employment in this line, I would not convert them into mariners, artisans, or any thing else. But our citizens will find emploiment in this line till their numbers, and of course their productions, become too great for the demand both internal and foreign.
—*THOMAS JEFFERSON* (1743–1826)
Letter to John Jay,
August 23, 1785

I think our governments will remain virtuous for many centuries; as long as they remain chiefly agricultural; and this will be as long as there shall be vacant lands in any part of America. When they get piled upon one another in large cities as in Europe, they will become cor-rupt as in Europe, and go to eating one another as they do there.
—*THOMAS JEFFERSON*
Letter to James Madison,
December 20, 1787

I hope, some day or another, we shall become a storehouse and granary for the world.
—*GEORGE WASHINGTON* (1732–1799)
To Marquis de Lafayette,
June 19, 1788

In my opinion, it would be proper also, for gentlemen to consider the means of encouraging the great staple of America, I mean agriculture, which I think may justly be styled the staple of the United States; from the spontane-ous productions which nature fur-nishes, and the manifest preference it has over every other object of emolu-ment in this country.
—*JAMES MADISON* (1751–1836)
Speech in Congress,
April 9, 1789

It is evident that the exertions of the husbandman will be steady or fluctuat-ing, vigorous or feeble, in proportion to the steadiness or fluctuation, ad-equateness or inadequateness, of the markets on which he must depend for the vent of the surplus which may be produced by his labor . .... This idea of an extensive domestic market for the surplus produce of the soil, is of the first consequence. It is, of all things, that which most effectually conduces to a flourishing state of agriculture.
—*ALEXANDER HAMILTON* (1755–1804)
Report to the House of Representa-tives on the Subject of Manufactures,
December 5, 1791

The class of citizens who provide at once their own food and their own raiment, may be viewed as the most truly independent and happy. They are more: they are the best basis of public liberty, and the strongest bulwark of public safety. It follows, that the greater the proportion of this class to the whole society, the more free, the more independent, and the more happy must be the society itself.

—JAMES MADISON
Essay in the *National Gazette*,
March 3, 1792

The life of the husbandman is preeminently suited to the comfort and happiness of the individual. *Health*, the first of blessings, is an appurtenance of his property and his employment. *Virtue*, the health of the soul, is another part of his patrimony, and no less favored by his situation. *Intelligence* may be cultivated in this as well as in any other walk of life. If the mind be less susceptible of plish in retirement than in a crowd, it is more capable of profound and comprehensive efforts. Is it more ignorant of some things? It has a compensation in its ignorance of others. *Competency* is more universally the lot of those who dwell in the country, when liberty is at the same time their lot. The extremes both of want and of waste have other abodes.

—JAMES MADISON
Essay in the *National Gazette*,
March 3, 1792

I know of no pursuit in which more real and important services can be rendered to any country than by improving its agriculture, its breed of useful animals, and other branches of a husbandman's cares.

—GEORGE WASHINGTON
Letter to John Sinclair,
July 20, 1794

Cultivation is, at least, one of the greatest natural improvements ever made by human invention. It has given to created earth a ten-fold value.

—THOMAS PAINE
Agrarian Justice
1797

How dear to my heart are the scenes
of my childhood
When fond recollection presents them
to view
The orchard, the meadow, the deep
tangled wildwood,
And ev'ry loved spot which my infancy
knew
The wide spreading pond, and the mill
that stood by it,
The bridge and the rock where the cataract fell;
The cot of my father, the dairy house
nigh it,
And e'en the rude bucket that hung in
the well.
The old oaken bucket, the iron bound
bucket,
The moss covered bucket that hung in
the well.
The moss covered bucket I hailed as a
treasure,
For often at noon, when returned from
the field,
I found it the source of an exquisite
pleasure,
The purest and sweetest that nature can
yield.
How ardent I seized it, with hands that
were glowing,

7

And quick to the white pebbled bottom
it fell
Then soon, with the emblem of turth
overflowing,
And dripping with coolness, it rose
from the well.
The old oaken bucket, the iron bound
bucket,
The moss covered bucket that hung in
the well.
—*Samuel Woodworth* (1785–1842)
The Old Oaken Bucket
1818

Horticulture is a valuable and interesting Section of Agriculture, the main
resource of human subsistence. Apart
from the ornamental, the scientific, and
experimental uses, which it may embrace, it affords a cheap and wholesome substitute for the disproportion-
ate consumption of animal food, which
has long been a habit of our Country,
resulting from the exuberant supply it
has enjoyed of this article. In promoting a reform of this habit, horticultural
Societies can not fail of a happy tendency.
—*James Madison* (1751–1836)
To George Watterson,
March 8, 1824

Those who labor in the earth are the
chosen people of God, if He ever had a
chosen people.
—*Thomas Jefferson*
Notes on the State of Virginia
1781–1785

Alcohol, Alcoholism, & Drunkenness

He that drinks fast pays slow.
—*Benjamin Franklin* (1706–1790)

Poor Richard's Almanack
1733

Drink does not drown care, but waters
it and makes it grow faster.
—*Benjamin Franklin*
Poor Richard's Almanack
1749

He who spills the rum loses that only;
he that drinks it, often loses both that
and himself.
—*Benjamin Franklin*
Poor Richard's Almanack
1750

Drunkenness, that worst of evils,
makes some mere fools, some beasts,
and some devils.
—*Benjamin Franklin*
Poor Richard's Almanack
1751

Spiritous liquors are injurious inasmuch
as they add an internal fire to the external heat of the sun. They relax the stom-
ach, quicken the circulation of the
blood, and thus dispose it to putrefac-
tion. I believe there are few instances
of people dropping down dead in a harvest field from excess of heat or labor.
Upon inquiry, it is generally found that
the sudden deaths which sometimes
occur in this country in this season have
been occasioned by the excessive use
of spiritous liquors. After the stimulating effects of spirits are over; they act
as sedatives upon the system; that is,
they produce relaxation and languor.
The system it is true may be roused in
these cases by fresh and increased
draughts of spirits, but these produce
corresponding degrees of debility, so
that in the evening of a day spent in the

alternate and compound exertions of working and drinking, a laborer is a proper subject for a physician; he often stands in more need of a flesh brush or warm bath than of a supper or a bed.
—BENJAMIN RUSH (1745–1813)
To the Editor of *The Pennsylvania Journal*,
June 22, 1782

A *compleat* suppression of every species of stimulating indulgence, if attainable at all, must be a work of peculiar difficulty, since it has to encounter not only the force of habit, but a propensity in human nature. In every age and nation, some exhilarating or exciting substance seems to have been sought for, as a relief from the languor of idleness, or the fatigues of labor. In the rudest state of Society, whether in hot or cold climates, a passion for ardent spirits is in a manner universal. In the progress of refinement, beverages less intoxicating, but still of an exhilarating quality, have been more or less common. And where all these sources of excitement have been unknown, or been totally prohibited by a religious faith, substitutes have been found in opium, in the nut of the betel, the root of the Ginseng, or the leaf of the Tobacco plant.
—JAMES MADISON (1751–1836)
To Thomas Hertell,
December 20, 1819

It would doubtless be a great point gained for our Country ... if ardent spirits could be made only to give way to malt liquors, to those afforded by the apple and the pear, and to the lighter and cheaper varieties of wine. It is remarkable that in the Countries where the grape supplies the common bever-

age, habits of intoxication are rare; and in some places almost without example.
—JAMES MADISON
To Thomas Hertell,
December 20, 1819

They who drink beer will think beer.
—WASHINGTON IRVING (1783–1859)
Sketch Book of Geoffrey Crayon
1820

The practicability and national economy of substituting to a great extent at least, for the foreign wines on which so large a sum is expended, those which can be produced at home, without withdrawing labour from objects not better rewarding it, is strongly illustrated by your experiments and statements; The introduction of a native wine is not a little recommended moreover, by its tendency to substitute a beverage favorable to temperate habits for the ardent liquors so destructive to the morals, the health, and the social happiness of the American people.
—JAMES MADISON
To John Adlum,
April 12, 1823

AMBITION

The tallest trees are most in the power of the winds, and ambitious men of the blasts of fortune.
—WILLIAM PENN (1644–1718)
More Fruits of Solitude
1702

They that soar too high, often fall hard; which makes a low and level dwelling preferable.
—WILLIAM PENN
More Fruits of Solitude
1702

9

Strive to be the greatest man in your country, and you may be disappointed. Strive to be the best and you may succeed: he may well win the race that runs by himself.
—*BENJAMIN FRANKLIN* (1706–1790)
Poor Richard's Almanack
1747

While avarice and ambition have a place in the heart of man, the weak will become a prey to the strong.
—*THOMAS PAINE* (1737–1809)
Thoughts on Defensive War
1775

There is no saying to what length an enterprising man may push his good fortune.
—*GEORGE WASHINGTON* (1732–1799)
To the New York Council of Safety,
August 4, 1777

How pitiful, in the eye of reason and religion, is that false ambition which desolates the world with fire and sword for the purposes of conquest and fame.
—*GEORGE WASHINGTON*
To John Lathrop,
June 22, 1788

I had rather be shut up in a very modest cottage, with my books, my family and a few old friends, dining on simple bacon, and letting the world roll on as it liked, than to occupy the most splendid post which any human power can give.
—*THOMAS JEFFERSON* (1743–1826)
Letter to A. Donald,
1789

Ambition is the subtlest Beast of the Intellectual and Moral Field. It is won-

derfully adroit in concealing itself from its owner.
—*JOHN ADAMS* (1735–1826)
Letter to John Quincy Adams,
January 3, 1794

I am not an ambitious man, but perhaps I have been an ambitious American. I have wished to see America the *Mother Church* of government.
—*THOMAS PAINE*
To James Monroe,
September 10, 1794

I leave to others the sublime delights of riding in the storm, better pleased with sound sleep & a warmer berth below it encircled, with the society of neighbors, friends & fellow laborers of the earth rather than with spies & sycophants. ... I have no ambition to govern men. It is a painful and thankless office.
—*THOMAS JEFFERSON*
To John Adams
December 28, 1796

Ambition is so vigilant, and where it has a model always in view as in the present case, is so prompt in seizing its advantages, that it can not be too closely watched, or too vigorously checked.
—*JAMES MADISON* (1751–1836)
To Thomas Jefferson,
December 25, 1797

Great ambition, unchecked by principle or the love of glory, is an unruly tyrant.
—*ALEXANDER HAMILTON* (1755–1804)
To James A. Bayard,
January 16, 1801

Whenever a man has cast a longing eye

on offices, a rottenness begins in his conduct.

—THOMAS JEFFERSON
1820

AMERICA & AMERICANISM

Westward the course of empire takes
its way;
The first four acts already past,
A fifth shall close the drama with the
day:
Time's noblest offspring is the last.

—GEORGE BERKELEY (1685–1753)
*On the Prospect of Planting Arts and
Learning in America*
1726

There ought to be no New England men, no New Yorker, &c., known on the Continent, but all of us Americans.

—CHRISTOPHER GADSEN (1724–1805)
To Charles Garth,
1765

When we view this country in its extent and variety of climates, soils, and produce, we ought to be exceeding thankful to divine goodness in bestowing it upon our forefathers, and giving it as an heritage for their children. We may call it the promised land, a good land and a large—a land of hills and vallies, of rivers, brooks, and springs of water—a land of milk and honey, and wherein we may eat bread to the full. A land whose stones are iron, the most useful material in all nature, and of other choice mines and minerals; and a land whose rivers and adjacent seas are stored with the best of fish. In a word, no part of the habitable world can boast of so many natu-

ral advantages as this northern part of *America*.

—SILAS DOWNER (1729–1785)
*A Discourse at the Dedication of
the Tree of Liberty*
1768

But we want no excuse for any *supposed* mistakes of our ancestors. Let us first see it prov'd that they were mistakes. 'Till then we must hold ourselves obliged to them for sentiments transmitted to us so worthy of their character, and so important to our security.

—SAMUEL ADAMS (1722–1803)
Essay in the *Boston Gazette*,
1771

May we ever be a people favoured of GOD. May our land be a land of liberty, the seat of virtue, the asylum of the oppressed, a name and a praise in the whole earth, until the last shock of time shall bury the empires of the world in one common undistinguished ruin!

—JOSEPH WARREN (1741–1775)
Boston Massacre Oration,
March 5, 1772

To one however who adores liberty, and the noble virtues of which it is the parent, there is some consolation in seeing, while we lament the fall of British liberty, the rise of that of America. Yes, my friend, like a young phoenix she will rise full plumed and glorious from her mother's ashes.

—ARTHUR LEE (1740–1792)
Letter to Samuel Adams,
December 24, 1772

The next Augustan age will dawn on the other side of the Atlantic. There will, perhaps, be a Thucydides at Boston, a

Xenophon at New York, and, in time, a Virgil at Mexico, and a Newton at Peru. At last, some curious traveler from Lima will visit England and give a description of the ruins of St. Paul's, like the editions of Balbec and Palmyra.
—*HORACE WALPOLE* (1717–1797)
Letter To Horace Mann,
November 24, 1774

I am not a Virginian, but an American.
—*PATRICK HENRY* (1736–1799)
Speech in the First Continental
Congress, Philadelphia
1774

America is a great, unwieldy body. Its progress must be slow. It is like a large fleet sailing under convoy. The fleetest sailers must wait for the dullest and slowest.
—*JOHN ADAMS* (1735–1826)
Letter to Abigail Adams,
June 17, 1775

Young man, there is America—which at this day serves for little more than to amuse you with stories of savage men and uncouth manners; yet shall, before you taste of death, show itself equal to the whole of that commerce which now attracts the envy of the world.
—*EDMUND BURKE* (1729–1797)
March 22, 1775

Sir, [the American colonists] are a race of convicts, and ought to be thankful for anything we allow them short of hanging.
—*SAMUEL JOHNSON* (1709–1784)
The Life of Samuel Johnson
by James Boswell
1775

The cause of America is in a great measure the cause of all mankind.
—*THOMAS PAINE* (1737–1809)
Common Sense
1776

The time. . . at which the continent was discovered, adds weight to the argument [for independence], and the manner in which it was peopled increases the force of it. The reformation as preceded by the discovery of America, as if the Almighty graciously meant to open a sanctuary to the persecuted in the future years, when home should afford neither friendship nor safety.
—*THOMAS PAINE*
Common Sense
1776

This new world hath been the asylum for the persecuted lovers of civil and religious liberty from every part of Europe. Hither have they fled, not from the tender embraces of the mother, but from the cruelty of the monster.
—*THOMAS PAINE*
Common Sense
1776

Columbia, Columbia, to glory arise, The queen of the world, and the child of the skies!
—*TIMOTHY DWIGHT* (1752–1817)
Columbia, Gem of the Ocean
1777

This Continent is too extensive to sleep all at once, and too watchful, even in its slumbers, not to startle at the unhallowed foot of an invader.
—*THOMAS PAINE*
The Crisis
1777

What charms me [in America] is that all citizens are brethren.

—MARQUIS DE LAFAYETTE (1757–1834)
To his Wife,
1777

America is her own mistress and can do what she pleases.

—THOMAS PAINE
The Crisis
1778

Could the mist of antiquity be taken away, and men and things viewed as they then really were, it is more than probable that they [the ancient Greeks and Romans] would admire us, rather than we them. America has surmounted a greater variety and combination of difficulties than, I believe, ever fell to the share of any one people, in the same space of time, and has replenished the world with more useful knowledge and sounder maxims of civil government than were ever produced in any age before. Had it not been for America there had been no such thing as freedom left throughout the whole universe.

—THOMAS PAINE
The Crisis
1778

America ever is what she thinks herself to be.

—THOMAS PAINE
The Crisis
1780

A European, when he first arrives, seems limited in his intentions, as well as in his views; but he very suddenly alters his scale; 200 miles formerly appeared a very great distance, it is now but a trifle; he no sooner breathes our air than he forms schemes, and embarks on designs he never would have thought of in his own country. There the plentitude of society confines many useful ideas, and often extinguishes the most laudable schemes which here ripen into maturity. Thus Europeans become Americans.

—MICHEL GUILLAUME JEAN DE
CRÈVECOEUR (1735–1813)
Letters from an American Farmer
1782

After a foreigner from any part of Europe is arrived, and become a citizen; let him devoutly listen to the voice of our great parent, which says to him, "Welcome to our shores, distressed European; bless the hour in which thou didst seek my verdant fields, my fair navigable rivers, and my green mountains! If thou wilt work, I have bread for thee; if thou wilt be honest, sober, and industrious, I have greater rewards to confer on thee—ease and independence. I will give thee fields to feed and clothe thee; a comfortable fireside to sit by, and tell thy children by what means thou hast prospered; and a decent bed to repose on. I shall endow thee beside with the immunities of a freeman. If thou wilt carefully educate thy children, teach them gratitude to God, and reverence to that philanthropic government, which has collected here so many men and made them happy, I will also provide for thy progency; and to every good man this ought to be most holy, the most Powerful, the most earnest wish he can possibly form, as well as the most consolatory prospect when he dies. Go thou and work and till; thou shalt prosper, provided thou be just, grateful and industrious."

—*MICHEL GUILLAUME JEAN DE CRÈVECOEUR*
Letters from an American Farmer
1782

Here individuals of all nations are melted into a new race of men, whose labors and posterity will one day cause great changes in the world.

—*MICHEL GUILLAUME JEAN DE CRÈVECOEUR*
Letters from an American Farmer
1782

I could point out to you a family whose grandfather was an Englishman, whose wife was Dutch, whose son married a French woman, and whose present four sons now have four wives of different nations. *He* is an American, who leaving behind him all his ancient prejudices and manners, receives new ones from the new life he has embraced, the new government he obeys, and the new rank he holds. ... The American is a new man, who acts upon new principles; he must therefore entertain new ideas, and form new opinions

—*MICHEL GUILLAUME JEAN DE CRÈVECOEUR*
Letters from an American Farmer
1782

Men are like plants; the goodness and flavor of the fruit proceeds from the peculiar soil and exposition in which they grow. We are nothing but what we derive from the air we breathe, the climate we inhabit, the government we obey, the system of religion we

profess, and the nature of our employment.

—*MICHEL GUILLAUME JEAN DE CRÈVECOEUR*
Letters from an American Farmer
1782

What then is the American? This new man? He is either a European, or a descendant of a European, hence that strange mixture of blood, which you will find in no other country.

—*MICHEL GUILLAUME JEAN DE CRÈVECOEUR*
Letters from an American Farmer
1782

America is a new character in the universe. She started with a cause divinely right, and struck at an object vast and valuable. Her reputation for political integrity, perseverance, fortitude, and all the manly excellences, stands high in the world.

—*THOMAS PAINE*
The Necessity of Taxation
1782

... an asylum for the poor and oppressed of all nations and religions.

—*GEORGE WASHINGTON* (1732–1799)
General Orders
April 18, 1783

I have an indifferent opinion of the honesty of this country, and ill forebodings as to its future system.

—*ALEXANDER HAMILTON* (1755–1804)
To George Washington,
March 25, 1783

At this auspicious period, the United States came into existence as a nation, and if their citizens should not be completely free and happy, the fault will be entirely their own.

—GEORGE WASHINGTON
Circular to the States,
June 8, 1783

It was my object to make Americans hold up their heads, and look down upon any nation that refused to do them justice; ... in my opinion, Americans had nothing to fear but from the meekness of their own hearts; as Christians, I wished them meek; as statesmen, I wished them proud; and I thought the pride and the meekness very consistent.

—JOHN ADAMS
Diary Entry,
April 30, 1783

To see it in our power to make a world happy—to teach mankind the art of being so—to exhibit on the theater of the universe a character hitherto unknown—and to have, as it were, a new creation entrusted to our hands, are honors that command reflection, and can neither be too highly estimated, nor too gratefully received.

—THOMAS PAINE
The Crisis
1783

Nothing is more favorable to nourishing successful seeds of liberty in Americans than the land they inhabit. Spread far and wide in an immense continent, free as the nature that surrounds them, among the crags and the mountains, the vast plains and the deserts, at the edge of forests where all is still wild, where nothing reminds them of servitude or man's tyranny, they encounter the lessons of liberty and independence in all the physical objects around them.

—JOSEPH MANDRILLON (1743–1794)
The American Spectator
1784

Its soul, its climate, its equality, liberty, laws, people, and manners. My God! how little do my countrymen know what precious blessings they are in possession of, and which no other people on earth enjoy!

—THOMAS JEFFERSON (1743–1826)
Letter to James Monroe,
June 17, 1785

Most of the *distresses* of our country, and of the *mistakes* which Europeans have formed of us, have arisen from the mistaken belief that the American Revolution is *over*. This is so far from being the case that we have only finished the first act of the great drama. We have changed our forms of government, but it remains yet to effect a revolution in our principles, opinions, and manners so as to accommodate them to the forms of government we have adopted.

—BENJAMIN RUSH (1745–1813)
To Richard Price,
May 25, 1786

Is it not the glory of the people of America, that, whilst they have paid a decent regard to the opinions of former times and other nations, they have not suffered a blind veneration for antiquity, for custom, or for names, to overrule the suggestions of their own good sense, the knowledge of their own situation, and the lessons of their own experience? To this manly spirit, posterity will be indebted for the possession, and the world for the example, of the numerous innovations displayed on the American theatre, in favor of private rights and public happiness.

—*JAMES MADISON* (1751–1836)
The Federalist Papers
1787

All Europe must by degrees be aroused to the recollection and assertion of the rights of human nature. Your good will to Mankind will be gratified with this prospect, and your pleasure as an American be enhanced by the reflection that the light which is chasing darkness and despotism from the old world, is but an emanation from that which has procured and succeeded the establishment of liberty in the New.

—*JAMES MADISON*
The Federalist Papers
1787

It is part of the American character to consider nothing as desperate; to surmount every difficulty by resolution and contrivance. In Europe there are shops for every want. Its inhabitants therefore have no idea that their wants can be furnished otherwise. Remote from all other aid, we are obliged to invent and to execute; to find means within ourselves, and not to lean on others.

—*THOMAS JEFFERSON*
To Martha Jefferson,
1787

Thirteen governments [of the original states] thus founded on the natural authority of the people alone, without a pretence of miracle or mystery, and which are destined to spread over the northern part of that whole quarter of

the globe, are a great point gained in favor of the rights of mankind.

—*JOHN ADAMS*
A Defence of the Constitutions of Government of the United States of America
1787–1788

There is a modesty often which does itself injury. Our coutnrymen possess this. They do not know their own superiority.

—*THOMAS JEFFERSON*
To John Rutledge, Jr.,
February 2, 1788

Nothing but harmony, honesty, industry, and frugality are necessary to make us a great and happy people.

—*GEORGE WASHINGTON*
To Marquis de Lafayette,
January 29, 1789

The preservation of the sacred fire of liberty and the destiny of the republican model of government are justly considered, perhaps as *deeply*, as *finally*, staked on the experiment intrusted to the hands of the American people.

—*GEORGE WASHINGTON*
First inaugural address,
April 30, 1789

Never was a finer canvas presented to work on that our countrymen. All of them engaged in agriculture or the pursuits of honest industry, independent in their circumstances, enlightened as to their rights, and firm in their habits of order & obedience to the laws. This I hope will be the age of experiments in government, and that their basis will be founded principles of honesty, not of mere force. We have seen no instance

of this since the days of Roman republic, nor do we read of any before that.
—THOMAS JEFFERSON
To John Adams,
February 28, 1796

I am sure the mass of citizens in these United States mean well, and I firmly believe they will always act well, whenever they can obtain a right understanding of matters.
—GEORGE WASHINGTON
To John Jay,
May 8, 1796

Citizens by birth or choice, of a common country, that country has a right to concentrate your affections. The name of American, which belongs to you in your national capacity, must always exalt the just pride of patriotism more than any appellation derived from local discriminations. With slight shades of difference, you have the same religion, manners, habits and political principles. You have in common cause fought and triumphed together. The independence and liberty you possess are the work of joint councils and joint efforts, of common dangers, sufferings, and successes.
—GEORGE WASHINGTON
Farewell Address,
September 17, 1796

We are laboring hard to establish in this country principles more and more *national* and free from all foreign ingredients, so that we may be neither "Greeks nor Trojans," but truly American.
—ALEXANDER HAMILTON
To Rufus King,
December 16, 1796

Hail, Columbia! happy land!
Hail, ye heroes! heaven-born band!
Who fought and bled in Freedom's cause.
—JOSEPH HOPKINSON (1770–1842)
Hail, Columbia
1798

This country will, erelong, assume an attitude correspondent with its great destinies—majestic, efficient, and operative of great things. A noble career lies before it.
—ALEXANDER HAMILTON
To Rufus King,
October 2, 1798

America, if she attains to greatness, must *creep* to it. ... Slow and sure is no bad maxim. Snails are a wise generation.
—ALEXANDER HAMILTON
To Theodore Sedgwick,
February 17, 1800

The wisdom and justice of the American governments, and the virtue of the inhabitants, may, if they are not deficient in the improvement of their own advantages, render the United States of America an enviable example to all the world, of peace, liberty, righteousness, and truth.
—MERCY OTIS WARREN (1728–1814)
History of the Rise, Progress and Termination of the American Revolution
1805

The station which we occupy among the nations of the earth is honorable, but awful. Trusted with the destinies of this solitary republic of the world, the only monument of human rights,

& the sole depository of the sacred fire of freedom & self-government from hence it is to be lighted up in other regions of the earth, if other regions of the earth shall ever become susceptible of its benign influence. All mankind ought then, with us, to rejoice in its prosperous, & sympathize in its adverse fortunes, as involving every thing dear to man.

—*THOMAS JEFFERSON*
To the Citizens of Washington,
March 4, 1809

Here [in the United States], we are, on the whole, doing well, and giving an example of a free system, which I trust will be more of a pilot to a good port, than a Beacon, warning from a bad one. We have, it is true, occasional fevers; but they are of the transient kind, flying off through the surface, without preying on the vitals. A Government like ours has so many safety-valves, giving vent to overheated passions, that it carries within itself a relief against the infirmities from which the best of human Institutions can not be exempt.

—*JAMES MADISON*
To Marquis de Lafayette,
November 25, 1820

The U.S. are now furnishing models and lessons to all the world, a great, soon to be the most hopeful portion of it, is receiving them with a happy docility; whilst the great European portion is either passively or actively gaining by them. The eyes of the world being thus on our Country, it is put more on its good behavior, and under the greater obligation also to do justice to the Tree of Liberty by an exhibition of the fine fruits we gather from it.

—*JAMES MADISON*
To James Monroe,
December 16, 1824

Let our object be, OUR COUNTRY, OUR WHOLE COUNTRY, AND NOTHING BUT OUR COUNTRY. And, by the blessing of God, may that country itself become a vast and splendid monument, not of oppression and terror, but of wisdom, of peace, and of liberty, upon which the world may gaze with admiration forever.

—*DANIEL WEBSTER* (1782–1852)
Address at the laying of the Bunker
Hill Monument Cornerstone,
June 17, 1825

ANGER

Not to be provoked is best: but if moved, never correct till the fume is spent: for every stroke our fury strikes is sure to hit ourselves at last.

—*WILLIAM PENN* (1644–1718)
The Fruits of Solitude
1693

Anger is never without a reason but seldom with a good one.

—*BENJAMIN FRANKLIN* (1706–1790)
Poor Richard's Almanack
1753

There are men too, who have not virtue enough to be angry.

—*THOMAS PAINE* (1737–1809)
The Forester's Letters
1776

A mind disarmed of its rage, feels no pleasure in contemplating a frantic quarrel. Sickness of thought ... leaves no ability for enjoyment, no relish for resentment; and though like a man in a fit, you feel not the injury of the struggle, nor distinguish between strength and disease, the weakness will nevertheless be proportioned to the violence, and the sense of pain increase within the recovery.

—THOMAS PAINE
The Crisis
1780

When angry, count ten before you speak; if very angry, a hundred.

—THOMAS JEFFERSON
A Decalogue of Canons for Observation in Practical Life,
February 21, 1825

APPEARANCES & VANITY

It is reported of the peacock that, priding himself in his gay feathers, he ruffles them up, but spying his black feet, he soon lets fall his plumes; so he that glories in his gifts and adornings should look upon his corruptions, and that will damp his high thoughts.

—ANNE BRADSTREET (c. 1612–1672)
Meditations Divine and Moral
c.1660

Show is not substance: realities govern wise men.

—WILLIAM PENN (1644–1718)
Some Fruits of Solitude
1693

Humility and knowledge in poor clothes excel pride and ignorance in costly attire.

—WILLIAM PENN
Some Fruits of Solitude
1693

Chose thy clothes by thine own eyes, not another's. The more plain and simple they are, the better. Neither unshapely nor fantastical; and for use and decency, and not for pride.

—WILLIAM PENN
Some Fruits of Solitude
1693

Excess in apparel is another costly folly: the very trimming of the vain world would clothe all the naked one.

—WILLIAM PENN
Some Fruits of Solitude
1693

In your apparel be modest and endeavor to accommodate nature, rather than to procure admiration.

—GEORGE WASHINGTON (1732–1799)
Rules of Civility
1745

A little of what you call frippery is very necessary towards looking like the rest of the world.

—ABIGAIL ADAMS (1744–1818)
Letter to John Adams,
May 1, 1780

Our pride is always hurt by the same propositions which offend our principles: for when we are shocked at the crime we are wounded by the supposition of our compliance.

—THOMAS PAINE (1737–1809)
The Crisis
1782

If you are not great enough to have ambition you are little enough to have vanity.

—THOMAS PAINE
To George Washington,
August 3, 1796

19

ARGUMENT & DEBATE

In disputes, be not so desirous to overcome as not to give liberty to each one to deliver his opinion.
—GEORGE WASHINGTON (1732–1799)
Rules of Civility
1745

Strive not with your superiors in argument, but always submit your judgment to others with modesty.
—GEORGE WASHINGTON
Rules of Civility
1745

A bad cause seldom fails to betray itself.
—JAMES MADISON (1751–1836)
The Federalist Papers
1788

I never saw an instance of one of two disputants convincing the other by argument.
—THOMAS JEFFERSON (1743–1826)
Letter to John Taylor,
June 1, 1798

Every difference of opinion is not a difference of principle. We have been called by different names brethren of the same principle. We are all Republicans—we are all Federalists. If there be any among us who would wish to dissolve this Union or to change its republican form, let them stand undisturbed as monuments to the safety with which error of opinion may be tolerated where reason is left free to combat it.
—THOMAS JEFFERSON
First Inaugural Address,
1801

I may sometimes differ in opinion from some of my friends, from those whose views are as pure & sound as my own. I censure none, but do homage to every one's right of opinion.
—THOMAS JEFFERSON
To William Duane,
March 28, 1811

In little disputes with your companions, give way rather than insist on trifles, for their love and the approbation of others will be worth more to you than the trifle in dispute.
—THOMAS JEFFERSON
To Francis Eppes,
May 21, 1816

A sharp tongue is the only edged tool that grows keener with constant use.
—WASHINGTON IRVING (1783–1859)
Rip Van Winkle
1820

BENEDICT ARNOLD

Our commander, Arnold, was of a remarkable character. He was brave, even to temerity, was beloved by the soldiery, perhaps for that quality only; he possessed great powers of persuasion, and was complaisant, but withal sordidly avaricious. Arnold was a short, handsome man, of a florid complexion, stoutly made, and forty years old at least.
—JOHN JOSEPH HENRY (1759–1811)
Journal entry,
1811

ARTS

The Science of Government it is my Duty to study, more than all other Sci-

20

ences: the Art of Legislation and Administration and Negotiation, ought to take Place, indeed to exclude in a manner all other Arts. I must study Politicks and War that my sons may have liberty to study Mathematicks and Philosophy. My sons ought to study Mathematicks and Philosophy, Geography, natural History, Naval Architecture, navigation, Commerce and Agriculture, in order to give their Children a right to study Painting, Poetry, Musick, Architecture, Statuary, Tapestry and Porcelaine.

—*JOHN ADAMS* (1735–1826)
Letter to Abigail Adams,
May 12, 1780

The arts and sciences esential to the prosperity of the state and to the ornament and happiness of human life have a primary claim to the encouragement of every lover of his country and mankind.

—*GEORGE WASHINGTON* (1732–1799)
To Joseph Willard,
March 22, 1781

You see I am an enthusiast on the subject of the arts. But it is an enthusiasm of which I am not ashamed, as its object is to improve the taste of my countrymen, to increase their reputation, to reconcile to them the respect of the world & procure them its praise.

—*THOMAS JEFFERSON* (1743-1826)
To James Madison,
September 20, 1785

I am so hackneyed to the touches of the painter's pencils that I am now altogether at their beck … at first I was as impatient and as restive under the operation as a colt is of the saddle. The next time I submitted very reluctantly, but with less flouncing. Now no dray horse moves more readily to his thill than I do to the painter's chair.

—*GEORGE WASHINGTON*
Letter to Francis Hopkinson,
1785

Architecture worth great attention. As we double our numbers every 20 years we must double our houses. Besides we build of such perishable materials that one half of our houses must be rebuilt in every space of 20 years. So that in that term, houses are to be built for three fourths of our inhabitants. It is then among the most important arts: and it is desireable to introduce taste into an art which shews so much.

—*THOMAS JEFFERSON*
Letter to John Rutledge, Jr.,
June 19, 1788

Well aware as I am, that public bodies are liable to be assailed by visionary projectors, I nevertheless wish to ascertain the probability of the magnetic theory. If there is any considerable probability that the projected voyage would be successful, or throw any valuable light on the discovery of longitude, it certainly comports with the honor and dignity of government to give it their countenance and support. Gentlemen will recollect, that some of the most important discoveries, both in arts and sciences, have come forward under very unpromising and suspicious appearances.

—*JAMES MADISON* (1751-1836)
Speech in Congress,
April 20, 1789

Every principal art has some science

for its parent, though the person who mechanically performs the work does not always, and but very seldom, perceive the connection.

—*THOMAS PAINE* (1737–1809)
Age of Reason, I
1794

To promote literature in this rising empire, and to encourage the arts, have ever been amongst the warmest wishes of my heart.

—*GEORGE WASHINGTON*
To the trustees of Washington Academy,
June 17, 1798

Don't forget among all of yr useful acquirements the comparatively trivial one of playing & singing several airs upon the harp. I will get one at Paris. That is an accomplishment that will be really useful to you.

—*JAMES MONROE* (1758–1831)
To his daughter Eliza,
March 1, 1805

ATTENTION & NEGLECT

A little neglect may breed mischief: for want of a nail the shoe was lost; for want of a shoe the horse was lost; and for want of a horse the rider was lost.

—*BENJAMIN FRANKLIN* (1706–1790)
Poor Richard's Almanack
1745

Little strokes / Fell great oaks.

—*BENJAMIN FRANKLIN*
Poor Richard's Almanack
1750

If the liberties of America are ever compleatly ruined, of which in my opinion there is now the utmost danger, it will in all probability be the consequence of a mistaken notion of *prudence*, which leads men to acquiesce in measures of the most destructive tendency for the sake of present ease. When designs are form'd to rase the very foundation of a free government, those few who are to erect their grandeur and fortunes upon the general ruin, will employ every art to sooth the devoted people into a state of indolence, inattention and security. … They are alarmed at nothing so much, as attempts to awaken the people to *jealousy* and *watchfulness*; and it has been an old game played over and over again, to hold up the men who would rouse their fellow citizens and countrymen to a sense of their *real* danger, and spirit them to the most zealous activity in the use of all proper means for the preservation of the public liberty, as '*pretended patriots,*' *intemperate politicans,*' *rash, hot-headed* men, *Incendiaries*, wretched *desperadoes*, who, as was said of the best of men, would turn the world upside down, or have done it already.

—*SAMUEL ADAMS* (1722–1803)
Essay in the *Boston Gazette*,
1771

B

BAD COMPANY

Associate yourself with Men of good Quality if you Esteem your own Reputation; for 'tis better to be alone than in bad Company.
—*GEORGE WASHINGTON* (1732–1799)
Rules of Civility
1745

It is easy to make acquaintances, but very difficult to shake them off, however irksome and unprofitable they are found, after we have once committed ourselves to them.
—*GEORGE WASHINGTON*
To Bushrod Washington,
January 15, 1783

BALTIMORE

This [Baltimore] is the dirtiest place in the world.
—*JOHN ADAMS* (1735–1826)
Diary Entry,
February 8, 1777

BANKS & BANKING

There is no practice more dangerous than that of borrowing money.
—*GEORGE WASHINGTON* (1732–1799)
To Samuel Washington,
July 12, 1797

The want of economy in the use of imported articles, enters very justly into the explanation given of the causes of the present general embarrassments [the panic of 1819]. Were every one to live within his income or even the savings of the prudent to exceed the devidicts of the extravagant, the balance in the foreign commerce of the nation, could not be against it. The want of a due economy has produced the unfavorable turn which has been experienced. ... It has been made a question whether Banks, when restricted to spheres in which temporary loans only are made to persons in active business promising quick returns, do not as much harm to imprudent, as good to prudent borrowers. But it can no longer be a doubt with any, that loan offices, carrying to every man's door, and even courting his acceptance of the monied means of gratifying his present wishes under a prospect or hope of procrastinated repayment, must, of all devices, be the one most fatal to a general frugality, and the benefits resulting from it.
—*JAMES MADISON* (1751–1836)
To Clarkson Crolius,
December 1819

BIGOTRY

Bigotry is the disease of ignorance, of

23

morbid minds; enthusiasm of the free and buoyant. Education & free discussion are the antidotes of both.
—*THOMAS JEFFERSON* (1743–1826)
To John Adams,
August 1, 1816

BILL OF RIGHTS

A bill of rights is what the people are entitled to against every government on earth.
—*THOMAS JEFFERSON* (1743–1826)
Letter to James Madison,
December 1787

There are certain maxims by which every wise and enlightened people will regulate their conduct. There are certain political maxims, which no free people ought ever to abandon. Maxims of which the observance is essential to the security of happiness. It is impiously irritating the avenging hand of Heaven, when a people who are in the full enjoyment of freedom, launch out into the wide ocean of human affairs, and desert those maxims which alone can preserve liberty. Such maxims, humble as they are, are those only which can render a nation safe or formidable. ... We have one, Sir, That all men are by nature free and independent, and have certain inherent rights, of which, when they enter into society, they cannot by any compact deprive or divest their posterity. We have a set of maxims of the same spirit, which must be beloved by every friend to liberty, to virtue, to mankind. Our Bill of Rights contains those admirable maxims.
—*PATRICK HENRY* (1736–1799)
To Edmund Randolph,
1788

What use then it may be asked can a bill of rights serve in popular Governments? I answer the two following which though less essential than in other Governments, sufficiently recommend the precaution.
I. The political truths declared in that solemn manner acquire by degrees the character of fundamental maxims of free Government, and as they become incorporated with the national sentiment, counteract the impulses of interest and passion.
2. Altho' it be generally true as above stated that the danger of oppression lies in the interested majorities of the people rather than in usurped acts of the Government, yet there may be occasions on which the evil may spring from the latter sources; and on such, a bill of rights will be a good ground for an appeal to the sense of the community.
—*JAMES MADISON* (1751–1836)
To Thomas Jefferson,
1788

In Europe, charters of liberty have been granted by power. America has set the example and France has followed it, of charters of power granted by liberty. This revolution in the practice of the world, may, with an honest praise, be pronounced the most triumphant epoch of its history, and the most consoling presage of its happiness.
—*JAMES MADISON*
Essay in the *National Gazette*,
January 18, 1792

In proportion as Government is influenced by opinion, must it be so by whatever influences opinion. This decides the question concerning a bill of rights, which acquires efficacy as time sanctifies and incorporates it with the public sentiment.

—*JAMES MADISON*
1792

BOOKS

A knowledge of books is the basis upon which other knowledge is to be built.
—*GEORGE WASHINGTON* (1732–1799)
To Jonathan Boucher,
July 9, 1771

A lively and lasting sense of filial duty is more effectually impressed on the mind of a son or daughter by reading King Lear, than by all the dry volumes of ethics, and divinity, that ever were written.
—*THOMAS JEFFERSON* (1743–1826)
Letter to Robert Skipwith,
August 3, 1771

Read good books because they will encourage as well as direct your feelings.
—*THOMAS JEFFERSON*
To Peter Carr,
August 10, 1787

Light reading (by this, I mean books of little importance) may amuse for the moment, but leaves nothing solid behind.
—*GEORGE WASHINGTON*
To George Washington Parke Custis,
November 13, 1796

Nothing would do more extensive good at small expense than the establishment of a small circulating library in every county.
—*THOMAS JEFFERSON*
To John Wyche,
1809

Books constitute capital. A library book lasts as long as a house, for hundreds of years. It is not, then, an article of mere consumption but fairly of capital, and often in the case of professional men, setting out in life, it is their only capital.
—*THOMAS JEFFERSON*
Letter to James Madison,
September 16, 1821

With us [in the United States] there are more readers than buyers of Books. In England there are more buyers than Readers. Hence those Gorgeous Editions, which are destined to sleep in the private libraries of the Rich, whose vanity aspires to that species of furniture; or who give that turn to their public spirit and patronage of letters.
—*JAMES MADISON* (1751–1836)
To Edward Everett,
March 19, 1823

BOSTON

This place [Boston] abounds with pritty women who … are, for the most part, free and affable as well as pritty. I saw not one prude while I was here.
—*ALEXANDER HAMILTON* (1712–1756)
Itinerarium
August 16, 1744

BOTANY & GARDENING

But though I am an old man, I am but a young gardener.
—*THOMAS JEFFERSON* (1743–1826)
Letter to Charles Wilson Peale,
August 20, 1811

Botany I rank with the most valuable sciences, whether we consider its subjects as furnishing the principal subsis-

tence of life to man & beast, delicious varieties for our table, refreshments from our orchards, the adornments of our flower-borders, shade and perfume of our groves, materials for our building, or medicaments for our bodies.
—*THOMAS JEFFERSON*
To Thomas Cooper,
October 7, 1814

BRAVERY & COURAGE

… we dread nothing but slavery. Death is the creature of a poltroon's brains; 'tis immortality to sacrifice ourselves for the salvation of our country. We fear not death. That gloomy night, the pale-faced moon, and the affrighted stars that hurried through the sky, can witness that we fear not death. Our hearts which, at the recollection, glow with rage that four revolving years have scarcely taught us to restrain, can witness that we fear not death …
—*JOHN HANCOCK* (1737–1793)
Boston Massacre Oration,
March 5, 1774

We are not weak if we make a proper use of those means which the God of Nature has placed in our power. … The battle, sir, is not to the strong alone; it is to the vigilant, the active, the brave.
—*PATRICK HENRY* (1736–1799)
Speech in Virginia Convention,
March 23, 1775

Men who are familiarized to danger, meet it without shrinking, whereas those who have never seen service often apprehend danger where no danger lies.
—*GEORGE WASHINGTON* (1732–1799)
Letter to Continental Congress,
February 9, 1776

'Tis the business of little minds to shrink; but he whose heart is firm, and whose conscience approves his conduct, will pursue his principles unto death.
—*THOMAS PAINE* (1737–1809)
The Crisis
1776

Bravery is a quality not to be dispensed within officers—like charity, it covers a great many defects.
—*BENJAMIN STODDERT* (1751–1813)
Letter to James Simons,
December 13, 1798

It is part of a sailor's life to die well.
—*STEPHEN DECATUR* (1779–1820)
On Captain James Lawrence, after his
death in action,
June 1, 1813

AARON BURR

I fear the other gentleman is unprincipled both as a public and a private man. When the Constitution was in deliberation, his conduct was equivocal, but its enemies, who, I believe, best understood him, considered him as with them. In fact, I take it, he is for or against nothing, but as it suits his interest or ambition. He is determined, as I conceive, to make his way to be the head of the popular party, and to climb *per fas et nefas* to the highest honor of the State, as much higher as circumstances may permit … I am mistaken if it be not his object to play the game of confusion, and I feel it a religious duty to oppose his career.
—*ALEXANDER HAMILTON* (1755–1804)
Hamilton papers,
Dated September 21, 1792

He is in every sense a profligate; a voluptuary in the extreme, with uncommon habits of expense. ... He is artful and intriguing to an inconceivable degree ... bankrupt beyond redemption except by the blunder of his country. ... he will certainly attempt to reform the government a la Bonaparte ... as unprincipled and dangerous a man as any country can boast—as true a Catiline as ever met in midnight conclave.
—ALEXANDER HAMILTON
Letter to James A. Bayard,
August 6, 1800

He will never choose to lean on good men, because he knows that they will never support his bad projects; but, instead of this he will endeavor to disorganize both parties, and to form out of them a third, composed of men fitted by their characters to be conspirators and instruments of such projects.
—ALEXANDER HAMILTON
Letter to James A. Bayard,
December 26, 1800

Secretly turning liberty into ridicule, he knows as well as most men how to make use of that name. In a word, if we have an embryo Caesar in the United States, 'tis Burr.
—ALEXANDER HAMILTON
c. 1800

Burr's conspiracy had been one of the most flagitious of which history will ever furnish an example ... but he who could expect to effect such objects by the aid of American citizens, must be perfectly ripe for Bedlam.
—THOMAS JEFFERSON (1743–1826)
Letter to E. Du Pont de Nemours,
July 14, 1807

I never thought him an honest, frank-dealing man, but considered him as a crooked gun or other perverted machine, whose aim or shot you could never be sure of.
—THOMAS JEFFERSON
Letter to William B. Giles,
April 1807

BUSINESS & TRADE

Corporations have neither bodies to be kicked nor souls to be damned.
—ANONYMOUS
Cited by Arthur Schlesinger, Jr.,
in *The Age of Jackson* (1945)
Date unknown

The creditors are a superstitious sect, great observers of set days and times.
—BENJAMIN FRANKLIN (1706–1790)
Poor Richard's Almanack
1737

Let your discourse with men of business be short and comprehensive.
—GEORGE WASHINGTON (1732–1799)
Rules of Civility
1745

Now everybody knows that the greatest part of the trade of Great Britain is with her colonies. This she enjoyeth, exclusive of any other European country, and hath entirely at her own command. Further, it may be made out that the greatest part of the profits of the trade of the colonies, at least on the continent, centers in Great Britain. ... *Trade* is a nice and delicate lady; she must be courted and won by soft and fair addresses. She will not bear the rude hand of a ravisher. Penalties increased, heavy taxes laid on, the checks of oppression and violence removed; these things must drive her from her present abode.

Hence, one or other of these consequences will follow: either (1) the colonies will universally go into such manufactures as they are capable of doing within themselves, or (2) they will do without them, and being reduced to mere necessaries, will be clothed like their predecessors the Indians with the skins of beasts, and sink into like barbarism. ... Now, either of these events taking place, how will it affect the island of Great Britain? The answer is obvious . ... Doth not this resemble the conduct of the good wife in the fable who killed her hen that every day laid her a *golden egg*?

—OXENBRIDGE THACHER (1720–1765)
The Sentiments of a British American
1764

[M]onopolies are odious, contrary to the spirit of a free government, and the principles of commerce; and ought not to be suffered.

—MARYLAND CONSTITUTION OF 1776
Section 39,
1776

Commerce and industry are the best mines of a nation.

—GEORGE WASHINGTON
To Joseph Reed,
May 28, 1780

There are some who maintain that trade will regulate itself, and it is not to be benefited by the encouragements or restraints of government. Such persons will imagine that there is no need of a common directing power. This is one of those wild speculative paradoxes, which have grown into credit among

us, contrary to the uniform practice and sense of the most enlightened nations.

—ALEXANDER HAMILTON (1755–1804)
The Continentalist, No. 5, New York
Packet,
April 18, 1782

Wherever Commerce prevails there will be an inequality of wealth, and wherever the latter does a simplicity of manners must decline.

—JAMES MADISON (1751–1836)
To Edmund Randolph,
September 30, 1783

A people ... who are possessed of the spirit of commerce, who see and who will pursue their advantages, may achieve almost anything.

—GEORGE WASHINGTON
To Benjamin Harrison,
October 10, 1784

Merchants love nobody.

—THOMAS JEFFERSON (1743–1826)
Letter to John Langdon,
1785

The period is not very remote when the benefits of a liberal and free commerce will, pretty generally, succeed to the devastations and horrors of war.

—GEORGE WASHINGTON
To Marquis de Lafayette,
August 15, 1786

Merchants are the least virtuous citizens and possess the least of the *amor patriae*.

—THOMAS JEFFERSON
Letter to M. de Meunier,
1786

I own myself the friend to a very free system of commerce, and hold it as a

28

truth, that commercial shackles are generally unjust, oppressive and impolitic—it is also a truth, that if industry and labour are left to take their own course, they will generally be directed to those objects which are the most productive, and this in a more certain and direct manner than the wisdom of the most enlightened legislature could point out.

—*JAMES MADISON*
Speech in Congress,
April 9, 1789

System to all things is the soul of business. To deliberate maturely and execute promptly is the way to conduct it to advantage.

—*GEORGE WASHINGTON*
To James Anderson,
December 21, 1797

Money, and not morality, is the principle of commercial nations.

—*THOMAS JEFFERSON*
Letter to John Langdon,
1810

C

CHANGE

I am well aware that the moment of any great change ... is unavoidably the moment of terror and confusion. The mind, highly agitated by hope, suspicion, and apprehension, continues without rest till the change be accomplished.
—*THOMAS PAINE* (1737–1809)
Letter to the People of France,
1792

There is a certain relief in change, even though it be from bad to worse; as I have found in travelling in a stage coach, that it is often a comfort to shift one's position and be bruised in a new place.
—*WASHINGTON IRVING* (1783–1859)
Tales of a Traveller
1824

CHARACTER

There is no object that we see, no action that we do, no good that we enjoy, no evil that we feel or fear, but we may make some spiritual advantage of all; and he that makes such improvement is wise as well as pious.
—*ANNE BRADSTREET* (c. 1612–1672)
Meditations Divine and Moral
c. 1660

Rarely promise. But, if lawful, constantly perform.
—*WILLIAM PENN* (1644–1718)
Some Fruits of Solitude
1693

There are some men like dictionaries; to be looked into upon occasion, but have no connection, and are little entertaining.
—*WILLIAM PENN*
Some Fruits of Solitude
1693

When a man does all he can, though it succeeds not well, blame not him that did it.
—*GEORGE WASHINGTON* (1732–1799)
Rules of Civility
1745

Nothing is more essential to the establishment of manners in a State than that all persons employed in places of power and trust must be men of unexceptionable characters.
—*SAMUEL ADAMS* (1722–1803)
To James Warren,
1775

The public cannot be too curious concerning the characters of public men.
—*SAMUEL ADAMS*
To James Warren,
1775

No reflection ought to be made on any man on account of birth, provided that his manners rise decently with his circumstances, and that he affects not to forget the level he came from; when he does, he ought to be led back and shown the mortifying picture of originality.
—*THOMAS PAINE* (1737–1809)
Four Letters on Interesting Subjects
1776

It is to be lamented ... that great characters are seldom without a blot.
—*GEORGE WASHINGTON*
To Marquis de Lafayette
May 10, 1786

Men's minds are as variant as their faces.
—*GEORGE WASHINGTON*
To Benjamin Harrison,
March 9, 1789

Good moral character is the first essential in a man.
—*GEORGE WASHINGTON*
TO GEORGE STEPTOE WASHINGTON,
DECEMBER 5, 1790

The uniform tenor of a man's life furnishes better evidence of what he has said or done on any particular occasion than the world of any enemy.
—*THOMAS JEFFERSON* (1743–1826)
To George Clinton,
December 31, 1803

Adore God. Reverence and cherish your parents. Love your neighbor as yourself, and your country more than yourself. Be just. Be true. Murmur not at the ways of Providence.
—*THOMAS JEFFERSON*
To Thomas Jefferson Smith,
February 21, 1825

CHARITY

Do good with what thou hast, or it will do thee no good.
—*WILLIAM PENN* (1644–1718)
Some Fruits of Solitude
1693

Do thine own work honestly and cheerfully: and when that is done, help thy fellow; that so another time he may help thee.
—*WILLIAM PENN*
Some Fruits of Solitude
1693

Frugality is good, if liberality be joined with it. The first is leaving off superfluous expenses; the last bestowing them to the benefit of others that need. The first without the last begins covetousness; the last without the first begins prodigality; both together make an excellent temper. Happy the place where that is found.
—*WILLIAM PENN*
Some Fruits of Solitude
1693

It imparts, first, the commiseration of the poor and unhappy of mankind, and extends a helping hand to mend their condition.
—*WILLIAM PENN*
More Fruits of Solitude
1702

God sends the poor to try us, as well as He tries them by being such: and he that refuses them a little out of the great deal that God has given him lays up poverty in store for his own posterity.
—*WILLIAM PENN*
More Fruits of Solitude
1702

Proportion your charity to the strength of your estate, or God will proportion your estate to the weakness of your charity.

—BENJAMIN FRANKLIN (1706–1790)
Poor Richard's Almanack
1757

The more we bestow the richer we become.

—THOMAS PAINE (1737–1809)
The Crisis Extraordinary
1780

Let your heart feel for the afflictions and distresses of everyone, and let your hand give in proportion to your purse, remembering ... that it is not everyone who asketh that deserveth charity.

—GEORGE WASHINGTON (1732–1799)
To Bushrod Washington,
January 15, 1783

Liberality and charity ... ought to govern in all disputes.

—GEORGE WASHINGTON
To Benjamin Harrison,
March 9, 1789

Never let an indigent person ask without receiving something, if you have the means.

—GEORGE WASHINGTON
To George Washington Parke Custis,
November 15, 1796

Private charities, as well as contributions to public purposes in proportion to every one's circumstances, are certainly among the duties we owe to society.

—THOMAS JEFFERSON (1743–1826)
To Charles Christian,
March 21, 1812

CHILDREN & PARENTING

If thou wouldst be obeyed, being a father; being a son, be obedient.

—WILLIAM PENN (1644–1718)
Some Fruits of Solitude
1693

Men are generally more careful of the breed of their horses and dogs, than of their children.

—WILLIAM PENN
Some Fruits of Solitude
1693

Is it [parental love] not the strongest affection known? Is it not greater than even that of self-preservation?

—THOMAS JEFFERSON (1743–1826)
A Bill for Proportioning Crime and
Punishment,
November 1778

The easiest way of becoming acquainted with the modes of thinking, the rules of conduct, and the prevailing manners of any people, is to examine what sort of education they give their children; how they treat them at home, and what they are taught in their places of public worship.

—MICHEL GUILLAUME JEAN DE
CRÈVECOEUR (1735–1813)
Letters From an American Farmer
1782

What is it that affectionate parents require of their Children for all their care, anxiety, and toil on their accounts? Only that they would be wise and virtuous, Benevolent and kind.

—ABIGAIL ADAMS (1744–1818)
To John Quincy Adams,
November 20, 1783

Mrs. Monroe hath added a daughter to our society, who tho' noisy, contributes greatly to its amusement.
—*JAMES MONROE* (1758–1831)
To Thomas Jefferson on the birth of Monroe's first daughter, Eliza, July 27, 1787

The rights of minors are as sacred as the rights of the aged.
—*THOMAS PAINE* (1737–1809)
Dissertation on First Principles of Government
1795

It has been some time since that I conceived of any event in this Life which could call forth feelings of mutual sympathy. But I know how closely entwined around a parent's heart are those chords which bind the filial to the parental Bosom, and when snapped assunder, how agonizing the pangs of separation.

I have tasted the bitter cup, and bow with reverence and humility before the great dispenser of it, without whose permission and overruling providence not a sparrow falls to the ground.
—*ABIGAIL ADAMS* (1744–1818)
A letter of condolence to Thomas Jefferson on the death of his daughter, Polly, May 20, 1804

The article of discipline is the most difficult in American education. Premature ideas of independence, too little repressed by parents, beget a spirit of insubordinate, which is the great obstacle.
—*THOMAS JEFFERSON*
To Dr. Thomas Cooper, November 2, 1822

CITIES

The mobs of great cities add just so much to the support of pure government, as sores do to the strength of the human body.
—*THOMAS JEFFERSON* (1743–1826)
Notes on the State of Virginia
1782

When we get piled upon one another in large cities as in Europe, we shall become corrupt as in Europe, and go to eating one another as they do there.
—*THOMAS JEFFERSON*
Letter to James Madison, December 20, 1787

The tumultuous populace of large cities are ever to be dreaded. Their indiscriminate violence prostrates for the time all public authority, and its consequences are sometimes extensive and terrible.
—*GEORGE WASHINGTON* (1732–1799)
To Marquis de Lafayette, July 28, 1791

'Tis not the country that peoples either the Bridewells or the Bedlams. These mansions of wretchedness are tenanted from the distresses and vices of overgrown cities.
—*JAMES MADISON* (1751–1836)
Essay in the *National Gazette*, March 3, 1792

I view great cities as pestilential to the morals, the health and the liberties of man.
—*THOMAS JEFFERSON*
To Benjamin Rush, September 23, 1800

CIVIL RIGHTS

In a free government, the security for civil rights must be the same as that for religious rights. It consists in the one case in the multiplicity of interests, and in the other, in the multiplicity of sects.

—*JAMES MADISON* (1751–1836)
The Federalist Papers
1788

COMPROMISE & MODERATION

All government—indeed, every human benefit and enjoyment, every virtue and every prudent act—is founded on compromise and barter.

—*EDMUND BURKE* (1729–1797)
Second Speech on Conciliation
with America,
March 22, 1775

Magnanimity in politics is not seldom the truest wisdom; and a great empire and little minds go ill together.

—*EDMUND BURKE*
Second Speech on Conciliation
with America,
March 22, 1775

I agree with you that in politics the middle way is none at all.

—*JOHN ADAMS* (1735–1826)
Letter to Horatio Gates,
March 23, 1776

A thing moderately good is not so good as it ought to be. Moderation in temper is always a virtue; but moderation in principle is always a vice.

—*THOMAS PAINE* (1737–1809)
The Rights of Man
1791

CONGRESS

The business of Congress is tedious beyond expression. ... Every man in it is a great man, an orator, a critic, a statesman; and therefore every man ... must show his oratory, his criticism, and his political abilities.

—*JOHN ADAMS* (1735–1826)
Letter to Abigail Adams on the
Continental Congress,
October 9, 1774

For heaven's sake, who are Congress? Are they not the creatures of the people, amenable to them for their conduct and dependent from day to day on their breath?

—*GEORGE WASHINGTON* (1732–1799)
To William Gordon,
July 8, 1783

At the commencement of the revolution, it was supposed that what is called the executive part of government was the only dangerous part; but we now see that quite as much mischief, if not more, may be done, ... by a legislature.

—*THOMAS PAINE* (1737–1809)
On the Affairs of Pennsylvania
1786

In order to judge the form to be given to this institution [the Senate], it will be proper to take a view of the ends to be served by it. These were, first, to protect the people against their rulers, secondly, to protect the people against the transient impressions into which they themselves might be led.

—*JAMES MADISON* (1751–1836)
Debate in the Constitutional
Convention,
June 26, 1787

I have observed, that gentlemen suppose, that the general legislature will do every mischief they possibly can, and that they will omit to do every thing good which they are authorised to do. If this were a reasonable supposition, their objections would be good. I consider it reasonable to conclude, that they will as readily do their duty, as deviate from it: Nor do I go on the grounds mentioned by gentlemen on the other side—that we are to place unlimited confidence in them, and expect nothing but the most exalted integrity and sublime virtue. But I go on this great republican principle, that the people will have virtue and intelligence to select men of virtue and wisdom.

—JAMES MADISON
Speech to the Virginia Ratifying
Convention,
June 20, 1788

It is certainly inconsistent with the established principles of republicanism, that the senate should be a fixed and unchangeable body of men. There should be then some constitutional provision against this evil. A rotation I consider as the best possible mode of affecting a remedy. The amendment will not only have a tendency to defeat any plots, which may be formed against the liberty and authority of the state governments, but will be the best means to extinguish the factions which often prevail, and which are sometimes so fatal to legislative bodies.

— MELANCTON SMITH (1744–1798)
New York Ratifying Convention,
1788

The executive in our government is not the sole, it is scarcely the principal object

of my jealousy. The tyranny of the legislatures is the most formidable dread at present and will be for many years. That period of the executive will come in its turn, but it will be at a remote period.

—THOMAS JEFFERSON (1743–1826)
Letter to James Madison,
1789

But is not man, in the shape of a senator or a representative, as fond of power as a president? … Are not ambition and favoritism, and all other vicious passions and sinister interests, as strong and active in a senator or a representative as in a president? Cannot, indeed, the members of the legislature conceal their private views and improper motives more easily than a president?

—JOHN ADAMS
Review of propositions to amend the
Constitution,
1808

If there be any thing amiss therefore, in the present state of our affairs, as the formidable deficit lately unfolded to us indicates, I ascribe it to the inattention of Congress to its duties, to their unwise dissipation & waste of the public contributions. They seemed, some little while ago to be at a loss for objects whereon to throw away the supposed fathomless funds of the treasury.

—THOMAS JEFFERSON
To Thomas Ritchie,
December 25, 1820

CONNECTICUT

The land of steady habits.

—ANONYMOUS
A traditional epithet for Connecticut,
Date Unknown

"Farewell Connecticut," said I, as I passed along the bridge. "I have had a surfeit of your ragged money, rough roads, and enthusiastic people."
—ALEXANDER HAMILTON (1712–1756)
Itinerarium
August 30, 1744

Connecticut in her blue-laws, laying it down as a principle, that the laws of God should be the laws of man.
—THOMAS JEFFERSON (1743–1826)
Letter to John Adams,
January 24, 1814

The last [state] expected to yield its steady habits (which were essentially bigoted in politics as well as religion).
—THOMAS JEFFERSON
Letter to Marquis de Lafayette,
May 14, 1817

'Tis a rough land of earth and stone
and tree,
Where breathes no castled lord or
cabined slave;
Where thought, and tongues, and hands
are bold and free,
And friends will find a welcome, foes
a grave;
And where none kneel, save when to
Heaven they pray,
Nor even then, unless in their own way.
—FITZ-GREENE HALLECK (1790–1867)
Connecticut
c. 1820

CONSCIENCE

Would you live with ease, do what you ought, not what you please.
—BENJAMIN FRANKLIN (1706–1790)
Poor Richard's Almanack
1734

Labor to keep alive in your breast that little spark of celestial fire called conscience.
—GEORGE WASHINGTON (1732–1799)
Rules of Civility
1745

He that carries a small Crime easily, will carry it on when it comes to be an ox.
—BENJAMIN FRANKLIN
Poor Richard's Almanack
1758

Driven from every other corner of the earth, freedom of thought and the right of private judgment in matters of conscience direct their course to this happy country as their last asylum.
—SAMUEL ADAMS (1722–1803)
Speech delivered in Philadelphia,
August 1, 1776

Conscience ... seldom comes to a man's aid while he is in the zenith of health and reveling in pomp and luxury upon ill-gotten spoils; it is generally the *last* act of his life and comes too late to be of much service to others here, or to himself hereafter.
—GEORGE WASHINGTON
To John Price Posey,
August 7, 1782

The moral sense, or conscience, is as much a part of man as his leg or arm. It is given to all human beings in a stronger or weaker degree, as force of members is given them in a greater or less degree. It may be strengthened by exercise, as may any particular limb of the body. This sense is submitted indeed in some degree to the guidance of reason; but it is a small stock which is required for this: even a less one than what we call Common sense. State a moral case to a ploughman & a professor. The former will decide it as well, & often better than the latter, because he has not been led astray by artificial rules.

—THOMAS JEFFERSON (1743–1826)
To Peter Carr,
August 10, 1787

But there is a question of great magnitude, which I am desirous of having determined. I shall therefore take the liberty of moving it: That we add to the end of the amendment, the words, "and persons conscientiously scrupulous of bearing arms" [be exempt from militia service]. I agree with the gentleman who was last up, that [it] is the glory of this country, the boast of the revolution, and the pride of the present constitution, that here the rights of mankind are known and established on a basis more certain, and I trust, more durable, than any heretofore recorded in history, or existing in any other part of this globe; but above all, it is the particular glory of this country, to have secured the rights of conscience which in other nations are least understood or most strangely violated.

—JAMES MADISON (1751–1836)
Speech in Congress,
December 22, 1790

Conscience is the most sacred of all property. ... To guard a man's house as his castle, to pay public and enforce private debts with the most exact faith, can give no title to invade a man's conscience which is more sacred than his castle.

—JAMES MADISON
Article in the *National Gazette*,
March 29, 1792

Opinion, & the just maintenance of it, shall never be a crime in my view; nor bring injury on the individual.

—THOMAS JEFFERSON
To Samuel Adams,
March 29, 1801

CONSISTENCY

The Greeks used to say, all cases are governed by their circumstances. The same thing may be well and ill as they change or vary the matter.

—WILLIAM PENN (1644–1718)
Some Fruits of Solitude
1693

I may venture to say that there never was a Man eminently famous but what was distinguish'd by this very Qualification [constancy], and few if any can live comfortably even in a private Life without it; for a Man who has no End in View, no Design to pursue, is like an irresolute Master of a Ship at Sea, that can fix upon no one Port to steer her to, and consequently can call not one Wind favourable to his Wishes.

—BENJAMIN FRANKLIN (1706–1790)
"On Constancy," in the
Pennsylvania Gazette,
April 4, 1734

Experience constantly teaches that new members of a public body do not feel the necessary respect or responsibility for the acts of their predecessors, and that a change of members and *of circumstances* often proves fatal to consistency and stability of public measures.

—JAMES MADISON (1751–1836)
Notes on Debates,
January 6, 1783

CONSTITUTION

... this eternal truth, that *public happiness depends on a virtuous and unshaken attachment to a free constitution.*
—*JOSEPH WARREN* (1741–1775)
Boston Massacre Oration,
March 5, 1772

I wish most sincerely ... that a Constitution [were] formed ... for America, that we might know what we are and what we have, what our Rights and what our Duties, in the Judgment of this Country as well as in our own. Till such a Constitution is settled, different Sentiments will ever occasion Misunderstandings.
—*BENJAMIN FRANKLIN* (1706–1790)
To Joseph Galloway,
February 18, 1774

A constitution, which is to render millions happy or miserable ... [is] a matter of such moment [that it] cannot be the work of a day.
—*GEORGE WASHINGTON* (1732–1799)
To John Augustine Washington,
May 31, 1776

A constitution founded on these principles introduces knowledge among the people, and inspires them with a conscious dignity becoming freemen; a general emulation takes place, which causes good humor, sociability, good manners, and good morals to be general. That elevation of sentiment inspired by such a government, makes the common people brave and enterprising. That ambition which is inspired by it makes them sober, industrious, and frugal.
—*JOHN ADAMS* (1735–1826)
Thoughts on Government
1776

We, the people of the United State, in order to form a more perfect union, establish justice, insure domestic tranquility, provide for the common defense, promote the general welfare, and secure the blessings of liberty to ourselves and our posterity, do ordain and establish this Constitution for the United States of America.
—*CONSTITUTION OF THE UNITED STATES*
Preamble,
September 17, 1787

I confess that there are several parts of this Constitution which I do not at present approve, but I am not sure I shall ever approve them. For having lived long, I have experienced many instances of being obliged by better information, or fuller consideration, to change opinions even on important subjects, which I once thought right, but found to be otherwise.
—*BENJAMIN FRANKLIN*
Speech at the Constitutional
Convention,
September 17, 1787

I doubt ... whether any other Convention ... may be able to make a better constitution; for, when you assemble a number of men, to have the advantage of their joint wisdom, you inevitably assemble with those men all their prejudices, their passions, their errors of opinion, their local interests, and their selfish views. From such an assembly can a *perfect* production be expected? It therefore astonishes me, Sir, to find this system approaching so near to perfection ...
—*BENJAMIN FRANKLIN*
Speech at the Constitutional
Convention,
September 17, 1787

In these sentiments, sir, I agree to this Constitution, with all its faults, if they are such; because I think a General Government necessary for us, and there is no form of government, but what may be a blessing to the people if well administered; and believe further, that this is likely to be well administered for a course of years, and can only end in despotism, as other forms have done before it, when the people shall become so corrupted as to need despotic government, being incapable of any other.
—BENJAMIN FRANKLIN
Speech at the Constitutional Convention,
September 17, 1787

On the whole, Sir, I cannot help expressing a wish, that every member of the Convention who may still have objections to it, would with me on this occasion doubt a little of his own infallibility, and, to make *manifest* our *unanimity*, put his name to this Instrument.
—BENJAMIN FRANKLIN
Speech at the Constitutional Convention,
September 17, 1787

I have the happiness to know that it is a rising, and not a setting sun.
—BENJAMIN FRANKLIN
Franklin spoke these words as members of the Constitutional Convention signed the engrossed document.
September 17, 1787

A republic, if you can keep it.
—BENJAMIN FRANKLIN
In answer to a question by Mrs. Powel: "Well, doctor, what have we got, a republic or a monarchy?" Franklin had just emerged from the

Constitutional Convention, and his answer was recorded by Joseph McHenry.
September 18, 1787

I wish the Constitution, which is offered, had been made more perfect; but I sincerely believe it is the best that could be obtained at this time. And, as a constitutional door is opened for amendment hereafter, the adoption of it, under the present circumstances of the Union, is in my opinion desirable.
—GEORGE WASHINGTON
To Patrick Henry,
September 24, 1787

Perfection is not the lot of humanity. Instead of censuring the small faults of the constitution, I am astonished, that so many clashing interests have been reconciled—and so many sacrifices made to the *general interest*! The mutual concessions made by the gentlemen of the convention, reflect the highest honor on their candor and liberality; at the same time, they prove that their minds were deeply impressed with a conviction, that such mutual sacrifices are *essential to our union*.
—NOAH WEBSTER (1758–1843)
An Examination into the Leading Principles of the Federal Constitution,
Philadelphia,
October 17, 1787

The great objects which presented themselves were:
1. to unite a proper energy in the Executive and a proper stability in the Legislative departments, with the essential characters of Republican Government.
2. to draw a line of demarkation which would give to the General Government

CONSTITUTION

every power requisite for general purposes, and leave to the States every
power which might be most beneficially administered by them.
3. to provide for the different interests
of different parts of the Union.
4. to adjust the clashing pretensions of
the large and small States. Each of these
objects was pregnant with difficulties.
  The whole of them together formed
a task more difficult than can be well
conceived by those who were not concerned in the execution of it.
  —JAMES MADISON (1751–1836)
        To Thomas Jefferson,
          October 24, 1787

Nothing is more common here, and I
presume the case must be the same with
you, than to see companies of intelligent people equally divided, and equally
earnest [on the question of adopting the
U.S. Constitution], in maintaining on
one side that the General Government
will overwhelm the State Governments,
and on the other that it will be a prey to
their encroachments; on the one side
that the structure of the Government is
too firm and too strong, and on the other
that it partakes too much of the weakness and instability of the Governments
of the particular States. What is the
proper conclusion from all this? That
unanimity is not to be expected in any
great political question: that the danger
is probably exaggerated on each side,
when an opposite danger is conceived
on the opposite side—that if any Constitution is to be established by deliberation and choice, it must be examined with many allowances, and must
be compared not with the theory, which
each individual may frame in his own
mind, but with the system which it is

meant to take the place of, and with
any other which there might be a probability of obtaining.
          —JAMES MADISON
          To Archibald Stuart,
            October 30, 1787

The diversity of opinions on so interesting a subject [the Constitution],
among men of equal integrity and discernment, is at once a melancholy proof
of the fallibility of the human judgment,
and of the imperfect progress yet made
in the science of Government.
          —JAMES MADISON
          To Archibald Stuart,
            October 30, 1787

Should the States reject this excellent
Constitution, the probability is, an opportunity will never again offer to can-
cel another in peace—the next will be
drawn in blood.
        —GEORGE WASHINGTON
  Attributed to George Washington,
    Pennsylvania Journal and Weekly
                    Advertiser,
            November 14, 1787

After the lapse of six thousand years
since the Creation of the world, America
now presents the first instance of a
people assembled to weigh deliberately
and calmly, and to decide leisurely and
peaceably, upon the form of government by which they will bind themselves
and their posterity.
    —JAMES WILSON (1741–1798)
      Speech on Proposed Federal
                  Constitution,
            November 24, 1787

In giving a definition of the simple kinds
of government known throughout the

world, I had occasion to describe what I meant by a democracy; and I think I termed it, that government in which the people retain the supreme power, and exercise it either collectively or by representation. This Constitution declares this principle, in its terms and in its consequences, which is evident from the manner in which it is announced. "We, the People of the United States."

—JAMES WILSON
Pennsylvania Ratification Convention,
November 26, 1787

There are very good articles in it, and very bad. I do not know which preponderate.

—THOMAS JEFFERSON (1743–1826)
Letter to W. S. Smith,
November 1787

In the formation of our constitution the wisdom of all ages is collected—the legislators of antiquity are consulted, as well as the opinions and interests of the millions who are concerned. In short, it is an empire of reason.

—NOAH WEBSTER
An Examination into the Leading
Principles of the Federal Constitution
1787

It is an excellency of this Constitution that it is expressed with brevity, and in the plain, common language of mankind.

—OLIVER ELLSWORTH (1745–1807)
Statement made during the
ratification debates,
1787–1788

We are a young, virtuous, and growing people; we have the good wishes of all

mankind; nature has bountifully bestowed upon us the blessings of climate and soil; the extent of our country affords room for our rapid increase for ages to come; a wise system of government we want; a wise system of government is offered for our acceptance; receive the offered good; put it in practice with wisdom, moderation, and virtue; and you may become a great, flourishing and happy nation.

—ANONYMOUS
Article in the Connecticut Courant,
January 7, 1788

A constitution cannot set bounds to a nation's wants; it ought not, therefore, to set bounds to its resources. Unexpected invasions, long and ruinous wars, may demand all the possible abilities of the country. Shall not your government have power to call these abilities into action? The contingencies of society are not reducible to calculations. They cannot be fixed or bounded, even in imagination.

—ALEXANDER HAMILTON (1755–1804)
New York Ratification Convention,
June 27, 1788

Have they said, we the States? Have they made a proposal of a compact between States? If they had, this would be a confederated government. The question turns, Sir, on … the expression, We, the People, instead of the States of America. …

[T]he principles of this system are extremely pernicious, impolitic, and dangerous. … It is not a democracy, wherein the people retain all their rights securely. …

Here is a revolution as radical as that which separated us from Great Britain.

It is as radical, if in this transition our rights and privileges are endangered, and the sovereignty of the States be relinquished: And cannot we plainly see, that this is actually the case?

The rights of conscience, trial by jury, liberty of the press, all our immunities and franchises, all pretensions to human rights and privileges, are rendered insecure, if not lost, by this change so loudly talked of by some, and inconsiderately by others. Is this same relinquishment of rights worthy of freeman?
—PATRICK HENRY (1736–1799)
Speech at the Virginia Convention to ratify the new Constitution,
June 5, 1788

Revolutions in government have in general been the tumultuous exchange of one tyrant for another, or the elevation of a few aspiring nobles upon the ruins of a better system. Never before has the collected wisdom of any nation been permitted quietly to deliberate, and determine upon the form of government best adapted to the genius, views and circumstances of the citizens. Never before have the people of any nation been permitted, candidly to examine, and then delierately adopt or reject the constitution proposed.
—SIMEON BALDWIN (1761–1851)
Oration at New Haven,
July 4, 1788

'Tis done. We have become a nation.
—BENJAMIN RUSH (1745–1813)
To Elias Boudinot, referring to the ratification of the Constitution,
July 9, 1788

The people are the only legitimate fountain of power, and it is from them that the constitutional character, under which the several branches of government hold their power, is derived.
—JAMES MADISON
The Federalist Papers
1788

It may be considered as an objection inherent in the principle, that as every appeal to the people would carry an implication of some defect in the government, frequent appeals would in great measure deprive the government of that veneration which time bestows on every thing, and without which perhaps the wisest and freest governments would not possess the requisite stability. If it be true that all governments rest on opinion, it is no less true that the strength of opinion in each individual … depend much on the number which he supposes to have entertained the same opinion. The reason of man, like man himself, is timid and cautious, when left alone; and acquires firmness and confidence, in proportion to the number with which it is associated. When the examples, which fortify opinion, are *ancient* as well as *numerous*, they are known to have a double effect. In a nation of philosophers, this consideration ought to be disregarded. A reverence for the laws, would be sufficiently inculcated by the voice of an enlightened reason. But a nation of philosophers is as little to be expected as the philosophical race of kings wished for by Plato. And in every other nation, the most rational government will not find it a superfluous advantage to have the prejudices of the community on its side.
—JAMES MADISON
The Federalist Papers
1788

42

The danger of disturbing the public tranquility by interesting too strongly the public passions, is a still more serious objection against a frequent reference of constitutional questions, to the decision of the whole society. ... We are to recollect that all the existing constitutions were formed in the midst of a danger which repressed the passions most unfriendly to order and concord; of an enthusiastic confidence of the people in their patriotic leaders, which stifled the ordinary diversity of opinions on great national questions; of a universal ardor for new and opposite forms, produced by a universal resentment and indignation against the ancient government; and whilst no spirit of party, connected with the changes to be made, or the abuses to be reformed, could mingle its leaven in the operation. The future situations in which we must expect to be usually placed, do not present any equivalent security against the danger which is apprehended.
—JAMES MADISON
The Federalist Papers
1788

[T]he Constitution ought to be the standard of construction for the laws, and that wherever there is an evident opposition, the laws ought to give place to the Constitution. But this doctrine is not deducible from any circumstance peculiar to the plan of convention, but from the general theory of a limited Constitution.
—ALEXANDER HAMILTON
The Federalist Papers
1788

There is no position which depends on clearer principles, than that every act of a delegated authority, contrary to the tenor of the commission under which it is exercised, is void. No legislative act therefore contrary to the constitution, can be valid. To deny this would be to affirm that the deputy is greater than his principal; that the servant is above his master; that the representatives of the people are superior to the people themselves; that men acting by virtue of powers may do not only what their powers do not authorise, but what they forbid.
—ALEXANDER HAMILTON
The Federalist Papers
1788

The interpretation of the laws is the proper and peculiar province of the courts. A constitution is in fact, and must be, regarded by the judges as a fundamental law. It therefore belongs to them to ascertain its meaning as well as the meaning of any particular act proceeding from the legislative body. If there should happen to be an irreconcilable variance between the two, that which has the superior obligation and validity ought of course to be preferred; or in other words, the constitution ought to be preferred to the statute, the intention of the people to the intention of their agents.
—ALEXANDER HAMILTON
The Federalist Papers
1788

The truth is, after all the declamations we have heard, that the Constitution is itself, in every rational sense, and to every useful purpose, A BILL OF RIGHTS.
—ALEXANDER HAMILTON
The Federalist Papers
1788

{T}he powers reserved by the people [under the Constitution] render them secure, and, until they themselves become corrupt, they will always have upright and able rulers. I give my assent to the Constitution.
—*JOHN HANCOCK* (1737–1793)
Massachusetts Ratifying Convention, 1788

Can any government be devised, that will be more suited to citizens, who wish for equal freedom and common prosperity? better calculated for preventing corruption of manners? for advancing the improvements that endear or adorn life? or that can be more conformed to the nature and understanding, to the best and the last end of man? What harvests of happiness may grow from the seeds of liberty that are now sowing? The cultivation will indeed demand continual care, unceasing diligence, and frequent conflicts with difficulties. This too is consonant to the laws of our nature. As we pass through night into day, so we do through trouble into joy. Generally, the higher the prize, the deeper the suffering. We die into immortality. To object against the benefits offered to us by our Creator, by excepting to the terms annexed, is a crime to be equaled only by its folly.
—*JOHN DICKINSON* (1732–1794)
Observations on the Constitution Proposed by the Federal Convention
1788

The idea of a constitution, limiting and superintending the operations of legislative authority, seems not to have been accurately understood in Britain. There are, at least, no traces of practice conformable to such a principle. The Brit-ish Constitution is just what the British Parliament pleases. ... To control the power and conduct of the legislature, by an overruling constitution, was an improvement in the science and practice of government reserved to the American States.
—*JAMES WILSON*
Speech in Pennsylvania Ratifying Convention, 1788

The Constitution ... is unquestionably the wisest ever yet presented to men.
—*THOMAS JEFFERSON*
Letter to David Humphreys, March 1789

No society can make a perpetual constitution, or even a perpetual law.
—*THOMAS JEFFERSON*
Letter to James Madison, September 6, 1789

The earth belongs always to the living generation: they may manage it, then and what proceeds from it, as they please, during their usufruct. They are masters, too, of their own persons, and consequently may govern them as they please. But persons and property make the sum of the objects of government. The constitution and the laws of their predecessors are extinguished then, in their natural course, with those whose will gave them being. This could preserve that being, till it ceased to be itself, and no longer. Every constitution, then, expires at the end of thirty-four years. If it be enforced longer, it is an act of force, not of right.
—*THOMAS JEFFERSON*
Letter to James Madison, September 6, 1789

Our new Constitution is now established, and has an appearance that promises permanency; but in this world nothing can be said to be certain, except death and taxes.
—BENJAMIN FRANKLIN
Letter to Jean-Baptiste Leroy,
November 13, 1789

The American constitutions were to liberty, what a grammar is to language: they define its parts of speech, and practically construct them into syntax.
—THOMAS PAINE (1737–1809)
The Rights of Man
1791

The federal Government has been hitherto limited to the Specified powers, by the greatest Champions for Latitude in expounding those powers. If not only the *means*, but the *objects* are unlimited, the parchment had better be thrown into the fire at once.
—JAMES MONROE (1758–1831)
To Henry Lee,
January 1, 1792

If in the opinion of the People, the distribution or modification of the Constitutional powers be in any particular wrong, let it be corrected by an amendment in the way which the Constitution designates. But let there be no change by usurpation; for though this, in one instance, may be the instrument of good, it is the customary weapon by which free governments are destroyed.
—GEORGE WASHINGTON
Farewell Address,
September 17, 1796

The basis of our political system is the

right of the people to make and to alter their constitutions of government. But the constitution which at any time exists, till changed by an explicit and authentic act of the whole people, is sacredly obligatory upon all.
—GEORGE WASHINGTON
Farewell Address,
September 17, 1796

Free government is founded in jealousy, and not in confidence, which prescribes limited constitutions, to bind down those whom we are obliged to trust with power.
—THOMAS JEFFERSON
The Kentucky Resolutions
1798

In questions of power let no more be heard of confidence in man, but bind him down from mischief by the chains of the constitution.
—THOMAS JEFFERSON
The Kentucky Resolutions
1798

So far is the political system of the United States distinguishable from that of other countries, by the caution with which powers are delegated and defined; that in one very important case, even of commercial regulation and revenue, the power is absolutely locked up against the hands of both governments. A tax on exports can be laid by no Constitutional authority whatever.
—JAMES MADISON
"The Report of 1800"
January 7, 1800

Our Constitution professedly rests upon the good sense and attachment of the people. This basis, weak as it may appear, has not yet been found to fail.

—JOHN QUINCY ADAMS (1767–1848)
Letter to William Vans Murray,
January 27, 1801

I join cordially in admiring and revering the Constitution of the Untied States, the result of the collected wisdom of our country. That wisdom has committed to us the important task of proving by example that a government, if organized in all its parts on the Representative principle unadulterated by the infusion of spurious elements, if founded, not in the fears & follies of man, but on his reason, on his sense of right, on the predominance of the social over his dissocial passions, may be so free as to restrain him in no moral right, and so firm as to protect him from every moral wrong.

—THOMAS JEFFERSON
To Amos March,
November 20, 1801

Tho' written constitutions may be violated in moments of passion or delusion, yet they furnish a text to which those who are watchful may again rally & recall the people: they fix too for the people the principles for their political creed.

—THOMAS JEFFERSON
To Joseph Priestley,
June 19, 1802

It is also not entirely unworthy of observation, that in declaring what shall be the *supreme* law of the land, the *Constitution* itself is first mentioned, and not the laws of the United States generally, but those only which shall be made in *pursuance* of the Constitution, have that rank. Thus, the particular phraseology of the Constitution of the United States confirms and strengthens the principle, supposed to be essential to all written constitutions, that a law repugnant to the Constitution is void; and that *courts*, as well as other departments, are bound by that instrument.

—JOHN MARSHALL (1755–1835)
Marbury v. Madison
1803

Certainly all those who have framed written constitutions contemplate them as forming the fundamental and paramount law of the nation, and consequently the theory of every such government must be, that an act of the legislature, repugnant to the constitution, is void.

—JOHN MARSHALL
Marbury v. Madison
1803

The powers of the legislature are defined, and limited; and that those limits may not be mistaken, or forgotten, the constitution is written. To what purpose are powers limited, and to what purpose is that limitation committed to writing, if these limits may, at any time, be passed by those intended to be restrained? The distinction, between a government with limited and unlimited powers, is abolished, if those limits do not confine the persons on whom they are imposed, and if acts prohibited and acts allowed, are of equal obligation.

—JOHN MARSHALL
Marbury v. Madison
1803

By the tables of mortality, of the adults living at one moment of time, a majority will be dead in about nineteen years.

At the end of that period, then, a new majority is come into place; or, in other words, a new generation. Each generation is as independent of the one preceding. ... It has, like them, a right to choose for itself the form of government it believes most promotive of its own happiness; consequently, a solemn opportunity of doing this every nineteen or twenty years should be provided by the Constitution.

—THOMAS JEFFERSON
Letter to W. H. Torrance,
1815

Some men look at constitutions with sanctimonious reverence, and deem them, like the Ark of the Covenant, too sacred to be touched. They ascribe to the men of the preceding age a wisdom more than human, and suppose what they did to be beyond amendment. I knew that age well; I belonged to it, and labored with it. It deserved well of its country. It was very like the present, but without the experience of the present, and forty years of experience in government is worth a century of book-learning.

—THOMAS JEFFERSON
Letter to Samuel Kercheval,
July 12, 1816

A constitution, to contain an accurate detail of all the subdivisions of which its great powers will admit, and of all the means by which they may be carried into execution, would partake of the prolixity of a legal code, and could scarcely be embraced by the human mind. It would probably never be understood by the public. Its nature, therefore, requires that only its great outlines should be marked, its important objects designated, and the minor ingredients which compose those objects be deduced from the nature of the objects themselves. That this idea was entertained by the framers of the American constitution, is not only to be inferred from the nature of the instrument, but from the language.

—JOHN MARSHALL
McCulloch v. Maryland
1819

Let the end be legitimate, let it be within the scope of the constitution, and all means which are appropriate, which are plainly adapted to that end, which are not prohibited, but consistent with the letter and spirit of the constitution, are constitutional.

—JOHN MARSHALL
McCulloch v. Maryland
1819

This provision is made in a constitution, intended to endure for ages to come, and consequently, to be adapted to the various crises of human affairs.

—JOHN MARSHALL
McCulloch v. Maryland
1819

We must never forget that it is a constitution we are expounding.

—JOHN MARSHALL
McCulloch v. Maryland
1819

A constitution is framed for ages to come, and is designed to approach immortality as nearly as human institutions can approach it.

—JOHN MARSHALL
Cohens v. Virginia
1821

The people made the Constitution, and the people can unmake it. It is the creature of their own will, and lives only by their will.

—*JOHN MARSHALL*
Cohens v. Virginia
1821

Frame constitutions of government with what wisdom and foresight we may, they must be imperfect, and leave something to discretion, and much to public virtue.

—*JOSEPH STORY* (1779–1845)
Address to the Suffolk Bar,
1821

As men, whose intentions require no concealment, generally employ the words which most directly and aptly express the ideas they intend to convey, the enlightened patriots who framed our constitution, and the people who adopted it, must be understood to have employed words in their natural sense, and to have intended what they have said.

—*JOHN MARSHALL*
Gibbons v. Ogden
1824

I entirely concur in the propriety of resorting to the sense in which the Constitution was accepted and ratified by the nation. In that sense alone it is the legitimate Constitution. And if that be not the guide in expounding it, there can be no security for a consistent and stable, more than for a faithful exercise of its powers. If the meaning of the text be sought in the changeable meaning of the words composing it, it is evident that the shape and attributes of the Government must partake of the changes to which the words and

phrases of all living languages are constantly subject. What a metamorphosis would be produced in the code of law if all its ancient phraseology were to be taken in its modern sense. And that the language of our Constitution is already undergoing interpretations unknown to its founders, will I believe appear to all unbiased Enquirers into the history of its origin and adoption.

—*JAMES MADISON*
To Henry Lee,
June 25, 1824

CORRUPTION & BRIBERY

[N]either the wisest constitution nor the wisest laws will secure the liberty and happiness of a people whose manners are universally corrupt.

—*SAMUEL ADAMS* (1722–1803)
Essay in *The Public Advertiser*
1749

The time to guard against corruption and tyranny is before they shall have gotten hold of us. It is better to keep the wolf out of the fold than to trust to drawing his teeth and talons after he shall have entered.

—*THOMAS JEFFERSON* (1743–1826)
Notes on Virginia
1782

He is a man of splendid abilities but utterly corrupt. He shines and stinks like rotten mackerel by moonlight.

—*JOHN RANDOLPH* (1773–1833)
Speaking of Rep. Edward Livingston,
c. 1800

CRIME & PUNISHMENT

When justice on offenders is not done,

Law, government, and commerce are o'erthrown.
—SIR JOHN DENHAM
Of Justice
c. 1668

No man shall be twise sentenced by Civill Justice for one and the same Crime, offence, or Trespasse.
—ANONYMOUS
"Massachusetts Body of Liberties of 1641"

I always hear of capital executions with concern, and regret that there should occur so many instances in which they are necessary.
—GEORGE WASHINGTON (1732–1799)
To James Clinton,
December 31, 1778

I am now engaged in the most disagreeable part of my duty, trying criminals. … Punishment must of course become certain, and mercy dormant—a harsh system, repugnant to my feelings, but nevertheless necessary.
—JOHN JAY (1745–1829)
1778

Silence becomes a kind of crime when it operates as a cover or an encouragement to the guilty.
—THOMAS PAINE (1737–1809)
Pennsylvania Packet,
January 23, 1779

No subject shall be liable to be tried, after an acquittal, for the same crime or offence.
—ANONYMOUS
New Hampshire Constitution of 1784

Excessive bail shall not be required, nor excessive fines imposed, nor cruel and unusual punishments inflicted.
—CONSTITUTION OF THE UNITED STATES
Amendment 8, The Bill of Rights
1787

Errors, or caprices of the temper, can be pardoned and forgotten; but a cold, deliberate crime of the heart … is not to be washed away.
—THOMAS PAINE
To George Washington,
February 22, 1795

An avidity to punish is always dangerous to liberty. It leads men to stretch, to misinterpret and to misapply even the best of laws.
—THOMAS PAINE
Dissertation on First Principles of Government
1795

Penitence must precede pardon.
—JOHN ADAMS (1735–1826)
The Sedition Act
1798

The sword of the law should never fall but on those whose guilt is so apparent as to be pronounced by their friends as well as foes.
—THOMAS JEFFERSON (1743–1826)
Letter to Sarah Mease,
March 1801

CYNICISM

He who says there is no such thing as an honest man, you may be sure is himself a knave.
—GEORGE BERKELEY (1685–1753)
Maxims Concerning Patriotism
c. early 1700s

There is no act, however virtuous, for which ingenuity may not find some bad motive.
—*THOMAS JEFFERSON* (1743–1826)
To Edward Dowse,
April 19, 1803

To believe all men honest would be folly. To believe none so, is something worse.
—*JOHN QUINCY ADAMS* (1767–1848)
Letter to William Eustis,
June 22, 1809

I cannot act as if all men were unfaithful because some are so; nor believe that all will betray me, because some do. I had rather be the victim of occasional infidelities, than relinquish my general confidence in the honesty of man.
—*THOMAS JEFFERSON*
To Thomas Leiper,
January 1, 1814

D

DEATH

Death is but crossing the world, as friends do the seas; they live in one another still.
—*WILLIAM PENN* (1644–1718)
Some Fruits of Solitude
1693

[T]ough death be a dark passage, it leads to immortality, and that is recompense enough for suffering of it. And yet faith lights us, even through the grave. … And this is the comfort of the good, that the grave cannot hold them, and that they live as soon as they die. For death is no more than a turning of us over from time to eternity.
—*WILLIAM PENN*
Some Fruits of Solitude
1693

Death observes no ceremony.
—*JOHN WISE* (1652–1725)
A Vindication of the Government of New England Churches
1717

I condole with you, we have lost a most dear and valuable relation, but it is the will of God and Nature that these mortal bodies be laid aside, when the soul is to enter into real life. … We are spirits. That bodies should be lent us, while

they can afford us pleasure, assist us in acquiring knowledge, or doing good to our fellow creatures, is a kind and benevolent act of God—when they become unfit for these purposes and afford us pain instead of pleasure—instead of an aid, become an incumbrance and answer none of the intentions for which they were given, it is equally kind and benevolent that a way is provided by which we may get rid of them. Death is that way.
—*BENJAMIN FRANKLIN* (1706–1790)
Letter to his stepdaughter on the death of his brother,
February 22, 1756

A man is not completely born until he is dead. Why then should we grieve that a new child is born among the immortals, a new member added to their happy society?
—*BENJAMIN FRANKLIN*
Letter to Miss Elizabeth Hubbard,
February 23, 1756

Death is not the monarch of the dead, but of the dying. The moment he obtains a conquest he loses a subject.
—*THOMAS PAINE* (1737–1809)
The Crisis
1778

However men may differ in their ideas

51

of grandeur or of government here, the grave is nevertheless a perfect republic.
—*THOMAS PAINE*
The Crisis
1778

I will move gently down the stream of life until I sleep with my fathers.
—*GEORGE WASHINGTON* (1732–1799)
To Marquis de Lafayette,
February 1, 1782

… that abyss from whence no traveler is permitted to return.
—*GEORGE WASHINGTON*
To Marquis de Lafayette,
April 5, 1783

That the earth belongs in usufruct to the living: that the dead have neither powers nor rights over it. The portion occupied by any individual ceases to be his when [he] himself ceases to be, & reverts to the society.
—*THOMAS JEFFERSON* (1743–1826)
To James Madison,
September 6, 1789

Enough of life and all life's idle pomp-
    Nor by a tyrant's fiat will I live-
I leave the busy, vain, ambitious world
    To cheat itself anew, and o'er and o'er
    Treat the same ground their ancesters have trod,
    In chance of thrones, of scepters, or of crowns,
    'Till all these bubbles break in empty air,
    Nor leave a trace of happiness behind.
—*MERCY OTIS WARREN* (1728–1814)
The Sack of Rome, Act V, Sc. 3
c. 1790

It is the nature of man to die, and he will continue to die as long as he continues to be born.
—*THOMAS PAINE*
Rights of Man, I
1791

I thank you for your kind condolence on the death of my nephew. It is a loss I sincerely regret, but as it is the will of Heaven, whose decrees are always just and wise, I submit to it without a murmur.
—*GEORGE WASHINGTON*
To Bryan Fairfax,
March 6, 1793

Nothing, they say, is more certain than death, and nothing more uncertain than the time of dying.
—*THOMAS PAINE*
Decline and Fall of the English System of Finance
1796

The death of near relations always produces awful and affecting emotions, under whatsoever circumstances it may happen.
—*GEORGE WASHINGTON*
To Burgess Ball,
September 22, 1799

When the summons comes, I shall endeavor to obey it with a good grace.
—*GEORGE WASHINGTON*
To Burgess Ball,
September 22, 1799

It is well. I die hard, but I am not afraid to go.
—*GEORGE WASHINGTON*
His last words
December 14, 1799

I have lived an honest and useful life to mankind; my time has been spent in doing good, and I die in perfect composure and resignation to the will of my Creator, God.
—THOMAS PAINE
Last Will and Testament,
January 18, 1809

In the month of March last I was called to the house in another part of town which was built by my father, in which he lived and died and from which I buried him; and in the chamber in which I was born I could not forbear to weep over the remains of a beautiful child of my son Thomas that died of the whooping cough. Why was I preserved 3/4 of a century, and that rose cropped in the bud? I, almost dead at top and in all my limbs and wholly useless to myself and the world?
—JOHN ADAMS (1735–1826)
To Benjamin Rush,
July 19, 1812

There is a ripeness of time for death, regarding others as well as ourselves, when it is reasonable we should drop off, and make room for another growth. When we have lived our generation out, we should not wish to encroach on another.
—THOMAS JEFFERSON
To John Adams,
August 1, 1816

Tried myself, in the school of affliction, by the loss of every form of connection which can rive the human heart, I know well, and feel what you have lost, what you have suffered, are suffering, and have yet to endure. The same trials have taught me that, for ills so immeasurable, time and silence are the only medicines. I will not therefore, by useless condolences, open afresh the sluices of your grief nor, altho' mingling sincerely my tears with yours, will I say a word more, where words are vain, but that it is of some comfort to us both that the term is not very distant at which we are to deposit, in the same cerement, our sorrows and suffering bodies, and to ascend in essence to an ecstatic meeting with the friends we have loved and lost and whom we shall still love and never lose again.
—THOMAS JEFFERSON
Letter of condolence to John Adams upon the death of Abigail Adams,
November 13, 1818

Green be the turf above thee,
Friend of my better days!
None knew thee but to love thee,
Nor named thee but to praise.
—FITZ-GREENE HALLECK (1790–1867)
"On the Death of Joseph Rodman Drake"
1820

Mine is the next turn, and I shall meet it with good will, for after one's friends are all gone before them, and our faculties leaving us, too, one by one, why wish to linger in mere vegetation—as a solitary trunk in a desolate field, from which all its former companions have disappeared?
—THOMAS JEFFERSON
To Maria Cosway,
December 27, 1820

DECLARATION OF INDEPENDENCE

We hold these truths to be self-evident: That all men are created equal; that they are endowed by their Creator with certain unalienable rights; that among these are life, liberty, and the pursuit of happiness; that, to secure these rights, governments are instituted among men, deriving their just powers from the consent of the governed; that whenever any form of government becomes destructive of these ends, it is the right of the people to alter or to abolish it, and to institute new government, laying its foundation on such principles, and organizing its powers in such form, as to them shall seem most likely to effect their safety and happiness. Prudence, indeed, will dictate that governments long established should not be changed for light and transient causes; and accordingly all experience hath shown that mankind are more disposed to suffer, while evils are sufferable than to right themselves by abolishing the forms to which they are accustomed. But when a long train of abuses and usurpations, pursuing invariably the same object, evinces a design to reduce them under absolute despotism, it is their right, it is their duty, to throw off such government, and to provide new guards for their future security.

—*THOMAS JEFFERSON* (1743–1826)
The Declaration of Independence
1776

We, therefore, the representatives of the United States of America, in General Congress assembled, appealing to the Supreme Judge of the world for the rectitude of our intentions, do, in the name and by the authority of the good people of these colonies solemnly publish and declare, That these United Colonies are, and of right ought to be, FREE AND INDEPENDENT STATES; that they are absolved from all allegiance to the British crown and that all political connection between them and the state of Great Britain is, and ought to be, totally dissolved; and that, as free and independent states, they have full power to levy war, conclude peace, contract alliances, establish commerce, and do all other acts and things which independent states may of right do. And for the support of this declaration, with a firm reliance on the protection of Divine Providence, we mutually pledge to each other our lives, our fortunes, and our sacred honor.

—*THOMAS JEFFERSON*
The Declaration of Independence
1776

When in the course of human events, it becomes necessary for one people to dissolve the political bands which have connected them with another, and to assume among the powers of the earth, the separate and equal station to which the laws of nature and of nature's God entitle them, a decent respect to the opinions of mankind requires that they should declare the causes which impel them to the separation.

—*THOMAS JEFFERSON*
The Declaration of Independence
1776

The 4th of July has been celebrated in Philadelphia in the manner I expected. The military men, and particularly one of them, ran away with all the glory of the day. Scarcely a word was said of the solicitude and labors and fears and sorrows and sleepless nights of the men who projected, proposed, defended, and subscribed the Declaration of Independence. Do you recollect your memorable speech upon the day on which the vote was taken? Do you recollect

the pensive and awful silence which pervaded the house when we were called up, one after another, to the table of the president of Congress to subscribe what was believed by many at that time to be our own death warrants? The silence and the gloom of the morning were interrupted, I well recollect, only for a moment by Colonel Harrison of Virginia, who said to Mr. Gerry at the table: "I shall have a great advantage over you, Mr. Gerry, when we are all hung for what we are now doing. From the size and weight of my body I shall die in a few minutes, but from the lightness of your body you will dance in the air an hour or two before you are dead." This speech procured a transient smile, but it was soon succeeded by the solemnity with which the whole business was conducted.
—BENJAMIN RUSH (1745–1813)
To John Adams,
July 20, 1811

I prepared a draught of the Declaration committed to us. It was too strong for Mr. Dickinson. He still retained the hope of reconciliation with the mother country, and was unwilling it should be lessened by offensive statements. He was so honest a man, & so able a one that he was greatly indulged even by those who could not feel his scruples. We therefore requested him to take the paper, and put it into a form he could approve. He did so, preparing an entire new statement, and preserving of the former only the last 4 paragraphs & half of the preceding one. We approved & reported it to Congress, who accepted it. Congress gave a signal proof of their indulgence to Mr. Dickinson, and of their great desire not to go too fast for

any respectable part of our body, in permitting him to draw their second petition to the King according to his own ideas, and passing it with scarcely any amendment. The disgust against this humility was general; and Mr. Dickinson's delight at its passage was the only circumstance which reconciled them to it. The vote being passed, altho' further observn on it was out of order, he could not refrain from rising and expressing his satisfaction and concluded by saying "there is but one word, Mr. President, in the paper which I disapprove, & that is the word *Congress*," on which Ben Harrison rose and said "there is but on word in the paper, Mr. President, of which I approve, and that is the word *Congress*."
—THOMAS JEFFERSON
Autobiography
1821

It [the Declaration of Independence] stands, and must forever stand, alone, a beacon on the summit of the mountain, to which all the inhabitants of the earth may turn their eyes for a genial and saving light till time shall be lost in eternity, and this globe itself dissolve, nor leave a wreck behind. It stands for ever, a light of admonition to the rulers of men, a light of salvation and redemption to the oppressed ... [as the delineation of] the boundaries of their respective rights and duties, founded in the laws of nature, and of nature's God.
—JOHN QUINCY ADAMS (1767–1848)
July 4th Oration
1821

It [the Declaration of Independence] was the first solemn declaration by a nation of the only *legitimate* founda-

tion of civil government. It was the corner stone of a new fabric, destined to cover the surface of the globe. It demolished at a stroke the lawfulness of all governments founded upon conquest. It swept away all the rubbish of accumulated centuries of servitude. It announced in practical form to the world the transcendent truth of the unalienable sovereignty of the people. It proved that the social compact was no figment of the imagination; but a real, solid, and sacred bond of the social union.
—*JOHN QUINCY ADAMS*
July 4th Oration
1821

There were other expressions which I would not have inserted if I had drawn it up, particularly that which called the King tyrant. I thought this too personal, for I never believed George to be a tyrant in disposition and in nature; I always believed him to be deceived by his courtiers on both sides of the Atlantic, and in his official capacity, only, cruel. I thought the expression too passionate, and too much like scolding, for so grave and solemn a document; but as Franklin and Sherman were to inspect it afterwards, I thought it would not become me to strike it out.
—*JOHN ADAMS* (1735–1826)
To Timothy Pickering,
August 6, 1822

DEFAMATION & PERSONAL ATTACKS

Don't throw stones at your neighbors, if your own windows are glass.
—*BENJAMIN FRANKLIN* (1706–1790)
Poor Richard's Almanack
1736

We must not in the course of public life expect immediate approbation and immediate grateful acknowledgment of our services. But let us persevere through abuse and even injury. The internal satisfaction of a good conscience is always present, and time will do us justice in the minds of the people, even those at present the most prejudiced against us.
—*BENJAMIN FRANKLIN*
Letter to Joseph Galloway,
December 2, 1765

[E]very one who takes delight in publicly or privately taking away any person' s good name, or striving to render him ridiculous, are in the gall of bitterness, and in the bonds of iniquity, whatever their pretences may be for it.
—*SARAH UPDIKE GODDARD*
(c. 1700–1770)
Letter to her son, William Goddard,
1765

The same fidelity to the public interest which obliges those who are its appointed guardians, to pursue with every vigor a perfidious or dishonest servant of the public requires them to confront the imputations of malice against the good and faithful one.
—*JAMES MADISON* (1751–1836)
To Edmund Randolph,
June 4, 1782

I find the pain of a little censure, even when it is unfounded, is more acute than the pleasure of much praise.
—*THOMAS JEFFERSON* (1743-1826)
Letter to Francis Hopkinson,
March 13, 1789

It is a curious phenomenon in political

history (not easy to be paralleled), that a measure which has elevated the credit of the country from a state of exalted pre-eminence, should bring upon the authors of it reprobation and censure.
—*ALEXANDER HAMILTON* (1755–1804)
"Vindication of the Funding System"
1791

To speak evil of anyone, unless there is unequivocal proofs of their deserving it, is an injury for which there is no adequate reparation.
—*GEORGE WASHINGTON* (1732–1799)
To George Washington Parke Custis,
November 28, 1796

Defamation is becoming a necessary of life; insomuch that a dish of tea, in the morning or evening, cannot be digested without this stimulant. Even those who do not believe these abominations, still read them with complacence to their auditors, and instead of the abhorrence & indignation which should fill a virtuous mind, betray a secret pleasure in the possibility that some may believe them, tho they do not themselves. It seems to escape them that it is not he who prints, but he who pays for printing a slander, who is its real author.
—*THOMAS JEFFERSON*
To John Norvell,
June 11, 1807

Attacks on me will do no harm, and silent contempt is the best answer to them.
—*JAMES MONROE* (1758–1831)
To George Hay,
April 29, 1808

It has been my poor fortune to be much harassed and calumniated let me serve under whom I may. It seems as if I can never get home after the discharge of important trusts abroad, and most faithfully, peace. My head must be pelted by the storm if ever I expose myself to it.
—*JAMES MONROE*
To David Gelston,
February 7, 1809

I laid it down as a law to myself, to take no notice of the thousand calumnies issued against me, but to trust my own conduct, and the good sense and candor of my fellow citizens.
—*THOMAS JEFFERSON*
Letter to Wilson C. Nicholas,
1809

They [journalists] are a sort of assassins who sit with loaded blunderbusses at the corner of streets and fire them off for hire or for sport at any passenger they select.
—*JOHN QUINCY ADAMS* (1767–1848)
Diary Entry,
September 7, 1820

DEMOCRACY & REPUBLICANISM

A democracy. This is a form of government which the light of nature does highly value, and often directs to as most agreeable to the just and natural prerogatives of human beings. This was of great account in the early times of the world. And not only so, but upon the experience of several thousand years, after the world had been tumbled and tossed from one species of government to another, at a great expense of blood and treasure, many of the wise nations of the world have sheltered themselves under it again; or at least

57

have blendished and balanced their governments with it.
—*JOHN WISE* (1652–1725)
A Vindication of the Government of New England Churches
1717

Our real disease ... is democracy.
—*ALEXANDER HAMILTON* (1712–1756)
Letter to Theodore Sedgwick,
c. 1740s

In the strict sense of the term, a true democracy has never existed, and never will exist.
—*JEAN JACQUES ROUSSEAU* (1712–1778)
The Social Contract, III
1762

The first principle and great end of government being to provide for the best good of all the people, this can be done only by a supreme legislative and executive ultimately in the people or whole community where GOD has placed it; but the inconveniences, not to say impossibility, attending the consultations and operations of a large body of people have made it necessary to transfer the power of the whole to a *few*. This necessity gave rise to deputation, proxy, or a right of representation.
—*JAMES OTIS* (1725–1783)
The Rights of the British Colonies Asserted and Proved
1764

All men are Republicans by nature and Royalists only by fashion.
—*THOMAS PAINE* (1737–1809)
The Forester's Letters
1776

If there is a form of government, then,

whose principle and foundation is virtue, will not every sober man acknowledge it better calculated to promote the general happiness that any other form?
—*JOHN ADAMS* (1735–1826)
"Thoughts on Government"
1776

Besides the unsuitableness of the republican form to the genius of the people, America is too extensive for it. That form may do well enough for a single city, or small territory; but would be utterly improper for such a continent as this. America is too unwieldy for the feeble, dilatory administration of democracy. Rome had the most extensive dominions of any ancient republic. But it should be remembered, that very soon after the spirit of conquest carried the Romans beyond the limits that were proportioned to their constitution, they fell under a despotic yoke. A very few years had elapsed from the time of their conquering Greece and first entering Asia, till the battle of Pharsalia, where Julius Caesar put an end to the liberties of his country.
—*ANONYMOUS*
The True Interest of America Impartially Stated
1776

But a representative democracy, where the right of election is well secured and regulated, and the exercise of the legislative, executive and judiciary authorities is vested in select persons chosen really and not nominally by the people, will in my opinion be most likely to be happy, regular and durable.
—*ALEXANDER HAMILTON* (1755–1804)
To Robert R. Livingston,
March 19, 1777

Europe contains hardly any other distinctions but lords and tenants; this fair country alone is settled by freeholders, the possessors of the soil they cultivate, members of the government they obey, and the framers of their own laws, by means of their representatives.
—MICHEL GUILLAUME JEAN DE CRÈVECOEUR (1735–1813)
Letters from an American Farmer
1782

Democratical states must always feel before they can see: it is this that makes their governments slow, but the people will be right at last.
—GEORGE WASHINGTON (1732–1799)
To Marquis de Lafayette,
July 25, 1785

It has ever been my hobby-horse to see rising in America an empire of liberty, and a prospect of two or three hundred millions of freemen, without one noble or one king among them. You say it is impossible. If I should agree with you in this, I would still say, let us try the experiment, and preserve our equality as long as we can.
—JOHN ADAMS
To Count Sarsfield,
February 3, 1786

We are now forming a republican government. Real liberty is neither found in despotism or the extremes of democracy, but in moderate governments.
—ALEXANDER HAMILTON
Debates of the Federal Convention,
June 26, 1787

I have no fear that the result of our experiment will be that men may be trusted to govern themselves without a mas-

ter. Could the contrary of this be proved I should conclude either that there is no God or that He is a malevolent being.
—THOMAS JEFFERSON (1743–1826)
Letter to David Hartley,
1787

One of the worst forms of government is a pure democracy, that is, one in which the citizens enact and administer the laws directly. Such a government is helpless against the mischiefs of faction.
—JAMES MADISON (1751–1836)
The Federalist Papers
1787

Our true situation appears to me to be this—a new extensive Country containing within itself the materials for forming a Government capable of extending to its citizens all the blessings of civil & religious liberty—capable of making them happy at home. This is the great end of Republican Establishments.
—CHARLES PINCKNEY (1757–1824)
Speech in Framing Convention,
1787

The known propensity of a democracy is to licentiousness which the ambitious call, and ignorant believe to be liberty.
—FISHER AMES (1758–1808)
Speech in the Massachusetts Ratifying Convention,
January 15, 1788

When a people shall have become incapable of governing themselves, and fit for a master, it is of little consequence from what quarter he comes.
—GEORGE WASHINGTON
Letter to Marquis de Lafayette,
April 28, 1788

It has been observed, by an honorable gentleman, that a pure democracy, if it were practicable, would be the most perfect government. Experience has proved that no position in politics is more false than this. The ancient democracies, in which the people themselves deliberated, never possessed one feature of good government. Their very character was tyranny; their figure, deformity. When they assembled, the field of debate presented an ungovernable mob, not only incapable of deliberation, but prepared for every enormity.

—ALEXANDER HAMILTON
New York Ratification Convention,
June 21, 1788

It has been advanced as a principle, that no government but a despotism can exist in a very extensive country. This is a melancholy consideration indeed. If it were founded on truth, we oughnt to dismiss the idea of a republican government, even for the state of New York. This idea ... has been misapprehended; and its application is entirely false and unwarrantable; it relates only to democracies, where the whole body of the people meet to transact business, and where representation is unknown.

—ALEXANDER HAMILTON
New York Ratification Convention,
June 27, 1788

We may define a republic ... as a government which derives all its powers directly or indirectly from the great body of the people, and is administered by persons holding their offices during pleasure, for a limited period, or during good behavior. It is *essential* to such a government that it be derived from the great body of the society, not from an inconsiderable proportion, or a favoured class of it.

—JAMES MADISON
The Federalist Papers
1788

The republican is the only form of government which is not eternally at open or secret war with the rights of mankind.

—THOMAS JEFFERSON
Letter to William Hunter,
March 11, 1790

The extension of the theory and practice of representation through all the different departments of the state is another very important acquisition made, by the Americans, in the science of jurisprudence and government. To the ancients, this theory and practice seem to have been altogether unknown. To this moment, the representation of the people is not the sole principle of any government in Europe. ... The American States enjoy the glory and the happiness of diffusing this vital principle [of representation] throughout all the different divisions and departments of the government.

—JAMES WILSON (1741–1798)
Lectures,
1790–1791

The greatest characters the world have known, have rose on the democratic floor. Aristocracy has not been able to keep a proportionate pace with democracy.

—THOMAS PAINE
Rights of Man, I
1791

A government deriving its energy from the will of the society ... is the government for which philosophy has been searching, and humanity been fighting

from the most remote ages. Such are republican governments which it is the glory of America to have invented, and her unrivaled happiness to possess.
—JAMES MADISON
Article in the *National Gazette*,
February 20, 1792

Republican government is no other than government established and conducted for the interest of the public, as well individually as collectively.
—THOMAS PAINE
Rights of Man
1792

A monarchy is a merchantman which sails well, but will sometimes strike on a rock, and go to the bottom; a republic is a raft which will never sink, but then your feet are always in the water.
—FISHER AMES
Speech in House of Representatives,
1795

Republicanism is not the phantom of a deluded imagination. On the contrary ... under no form of government, will laws be better supported, liberty and property better secured, or happiness be more effectually dispensed to mankind.
—GEORGE WASHINGTON
To Edmund Pendleton,
January 22, 1795

The conviction that government, by representation, is the true system of government, is spreading itself fast in the world. The reasonableness of it can be seen by all. The justness of it makes itself felt even by its opposers.
—THOMAS PAINE
Agrarian Justice
1797

Sometimes it is said that man can not be trusted with the government of himself. Can he, then, be trusted with the government of others? Or have we found angels in the form of kings to govern him? Let history answer this question.
—THOMAS JEFFERSON
First inaugural address,
March 4, 1801

A republic must not only be so in its principles but in its form.
—THOMAS PAINE
"To the Citizens of the United States"
1802

It is the almost universal mistake of our countrymen, that democracy would be mild and safe in America. They charge the horrid excesses of France not so much to human nature, which will never act better when the restraints of government, morals, and religion are thrown off, but to the characteristic cruelty and wickedness of Frenchmen.

The truth is, and let it humble our pride, the most ferocious of all animals, when his passions are roused to fury and are uncontrolled, is man; and of all governments, the worst is that which never fails to excite, but was never found to restrain those passions, that is, democracy. It is an illuminated hell, that in the midst of remorse, horror, and torture, rings with festivity; for experience shows, that one joy remains to this most malignant description of the damned, the power to make others wretched.
—FISHER AMES
The Dangers of American Liberty
1805

A democracy cannot last. Its nature ordains, that its next change shall be

61

into a military despotism, of all known governments, perhaps, the most prone to shift its head, and the slowest to mend its vices. The reason is, that the tyranny of what is called the people, and that by the sword, both operate alike to debase and corrupt, till there are neither men left with the spirit to desire liberty, nor morals with the power to sustain justice.

—FISHER AMES
The Dangers of American Liberty,
1805

America has the high honor and happiness of being the first nation that gave to the world the example of forming written constitutions by conventions elected expressly for the purpose, and of improving them by the same procedure, as time and experience shall show necessary. Government in other nations … has been established by bloodshed. Not a drop of blood has been shed in the United States in consequence of establishing constitutions and governments by her own peaceful system. The silent vote, or the simple *yea or nay* is more powerful than the bayonet.

—THOMAS PAINE
To the Citizens of Pennsylvania on the
Proposal for Calling a Convention
1805

Brothers! between you and me
    Whirlwinds sweep and billows roar:
Yet in spirit oft I see
    On thy wild and winding shore
Freedom's bloodless banners wave,—
    Feel the pulses of the brave
Unextinguished in the grave,—
    See them drenched in sacred gore,—
Catch the warrior's gasping breath
Murmuring "Liberty or death!"

Shout aloud! Let every slave,
    Crouching at Corruption's throne,
Start into a man, and brave
    Racks and chains without a groan:
And the castle's heartless glow,
    And the hovel's vice and woe,
Fade like gaudy flowers that blow—
    Weeds that peep, and then are gone
Whilst, from misery's ashes risen,
    Love shall burst the captive's prison.

Cotopaxi! bid the sound
    Through thy sister mountains ring,
Till each valley smile around
    At the blissful welcoming!
And, O thou stern Ocean deep,
    Thou whose foamy billows sweep
Shores where thousands wake to weep
    Whilst they curse a villain king,
On the winds that fan thy breast
Bear thou news of Freedom's rest!

Can the daystar dawn of love,
    Where the flag of war unfurled
Floats with crimson stain above
    The fabric of a ruined world?
Never but to vengeance driven
    When the patriot's spirit shriven
Seeks in death its native Heaven!
    There, to desolation hurled,
Widowed love may watch thy bier,
Balm thee with its dying tear.

—PERCY BYSSHE SHELLEY (1792–1822)
To the Republicans of North America
1812
(Shelley was English, but was sympathetic to all movements for democracy)

Remember, democracy never lasts long. … There never was a democracy yet that did not commit suicide. It is in vain to say that democracy is less vain, less proud, less selfish, less ambitious, or less avaricious than aristocracy or monarchy.

—*JOHN ADAMS* (1735–1826)
Letter to John Taylor, Speaking of direct, not representative, democracy, April 15, 1812

DEPENDENCE

Dependence begets subservience and venality, suffocates the germ of virtue, and prepares fit tools for the designs of ambition.

—*THOMAS JEFFERSON* (1743–1826)
Notes on the State of Virginia
1782

DIFFICULTIES & ADVERSITY

All great and honorable actions are accomplished with great difficulties.

—*WILLIAM BRADFORD* (1590–1657)
History of Plymouth Plantation Commenting on the departure of the Pilgrims from Holland to the New World in 1620
1630–1651

No pain, no palm; no thorns, no throne; no gall, no glory; no cross, no crown.

—*WILLIAM PENN* (1644–1718)
No Cross, No Crown
1669

There are no gains without pains.

—*BENJAMIN FRANKLIN* (1706–1790)
Poor Richard's Almanack
1745

We ought not to convert trifling difficulties into insuperable obstacles.

—*GEORGE WASHINGTON* (1732–1799)
To Marquis de Malmedy,
May 16, 1777

We should never despair; our situation before has been unpromising and has changed for the better, so I trust, it will again. If new difficulties arise, we must only put forth new exertions and proportion our efforts to the exigency of the times.

—*GEORGE WASHINGTON*
Letter to Major General Philip Schuyler on the fall of Fort Ticonderoga,
July 15, 1777

A long series of politics so remarkably distinguished by a succession of misfortunes, without one alleviating turn, must certainly have something in it systematically wrong. It is sufficient to awaken the most credulous into suspicion, and the most obstinate into thought.

—*THOMAS PAINE* (1737–1809)
The Crisis
1778

On this little shell, how very few are the spots where man can live and flourish? Even under those mild climates which seem to breathe peace and happiness, the poison of slavery, the fury of despotism, and the rage of superstition, are all combined against man!

—*MICHEL GUILLAUME JEAN DE CRÈVECOEUR* (1735–1813)
Letters From an American Farmer
1782

We are not to expect to be translated from despotism to liberty in a feather bed.

—*THOMAS JEFFERSON* (1743–1826)
To Marquis de Lafayette,
1790

While despair is preying on the mind, time and its effects are preying on despair;

and certain it is, the dismal vision will face away, and *Forgetfulness*, with her sister Ease, will change the scene.
—*THOMAS PAINE*
Forgetfulness
1794

A garden ... is a very useful refuge of a disappointed politician.
—*ALEXANDER HAMILTON* (1755–1804)
To Charles Cotesworth Pinckney,
December 29, 1802

The only temper that honors a nation is that which rises in proportion to the pressure upon it.
—*JOHN QUINCY ADAMS* (1767–1848)
September 14, 1814

Grief drives men into habits of serious reflection, sharpens the understanding, and softens the heart.
—*JOHN ADAMS* (1735–1826)
Letter to Thomas Jefferson,
May 6, 1816

Little minds are tamed and subdued by misfortune, but great minds rise above it.
—*WASHINGTON IRVING* (1783–1859)
Philip of Pokanoket in *The Sketchbook*
1820

Afflictions of every kind are the onerous conditions charged on the tenure of life; and it is a silencing if not a satisfactory vindication of the ways of Heaven to Man, that there are but few who do not prefer an acquiescence in them, to a surrender of the tenure itself.
—*JAMES MADISON* (1751–1836)
To John G. Jackson,
December 28, 1821

If thou wouldst be happy and easy in thy family, above all things observe discipline.
—*WILLIAM PENN* (1644–1718)
Some Fruits of Solitude
1693

Be not deceived with the first appearances of things, but give thy self time to be in the right.
—*WILLIAM PENN*
Some Fruits of Solitude
1693

Discipline is the soul of an army. It makes small numbers formidable; procures success to the weak and esteem to all.
—*GEORGE WASHINGTON* (1732–1799)
Letter to the captains of the Virginia
Regiments,
July 1759

The best advice I can give ... is to be strict in your discipline; that is, to require nothing unreasonable of your officers and men, but see that whatever is required be punctually complied with.
—*GEORGE WASHINGTON*
To William Woodford,
November 10, 1775

Nothing can be more hurtful to the service, than the neglect of discipline, for that discipline, more than numbers, gives one army the superiority over another.
—*GEORGE WASHINGTON*
General Orders,
July 6, 1777

The firmness requisite for the real business of fighting is only to be attained by a constant course of discipline and service.

—GEORGE WASHINGTON
To Samuel Huntington,
September 15, 1780

DUE PROCESS

No mans life shall be taken away, no mans honour or good name shall be stayned, no mans person shall be arested, restrayned, banished, dismembred, nor any wayes punished, no man shall be deprived of his wife or children, no mans goods or estaite shall be taken away from him, nor any way indammaged under colour of law or Countenance of Authoritie, unlesse it be by vertue or equitie of some expresse law of the Country waranting the same, established by a generall Court and sufficiently published, or in case of the defect of a law in any parteculer case by the word of God. And in Capital cases, or in cases concerning dismembring or banishment according to that word to be judged by the Generall Court.

—ANONYMOUS
Massachusetts Body of Liberties
of 1641

That no Person or Persons shall or may, at any Time hereafter, be obliged to answer any Complaint, Matter or Thing whatsoever, relating to Property, before the Governor and Council, or in any other Place, but in ordinary Course of Justice, unless Appeals thereunto shall be hereafter by Law appointed.

—WILLIAM PENN (1644–1718)
Pennsylvania Charter of Privileges
of 1701

It is better that ten guilty persons escape than one innocent suffer.

—SIR WILLIAM BLACKSTONE (1723–1780)
Commentaries on the Laws of England
1765–1769

That it is better one hundred guilty persons should escape than that one innocent person should suffer is a maxim that has been long and generally approved.

—BENJAMIN FRANKLIN (1706–1790)
Letter to Benjamin Vaughan,
March 14, 1785

No person shall be held to answer for a capital, or otherwise infamous crime, unless on a presentment or indictment of the grand jury, except in cases arising in the land or naval forces, or in the militia, when in actual service in time of war or public danger; nor shall any person be subject for the same offence to be twice put in jeopardy of life or limb; nor shall be compelled in any criminal case to be a witness against himself, nor be deprived of life, liberty, or property, without due process of law; nor shall private property be taken for public use; without just compensation.

—CONSTITUTION OF THE UNITED STATES
Amendment 5, The Bill of Rights
1787

In all criminal prosecutions, the accused shall enjoy the right to a speedy and public trial, by an impartial jury of the state and district wherein the crime shall have been committed, which district shall have been previously ascertained by law, and to be informed of the nature and cause of the accusation; to be confronted with the witnesses against him; to have compulsory process for obtaining witnesses in his favor, and to have the assistance of counsel for his defence.

—CONSTITUTION OF THE UNITED STATES
Amendment 6, The Bill of Rights
1787

DUTY

Nor is a duty beneficial because it is commanded, but it is commanded because it is beneficial.

—BENJAMIN FRANKLIN (1706–1790)
Poor Richard's Almanack
1739

Only aim to do your duty, and mankind will give you credit where you fail.

—THOMAS JEFFERSON (1743–1826)
The Rights of British America
1774

There is one reward that nothing can deprive me of, and that is the consciousness of having done my duty with the strictest rectitude and most scrupulous exactness.

—GEORGE WASHINGTON (1732–1799)
To Lund Washington,
May 19, 1780

$\mathcal{E}$

ECONOMICS

Every individual necessarily labors to render the annual revenue of the society as great as he can. He generally indeed neither intends to promote the public interest, nor knows how much he is promoting it. ... He intends only his own gain, and he is in this, as in many other cases, led by an invisible hand to promote an end which was no part of his intention. ... By pursuing his own interest he frequently promotes that of the society more effectually than when he really intends to promote it. I have never known much good done by those who affected to trade for the public good.
—*ADAM SMITH* (1723–1790)
An Inquiry into the Nature and Causes of the Wealth of Nations
1776

It is not from the benevolence of the butcher, the brewer, or the baker that we expect our dinner, but from their regard to their own interest. We address ourselves, not to their humanity but to their self-love.
—*ADAM SMITH*
An Inquiry into the Nature and Causes of the Wealth of Nations
1776

People of the same trade seldom meet together, even for merriment and diversion, but the conversation ends in a conspiracy against the public, or in some contrivance to raise prices.
—*ADAM SMITH*
An Inquiry into the Nature and Causes of the Wealth of Nations
1776

Let the influx of money be ever so great, if there be no confidence, property will sink in value. ... The circulation of confidence is better than the circulation of money.
—*JAMES MONROE* (1758–1831)
Speech, Virginia Convention,
June 20, 1788

EDUCATION

Children had rather be making of tools and instruments of play; shaping, drawing, framing and bulding, &c. than getting some rules of propriety of speech by heart: and those also would follow with more judgment, and less trouble and time.
—*WILLIAM PENN* (1644–1718)
Some Fruits of Solitude
1693

The first thing obvious to children is what is sensible: and that we make no part of their rudiments.

We press their memory too soon, and puzzle, strain and load them with words and rules; to know grammar and rhetoric, and a strange tongue or two, that it is ten to one may never be useful to them; leaving their natural genius to mechnical and physical natural knowledge uncultivated and neglected; which would be of exceeding use and pleasure to them through the whole course of their life.

—*WILLIAM PENN*
Some Fruits of Solitude
1693

We shall have the more merchants and husbandmen, or ingenious naturalists, if the government be but any thing solicitous of the education of their youth: Which, next to the present and immediate happiness of any country, ought of all things, to be the care and skill of the government. For such as the youth of any country is bred, such is the next generation, and the government in good or bad hands.

—*WILLIAM PENN*
An Essay Towards the Present and Future Peace of Europe
1693

That none may Expect to be admitted into this College unless upon Examination of the Praesident and Tutors, They shall be found able Extempore to Read, Construe and Parce Tully, Virgil and the Greek Testament: and to write True Latin Prose and to understand the Rules of Prosodia, and Common Arithmetic, and shall bring Sufficient Testamony of his Blameless and inoffensive Life.

—*ANONYMOUS*
Regulations at Yale College
1745

On education all our lives depend / And few to that, too few, with care attend.

—*BENJAMIN FRANKLIN* (1706–1790)
Poor Richard's Almanack
1748

It should be your care, therefore, and mine, to elevate the minds of our children and exalt their courage; to accelerate and animate their industry and activity; to excite in them an habitual contempt of meanness, abhorrence of injustice and inhumanity, and an ambition to excel in every capacity, faculty, and virtue. If we suffer their minds to grovel and creep in infancy, they will grovel all their lives.

—*JOHN ADAMS* (1735–1826)
Dissertation on the Canon and Feudal Law
1765

Liberty cannot be preserved without general knowledge among people.

—*JOHN ADAMS*
Dissertation on the Canon and Feudal Law
1765

The preservation of the means of knowledge among the lowest ranks is of more importance to the public than all the property of all the rich men in the country.

—*JOHN ADAMS*
Dissertation on the Canon and Feudal Law
1765

The infant mind is pregnant with a variety of passions; But I apprehend it is in the power of those who are entrusted with the education of youth in a considerable degree to determine the bent of the noble passions and to fix them on salutary objects, or let them loose to such as are pernicious or destructive. Here then lies the foundation of civil liberty; in forming the habits of the youthful mind, in forwarding every passion that may tend to the promotion of the happiness of the community, in fixing in ourselves right ideas of benevolence, humanity, integrity and truth.

—*Nathanael Greene* (1742–1786)
To Samuel Ward Jr.,
1771

The principles and modes of government are too important to be disregarded by an inquisitive mind and I think are well worthy a critical examination by all students that have health and leisure.

—*James Madison* (1751–1836)
To William Bradford,
December 1, 1773

The slavery of a people is generally founded in ignorance of some kind or another; and there are not wanting such facts as abundantly prove the human mind may be so sunk and debased, through ignorance and its natural effects, as even to adore its enslaver, and kiss its chains. Hence knowledge and learning may well be considered as most essentially requisite to a free, righteous government.

— *Samuel Phillips Payson* (1736–1801)
A Sermon delivered in Boston,
1778

Illuminate, as far as practicable, the minds of the people at large, and more especially to give them knowledge of those facts, which history exhibiteth, that, possessed thereby of the experi-

ence of other ages and countries, they may be enabled to know ambition under all its shapes, and prompt to exert their natural powers to defeat its purposes.

—*Thomas Jefferson* (1743–1826)
1779

I consider knowledge to be the soul of a republic, and as the weak and the wicked are generally in alliance, as much care should be taken to diminish the number of the former as of the latter. Education is the way to do this, and nothing should be left undone to afford all ranks of people the means of obtaining a proper degree of it at a cheap and easy rate.

—*John Jay* (1745–1829)
To Benjamin Rush,
March 21, 1785

It is favourable to liberty. Freedom can exist only in the society of knowledge. Without learning, men are incapable of knowing their rights, and where learning is confined to a few people, liberty can be neither equal nor universal.

—*Benjamin Rush* (1745–1813)
Essay,
1786

Let our common people be compelled by law to give their children (what is commonly called) a good English education. Let schoolmasters of every description be supported in part by the public, and let their principles and morals be subjected to examination before we employ them. ... This plan of general education alone will render the American Revolution a blessing to mankind.

—*Benjamin Rush*
To Richard Price,
May 25, 1786

69

But while *property* is considered as the *basis* of the freedom of the American yeomanry, there are other auxiliary supports; among which is the *information of the people*. In no country, is education so general—in no country, have the body of the people such a knowledge of the rights of men and the principles of government. This knowledge, joined with a keen sense of liberty and a watchful jealousy, will guard our constitutions, and awaken the people to an instantaneous resistance of encroachments.

—*NOAH WEBSTER* (1758–1843)
"An Examination into the Leading Principles of the Federal Constitution"
October 17, 1787

The blessings of knowledge can be extended to the poor and laboring part of the community only by the means of FREE SCHOOLS. ... To a people enlightened in the principles of liberty and Christianity, arguments, it is to be hoped, will be unnecessary to persuade them to adopt these necessary and useful institutions.

—*BENJAMIN RUSH*
To the Citizens of Philadelphia,
March 28, 1787

Children should be educated and instructed in the principles of freedom.

—*JOHN ADAMS*
Defense of the Constitutions
1787

Every child in America should be acquainted with his own country. He should read books that furnish him with ideas that will be useful to him in life and practice. As soon as he opens his lips, he should rehearse the history of his own country.

—*NOAH WEBSTER*
On the Education of Youth in America
1788

It is an object of vast magnitude that systems of education should be adopted and pursued which may not only diffuse a knowledge of the sciences but may implant in the minds of the American youth the principles of virtue and of liberty and inspire them with just and liberal ideas of government and with an inviolable attachment to their own country.

—*NOAH WEBSTER*
On the Education of Youth in America
1788

In a country like this ... if there cannot be money found to answer the common purposes of education ... it is evident that there is something amiss in the ruling political power.

—*GEORGE WASHINGTON* (1732–1799)
To John Armstrong,
April 25, 1788

Let public schools then be established in every county of the United States, at least as many as are necessary for the present population; and let those schools be supported by a general tax.

—*ROBERT CORAM* (1761–1796)
"Political Inquiries, to which is added a plan for the establishment of schools throughout the United States"
1791

The class of literati is not less necessary than any other. They are the cultivators of the human mind—the manufacturers of useful knowledge—the agents of the commerce of ideas—the censors of public manners—the teachers of the arts of life and the means of happiness.

—*JAMES MADISON*
Notes for Essays,
December 1791

There is existing in man, a mass of sense lying in a dormant state, and which, unless something excites it to action, will descend with him, in that condition, to the grave.

—*THOMAS PAINE* (1737–1809)
Rights of Man, II
1792

In a government founded on the sovereignty of the people the education of youth is an object of the first importance. In such a government knowledge should be diffused throughout the whole society, and for that purpose the means of acquiring it made not only practicable but easy to every citizen.

—*JAMES MONROE* (1758–1831)
Address to the Virginia General
Assembly,
December 6, 1801

It is universally admitted that a well-instructed people alone can be permanently a free people.

—*JAMES MADISON*
Second annual message to Congress,
December 5, 1810

Enlighten the people generally, and tyranny and oppressions of body and mind will vanish like evil spirits at the dawn of the day.

—*THOMAS JEFFERSON*
Letter to P. S. du Pont de Nemours,
April 24, 1816

It is only when the People become ignorant and corrupt, when they degenerate into a populace, that they are incapable of exercizing their sovereignty. … The people themselves become the willing instruments of their own debasement and ruin. … Let us, by all wise and constitutional measures, promote intelligence among the People, as the best means of preserving our liberties.

JAMES MONROE
First Inaugural Address,
March 4, 1817

An institution which endeavors to rear American youth in pure love of truth and duty, and while it enlightens their minds by ingenious and liberal studies, endeavors to awaken a love of country, to soften local prejudices, and to inoculate Christian faith and charity, cannot but acquire, as it deserves, the confidence of the wise and good.

—*JAMES MONROE*
Commenting on Harvard University
in "A Narrative of a Tour of
Observation"
1818

I take a deep interest, as a parent and a citizen, in the success of female education, and have been delighted whenever I have been, to witness the attention paid to it.

—*JAMES MONROE*
Commenting on Harvard University
in "A Narrative of a Tour of
Observation"
1818

If the condition of man is to be progressively ameliorated, as we fondly

71

hope & believe, education is to be the chief instrument in effecting it.
—THOMAS JEFFERSON
To M. Jullien,
1818

I know no safe depository of the ultimate powers of the society but the people themselves: and if we think them not enlightened enough to exercise their control with a wholesome discretion, the remedy is not to take it from them, but to inform their discretion by education. This is the true corrective of abuses of constitutional power.
—THOMAS JEFFERSON
To William Charles Jarvis,
September 28, 1820

Learned Institutions ought to be favorite objects with every free people. They throw that light over the public mind which is the best security against crafty & dangerous encroachments on the public liberty.
—JAMES MADISON
Letter to W. T. Barry,
August 4, 1822

There is no royal road to Learning.
—RALPH WALDO EMERSON (1803–1882)
Journal
1824

A diffusion of knowledge is the only guardian of true liberty.
—JAMES MADISON
To George Thompson,
1825

A military instructor whose duty it should be, to call the roll, and parade the youth, at such times as should be appointed, to instruct them in military tactics and see

that they are in place. To educate the youth in all the sciences, and rear them to elevated and useful purposes, an appeal must be made to generous and noble sentiments, but at the same time the discipline must be exact and strict. Their duties should be regulated by the hour, and they should always be in place at the time appointed. A departure from the rule is sure to degenerate into licentiousness.
—JAMES MONROE
Monroe on students at the University of Virginia,
August 25, 1828

ELECTIONS & POLITICS

I entreat you to consider that, when you choose magistrates, you take them from among yourselves, men subject to like passions as you are.
—JOHN WINTHROP (1588–1649)
Speaking in a court case,
1645

Political contests are necessary sometimes, as well as military, to afford exercise and practice, and to instruct in the art of defending liberty and property.
—JAMES MADISON (1751–1836)
Letter to William Bradford, Jr.,
January 24, 1774

Whenever politics are applied to debauch mankind from their integrity, and dissolve the virtue of human nature, they become detestable; and to be a statesman on this plan, is to be a commissioned villain. He who aims at it, leaves a vacancy in his character, which may be filled up with the worst of epithets.
—THOMAS PAINE (1737–1809)
To the Abbe Raynal,
1782

An auxiliary desideratum for the melio-
ration of the Republican form is such a
process of elections as will most certainly extract from the mass of the Society the purest and noblest characters
which it contains; such as will at once
feel most strongly the proper motives
to pursue the end of their appointment,
and be most capable to devise the proper
means of attaining it.

—JAMES MADISON
"Vices of the Political System"
April 1787

Can we forget for whom we are forming a Government? Is it for *man*, or
for the imaginary beings called *States*?
Will our honest constituents be satisfied with metaphysical distinctions? ...
The rule of suffrage ought on every
principle to be the same in the 2d as in
the 1st branch [of the legislature]. If
the Government be not laid on this foundation, it can be neither solid nor lasting, any other principle will be local,
confined and temporary.

—JAMES WILSON (1742–1798)
Constitutional Convention,
June 30, 1787

In this system, it is declared that the
electors in each state shall have the
qualifications requisite for electors of
the most numerous branch of the state
legislature. This being made the criterion of the right of suffrage, it is consequently secured, because the same
Constitution guaranties to every state
in the Union a republican form of government. The right of suffrage is fundamental to republics.

—JAMES WILSON
Pennsylvania Ratification Convention,
November 26, 1787

After all, Sir, we must submit to this
idea, that the true principle of a republic is that the people should choose
whom they please to govern them.
Representation is imperfect in proportion as the current of popular favor is
checked. This great source of free government, popular election, should be
perfectly pure, and the most unbounded
liberty allowed.

—ALEXANDER HAMILTON (1755–1804)
Speech in the New York Assembly,
June 21, 1788

I am now pressed by some of my friends
to repair to Virginia as a requisite expedient for counteracting the machinations
against my election into the House of
Representatives. To this again I am extremely disinclined. ... It will have an
electioneering appearance which I always despised and wish to shun.

—JAMES MADISON
To Edmund Randolph,
November 23, 1788

It is a just observation that the people
commonly intend the Public Good. This
often applies to their very errors. But
their good sense would despise the adu-
lator who should pretend they always
reason right about the means of promoting it.

—ALEXANDER HAMILTON
The Federalist Papers
1788

Corruption in Elections has heretofore
destroyed all Elective Governments.
What Regulations or Precautions may
be devised to prevent it in future, I am
content with you to leave Posterity to
consider. You and I shall go to the Kingdom of the just or at least shall be re-

leased from the Republic of the Unjust, with Hearts pure and hands clean of all Corruption in Elections; so much I firmly believe.

—*JOHN ADAMS* (1735–1826)
Letter to Thomas Jefferson,
April 6, 1796

In all free governments, contentions in elections will take place, and, whilst it is confined to our own citizens, it is not to be regretted; but severely indeed ought it to be reprobated, when occasioned by foreign machinations.

—*GEORGE WASHINGTON* (1732–1799)
To Jonathan Trumbull,
March 3, 1797

I am sensible that by being removed from the turbulent and disgusting scene of perpetual electioneering I am spared many a detail of vexation...

—*JOHN QUINCY ADAMS* (1767–1848)
Letter to Thomas Boylston Adams,
December 20, 1800

Politics is such a torment that I would advise everyone I love not to mix with it.

—*THOMAS JEFFERSON* (1743–1826)
Letter to Martha Jefferson Randolph,
1800

I have taken final leave [of politics]. I think little of them and say less. I have given up newspapers in exchange for Tacitus and Thucydides, for Newton and Euclid, and I find myself much happier.

—*THOMAS JEFFERSON*
Letter to John Adams,
January 21, 1821

I would take no one step to advance or promote pretensions to the Presidency. If that office was to be the prize of cabal and intrigue, or purchasing newspapers, bribing by appointments, or bargaining for foreign missions, I had no ticket in that lottery.

—*JOHN QUINCY ADAMS*
Diary entry,
February 25, 1821

ENGLAND (UNITED KINGDOM)

Blessed by thy Commons, who for
    common good,
And thy infringed Laws have boldly
    stood.

—*ANNE BRADSTREET* (c. 1612–1672)
"A Dialogue Between Old England
and New: New England"
1642

We all think ourselves happy under Great Britain. We love, esteem, and reverence our mother country, and adore our King. And could the choice of independency be offered the colonies or subjection to Great Britain upon any terms above absolute slavery, I am convinced they would accept the latter.

—*JAMES OTIS* (1725–1783)
*Rights of the British Colonies
Asserted and Proved*
1764

The union between our Mother Country and these Colonies, and the energy of mild and just Government, produce benefits so remarkably important, and afforded such an assurance of their permanency and increase, that the wonder and envy of other nations were excited, while they beheld Great Britain rising to a power the most extra-ordinary the world had ever known.

—ANONYMOUS

Olive Branch Petition, a last attempt by moderate colonists to avoid war with Great Britain. It was signed by representatives of the colonies on July 8, 1775 and presented to King George III. Among the 48 signatories were John Adams, Stephen Hopkins, Benjamin Franklin, Thomas Jefferson and others who would later sign the Declaration of Independence.

July 8, 1775

The history of the present King of Great Britain is a history of repeated injuries and usurpations, all having in direct object the establishment of an absolute tyranny over these states. To prove this, let facts be submitted to a candid world.

He has refused his assent to laws, the most wholesome and necessary for the public good.

He has forbidden his governors to pass laws of immediate and pressing importance, unless suspended in their operation till his assent should be obtained; and, when so suspended, he has utterly neglected to attend to them.

He has refused to pass other laws for the accommodation of large districts of people, unless those people would relinquish the right of representation in the legislature, a right inestimable to them, and formidable to tyrants only.

He has called together legislative bodies at places unusually uncomfortable, and distant from the depository of their public records, for the sole purpose of fatiguing them into compliance with his measures.

He has dissolved representative houses repeatedly, for opposing, with manly firmness, his invasions on the rights of the people.

He has refused for a long time, after such dissolutions, to cause others to be elected; whereby the legislative powers, incapable of annihilation, have returned to the people at large for their exercise; the state remaining, in the mean time, exposed to all the dangers of invasions from without and convulsions within.

He has endeavored to prevent the population of these states; for that purpose obstructing the laws for naturalization of foreigners; refusing to pass others to encourage their migration hither, and raising the conditions of new appropriations of lands.

He has obstructed the administration of justice, by refusing his assent to laws for establishing judiciary powers.

He has made judges dependent on his will alone, for the tenure of their offices, and the amount and payment of their salaries.

He has erected a multitude of new offices, and sent hither swarms of officers to harass our people and eat out their substance.

He has kept among us, in times of peace, standing armies, without the consent of our legislatures.

He has affected to render the military independent of, and superior to, the civil power.

He has combined with others to subject us to a jurisdiction foreign to our Constitution and unacknowledged by our laws, giving his assent to their acts of pretended legislation:

For quartering large bodies of armed troops among us;

For protecting them, by a mock trial, from punishment for any murders which they should commit on the inhabitants of these states;

For cutting off our trade with all parts of the world;

For imposing taxes on us without our consent;

For depriving us, in many cases, of the benefits of trial by jury;

For transporting us beyond seas, to be tried for pretended offenses;

For abolishing the free system of English laws in a neighboring province, establishing therein an arbitrary government, and enlarging its boundaries, so as to render it at once an example and fit instrument for introducing the same absolute rule into these colonies;

For taking away our charters, abolishing our most valuable laws, and altering fundamentally the forms of our governments;

For suspending our own legislatures, and declaring themselves invested with power to legislate for us in all cases whatsoever.

He has abdicated government here, by declaring us out of his protection and waging war against us.

He has plundered our seas, ravaged our coasts, burned our towns, and destroyed the lives of our people.

He is at this time transporting large armies of foreign mercenaries to complete the works of death, desolation, and tyranny already begun with circumstances of cruelty and perfidy scarcely paralleled in the most barbarous ages, and totally unworthy the head of a civilized nation.

He has constrained our fellow-citizens, taken captive on the high seas, to bear arms against their country, to become the executioners of their friends and brethren, or to fall themselves by their hands.

He has excited domestic insurrection among us, and has endeavored to bring on the inhabitants of our frontiers the merciless Indian savages, whose known rule of warfare is an undistinguished destruction of all ages, sexes, and conditions.

In every stage of these oppressions we have petitioned for redress in the most humble terms; our repeated petitions have been answered only by repeated injury. A prince, whose character is thus marked by every act which may define a tyrant, is unfit to be the ruler of a free people.

Nor have we been wanting in our attentions to our British brethren. We have warned them, from time to time, of attempts by their legislature to extend an unwarrantable jurisdiction over us. We have reminded them of the circumstances of our emigration and settlement here. We have appealed to their native justice and magnanimity; and we have conjured them, by the ties of our common kindred, to disavow these usurpations which would inevitably interrupt our connections and correspondence. They too, have been deaf to the voice of justice and of consanguinity. We must, therefore, acquiesce in the necessity which denounces our separation, and hold them as we hold the rest of mankind, enemies in war, in peace friends.

—*THOMAS JEFFERSON* (1743–1826)
The Declaration of Independence
1776

Your [the citizens of the 13 colonies] adversaries are composed of wretches who laugh at the rights of humanity, who turn religion into derision, and would, for higher wages, direct their swords against their leaders or their country.

—SAMUEL ADAMS (1722–1803)
Speech to Continental Congress,
1776

After the coolest reflections on the matter, *this must* be allowed, that Britain was too jealous of America, to govern it justly; too ignorant of it, to govern it well; and too distant from it, to govern it at all.

—THOMAS PAINE (1737–1809)
The Crisis
1777

In 1764 the plan for raising a revenue from this country was resolved on by the British ministry, and their obsequious parliament were instructed to pass an act for that purpose. Not content with having for a century directed the entire commerce of America, and centered its profits in their own island, thereby deriving from the colonies every substantial advantage which the situation and transmarine distance of the country could afford them: not content with appointing the principal officers in the different governments, while the king had a negative upon every law that was enacted: not content with our supporting the whole charge of our municipal establishments, although their own creatures held the chief posts therein not content with laying external duties upon our mutilated and shackled commerce, they, by this statute, attempted to rob us of even the curtailed property, the hard-earned peculium which still remained to us to create a revenue for the support of a fleet and army, in reality to overawe and secure our subjection, not (as they insidiously pretended) to protect our trade, or defend our frontiers; the first of which they annoyed, and the latter deserted.

—WILLIAM TUDOR (dates unknown)
Boston Massacre Oration,
March 5, 1779

I wish you, Sir, to believe, and that it may be understood in America, that I have done nothing in the late contest, but what I thought myself indispensably bound to do by the Duty which I owed to my people. I will be very frank with you. I was the last to consent to the separation; but the separation having been made, and having become inevitable, I have always said as I say now, that I would be the first to meet the Friendship of the United States as an independent Power.

—KING GEORGE III (1738–1820)
Letter of John Adams to John Jay.
Adams had an audience with King George III and reported what had been said in this letter.
June 2, 1785

I believe the British government forms the best model the world ever produced. … This government has for its object public strength and individual security.

—ALEXANDER HAMILTON (1755–1804)
Debates of the Federal Convention,
June 18, 1787

Great Britain's governing principles are conquest, colonization, commerce, monopoly.

—THOMAS JEFFERSON
Letter to William Carmichael,
1790

England presents a singular phenomenon of an honest people whose constitution, from its nature, must render their government forever dishonest.

—*THOMAS JEFFERSON*
Letter to James Ronaldson,
1810

The extremes of opulence and of want are more remarkable, and more constantly obvious, in this country than in any other that I ever saw.

—*JOHN QUINCY ADAMS* (1767–1848)
Diary entry,
November 8, 1816

ENVY & MALICE

Believe nothing against another, but upon good authority: nor report what may hurt another, unless it be a greater hurt to others to conceal it.

—*WILLIAM PENN* (1644–1718)
Some Fruits of Solitude
1693

Jealousy is a kind of civil war in the soul, where judgment and imagination are at perpetual jars. This civil dissension in the mind, like that of the body politic, commits great disorders, and lays all waste. Nothing stands safe in its way: nature, interest, religion, must yield to its fury. It violates contracts, dissolves society, breaks wedlock, betrays friends and neighbours. No body is good, and every one is either doing or designing them a mischief.

—*WILLIAM PENN*
More Fruits of Solitude
1702

Some men do as much begrudge others a good name, as they want one themselves; and perhaps that is the reason of it.

—*WILLIAM PENN*
More Fruits of Solitude
1702

Let your conversation be without malice or envy, for 'tis a sign of a tractable and commendable nature.

—*GEORGE WASHINGTON* (1732–1799)
Rules of Civility
1745

There are two distinct species of popularity: the one excited by merit, the other by resentment.

—*THOMAS PAINE* (1737–1809)
Rights of Man, I
1791

EQUALITY & EQUAL RIGHTS

Every person within this Jurisdiction, whether Inhabitant or forreiner shall enjoy the same justice and law, that is generall for the plantation, which we constitute and execute one towards another without partialitie or delay.

—*ANONYMOUS*
Massachusetts Body of Liberties of
1641

When the Lord sent me forth into the world, He forbade me to put off my hat to any, high or low.

—*GEORGE FOX* (1624–1691)
Journal
1694

The third capital immunity belonging to man's nature is an equality amongst men, which is not to be denied by the law of nature till man has resigned himself with all his rights for the sake of a

civil state, and then his personal liberty and equality is to be cherished and preserved to the highest degree as will consist with all just distinctions amongst men of honor and shall be agreeable with the public good.
—JOHN WISE (1652–1725)
A Vindication of the Government of New England Churches
1717

Reason teaches that *all Men* are *naturally equal* in Respect of *Jurisdiction* or *Dominion* one over another.
—REV. ELISHA WILLIAMS (1694–1755)
A Seasonable Plea
1744

The dons, the bashaws, the grandees, the patricians, the sachems, the nabobs, call them by what names you please, sigh and groan and fret, and sometimes stamp and foam and curse, but all in vain. The decree is gone forth, and it cannot be recalled, that a more equal liberty than has prevailed in other parts of the earth must be established in America.
—JOHN ADAMS (1735–1826)
To Patrick Henry,
June 3, 1776

All men are created equally free and independent, and have certain inherent rights, of which they cannot, by any compact, deprive or divest their posterity: among which are the enjoyment of life and liberty, with the means of acquiring and possessing property, and pursuing the obtaining happiness and safety.
—GEORGE MASON (1725–1792)
First draft, Virginia Declaration
of Rights,
c. 1776

The foundation on which all [our constitutions] are built is the natural equality of man, the denial of every preeminence but that annexed to legal office, and particularly the denial of a preeminence by birth.
—THOMAS JEFFERSON (1743–1826)
Letter to George Washington,
1784

The earth is given as a common stock for man to labor and live on.
—THOMAS JEFFERSON
Letter to James Madison,
1785

The people of the U. States are perhaps the most singular of any we are acquainted with. Among them there are fewer distinctions of fortune and less of rank, than among the inhabitants of any other nation. Every freeman has a right to the same protection and security; and a very moderate share of property entitles them to the possession of all the honors and privileges the public can bestow: hence arises a greater equality, than is to be found among the people of any other country, and an equality which is more likely to continue.
—CHARLES PINCKNEY (1757–1824)
"Plan of a Government for America"
June 25, 1787

That all men are by nature equal was once the fashionable phrase of the times, and men gloried in this equality and really believed it, or else they acted their parts to the life! Latterly, however, this notion is laughed out of countenance, and some very grave personages have not scrupled to assert that as we have copied the English in our form of federal government, we ought to

79

imitate them in the establishment of a nobility also.

—TIMOTHY DWIGHT (1752–1817)
"Political Inquiries, to which is added a plan for the establishment of schools throughout the United States"
1791

The true and only basis of representative government is equality of rights. Every man has a right to one vote, and no more in the choice of representatives.

—THOMAS PAINE (1737–1809)
Dissertation on First Principles of Government
1795

Equally fallacious is the doctrine of equality, of which much is said, and little understood. That one man in a state, has as good a right as another to his life, limbs, reputation and property, is a proposition that no man will dispute. Nor will it be denied that each member of a society, who has not forfeited his claims by misconduct, has an equal right to protection. But if by equality, writers understand an equal right to distinction, and influence; or if they understand an equal share of talents and bodily powers; in these senses, all men are not equal.

—NOAH WEBSTER (1758–1843)
"An Oration on the Anniversary of the Declaration of Independence"
1802

Equal laws protecting equal rights are … the best guarantee of loyalty & love of country.

—JAMES MADISON (1751–1836)
Letter to Jacob De La Motta,
August 1820

In regard to this principle, that all men are born free and equal, if there is an animal on earth to which it does not apply that is not born free, it is man— he is born in a state of the most abject want, and in a state of perfect helplessness and ignorance. … Who should say that all the soil in the world is equally rich, the first rate land in Kentucky and the Highlands of Scotland because the superficial content of the acre is the same, would be just as right as he who should maintain the absolute equality of man in virtue of his birth. The ricketty and scrofulous little wretch who first sees the light in a work-house, or in a brothel, and who feels the effects of alcohol before the effects of vital air, is not equal in any respect to the ruddy offspring of the honest yeoman; nay, I will go further, and say that a prince, provided he is no better born than royal blood will make him, is not equal to the healthy son of a peasant.

—JOHN RANDOLPH (1773–1833)
Remarks in the Senate,
c. 1826

ERROR

It is one thing to show a man that he is in an error, and another to put him in possession of truth.

—JOHN LOCKE (1632–1704)
"Essay Concerning Human Understanding"
1690

It will always happen, when a thing is originally wrong, that amendments do not make it right.

—THOMAS PAINE (1737–1809)
Rights of Man, I
1791

No man is prejudiced in favor of a thing knowing it to be wrong. He is attached to it on the belief of it being right.
—*THOMAS PAINE*
Rights of Man, I
1791

If there be any among us who would wish to dissolve this Union or to change its republican form, let them stand undisturbed as monuments of the safety with which error of opinion may be tolerated where reason is left free to combat it.
—*THOMAS JEFFERSON* (1743–1826)
Inaugural Address,
March 4, 1801

We are all liable to error, and those who are engaged in the management of public affairs are more subject to excitement and to be led astray by their particular interests and passions than the great body of our constituents, who, living at home in the pursuit of the ordinary avocations, are calm but deeply interested spectators of events and of the conduct of those who are parties to them.
—*JAMES MONROE* (1758–1831)
Seventh annual message to Congress,
December 2, 1823

EXCUSES

It is better to offer no excuse than a bad one.
—*GEORGE WASHINGTON* (1732–1799)
To Harriot Washington,
October 30, 1791

EXPANSION & MANIFEST DESTINY

The use of the Mississippi is given by

Nature to our Western Country, and no power on Earth can take it from them. Whilst we assert our title to it therefore with a becoming firmness let us not forget that we can not ultimately be deprived of it, and that for the present, war is more than all things to be deprecated.
—*JAMES MADISON* (1751–1836)
To James Monroe,
January 8, 1785

I know the acquisition of Louisiana has been disapproved by some, from a candid apprehension that the enlargement of our territory would endanger its union. But who can limit the extent to which the federative principle may operate effectively. The larger our association, the less will it be shaken by local passions; and in any view, is it not better that the opposite bank of the Mississippi should be settled by our own brethren and children, than by strangers of another family? With which shall we be most likely to live in harmony and friendly intercourse?
—*THOMAS JEFFERSON* (1743–1826)
Second Inaugural Address,
March 4, 1805

If this bill [for the admission of Orleans Territory as a State] passes, it is my deliberate opinion that it is virtually a dissolution of the Union; that it will free the States from their moral obligation; and, as it will be the right of all, so it will be the duty of some, definitely to prepare for a separation—amicably if they can, violently if they must.
—*JOSIAH QUINCY, JR.* (1772–1864)
Congressional Debates,
January 14, 1811

It is evident, that the further acquisi-

tion of territory, to the West and South, involves difficulties, of an internal nature, which menace the Union itself. We ought therefore to be cautious in making the attempt.
—*JAMES MONROE* (1758–1831)
Letter to Thomas Jefferson,
May 1820

So seducing is the passion for extending our territory, that is compelled to take our own redress it is quite uncertain within what limit it will be confined.
—*JAMES MONROE*
Letter to Albert Gallatin,
May 26, 1820

EXPERIENCE

Experience keeps a dear school, but fools will learn in no other.
—*BENJAMIN FRANKLIN* (1706–1790)
Poor Richard's Almanack
1743

I have but one lamp by which my feet are guided, and that is the lamp of experience. I know of no way of judging the future but by the past.
—*PATRICK HENRY* (1736–1799)
Speech in Virginia Convention,
March 23, 1775

To inveigh against things that are past and irremediable is unpleasing; but to steer clear of the shelves and rocks we have struck upon is the part of wisdom.
—*GEORGE WASHINGTON* (1732–1799)
To John Armstrong,
March 26, 1781

Experience is a severe preceptor, but it teaches useful truths, and however harsh, is always honest. Be calm and dispassionate, and listen to what it tells us.
—*JOHN JAY* (1745–1829)
Address to the People of
New York State,
1788

Some person of more advanc'd life and longer standing publick trust sho'd be selected. ... A person who had marked a line of conduct so decisively that you might tell what he would be hereafter by what he had been heretofore.
—*JAMES MONROE* (1758–1831)
To James Madison,
October 9, 1792

Experience is the oracle of truth; and where its responses are unequivocal, they ought to be conclusive and sacred.
—*JAMES MADISON* (1751–1836)
Annual Message to Congress,
December 5, 1810

FACTS & OPINIONS

New opinions are always suspected, and usually opposed, without any other reason but because they are not already common.
—*JOHN LOCKE* (1632–1704)
Essay Concerning Human Understanding
1690

Facts are stubborn things.
—*JOHN ADAMS* (1735–1826)
As defense attorney during the trial for the British soldiers accused in the Boston Massacre, December 1770

As long as the reason of man continues fallible, and he is at liberty to exercise it, different opinions will be formed.
—*JAMES MADISON* (1751–1836)
The Federalist Papers
1787

Conjectures are often substituted for facts.
—*GEORGE WASHINGTON* (1732–1799)
To George Washington Parke Custis, June 13, 1798

FAITH

The way to see by faith is to shut the eye of reason.
—*BENJAMIN FRANKLIN* (1706–1790)
Poor Richard's Almanack
1758

What is it that men cannot be made to believe!
—*THOMAS JEFFERSON* (1743–1826)
Letter to Richard Henry Lee, April 22, 1786

FAMILY

Ill thrives that hapless family that shows
A cock that's silent and a hen that crows;
I know not which lives more unnatural lives,
Obeying husbands or commanding wives.
—*BENJAMIN FRANKLIN* (1706–1790)
Poor Richard's Almanack
1734

The happiest moments of my life have been the few which I have past at home in the bosom of my family. ... public employment contributes neither to advantage nor happiness. It is but

honorable exile from one's family and affairs.
—*Thomas Jefferson* (1743–1826)
Letter to Francis Willis, Jr.,
April 18, 1790

I have here company enough, part of which is very friendly, part well enough disposed, part secretly hostile, and a constant succession of strangers. But this only serves to get rid of life, not to enjoy it; it is in the love of one's family that heartfelt happiness is known. I feel it when we are all together, and, when alone, beyond what can be imagined.
—*Thomas Jefferson*
To Mary Jefferson Eppes,
October 26, 1801

Be it ever so humble, there's no place like home.
—*John Howard Paine* (1791–1852)
From the play
Clari, the Maid of Milan
1823

First Settlers

And for the season it was winter, and they that know the winters of that country know them to be sharp and violent, and subject to cruel and fierce storms, dangerous to travel to known places, much more to search an unknown coast. … For summer being done, all things stand upon them with a weather-beaten face, and the whole country, full of woods and thickets, represented a wild and savage hue.
—*William Bradford* (1590–1657)
Of Plymouth Plantation
1620–1647

Thus out of small beginnings greater

things have been produced by His hand that made all things of nothing, and gives being to all things that are; and, as one small candle may light a thousand, so the light here kindled hath shone unto many, yea in some sort to our whole nation.
—*William Bradford*
Of Plymouth Plantation
(1620–1647)

Being thus arrived in a good harbor and brought safe to land, they fell upon their knees and blessed the God of heaven, who had brought them over the vast and furious ocean, and delivered them from all the perils and miseries thereof, again to set their feet on the firm and stable earth, their proper element.
—*William Bradford*
Of Plymouth Plantation
1620–1647

They began now to gather in the small harvest they had, and to fit up their houses and dwellings against winter, being all well recovered in health and strength and had all things in good plenty. For as some were thus employed in affairs abroad, others were exercised in fishing, about cod and bass and other fish, of which they took good store, of which every family had their portion. All the summer there was no want; and now began to come in store of fowl, as winter appproached, of which this place did abound when they came first (but afterward decreased by degrees). And besides waterfowl there was a great store of wild turkeys, of which they took many, besides venison, etc. Besides they had about a peck a meal a week to a person, or now since harvest, Indian corn to the proportion.

Which made many afterwards write so largely of their plenty here to their friends in England, which were not feigned but true reports.

—WILLIAM BRADFORD
Of Plymouth Plantation, describing the
first harvest of the Pilgrims
1620–1647

What could now sustain them but the Spirit of God and His grace? May not and ought not the children of these fathers rightly say: "Our fathers were Englishmen which came over this great ocean, and were ready to perish in this wilderness; but they cried unto the Lord, and He heard their voice and looked on their adversity," etc.

—WILLIAM BRADFORD
Of Plymouth Plantation
1620–1647

They knew they were pilgrims.

—WILLIAM BRADFORD
Of Plymouth Plantation
1620–1647

In the name of GOD, AMEN. We, whose names are underwritten, the Loyal Subjects of our dread Sovereign Lord King _James,_ by the Grace of God, of _Great Britain, France,_ and _Ireland,_ King, _Defender of the Faith,_ &c. Having undertaken for the Glory of God, and Advancement of the Christian Faith, and the Honour of our King and Country, a Voyage to plant the first Colony in the northern Parts of _Virginia;_ Do by these Presents, solemnly and mutually, in the Presence of God and one another, covenant and combine ourselves together into a civil Body Politick, for our better Ordering and Preservation, and Furtherance of the Ends

aforesaid: And by Virtue hereof do enact, constitute, and frame, such just and equal Laws, Ordinances, Acts, Constitutions, and Officers, from time to time, as shall be thought most meet and convenient for the general Good of the Colony; unto which we promise all due Submission and Obedience.

IN WITNESS whereof we have hereunto subscribed our names at _Cape-Cod_ the eleventh of November, in the Reign of our Sovereign Lord King James, of _England, France,_ and _Ireland,_ the eighteenth, and of _Scotland_ the fifty-fourth, _Anno Domini_ 1620.

—ANONYMOUS
The Mayflower Compact
1620

JAMES, by the Grace of God, King of England, Scotland, France and Ireland, Defender of the Faith, &c. to all whom these Presents shall come, Greeting, Whereas, upon the humble Petition of divers of our well disposed Subjects, that intended to make several Plantations in the Parts of America, between the Degrees of thirty-foure and fourty-five; We according to our princely Inclination, favouring much their worthy Disposition, ... have ... granted unto them divers Liberties, Priveliges, Enlargements, and Im-munityes, as in and by our severall Letters-Patents it doth and may more at large appears. ... We would likewise be graciously pleased to make certaine Adventurers, intending to erect and. establish fishery, Trade, and Plantacion, ... and their Successors, one several distinct and entire Body, and to grant unto them, such Estate, Liberties, Priveliges, Enlargements, and Im-munityes there, as in these our Letters-Pattents hereafter particularly expressed and declared. And for asmuch as We have been certainly given to understand by divers of our good Subjects, that have for these many Years past frequented those Coasts and Territoryes, between the Degrees of Fourty and Fourty-Eight, that there is noe other the Subjects of any Christian King or State, by any Authority from their Sover-aignes, Lords, or Princes, actually in Possession of any of the said Lands or Precincts, whereby any Right, Claim, Interest, or Title, may, might, or ought by that Meanes accrue, belong, or appertaine unto them, or any of them. And also for that We have been further given certainly to knowe, that within these late Yeares there hath by God's Visitation reigned a wonderfull Plague, together with many horrible Slaugthers, and Murthers, committed amoungst the Savages and brutish People there, heertofore inhabiting, in a Manner to the utter Destruction, Deuastacion, and Depopulacion of that whole Territorye, so that there is not left for many Leagues together in a Manner, any that doe claime or challenge any Kind of Interests therein, nor any other Superiour Lord or Souveraigne to make Claime hereunto, whereby We in our Judgment are persuaded and satisfied that the appointed Time is come in which Almighty God in his great Goodness and Bountie towards Us and our People, hath thought fitt and determined, that those large and goodly Territoryes, deserted as it were by their naturall Inhabitants, should be possessed and enjoyed by such of our Subjects and People as heertofore have and hereafter shall by his Mercie and Favour, and by his Powerfull Arme, be directed and conducted thither. In Contemplacion

and serious Consideracion whereof, Wee have thougt it fitt according to our Kingly Duty, soe much as in Us lyeth, to second and followe God's sacred Will, rendering reverend Thanks to his Divine Majestie for his gracious favour in laying open and revealing the same unto us, before any other Christian Prince or State, by which Meanes without Offence, and as We trust to his Glory, Wee may with Boldness goe on to the settling of soe hopefull a Work, which tendeth to the reducing and Conversion of such Sauages as remaine wandering in Desolacion and Distress, to Civil Societie and Christian Religion, to the Inlargement of our own Dominions, and the Aduancement of the Fortunes of such of our good Subjects as shall willingly intresse themselves in the said Imployment, to whom We cannot but give singular Commendations for their soe worthy Intention and Enterprize; Wee therefore, of our especiall Grace, mere Motion, and certaine Knowledge, by the Aduice of the Lords and others of our Priuy Councell have for Us, our Heyrs and Successors, graunted, ordained, and established, and in and by these Presents, Do for Us, our Heirs and Successors, grant, ordaine and establish, that all that Circuit, Continent, Precincts, and Limitts in America, lying and being in Breadth from Fourty Degrees of Northerly Latitude, from the Equnoctiall Line, to Fourty-eight Degrees of the said Northerly Latitude, and in length by all the Breadth aforesaid throughout the Maine Land, from Sea to Sea, with all the Seas, Rivers, Islands, Creekes, Inletts, Ports, and Havens, within the Degrees, Precincts and Limitts of the said Latitude and Longitude, shall be the Limitts; and Bounds, and Precints of the second Collony: And to the End that the said Territoryes may forever hereafter be more particularly and certainly known and distinguished, our Will and Pleasure is, that the same shall from henceforth be nominated, termed, and called by the Name of New-England, in America; and by that Name of New-England in America, the said Circuit, Precinct, Limitt, Continent, Islands, and Places in America, aforesaid, We do by these Presents, for Us, our Heyrs and Successors, name, call, erect, found and establish, and by that Name to have Continuance for ever.

—*King James I* (1566–1625)
The Charter of New England,
November 3, 1620

For we must consider that we shall be as a city upon a hill. The eyes of all people are upon us, so if we shall deal falsely with our God in this work we have undertaken, and so cause him to withdraw his present help from us, we shall be made a story and a byword through the world.

—*John Winthrop* (1588–1649)
"A Model of Christian Charity,"
a sermon delivered
on board the *Arabella*
1630

Now the only way to avoid this shipwreck, and to provide for our posterity, is to follow the counsel of Micah, to do justly, to love mercy, to walk humbly with our God. For this end, we must be knit together in this work as one man. We must entertain each other in brotherly affection, we must be willing to abridge ourselves of our superfluities, for the supply of each others' necessities. We must uphold a familiar

commerce together in all meekness, gentleness, patience, and liberality. We must delight in each other, make others' conditions our own, rejoice together, mourn together, labor and suffer together, always having before our eyes our commission and community in the work, our community as members of the same body.

—*John Winthrop*
"A Model of Christian Charity,"
a sermon delivered
on board the *Arabella*
1630

Whereas we all came into these parts of America with one and the same end and aim, namely, to advance the Kingdom of our Lord Jesus Christ and to enjoy the liberties of the Gospel in purity with peace; and whereas in our settling (by a wise providence of God) we are further dispersed upon the sea coasts and rivers than was at first intended, so that we can not according to our desire with convenience communicate in one government and jurisdiction; and whereas we live encompassed with people of several nations and strange languages which hereafter may prove injurious to us or our posterity. And forasmuch as the natives have formerly committed sundry Insolence and outrages upon several Plantations of the English and have of late combined themselves against us: and seeing by reason of those sad distractions in England which they have heard of, and by which they know vie are hindered from that humble way of seeking advice, or reaping those comfortable fruits of protection, which at other times we might well expect. We therefore do conceive it our bounder duty, without delay to enter into a present Consociation amongst ourselves, for mutual help and strength in all our future concernments: That, as in nation and religion, so in other respects, we be and continue one according to the tenor and true meaning of the ensuing articles: Wherefore it is fully agreed and concluded by and between the parties or Jurisdictions above named, and they jointly and severally do by these presents agree and conclude that they all be and henceforth be called by the name of the United Colonies of New England.

—ANONYMOUS
The Articles of Confederation of the
United Colonies of New England
May 19, 1643

Our forefathers, with the permission of their sovereign, emigrated from *England*, to avoid the unnatural oppressions which then took place in that country. They endured all sorts of miseries and hardships, before they could establish any tolerable footing in the new world. It was then hoped and expected that the blessing of freedom would be the inheritance of their posterity, which they preferred to every other temporal consideration. With the extremest toil, difficulty, and danger, our great and noble ancestors founded in *America* a number of colonies under the allegiance of the crown of *England*. They forfeited not the privileges of *Englishmen* by removing themselves hither, but brought with them every right, which they could or ought to have enjoyed had they abided in England.

—SILAS DOWNER (1729–1785)
A Discourse at the Dedication of
the Tree of Liberty,
1768

This country having been discovered by an English subject, in the year 1620, was ... deemed the property of the crown of England. Our ancestors, when they resolved to quit their native soil, obtained from king James, a grant of certain lands in North America. This they probably did to silence the cavils of their enemies, for it cannot be doubted, but that they despised the pretended right which he claimed thereto. Certain it is, that he might, with equal propriety and justice, have made them a grant of the planet Jupiter.

—JOSEPH WARREN (1741–1775)
Boston Massacre Oration,
March 5, 1775

Our forefathers, inhabitants of the island of Great-Britain, left their native land, to seek on these shores a residence for civil and religious freedom. At the expense of their blood, at the hazard of their fortunes, without the least charge to the country from which they removed, by unceasing labour, and an unconquerable spirit, they effected settlements in the distant and unhospitable wilds of America, then filled with numerous and warlike barbarians.

—JOHN DICKINSON (1732–1794)
"A Declaration by the Representatives
of the United Colonies of North-
America, Now Met in Congress at
Philadelphia, Setting Forth the Causes
and Necessity of Their
Taking Up Arms"
July 6, 1775

Liberty was the darling object of the first settlers of this country. Animated with the hope of enjoying those civil and religious rights, which Heaven designed for the virtuous, they bade adieu to the joys of a more social life, and, surrounded with the horrors of death in a thousand different shapes, they took possession of the fair territory we now inhabit. In the anticipation of liberty, plenty and peace, they braved all dangers and hardships.

—*SIMEON BALDWIN* (1761–1851)
Oration at New Haven, Connecticut,
July 4, 1788

THE FLAG

Oh, say, can you see by the dawn's early light.
What so proudly we hailed at the twilight's last gleaming?
Whose broad stripes and bright stars, through the perilous flight,
O'er the ramparts we watched were so gallantly streaming.
And the rockets' red glare, the bombs bursting in air,
Gave proof through the night that our flag was still there.
Oh, say, does that star-spangled banner yet wave
O'er the land of the free and the home of the brave.

— *FRANCIS SCOTT KEY* (1779–1843)
"The Star-Spangled Banner"
1814

O! thus be it ever when freemen shall stand
Between their loved homes and the foe's desolation;
Bless'd with victory and peace, may our Heaven-rescued land
Praise the Power that hath made and preserved us a nation.

— *FRANCIS SCOTT KEY*
"The Star-Spangled Banner"
1814

When Freedom from her mountain height,
Unfurled her standard to the air,
She tore the azure robe of night,
And set the stars of glory there.

—*JOSEPH RODMAN DRAKE* (1795–1820)
The American Flag
1819

FLATTERY & PRAISE

It is much easier for him to merit applause than hear of it: and he never doubts himself more, or the person that gives it, than when he hears so much of it.

—*WILLIAM PENN* (1644–1718)
More Fruits of Solitude
1702

[W]e cannot be too circumspect how we receive praise: for if we contemplate our selves in a false glass, we are sure to be mistaken about our dues; and because we are too apt to believe what is pleasing, rather than what is true, we may be too easily swelled beyond our just proportion, by the windy complements of men.

—*WILLIAM PENN*
More Fruits of Solitude
1702

We are too apt to love praise, but not to deserve it.

—*WILLIAM PENN*
More Fruits of Solitude
1702

Let those flatter who fear: it is not an American art.

—*THOMAS JEFFERSON* (1743–1826)
"The Rights of British America"
1774

The world is a severe schoolmaster, for its frowns are less dangerous than its smiles and flatteries, and it is a difficult task to keep in the path of wisdom.
—*PHYLLIS WHEATLEY* (c. 1753–1784)
Letter to John Thornton,
October 30, 1774

A little flattery will support a man through great fatigue.
—*JAMES MONROE* (1758–1831)
To F. A. Van Der Kemp,
January 24, 1818

FORCE & COERCION

Were some as Christian, as they boast themselves to be, it would save us all the labour we bestow in rendering persecution so unchristian, as it most truly is: nay were they those men of reason they character themselves, and what the civil law styles good citizens, it had been needless for us to tell them, that neither can any external coercive power convince the understanding of the poorest idiot, nor fines and prisons be judged fit and adequate penalties for faults purely intellectual; as well as that they are destructive of all civil government.
—*WILLIAM PENN* (1644–1718)
The Great Case of Liberty
and Conscience
1670

The strongest is never strong enough to be always the master, unless he transforms his strength into right, and obedience into duty.
—*JEAN JACQUES ROUSSEAU*
(1712–1778)
The Social Contract
1762

Let me now offer a few considerations to shew the obligations men are under to defend that liberty which providence has conferred upon them. This is a trust committed to us by heaven: we are accountable for the use we make of it, and ought therefore, to the best of our power to defend it. The servant, who hid his talent in a napkin, is condemned in our Lord's parable, and he who through inattention, indolence or cowardice, suffers it to be wrested from him, is little less criminal. Should a person, for instance, whose ability and circumstances enable him to do good in the world, to relieve his distressed brethren, and be an example of charity and other virtues, tamely yield up all his interest and become an absolute slave to some unjust and wicked oppressor, when he might by a manly resistance have secured his liberty, would he not be guilty of great unfaithfulness to God, and justly liable to his condemnation. This would in its consequences be really worse than hiding his talent in a napkin; it would be not only not improving it for the glory of the giver, but conveying it into hands which will, in all probability, employ it greatly to his dishonour. This reasoning is as applicable to a community as to an individual. A kingdom or commonwealth, as such, is accountable for the improvement it makes of it's advantages; It is bound to preserve them, and employ them for the honour of God! so far as it can, to be an example of virtue to neighbouring communities, and afford them relief when they are in distress: but by yielding up their possessions and liberties to an encroaching oppressive power, they become, in a great measure, incapable of their duties, and are liable to be made the ministers of sin through the compulsion of their masters. Out of faithfulness then, to God and in order to escape the doom of slothful servants, we should endeavour to defend our rights and liberties.

—SIMEON HOWARD (?–c. 1804)
Sermon preached to the Ancient
and Honorable Artillery
Company in Boston,
June 7, 1773

The use of force alone is but temporary. It may subdue for a moment; but it does not remove the necessity of subduing again: and a nation is not governed, which is perpetually to be conquered.

—EDMUND BURKE (1729–1797)
Second Speech on Conciliation with
America, the Thirteen Resolutions,
March 22, 1775

Suffer not yourselves to be betrayed with a kiss. Ask yourselves how this gracious reception of our petition comports with those warlike preparations which cover our waters and darken our land. Are fleets and armies necessary to a work of love and reconciliation? Have we shown ourselves so unwilling to be reconciled, that force must be called in to win back our love? Let us not deceive ourselves, sir. These are the implements of war and subjugation—the last arguments to which kings resort.

—PATRICK HENRY (1736–1799)
Speech at the Virginia Convention,
March 23, 1775

Subject opinion to coercion: whom will you make your inquisitor? Fallible men; men governed by bad passions, by private as well as public reasons. And why subject it to coercion? To produce uniformity. But is uniformity of opinion desirable? No more than of face and stature.

—THOMAS JEFFERSON (1743–1826)
Notes on the State of Virginia
1782

In politics, as in religion, it is equally absurd to aim at making proselytes by fire and sword. Heresies in either can rarely be cured by persecution.

—ALEXANDER HAMILTON (1755–1804)
The Federalist Papers
1787

That the laws of every country ought to be executed, cannot be denied. That force must be used if necessary cannot be denied. Can any government be established, that will answer any purpose whatever, unless force be provided for executing its laws?

—JAMES MADISON (1751–1836)
Speech at the Virginia Convention,
June 14, 1788

We will exercise the reason with which we are endued, or we possess it unworthily. If either of these can be rendered sufficiently extensive in a country, the machinery of Government goes easily on. Reason obeys itself; and Ignorance submits to whatever is dictated to it.

—THOMAS PAINE (1737–1809)
Address and Declaration
1791

Force cannot change right.

—THOMAS JEFFERSON
To John Cartwright,
June 5, 1824

FOREIGN INFLUENCE

The weak side of a republican government is the danger of foreign influence.
—*ALEXANDER HAMILTON* (1755–1804)
Constitutional Convention,
June 18, 1787

Against the insidious wiles of foreign influence ... the jealousy of a free people ought to be constantly awake; since history and experience prove that foreign influence is one of the most baneful foes of republican government.
—*GEORGE WASHINGTON* (1732–1799)
Farewell Address,
September 17, 1796

Our form of government, inestimable as it is, exposes us, more than any other, to the insidious intrigues and pestilent influence of foreign nations. Nothing but our inflexible neutrality can preserve us.
—*JOHN ADAMS* (1735–1826)
Letter in *The Boston Patriot*
c. 1809

FOREIGN RELATIONS & POLICY

Not a place upon earth might be so happy as America. Her situation is remote from all the wrangling world, and she has nothing to do but to trade with them.
—*THOMAS PAINE* (1737–1809)
"The American Crisis. No. 1" in
the *Pennsylvania Journal*,
December 19, 1776

America, remote from all the wrangling world, may live at ease. Bounded by the ocean and backed by the wilderness, what hath she to fear, but her GOD?
—*THOMAS PAINE*
The Forester's Letters
1776

As Europe is our market for trade, we ought to form no partial connection with any part of it. It is the true interest of America to steer clear of European contentions.
—*THOMAS PAINE*
Common Sense
1776

It is best mankind should mix. There is ever something to learn, either of manners or principle; and it is by a free communication, without regard to domestic matters, that friendship is to be extended and prejudice destroyed all over the world.
—*THOMAS PAINE*
"To the Abbe Raynal"
1782

We mistake the object of our government, if we hope or wish that it is to make us respectable abroad. Conquest or superiority among other powers is not or ought not ever to be the object of republican systems. If they are sufficiently active and energetic to rescue us from contempt and preserve our domestic happiness and security, it is all we can expect from them, it is more than almost any other Government ensures its citizens.
—*CHARLES PINCKNEY* (1757–1824)
Constitutional Convention,
June 25, 1787

No government could give us tranquility and happiness at home, which did

not possess sufficient stability and strength to make us respectable abroad.
—*ALEXANDER HAMILTON* (1755–1804)
At the Constitutional Convention,
June 29, 1787

The world may politically, as well as geographically, be divided into four parts, each having a distinct set of interests. Unhappily for the other three, Europe, by her arms and by her negotiations, by force and by fraud, has ... extended her dominion over them all. Africa, Asia, and America have successively felt her domination. The superiority she has long maintained has tempted her to plume herself as the Mistress of the World, and to consider the rest of mankind as created for her benefit.
—*ALEXANDER HAMILTON*
The Federalist Papers
1787

My commercial system turns very much on giving a free course to trade, and cultivating good humor with all the world.
—*ALEXANDER HAMILTON*
To Thomas Jefferson,
January 13, 1791

I believe it is among nations as with individuals, that the party taking advantage of the distresses of another will lose infinitely more in the opinion of mankind, and in subsequent events, than he will gain by the stroke of the moment.
—*GEORGE WASHINGTON* (1732–1799)
To Gouverneur Morris,
July 28, 1791

If there be one principle more deeply rooted than any other in the mind of every American, it is that we should have nothing to do with conquest.
—*THOMAS JEFFERSON* (1743–1826)
Letter to William Short,
1791

We certainly cannot deny to other nations that principle whereon our own government is founded, that every nation has a right to govern itself internally under what forms it pleases, and to change these forms at its own will: and externally to transact business with other nations thro' whatever organ it chuses. ... The only thing essential is the will of the nation.
—*THOMAS JEFFERSON*
To Thomas Pinckney,
December 30, 1792

It is the sincere wish of America to have nothing to do with the political intrigues, or squabbles of European nations.
—*GEORGE WASHINGTON*
Letter to Earl of Buchan,
April 22, 1793

There is a rank due to the United States among nations which will be withheld, if not absolutely lost, by the reputation of weakness.
—*GEORGE WASHINGTON*
Fifth Annual Address to Congress,
December 3, 1793

My ardent desire is ... to keep the United States free from political connections with every other country, to see them independent of all and under the influence of none.
—*GEORGE WASHINGTON*
Letter to Patrick Henry,
October 9, 1795

A treaty, which is a contract between nation and nation, abridges even the legislative discretion of the whole Legislature by the moral obligation of keeping its faith.

—ALEXANDER HAMILTON
To William Smith,
March 10, 1796

The nature of foreign negotiations requires caution and their success must often depend on secrecy. ... The necessity of such caution and secrecy was one cogent reason for vesting the power of making treaties in the President. To admit then a right in the House of Representatives to demand, and to have as a matter of course, all the Papers respecting a negotiation with a foreign power, would be to establish a dangerous precedent. It does not occur that the inspection of the papers asked for, can be relative to any purpose under the cognizance of the House of Representatives, except that of an impeachment, which the resolution has not expressed. I repeat, that I have no disposition to withhold any information which the duty of my station will permit, or the public good shall require to be disclosed: and in fact, all the Papers affecting the negotiation with Great Britain were laid before the Senate, when the Treaty itself was communicated for their consideration and advice. The course which the debate has taken, on the resolution of the House, leads to some observations on the mode of making treaties under the Constitution of the United States.

—GEORGE WASHINGTON
Address to the House of
Representatives,
March 30, 1796

It is the duty of every government to charge itself with the care of any of its citizens who may happen to fall under an arbitrary persecution abroad.

—THOMAS PAINE
To George Washington,
August 3, 1796

I have always given it as my decided opinion that no nation had a right to inter-meddle in the internal concerns of another; ... and that, if this country could, consistent with its engagements, maintain a strict neutrality and thereby preserve peace, it was bound to do so by motives of policy, interest, and every other consideration.

—GEORGE WASHINGTON
Letter to James Monroe,
August 25, 1796

Observe good faith and justice toward all nations. Cultivate peace and harmony with all. ... The nation which indulges toward another an habitual hatred or an habitual fondness is in some degree a slave. It is a slave to its animosity or to its affection, either of which is sufficient to lead it astray from its duty and its interest.

—GEORGE WASHINGTON
Farewell Address,
September 17, 1796

The great rule of conduct for us in regard to foreign nations is, in extending our commercial relations to have with them as little political connection as possible. ... Why, by interweaving our destiny with that of any part of Europe, entangle our peace and prosperity in the toils of European ambition, rivalship, interest, humor, or caprice? It is our true policy to steer clear of permanent alli-

ances with any portion of the foreign world. ... We may safely trust to temporary alliances for extraordinary emergencies. ... There can be no greater error than to expect or calculate upon real favors from nation to nation. It is an illusion which experience must cure, which a just pride ought to discard.
—GEORGE WASHINGTON
Farewell Address,
September 17, 1796

Peace, commerce, and honest friendship with all nations, entangling alliances with none should be our motto.
—THOMAS JEFFERSON
First Inaugural Address,
March 4, 1801

We consider the interests of Cuba, Mexico and ours as the same, and that the object of both must be to exclude all European influence from this hemisphere.
—THOMAS JEFFERSON
Letter to W. C. C. Claiborn,
October 1808

Indulging no passions which trespass on the rights or the repose of other nations, it has been the true glory of the United States to cultivate peace by observing justice, and to entitle themselves to the respect of the nations at war by fulfilling their neutral obligations with the most scrupulous impartiality.
—JAMES MADISON (1751–1836)
First Inaugural Address,
March 4, 1809

The less we do with the amities or enmities of Europe, the better.
—THOMAS JEFFERSON
Letter to Thomas Leiper,
1815

The national defense is one of the cardinal duties of a statesman.
—JOHN ADAMS (1735–1826)
To James Lloyd,
January 1815

A virtuous people may and will confine themselves within the limit of a strict neutrality, but it is not in their power to behold a conflict so vitally important to their neighbors without the sensibility and sympathy which naturally belong to such a case.
—JAMES MONROE (1758–1831)
Third annual message to Congress,
December 7, 1819

America ... well knows that by once enlisting under other banners than her own, were they even the banners of foreign independence, she would involve herself beyond the power of extraction, in all the wars of interest and intrigue, of individual avarice, envy, ambition, which assume the colors and usurp the standard of freedom. The fundamental maxims of her policy would insensibly change from liberty to force. ... She would be no longer the ruler of her own spirit.
—JOHN QUINCY ADAMS (1767–1848)
Address,
July 4, 1821

Wherever the standard of freedom and independence has been or shall be unfurled, there will be America's heart, her benedictions and her prayers. But she does not go abroad in search of monsters to destroy. She is the champion and vindicator only of her own.
—JOHN QUINCY ADAMS
Address,
July 4, 1821

Russia seems at present the great bug-bear of the European politicians on the land, as the British Leviathan is on the water.

—*JAMES MADISON*
Letter to Richard Rush,
November 20, 1821

In the wars of the European powers in matters relating to themselves we have never taken any part, nor does it comport with our policy so to do.

—*JAMES MONROE*
Annual message to Congress,
December 2, 1823

It is by rendering justice to other nations that we can expect it from them.

—*JAMES MONROE*
Annual message to Congress,
December 2, 1823

The American continents ... are henceforth not to be considered as subject for future colonization by any European powers.

—*JAMES MONROE*
Annual message to Congress,
December 2, 1823

We owe it, therefore, to candor and to the amicable relations existing between the United States and those [European] powers to declare that we should consider any attempt on their part to extend their system to any portion of this hemisphere as dangerous to our peace and safety. With the existing colonies or dependencies of any European Power we have not interfered, and shall not interfere. But with the governments who have declared their independence, and maintained it, ... we could not view any interposition for the purpose

of oppressing them, or controlling, in any other manner, their destiny, by any European Power, in any other light than as the manifestation of an unfriendly disposition towards the United States.

—*JAMES MONROE*
Annual message to Congress,
December 2, 1823

I confess I have the same fears for our South American brethren; the qualifications for self-government in society are not innate. They are the result of habit and long training, and for these they will require time and probably much suffering.

—*THOMAS JEFFERSON*
Letter to Edward Everett,
March 27, 1824

Separated as we are from Europe by the great Atlantic ocean, we can have no concern in the wars of the European Governments no[r] in the causes which produce them.

—*JAMES MONROE*
Annual message to Congress,
December 7, 1824

FRANCE

Our very good friend, the Marquis de Lafayette, has entrusted to my care the key of the Bastille, and a drawing handsomely framed, representing the demolition of that detestable prison, as a present to your Excellency, of which his letter will more particularly inform. I feel myself happy in being the person through whom the Marquis has conveyed this early trophy of the spoils of despotism, and the first ripe fruits of American principles transplanted to Europe, to his master and patron. When he mentioned to me the present he intended you, my heart leaped with joy. It is something so truly in character that no remarks can illustrate it, and is more happily expressive of his remembrance of his American friends than any letters can convey. That the principles of America opened the Bastille is not to be doubted; and therefore the key comes to the right place.

—THOMAS PAINE (1737–1809)
To George Washington,
May 1, 1790

Ask the travelled inhabitant of any nation, In what country on earth would you rather live?—Certainly in my own, where all my friends, my relations, and the earliest & sweetest affections and recollections of my life. Which would be your second choice? France.

—THOMAS JEFFERSON (1743–1826)
Autobiography
1821

BENJAMIN FRANKLIN

He snatched the lightning from heaven and the sceptre from tyrants.

—ANNE ROBERT JACQUES, BARON A
L'AULNE TURGOT (1727–1781)
Inscription for the Houdon bust of
Franklin,
1778

FREEDOM

Wear none of thine own chains; but keep free, whilst thou art free.

—WILLIAM PENN (1644–1718)
Some Fruits of Solitude
1693

Man is born free, and everywhere he is in chains.

—JEAN JACQUES ROUSSEAU (1712–1778)
The Social Contract
1762

Political freedom includes in it every other blessing. All the pleasures of riches, science, virtue, and even religion itself derive their value from liberty alone. No wonder therefore wise and prudent legislators have in all ages been held in such great veneration; and no wonder too those illustrious souls who have employed their pens and sacrificed their lives in defense of liberty have met with such universal applause. Their reputations, like some majestic river which enlarges and widens as it approaches its parent ocean, shall become greater and greater through every age and outlive the ruins of the world itself.

—BENJAMIN RUSH (1745–1813)
To Catharine Macaulay,
January 18, 1769

The liberties of our country, the freedom of our civil constitution, are worth defending at all hazards; and it is our duty to defend them against all attacks. We have received them as a fair inheritance from our worthy ancestors: they purchased them for us with toil and danger and expense of treasure and blood, and transmitted them to us with care and diligence. It will bring an everlasting mark of infamy on the present generation, enlightened as it is, if we should suffer them to be wrested from us by violence without a struggle, or be cheated out of them by the artifices of false and designing men.

—SAMUEL ADAMS (1722–1803)
Article in the *Boston Gazette*,
October 14, 1771

I believe that no people ever yet groaned under the heavy yoke of slavery but when they deserved it.
—SAMUEL ADAMS
Article in the *Boston Gazette*,
October 14, 1771

The truth is, all might be free if they valued freedom, and defended it as they ought.
—SAMUEL ADAMS
Article in the *Boston Gazette*,
October 14, 1771

If men through fear, fraud or mistake, should in terms renounce and give up any essential natural right, the eternal law of reason and the great end of society, would absolutely vacate such renunciation; the right to freedom being the gift of God Almighty, it is not in the power of Man to alienate this gift, and voluntarily become a slave.
—JOHN ADAMS (1735–1826)
Rights of the Colonists
1772

In every human breast, God has implanted a principle, which we call love of freedom; it is impatient of oppression and pants for deliverance.
—PHYLLIS WHEATLEY (c. 1753–1784)
The Boston Post-Boy
1774

Freedom and not servitude is the cure of anarchy; as religion, and not atheism, is the true remedy for superstition.
—EDMUND BURKE (1729–1797)
Second Speech on Conciliation with America, The Thirteen Resolutions,
March 22, 1775

Our contest is not only whether we ourselves shall be free, but whether there shall be left to mankind an asylum on earth for civil and religious liberty.
—SAMUEL ADAMS
Speech in Philadelphia,
August 1, 1776

Freedom hath been hunted round the globe. Asia and Africa have long expelled her. Europe regards her like a stranger, and England hath given her warning to depart. O! Receive the fugitive, and prepare in time an asylum for mankind.
—THOMAS PAINE (1737–1809)
Common Sense
1776

Our unalterable resolution should be to be free.
—SAMUEL ADAMS
To James Warren,
1776

Those who expect to reap the blessings of freedom, must, like men, undergo the fatigues of supporting it.
—THOMAS PAINE
The Crisis
1777

Remember, that in all countries where the freedom of the poor has been taken away, in whole or in part, that the freedom of the rich lost its defence. The circle has ever continued to constrict, till lessening to a point it became absolute.
—THOMAS PAINE
A Serious Address to the People of Pennsylvania
1778

Tis freedom's genius, nurs'd from age to age,

Matur'd in schools of liberty and law,
On virtue's page from sire to son
  convey'd,
E'er since the savage, fierce, barbarian
  hords,
Pour'd in. ...
　　　　　—MERCY OTIS WARREN (1728–1814)
　　　　　　　Don Juan De Padilla in
　　　　　　　"The Ladies of Castille"
　　　　　　　　　　　1790

Let freedom be the mistress of thy
heart.
　　　　　　　—MERCY OTIS WARREN
　　　　　　　Don Juan De Padilla in
　　　　　　　"The Ladies of Castille"
　　　　　　　　　　　1790

Although all men are born free, and all
nations might be so, yet too true it is,
that slavery has been the general lot of
the human race. Ignorant—they have
been cheated; asleep—they have been
surprised; divided—the yoke has been
forced upon them.

But what is the lesson? that because
the people *may* betray themselves,
they ought to give themselves up,
blindfolded, to those who have an interest in betraying them? Rather conclude that the people ought to be enlightened, to be awakened, to be
united, that after establishing a government they should watch over it,
as well as obey it.
　　　　　　—JAMES MADISON (1751–1836)
　　　　　　Essay in the *National Gazette*,
　　　　　　　　December 20, 1792

It is impossible to conquer a nation determined to be free!
　　　　　　　　　—THOMAS PAINE
　　　　　Letter to the People of France,
　　　　　　　　　　　1792

Let the human mind loose. It must be
loose. It will be loose. Superstition and
dogmatism cannot confine it.
　　　　　　　　　—JOHN ADAMS
　　　　　　　To John Quincy Adams,
　　　　　　　　November 13, 1816

The human mind will some day get
back to the freedom it enjoyed 2000
years ago. This country, which has
given to the world the example of
physical liberty, owes to it that of
moral emancipation also. For, as yet,
it is but nominal with us. The inquisition of public opinion overwhelms in
practice the freedom asserted by the
laws in theory.
　　　—THOMAS JEFFERSON (1743–1826)
　　　　　　　　To John Adams,
　　　　　　　　January 22, 1821

FREEDOM OF SPEECH & PRESS

Liberty of speech inviteth and pro-
voketh liberty to be used again, and
so bringeth much to a man's knowledge.
　　　　—FRANCIS BACON (1561–1626)
　　　　The Advancement of Learning
　　　　　　　　　1605

Give me the liberty to know, to utter,
and to argue freely according to conscience, above all liberties.
　　　　　—JOHN MILTON (1608–1674)
　　　　　　　　Areopagitica
　　　　　　　　　1644

Though all the winds of doctrine were
let loose to play upon the earth, so Truth
be in the field, we do injuriously, by
licensing and prohibiting, to mis-doubt
her strength. Let her and Falsehood
grapple; who ever knew Truth put to

the worse, in a free and open encounter?

—JOHN MILTON
Areopagitica
1644

Without Freedom of Thought, there can be no such Thing as Wisdom; and no such Thing as publick Liberty, without Freedom of Speech.

—BENJAMIN FRANKLIN (1706–1790)
Letter from "'Silence Dogood,"
printed in *The New England Courant*,
July 9, 1722

If all printers were determined not to print anything till they were sure it would offend nobody, there would be very little printed.

—BENJAMIN FRANKLIN
Apology for Printers
1731

Printers are educated in the Belief, that when Men differ in Opinion, both Sides ought equally to have the Advantage of being heard by the Publick; and that when Truth and Error have fair Play, the former is always an overmatch for the latter.

—BENJAMIN FRANKLIN
Apology for Printers
1731

In an absolute Monarchy, the Will of the Prince being the Law, a Liberty of the Press to complain of Grievances would be complaining against the Law, and the Constitution, to which they have submitted, or have been obliged to submit; and therefore, in one Sense, may be said to deserve Punishment, So that under an absolute Monarchy, I saw, such a Liberty is inconsistent with the Constitution, having no proper Subject in Politics, on

which it might be exercis'd, and if exercis'd would incur a certain Penalty.

—JOHN PETER ZENGER (1697–1746)
The New-York Weekly Journal,
November 12, 1733

No nation ancient or modern ever lost the liberty of freely speaking, writing, or publishing their sentiments, but forthwith lost their liberty in general and became slaves.

—JOHN PETER ZENGER
The New-York Weekly Journal,
November 12, 1733

The Liberty of the Press is a Subject of the greatest Importance, and in which every Individual is as much concern'd as he is in any other Part of Liberty.

—JOHN PETER ZENGER
The New-York Weekly Journal,
November 12, 1733

The loss of liberty in general would soon follow the suppression of the liberty of the press; for it is an essential branch of liberty, so perhaps it is the best preservative of the whole.

—JOHN PETER ZENGER
The New-York Weekly Journal,
November 12, 1733

There are two Sorts of Monarchies, an absolute and a limited one. In the first, the Liberty of the Press can never be maintained, it is inconsistent with it; for what absolute Monarch would suffer any Subject to animadvert to his Actions, when it is in his Power to declare the Crime, and to nominate the Punishment?

—JOHN PETER ZENGER
The New-York Weekly Journal,
November 12, 1733

That, to which nature and the laws of our country have given us a Right—That Liberty—both of exposing and opposing arbitrary power (in these parts of the world at least) by speaking and writing the Truth.

—ANDREW HAMILTON (?-1741)
In defense of John Peter Zenger, 1735

The question before the Court and you gentlemen of the Jury, is not of small or private concern, it is not the cause of a poor Printer, nor of New York alone, which you are now trying: No! It may in its consequence, affect every Freeman that lives under a British Government on the main of America. It is the best cause. It is the cause of Liberty.

—ANDREW HAMILTON
In defense of John Peter Zenger, 1735

But none of the means of information are more sacred, or have been cherished with more tenderness and care by the settlers of America, than the press.

—JOHN ADAMS (1735-1826)
Dissertation on the Canon and the Feudal Law
1765

As for the freedom of the press, I will tell you what it is: the liberty of the press is that a man may print what he pleases without license. As long as it remains so, the liberty of the press is not restrained.

—WILLIAM MURRAY, English jurist
(1705-1793)
Justice charge to the jury in the trial of H. W. Woodfall, 1772

The liberty of the press is essential to the security of the state.

—JOHN ADAMS
Free-Press Clause,
Massachusetts Constitution
1780

Reason and free inquiry are the only effectual agents against error.

—THOMAS JEFFERSON (1743-1826)
Notes on Virginia
1781-1782

For if Men are to be precluded from offering their Sentiments on a matter, which may involve the most serious and alarming consequences, that can invite the consideration of Mankind, reason is of no use to us; the freedom of Speech may be taken away, and, dumb and silent we may be led, like sheep, to the Slaughter.

—GEORGE WASHINGTON (1732-1799)
Address to the officers of the army,
March 15, 1783

Our liberty depends on the freedom of the press, and that cannot be limited without being lost.

—THOMAS JEFFERSON
Letter to Dr. J. Currie,
1786

Congress shall make no law respecting an establishment of religion, or prohibiting the free exercise thereof; or abridging the freedom of speech, or of the press; or the right of the people peaceably to assemble, and to petition the Government for a redress of grievances.

—CONSTITUTION OF THE UNITED STATES
Amendment 1, The Bill of Rights
(1787)

For instance, the liberty of the press, which has been a copious subject of declamation and opposition: what control can proceed from the federal government, to shackle or destroy that sacred palladium of national freedom? ... the proposed system possesses no influence whatever upon the press; and it would have been merely nugatory, to have introduced a formal declaration upon the subject; nay, that very declaration might have been construed to imply that some degree of power was given, since we undertook to define its extent.

—JAMES WILSON (1741–1798)
Address in Philadelphia,
1787

Were it left to me to decide whether we should have a government without newspapers, or newspapers without government, I should not hesitate a moment to prefer the latter.

—THOMAS JEFFERSON
Letter to Colonel Edward Carrington,
January 16, 1787

I confess I do not see in what cases the Congress can, with any pretense of right, make a law to suppress the freedom of the press.

—RICHARD HENRY LEE (1732–1794)
Letters of the Federal Farmer
1788

No government ought to be without censors, and, where the press is free, no one ever will.

—THOMAS JEFFERSON
Letter to George Washington,
1792

When the people have formed a con-

stitution, they retain those rights which they have not expressly delegated. It is a question whether what is thus retained can be legislated upon. Opinions are not the objects of legislation. You animadvert on the *abuse* of reserved rights—how far will this go? It may extend to the liberty of speech and the press.

—JAMES MADISON (1751–1836)
Speech in Congress,
November 27, 1794

It must be seen that no two principles can be either more indefensible in reason, or more dangerous in practice—than that 1. arbitrary denunciations may punish, what the law permits, & what the Legislature has no right, by law, to prohibit—and that 2. the Government may stifle all censures whatever on its misdoings; for if it be itself the Judge it will never allow any censures to be just, and if it can suppress censures flowing from one lawful source it may those flowing from any other—from the press and from individuals as well as from Societies.

—JAMES MADISON
To James Monroe,
December 4, 1794

To preserve the freedom of the human mind ... and the freedom of the press, every spirit should be ready to devote itself to martyrdom; for as long as we may think as we will, and speak as we think the condition of man will proceed in improvement.

—THOMAS JEFFERSON
Letter to William Green Mumford,
June 18, 1799

To the press alone, chequered as it is

with abuses, the world is indebted for all the triumphs which have been gained by reason and humanity over error and oppression.

—*THOMAS JEFFERSON*
Virginia and Kentucky Resolutions, 1799

It is better to leave a few of its [the press's] noxious branches to their luxuriant growth, than by pruning them away, to injure the vigor of those yielding the proper fruits.

—*JAMES MADISON*
"Report on The Virginia Resolutions" 1799–1800

So great is the influence of the information communicated from the press, in the formation of public opinion, that it ought not, it cannot be viewed with indifference by any, who are friendly to public happiness.

—*ZEPHANIAH SWIFT MOORE* (1770–1820)
"Oration on the Anniversary of the Independence of the United States" 1802

I have therefore long thought that a few prosecutions of the most prominent offenders would have a wholesome effect.

—*THOMAS JEFFERSON*
Letter from Jefferson to Thomas McKean, supporting trials of newspaper publishers for seditious libel, February 19, 1803

The firmness with which the people have withstood the late abuses of the press, the discernment they have manifested between truth and falsehood, show that they may safely be trusted to hear everything true and false, and

to form a correct judgment between them.

—*THOMAS JEFFERSON*
Letter to Judge John Taylor, June 28, 1804

The liberty of the press consists, in my idea, in publishing the truth, from good motives and for justifiable ends, though it reflect on the government, on magistrates, or individuals. If it be not allowed, it excludes the privilege of canvassing men, and our rulers. It is in vain to say, you may canvass measures. This is impossible without the right of looking to men.

—*ALEXANDER HAMILTON* (1755–1804)
People v. Croswell,
February 13, 1804

While we deny that Congress has a right to control the freedom of the press, we have ever asserted the right of the states, and their exclusive right, to do so.

—*THOMAS JEFFERSON*
Letter to Abigail Adams, 1804

The press, confined to truth, needs no other legal restraint; the public judgment will correct false reasonings and opinions, on a full hearing of all parties; and no other definite line can be drawn between the inestimable liberty of the press and its demoralizing licentiousness.

—*THOMAS JEFFERSON*
Second Inaugural Address, March 4, 1805

Nothing can now be believed which is seen in a newspaper.

—*THOMAS JEFFERSON*
Letter to J. Norville, 1805

I deplore with you the putrid state into which our newspapers have passed, and the malignity, the vulgarity, & mendacious spirit of those who write for them.

—*THOMAS JEFFERSON*
To Walter Jones,
January 2, 1814

If there is ever an amelioration of the condition of mankind, philosophers, theologians, legislators, politicians and moralists will find that the regulation of the press is the most difficult, dangerous and important problem they have to resolve. Mankind cannot now be governed without it, nor at present with it.

—*JOHN ADAMS*
To James Lord,
February 11, 1815

If a nation expects to be ignorant and free, in a state of civilization, it expects what never was and never will be. The functionaries of every government have propensities to command at will the liberty and property of their constituents. There is no safe deposit for these but with the people themselves; nor can they be safe with them without information. Where the press is free ... all is safe.

—*THOMAS JEFFERSON*
Letter to Colonel Charles Yancey,
January 6, 1816

The only security of all is in a free press.

—*THOMAS JEFFERSON*
Letter to Marquis de Lafayette,
1823

FRIENDS & FRIENDSHIP

A true friend unbosoms freely, advises justly, assists readily, adventures boldly,

takes all patiently, defends courageously, and continues a friend unchangeably.

—*WILLIAM PENN* (1644–1718)
Some Fruits of Solitude
1693

Friends are true twins in soul; they sympathize in every thing, and have the same love and aversion.

—*WILLIAM PENN*
Some Fruits of Solitude
1693

In short, choose a friend as thou dost a wife, till death separate you.

—*WILLIAM PENN*
Some Fruits of Solitude
1693

There can be no friendship where there is no freedom. Friendship loves a free air, and will not be penned up in straight and narrow enclosures. It will speak freely, and act so too; and take nothing ill, where no ill is meant; nay, where it is, it will easily forgive ...

—*WILLIAM PENN*
Some Fruits of Solitude
1693

A true friend is the best possession.

—*BENJAMIN FRANKLIN* (1706–1790)
Poor Richard's Almanack
1744

A false friend and a shadow attend only while the sun shines.

—*BENJAMIN FRANKLIN*
Poor Richard's Almanack
1756

Yet it is left to every man as he comes of age to choose *what society* he will continue to belong to. Nay, if one has a mind to turn *hermit*, and after he has been born, nursed, and brought up in the arms of society, and acquired the habits and passions of social life is wiling to run the risk of starving alone, which is generally most unavoidable in a state of hermitage, who shall hinder him? I know of no human law founded on the law of *nature* to restrain him from separating himself from all the species if he can find it in his heart to leave them, unless it should be said it is against the great law of *self-preservation*: but of this every man will think himself *his own judge*.

—*JAMES OTIS* (1725–1783)
The Rights of the British Colonies Asserted and Proved
1764

If you would know any man's affection towards you, consult his behavior; that is the best evidence of a virtuous mind. Though a person's professions be ever so voluminous, and his zeal ever so noisy, yet he is not entitled to our esteem, but only civility; for profession is but the shadow of friendship, and saying is not proving. If a person would be considered in the character of a friend, let it appear by generous and friendly actions; for that is the only testimony upon which we may safely ground our esteem. If a man professes friendship one day and proves himself an enemy the next, why should I give credit to one who so effectually contradicts himself?

—*NATHANIEL GREENE* (1742–1786)
To Samuel Ward, Jr.,
1772

Friendship like all Truth delights in plainness and simplicity and It is the

Counterfeit alone that needs Ornament and ostentation.

—*JAMES MADISON* (1751–1836)
To William Bradford,
April 28, 1773

The intimacy which is contracted in infancy, and the friendship which is formed in misfortune, are, of all others, the most lasting and unalterable.

—*THOMAS PAINE* (1737–1809)
Common Sense
1776

Be courteous to all, but intimate with few, and let those few be well tried before you give them your confidence.

—*GEORGE WASHINGTON* (1732–1799)
To Bushrod Washington,
January 15, 1783

Life is of no value but as it brings us gratifications. Among the most valuable of these is rational society. It informs the mind, sweetens the temper, cheers our spirits, and promotes health.

—*THOMAS JEFFERSON* (1743–1826)
To James Madison,
February 20, 1784

To correspond with those I love is among my highest gratifications.

—*GEORGE WASHINGTON*
To Henry Knox,
January 5, 1785

Friendship is but another name for an alliance with the follies & the misfortunes of others. Our own share of miseries is sufficient: why enter then as volunteers into those of another? ... A friend dies or leaves us: we feel as if a limb was cut off. He is sick: we must watch over him,

& participate of his pains. ... He loses a child, a parent or a partner: we must mourn the loss as if it was our own.
—*THOMAS JEFFERSON*
To Maria Cosway,
October 12, 1786

[F]riendship is precious, not only in the shade, but in the sunshine of life; and thanks to a benevolent arrangement of things, the greater part of life is sunshine.
—*THOMAS JEFFERSON*
Letter to Maria Cosway,
October 12, 1786

The friendships contracted earliest in life, are those which stand by us the longest.
—*THOMAS JEFFERSON*
To Elizabeth Blair Thompson,
January 19, 1787

I am always distressed at closing a letter, because it seems like taking leave of my friends after a parting conversation.
—*THOMAS PAINE*
To Kitty Nicholson Few,
1789

Trouble is a pleasure when it is to serve our friends living or dead.
—*THOMAS JEFFERSON*
To Elizabeth Wayles Eppes,
May 15, 1791

I am become so unprofitable a correspondent, and so remiss in my correspondencies, that nothing but the kindness of my friends in overlooking these deficiencies could induce them to favor me with a continuance of their letters.
—*GEORGE WASHINGTON*
To Gouverneur Morris,
December 22, 1795

I find friendship to be like wine, raw when new, ripened with age, the true old man's milk & restorative cordial.
—*THOMAS JEFFERSON*
To Benjamin Rush,
August 17, 1811

A line from my good old friends is like balm to my soul.
—*THOMAS JEFFERSON*
To Nathan Macon,
November 23, 1821

FUTURE

I must soon quit the scene, but you may live to see our country flourish; as it will amazingly and rapidly after the war is over; like a field of young Indian corn, which long fair weather and sunshine had enfeebled and discolored, and which in that weak state, by a sudden gust of violent wind, hail, and rain, seemed to be threatened with absolute destruction; yet the storm being past, it recovers fresh verdure, shoots up with double vigor, and delights the eye not of its owners only, but of every observing traveler.
—*BENJAMIN FRANKLIN* (1706–1790)
Letter to George Washington,
March 5, 1780

I like the dreams of the future better than the history of the past.
—*THOMAS JEFFERSON* (1743–1826)
Letter to John Adams,
August 1, 1816

ABRAHAM ALFONSE ALBERT GALLATIN

[A] man of most singular sagacity and penetration; he could read the very thoughts of men in their faces and develop their designs; a man of few words, made no promises but to real favorites [who] ever sought to enhance his own interest, power, and aggrandisement by the most insatiate avarice on the very vitals of the unsuspecting nation.

—*WILLIAM DUANE* (1760–1835)
In *Aurora*,
September 3, 1811

Gallatin is a man of first-rate talents, conscious and vain of them, tortuous in his paths, born in Europe, disguising and yet betraying a supercilious prejudice of European superiority of intellect, and holding principles pliable to circumstances, occasionally mistaking the left for the right-handed wisdom.

—*JOHN QUINCY ADAMS* (1767–1848)
Diary entry,
November 1821

GAMBLING

Avoid Gaming. This is a vice which is productive of every possible evil; equally injurious to the morals and health of its votaries. It is the child of avarice, the brother of iniquity, and father of mischief.

—*GEORGE WASHINGTON* (1732–1799)
To Bushrod Washington,
January 15, 1783

In a world which furnishes so many employments which are useful, and so many which are amusing, it is our own fault if we ever know what ennui is, or if we are ever driven to the miserable resource of gaming, which corrupts our dispositions, and teaches us a habit of hostility against all mankind.

—*THOMAS JEFFERSON* (1743–1826)
To Martha Jefferson,
May 21, 1787

I recollect there is a billiard table near you; let me warn you against it. A passion of this kind will controul [sic] as it always has every other. If it seizes you, yr. clients money will not be safe in yr. hands.

—*JAMES MONROE* (1758–1831)
To his brother Joseph,
June 16, 1794

GEOGRAPHY

However strongly the passionate politics of the moment may operate, the politics that arise from geographical

107

situation are the most certain, and will in all cases finally prevail.
—THOMAS PAINE (1737–1809)
Age of Reason, I
1794

GEORGIA

I pitched upon this place, not only for the pleasantness of the situation, but because ... I thought it healthy; for it is sheltered from the western and southern winds by vast woods of pine-trees.
—JAMES EDWARD OGLETHORPE
(1696–1785)
Letter,
February 20, 1733

GOD & PROVIDENCE

[A]s it is some men's duty to plow, some to sow, some to water, and some to reap; so it is the wisdom as well as duty of a man, to yield to the mind of providence, and cheerfully, as well as carefully, embrace and follow the guidance of it.
—WILLIAM PENN (1644–1718)
A Letter from William Penn
1683

Glorious Things are spoken of Thee, O thou City of God, whose Street be in thee, O New England; The interpretation of it, be unto you, O American Colonies... There are many Arguments to persuade us That our Glorious Lord will have an Holy City in America; a City, the street whereof shall be Pure Gold...
—COTTON MATHER (1663–1728)
"Theopolis Americana" Sermon
("God's City: America"),
1701

See the wonderous works of Providence! The uncertainty of human things!
—GEORGE WASHINGTON (1732–1799)
To Robert Jackson,
August 2, 1755

There is a destiny which has the sovereign control of our actions, not to be resisted by the strongest efforts of human nature.
—GEORGE WASHINGTON
To Sarah Cary (Sally) Fairfax,
1758

If we believe the power of hell to be limited, we must likewise believe that their agents are under some providential control.
—THOMAS PAINE (1737–1809)
The Crisis
1776

The determinations of Providence are always wise, often inscrutable, and though its decrees appear to bear hard upon us at times, is nevertheless meant for gracious purposes.
—GEORGE WASHINGTON
To Bryan Fairfax,
March 1, 1778

The Hand of providence has been so conspicuous in all this, that he must be worse than an infidel that lacks faith, and more than wicked, that has not gratitude enough to acknowledge his obligations.
—GEORGE WASHINGTON
To Thomas Nelson,
August 20, 1778

Is there then no superintending power who conducts the moral operations of

the world, as well as the physical? The same sublime hand which guides the planets round the sun with so much exactness, which preserves the arrangement of the whole with such exalted wisdom and paternal care, and prevents the vast system from falling into confusion; doth it abandon mankind to all the errors, the follies, and the miseries, which their most frantic rage, and their most dangerous vices and passions can produce?
—*MICHEL GUILLAUME JEAN DE*
CRÈVECOEUR (1735–1813)
Letters From an American Farmer
1782

A State, I cheerfully admit, is the noblest work of Man: But Man, himself, free and honest, is, I speak as to this world, the noblest work of God.
—*JAMES WILSON* (1742–1798)
Chisholm v. Georgia
February 18, 1793

I believe in one God, and no more; and I hope for happiness beyond this life.
—*THOMAS PAINE*
Age of Reason
1794

It is difficult beyond the power of man to conceive an eternal duration of what we call time; but it is more impossible to conceive a time when there shall be no time. In like manner of reasoning, every thing we behold carries in itself the internal evidence that it did not make itself ...; and it is the conviction arising from this evidence, that carries us on, as it were, by necessity, to the belief of a first cause eternally existing, of a nature totally different to any material existence we know of, and by the

power of which all things exist, and this first cause man calls God.
—*THOMAS PAINE*
Age of Reason
1794

The only idea man can affix to the name of God, is, that of a *first cause*, the cause of all things. And incomprehensibly difficult as it is for man to conceive what a first cause is, he arrives at the belief of it, from the tendfold greater difficulty of disbelieving it.
—*THOMAS PAINE*
Age of Reason
1794

[It] is not for man to scan the wisdom of Providence. The best he can do is to submit to its decrees.
—*GEORGE WASHINGTON*
To Henry Knox,
March 2, 1797

A man does not serve God when he prays, for it is himself he is trying to serve ... but instead of buffeting the Deity with prayers as if I distrusted him or must dictate to him, I reposed myself on his protection; and you, my friend, will find, even in your last moments, more consolation in the silence of resignation than in the murmuring wish of prayer.
—*THOMAS PAINE*
To Samuel Adams,
January 1, 1803

This belief in a God All Powerful wise and good, is so essential to the moral order of the world and to the happiness of man, that arguments which enforce it cannot be drawn from too many sources nor adapted with too much solicitude to the different characters and capacities to be impressed with it. ... This finiteness of the Human understanding betrays itself on all subjects, but more especially when it contemplates such as involve infinity. What may safely be said seems to be, that the infinity of time and space forces itself on our conception, a limitation of either being inconceivable: that the mind prefers at once the idea of a self existing cause to that of an infinite series of cause and effect, which arguments, instead of avoiding the difficulty: and that it finds more facility in assenting to the self existence of an invisible cause possessing infinite power, wisdom and goodness, than to the self existence of the universe, visibly destitute of those attributes, and which may be the effect of them.

—*JAMES MADISON* (1751–1836)
To Frederick Beasley,
November 29, 1825

GOOD & EVIL

We often see stones hang with drops not from any innate moisture, but from a thick air about them; so may we sometime see marble-hearted sinners seem full of contrition, but it is not from any dew of grace within but from some black clouds that impends them, which produces these sweating effects.

—*ANNE BRADSTREET* (c. 1612–1672)
Meditations Divine and Moral
c. 1600

A bad cause will ever be supported by bad means and bad men.

—*THOMAS PAINE* (1737–1809)
The Crisis
1777

How easy it is to abuse truth and language, when men, by habitual wickedness, have learned to set justice at defiance.

—*THOMAS PAINE*
"Common Sense on George III's
Speech"
1782

When great evils happen, I am in the habit of looking out for what good may arise from them as consolations to us; and Providence has in fact so established the order of things as that most evils are the means of producing some good.

—*THOMAS JEFFERSON* (1743–1826)
To Benjamin Rush,
September 23, 1800

It is the melancholy law of human societies to be compelled sometimes to choose a great evil in order to ward off a greater.

—*THOMAS JEFFERSON*
To William Short,
November 28, 1814

GOVERNMENT

Were we directed from Washington when to sow, & when to reap, we should soon want bread.

—*THOMAS JEFFERSON* (1743–1826)
From *The Writings of Thomas Jefferson*,
edited by Paul L. Ford,
Date of quote unknown

Governments, like clocks, go from the motion men give them, and as governments are made and moved by men, so by them they are ruined too. Wherefore governments rather depend upon men, than men upon governments. Let men be good, and the government cannot be bad; if it be ill, they will cure it. But if men be bad, let the government be never so good, they will endeavour to warp and soil it to their turn.

—*WILLIAM PENN* (1644–1718)
Preface to the First Frame of Government for Pennsylvania, which was formally adopted in England, April 25, 1682

Government is an expedient against confusion; a restraint upon all disorder; just weights and an even balance: that one may not injure another, nor himself, by intemperance.

—*WILLIAM PENN*
An Essay Towards the Present and Future Peace of Europe
1693

Government then is the prevention or cure of disorder, and the means of justice, as that is of peace: For this cause they have sessions, terms, assizes and parliaments, to overrule men's passions and resentments, that they may not be judges in their own cause, nor punishers of their own wrongs, which as it is very incident to men in their corrupt state, so for that reason, they would observe no measure; nor on the other hand would any be easily reduced to their duty. Not that men know not what is right, their excesses, and wherein they are to blame; by no means, nothing is plainer to them; but so depraved is human nature, that without compulsion, some way or other, too many would not readily be brought to do what they know is right and fit, or avoid what they are satisfied they should not do.

—*WILLIAM PENN*
An Essay Towards the Present and Future Peace of Europe
1693

[O]ut of society every man is his own king, does what he lists, at his own peril. But when he comes to incorporate himself, he submits that royalty to the conveniency of the whole, from whom he receives the returns of protection. So that he is not now his own judge nor avenger, neither is his antagonist, but the law, in indifferent hands between both. ...Thus while we are not our own, every body is ours, and we get more than we lose, the safety of the society being the safety of the particulars that constitute it. So that while we seem to submit to, and hold all we have from society, it is by society that we keep what we have.

—*WILLIAM PENN*
An Essay Towards the Present and Future Peace of Europe
1693

Let the people think they govern, and they will be governed.

—*WILLIAM PENN*
Some Fruits of Solitude
1693

Three things contribute much to ruin government: looseness, oppression and envy. Where the reins of government are too slack, there the manners of the people are corrupted: and that destroys industry, begets effiminacy, and provokes heaven against it. Oppression makes a poor country and a desperate people, who always wait an opportunity to change. He that ruleth over men must be just, ruling in the fear of God, said an old and wise king. Envy disturbs and distracts government, clogs the wheels, and perplexes the administration; and nothing contributes more to this disorder, than a partial dis-

tribution of rewards and punishments in the sovereign.
—WILLIAM PENN
Some Fruits of Solitude
1693

I shall consider man in a state of natural being, as a freeborn subject under the crown of Heaven, and owing homage to none but God himself. It is certain civil government in general is a very desirable result of Providence, and an incomparable benefit to mankind, yet must needs be acknowledged to be the effect of human free-compacts and not of divine institution; it is the produce of man's reason, of human and rational combinations, and not from any direct orders of infinite wisdom, in any positive law wherein is drawn up this or that scheme of civil government.
—JOHN WISE (1652–1725)
A Vindication of the Government of New England Churches
1717

The end of all good government is to cultivate humanity, and promote the happiness of all, and the good of every man in all his rights, his life, liberty, estate, honor, etc., without injury or abuse done to any.
—JOHN WISE
A Vindication of the Government of New England Churches
1717

The good-will of the governed will be starved if not fed by the good deeds of the governors.
—BENJAMIN FRANKLIN (1706–1790)
Poor Richard's Almanack
1753

We are therefore brought exactly to the same point at last, whether we consider government as it is originally an appointment of Heaven, or, more immediately, the voluntary choice of men. The security and happiness of all the members composing the political body must be the design and end thereof, considered in both these lights.
—JONATHAN MAYHEW (1720–1776)
Election sermon,
1754

The body politic, like the human body, begins to die from its birth, and bears in itself the causes of its destruction.
—JEAN JACQUES ROUSSEAU (1712–1778)
The Social Contract, III
1762

If life, liberty, and property could be enjoyed in as great perfection in *solitude* as in *society* there would be no need of government. But the experience of ages has proved that such is the nature of man, a weak, imperfect being, that the valuable ends of life cannot be obtained without the union and assistance of many.
—JAMES OTIS (1725–1783)
The Rights of the British Colonies Asserted and Proved
1764

[T]ho' it is also admitted that the security of property is one end of government, but that of little estimation even in the view of a miser when life and liberty of locomotion and further accumulation are placed in competition, it must be a very absurd way of speaking to assert that one end of government is the foundation of government ... [the people delegate power to government only to serve "the good of the whole"]

The end of government being the good of mankind, points out its great duties: It is above all things to provide for the security, the quiet, and happy enjoyment of life, liberty, and property. There is not one act which a government can have a right to make, that does not tend to the advancement of the security, tranquility and prosperity of the people.
—*JAMES OTIS*
The Rights of the British Colonies Asserted and Proved
1764

For who are a free people? Not *those*, over whom government is reasonably and equitably exercised, but *those*, who live under a government so *constitutionally checked and controlled*, that proper provision is made against its being otherwise exercised.
—*JOHN DICKINSON* (1732–1794)
Political Writings
1767–1768

Mankind being formed into society, the moral obligation they are under to civil government will appear from the same principle, as being necessary to secure to them those natural rights and privileges which are essential to their happiness. Life, liberty, and property, are the gifts of the creator, on the unmolested enjoyment of which their happiness chiefly depends: yet they are such an imperfect set of beings that they are liable to have these invaded by one another: But the preservation of them in every fit method is evidently their duty.
—*DANIEL SHUTE* (1722–1802)
An Election Sermon,
1768

Security to the persons and properties of the governed is so obviously the design and end of civil government, that to attempt a logical proof of it would be like burning tapers at noonday, to assist the sun in enlightening the world.
—*JOHN HANCOCK* (1737–1793)
Boston Massacre Oration,
March 5, 1774

Those who bear equally the burdens of government should equally participate of its benefits.
—*THOMAS JEFFERSON*
Address to Lord Dunmore,
1775

To form a new government requires infinite care and unbounded attention; for if the foundation is badly laid, the superstructure must be bad.
—*GEORGE WASHINGTON* (1732–1799)
To John Augustine Washington,
May 31, 1776

That government is, or ought to be instituted for the common benefit, protection, and security of the people, nation, or community ... and that when any government shall be found inadequate or contrary to these purposes, a majority of the community hath an indubitable, unalienable, and indefeasible right to reform, alter or abolish it, in such manner as shall be judged conducive to the publick weal.
—*GEORGE MASON* (1725–1792)
Draft of Virginia Declaration of Rights,
June 12, 1776

A government of our own is our natural right.
—*THOMAS PAINE* (1737–1809)
Common Sense
1776

Government, like dress, is the badge of lost innocence; the palaces of kings are built upon the ruins of the bowers of paradise.
—*THOMAS PAINE*
Common Sense
1776

Society in every state is a blessing, but government, even in its best state, is but a necessary evil; in its worst state, an intolerable one.
—*THOMAS PAINE*
Common Sense
1776

I draw my idea of the form in government from a principle in nature which no art can overturn, viz., That the more simple anything is, the less liable it is to be disordered, and the easier repaired when disordered. ... the constitution of England is so exceedingly complex, that the nation may suffer for years together without being able to discover in which part the fault lies. Some will say in one and some in another, and every political physician will advise a different medicine.
—*THOMAS PAINE*
Common Sense
1776

The happiness of society is the end of government.
—*JOHN ADAMS* (1735–1826)
Thoughts on Government
1776

Fear is the foundation of most governments; but it is so sordid and brutal a passion, and renders men in whose breasts it predominates so stupid and miserable, that Americans will not be likely to approve of any political institution which is founded on it.
—*JOHN ADAMS*
Thoughts on Government
1776

That, as a republic is the best of governments, so that particular arrangements of the powers of society, or, in other words, that form of government which is best contrived to secure an impartial and exact execution of the laws, is the best of republics.
—*JOHN ADAMS*
Thoughts on Government
1776

That no free government, or the blessings of liberty, can be preserved to any people, but by a firm adherence to justice, moderation, temperance, frugality and virtue, and by frequent recurrence to fundamental principles.
—*ANONYMOUS*
Virginia Declaration of Rights,
1776

That instability is inherent in the nature of popular government, I think very disputable; unstable democracy is an epithet frequently in the mouths of politicians; but I believe that from a strict examination of the matter, from the records of history, it will be found that the fluctuations of governments in which the popular principle has borne a considerable sway has proceeded from its being compounded with other principles; and from its being made to operate in an improper channel. Compound governments, though they may be harmonious in the beginning, will introduce different interests; and these interests will clash, throw the state into

convulsions, and produce a change or dissolution.
—*ALEXANDER HAMILTON* (1755–1804)
To Robert R. Livingston,
March 19, 1777

The people at large are governed much by custom.
—*GEORGE WASHINGTON*
To Henry Laurens,
December 15, 1777

A narrow system of politics, like a narrow system of religion, is calculated only to sour the temper, and live at variance with mankind.
—*THOMAS PAINE*
The Crisis
1777

Politics to be executively right, must have a unity of means and time, and a defect in either overthrows the whole.
—*THOMAS PAINE*
The Crisis
1777

A frequent recurrence to the fundamental principles of the constitution, and a constant adherence to those of piety, justice, moderation, temperance, industry and frugality, are absolutely necessary to preserve the advantages of liberty, and to maintain a free government.
—*ANONYMOUS*
Massachusetts Bill of Rights
1780

The legitimate powers of government extend to such acts only as are injurious to others.
—*THOMAS JEFFERSON*
Notes on the State of Virginia
1784

The form of government best calculated for preserving liberty in time of peace, is not the best form for conducting the operations of war.
—*THOMAS PAINE*
On the Affairs of Pennsylvania
1786

The views of the governed are often materially different from those who govern. The science of policy is the knowledge of human nature.
—*ALEXANDER HAMILTON*
Constitutional Convention,
June 22, 1787

Even to observe neutrality you must have a strong government.
—*ALEXANDER HAMILTON*
Constitutional Convention,
June 29, 1787

[T]he good people of the U. States in their late generous contest, contended for free government in the fullest, clearest, and strongest sense. That they had no idea of being brought under despotic rule under the notion of "Strong Government," or in the form of *elective despotism*: Chains being still Chains, whether made of gold or iron. The corrupting nature of power, and its insatiable appetite for increase ... [makes amendments necessary to safeguard natural rights].
—*RICHARD HENRY LEE* (1732–1794)
To Samuel Adams,
October 1787

Government, indeed, taken as a science, may yet be considered in its infancy; and with all its various modifications, it has hitherto been the result of force, fraud, or accident. For, after the lapse of six thousand years since the creation of the world, America now presents the first instance of a people assembled to weigh deliberately and calmly, and to decide leisurely and peacably, upon the form of government by which they will bind themselves and their posterity.

—*JAMES WILSON* (1742–1798)
Opening Address, Pennsylvania
Ratifying Convention,
November 24, 1787

I consider the people of the United States as forming one great community; and I consider the people of the different states as forming communities, again, on a lesser scale. From this great division of the people into distinct communities, it will be found necessary that different proportions of legislative powers should be given to the governments, according to the nature, number, and magnitude of their objects.

—*JAMES WILSON*
Pennsylvania Ratification Convention,
November 26, 1787

A free government has often been compared to a pyramid. This allusion is made with peculiar propriety in the system before you; it is laid on the broad basis of the people; its powers gradually rise, while they are confined, in proportion as they ascend, until they end in that most permanent of all forms. When you examine all its parts, they will invariably be found to preserve that essential mark of free governments—a chain of connection with the people.

—*JAMES WILSON*
Summation and Final Rebuttal,
Pennsylvania Ratifying Convention,
December 11, 1787

Nothing is more certain than the indispensable necessity of government, and it is equally undeniable, that whenever and however it is instituted, the people must cede to it some of their natural rights, in order to vest it with requisite powers.

—*JOHN JAY* (1745–1829)
The Federalist Papers
1787

Government implies the power of making laws. It is essential to the idea of a law, that is to be attended with a sanction; or, in other words, a penalty or punishment for disobedience.

—*ALEXANDER HAMILTON*
The Federalist Papers
1787

Every government ought to contain in itself the means of its own preservation.

—*ALEXANDER HAMILTON*
The Federalist Papers
1787

Consent of the people [is the] pure, original fountain of all legitimate authority.

—*ALEXANDER HAMILTON*
The Federalist Papers
1787

A government, the constitution of which renders it unfit to be trusted with all the powers which a free people ought to delegate to any government, would be an unsafe and improper depositary of the national interests.

—*ALEXANDER HAMILTON*
The Federalist Papers
1787

A government ought to contain in itself

every power requisite to the full accomplishment of the objects committed to its care ... free from every other control but a regard to the public good and to the sense of the people.

—ALEXANDER HAMILTON
The Federalist Papers
1787

If mankind were to resolve to agree in no institution of government, until every part of it had been adjusted to the most exact standard of perfection, society would soon become a general scene of anarchy, and the world a desert. Where is the standard of perfection to be found? Who will undertake to unite the discordant opinions of a whole community ... and to prevail upon one conceited projector to renounce his INFALLIBLE criterion for the FALLIBLE criterion of his more CONCEITED NEIGHBOR?

—ALEXANDER HAMILTON
The Federalist Papers
1787

The true test of a good government is its aptitude and tendency to produce a good administration.

—ALEXANDER HAMILTON
The Federalist Papers
1787

Why has government been instituted at all? Because the passions of men will not conform to the dictates of reason and justice, without constraint.

—ALEXANDER HAMILTON
The Federalist Papers
1787

Complaints are every where heard from our most considerate and virtuous citizens, equally the friends of public and private faith, and of public and personal liberty; that our governments are to [be] unstable; that the public good is disregarded in the conflicts of rival parties; and that measures are too often decided, not according to the rules of justice, and the rights of the minor party; but by the superior force of an interested and overbearing majority. ... It will be found indeed, on a candid review of our situation, that some of the distresses under which we labour, have been erroneously charged on the operation of our governments; but it will be found at the same time that other causes will not alone account for many of our heaviest misfortunes; and particularly, for that prevailing and increasing distrust of public engagements, and alarm for private rights, which are echoed from one end of the continent to the other. These must be chiefly, if not wholly, effects of the unsteadiness and injustice, with which a factious spirit has tainted our public administration.

—JAMES MADISON (1751–1836)
The Federalist Papers
1787

The natural progress of things is for liberty to yield and government to gain ground.

—THOMAS JEFFERSON
Letter to Edward Carrington,
May 27, 1788

Governments destitute of energy, will ever produce anarchy.

—JAMES MADISON
Speech to Virginia Convention,
June 7, 1788

There never was a government without force. What is the meaning of government? An institution to make people do their duty. A government leaving it to a man to do his duty, or not, as he pleases, would be a new species of government, or rather no government at all.

—JAMES MADISON
Speech in the Virginia Ratifying
Convention,
June 16, 1788

I will venture to assert that no combination of designing men under Heaven will be capable of making a government unpopular which is in its principles a wise and good one, and vigorous in its operations.

—ALEXANDER HAMILTON
Debates and Proceedings of the
Convention of the State of New York,
June 17, 1788

It is a melancholy reflection that liberty should be equally exposed to danger whether the Government have too much or too little power.

—JAMES MADISON
Letter to Thomas Jefferson,
October 17, 1788

A certain degree of impartiality or the appearance of it, is necessary in the most despotic Governments. In republics, this may be considered as the vital principle of the Administration. And in a *federal* Republic founded on local distinctions involving local jealousies, it ought to be attended to with a still more scrupulous exactness.

—JAMES MADISON
To Edmund Pendleton,
October 20, 1788

We have heard of the impious doctrine in the old world that the people were made for kings, not kings for the people. Is the same doctrine to be revived in the new, in another shape, that the solid happiness of the people is to be sacrificed to the views of political institutions of different form? It is too early for politicians to presume on our forgetting that the public good, the real welfare of the great body of the people is the supreme object to be pursued; and that no form of government whatever, has any other value, than as it may be fitted for the attainment of this object.

—JAMES MADISON
The Federalist Papers
1788

In all great changes of established governments, forms ought to give way to substance.

—JAMES MADISON
The Federalist Papers
1788

Energy in government is essential to that security against external and internal danger, and to that prompt and salutary execution of the laws which enter into the very definition of good government. Stability in government is essential to national character and to the advantages annexed to it, as well as to that repose and confidence in the minds of the people, which are among the chief blessings of civil society.

—JAMES MADISON
The Federalist Papers
1788

What is government itself, but the greatest of all reflections on human nature? If men were angels, no government would be necessary. If angels were to govern men, neither external nor internal controls on government would be necessary. In framing a government which is to be administered by men over men, the great difficulty lies in this; you must first enable the government to control the governed; and in the next place oblige it to control itself.

—JAMES MADISON
The Federalist Papers
1788

Justice is the end of government. It is the end of civil society. It ever has been and ever will be pursued until it be obtained, or until liberty be lost in the pursuit.

—JAMES MADISON
The Federalist Papers
1788

A good government implies two things: fidelity to the object of government, which is the happiness of the people; secondly, a knowledge of the means by which that object can be best attained.

—JAMES MADISON
The Federalist Papers
1788

[W]hen once an efficient national government is established, the best men in the country will not only consent to serve, but also will generally be appointed to manage it; for, although town or country, or other contracted influence, may place men in State assemblies, or senates, or courts of justice, or executive departments, yet more general and extensive reputation for talents and other qualifications will be necessary to recommend men to offices under the national government, especially as it will have the widest field for choice, and never experience that want of proper persons which is not uncommon in some of the states. Hence, it will result that the administration, the political counsels, and the judicial decisions of the national government will be more wise, systematical, and judicious than those of individual states, and consequently more satisfactory with respect to other nations, as well as more safe with respect to us.

—JOHN JAY
The Federalist Papers
1788

Government will always take its complexion from the habits of the people—habits are continually changing from age to age—a body of legislators taken from the people, will generally represent these habits at the time when they are chosen—hence these two important conclusions, 1st: That a legislative body should be frequently renewed and always taken from the people—2nd: That a government which is perpetual, or incapable of being accommodated to every change of national habits, must in time become a bad government.

—NOAH WEBSTER (1758–1843)
In *American Magazine*
1788

If I recollect right, it was observed by an honorable member from New York, that this amendment would be an infringement of the natural rights of the people. I humbly conceive, if the gentleman reflects maturely on the nature of his argument, he will acknowledge its weakness. What is government itself, but a restraint upon the natural rights of the people? What constitution was ever devised, that did not operate as a

119

restraint on their original liberties? What is the whole system of qualifications, which take place in all free governments, but a restraint? Why is a certain age made necessary? Why a certain term of citizenship? This constitution itself, Sir, has restraints innumerable. The amendment, it is true, may exclude two of the best men: but it can rarely happen, that the state will sustain any material loss by this. I hope and believe that we shall always have more than two men, who are capable of discharging the duty of a senator.

—MELANCTON SMITH (1744–1798)
New York Ratifying Convention,
1788

Our duty is to frame a government friendly to liberty and the rights of mankind, which will tend to cherish and cultivate a love of liberty among our citizens. If this government becomes oppressive it will be by degrees: It will aim at its end by disseminating sentiments of government opposite to republicanism; and proceed from step to step in depriving the people of a share in the government.

—MELANCTON SMITH
New York Ratifying Convention,
1788

The gentleman last on the floor, has informed us, that according to his idea of a complete representation, the extent of our country is too great for it. … I take it [however], that no federal government is worth having, unless it can provide for the general interests of the United States.

—JOHN JAY
New York Ratifying Convention,
1788

To look up to a government that establishes justice, insures order, cherishes virtue, secures property, and protects from every species of violence, affords a pleasure, that can only be exceeded by looking up in all circumstances to an overruling providence. Such a pleasure I hope is before us, and our posterity under the influence of the new government.

—BENJAMIN RUSH (1745–1813)
To David Ramsay,
1788

It is time we have a government established & Washington at its head. But we are too poor for Monarchy, too wise for despotism, too dissipated selfish & extravagant for Republicanism.

—MERCY OTIS WARREN (1728–1814)
To Catharine Macaulay,
September 20, 1789

The best frame of government is that which is most likely to prevent the greatest sum of evil.

—JAMES MONROE (1758–1831)
*Observations on the Federal
Government*
1789

That the government, though not absolutely perfect, is one of the best in the world, I have little doubt.

—GEORGE WASHINGTON
To Catherine Macaulay Graham,
January 9, 1790

The consequence is, that the happiness of society is the first law of every government. This rule is founded on the law of nature: it must control every political maxim: it must regulate the legislature itself. The people have a right to insist that this rule be observed; and are entitled to demand a moral security that the legislature will observe it. If they have not the first [that right], they are slaves; if they have not the second [that moral security], they are, every moment, exposed to slavery.

—JAMES WILSON
Lectures,
1790–1791

Government, in my humble opinion, should be formed to secure and to enlarge the exercise of the natural rights of its members; and every government, which has not this in view, as its principal object, is not a government of the legitimate kind.

—JAMES WILSON
Lectures,
1790–1791

It is not enough to constitute a good government; it is equally indispensable to adopt such methods as may assure the permanency of a good government.

—THOMAS PAINE
"Answers to Four Questions on Legislative and Executive Powers"
1791

Man is not the enemy of man, but through the medium of a false system of Government.

—THOMAS PAINE
Rights of Man
1791

We have established a common Government, which, being free in its principles, being founded in our own choice, being intended as the guardian of our common rights and the patron of our common interests, and wisely containing within itself a provision for its own amendment as experience may point out its errors, seems to promise everything that can be expected from such an institution; and if supported by wise counsels, by virtuous conduct, and by mutual and friendly allowances, must approach as near to perfection as any human work can aspire, and nearer than any which the annals of mankind have recorded.

—JAMES MADISON
To George Washington,
June 21, 1792

It is time that nations should be rational, and not be governed like animals, for the pleasure of their riders.

—THOMAS PAINE
Rights of Man, II
1792

The strength of government does not consist in any thing *within* itself, but in the attachment of a nation, and the interest which the people feel in supporting it. When this is lost, government is but a child in power; and though ... it may harass individuals for a while, it but facilitates its own fall.

—THOMAS PAINE
Rights of Man, II
1792

Governments by precedent, without any regard to the principle of the precedent, is one of the vilest systems that can be set up.

—THOMAS PAINE
Rights of Man, II
1792

The true system of Government consists, not in Kings, but in fair and honorable Representation.

—THOMAS PAINE
Speech to the French National
Convention,
January 15, 1793

There is no resource so firm for the government of the United States as the affections of the people guided by an enlightened policy.

—GEORGE WASHINGTON
Fifth Annual Address to Congress,
December 3, 1793

A state, useful and valuable as the contrivance is, is the inferior contrivance of man; and from his native dignity derives all its acquired importance. ... Let a state be considered as subordinate to the people: But let everything else be subordinate to the state.

—JAMES WILSON
Chisholm v. Georgia
1793

The very idea of the power and the right of the people to establish government presupposes the duty of every individual to obey established government.

—GEORGE WASHINGTON
Farewell Address,
September 17, 1796

I think every nation has a right to establish that form of government under which it conceives it shall live most happy, provided it infracts no right or is not dangerous to others.

—GEORGE WASHINGTON
To Marquis de Lafayette,
December 25, 1798

Beware, my dear sir, of magnifying a

riot into an insurrection, by employing, in the first instance, an inadequate force. 'Tis far better to err on the other side. Whenever the government appears in arms, it ought to appear like a Hercules, and inspire respect by the display of strength.

—ALEXANDER HAMILTON
To James McHenry,
March 18, 1799

A wise and frugal government, which shall restrain men from injuring one another, shall leave them otherwise free to regulate their own pursuits of industry and improvement, and shall not take from the mouth of labor the bread it has earned. This is the sum of good government, and this is necessary to close the circle of our felicities.

—THOMAS JEFFERSON
First Inaugural Address,
March 4, 1801

The very essense of civil liberty certainly consists in the right of every individual to claim the protection of the laws, whenever he receives an injury. One of the first duties of government is to afford that protection.

—JOHN MARSHALL (1755–1835)
Marbury v. Madison
1803

That government is the strongest of which every man feels himself a part.

—THOMAS JEFFERSON
Letter to H. D. Tiffin,
1807

I estimate the acts of my friends by the intentions only. Being satisfied on that point I can bear with patience any consequence which may casually result from them. I am aware that under free govt., it is difficult to avoid those of [a] kind ... for perhaps no important good was ever altogether free from some poison of alloy. I am however equally aware that the evils which are incident to the system ... even to the individual who suffers by them, are trifling when compared with the great bliss which it imparts.

—*JAMES MONROE*
To Thomas Jefferson,
March 22, 1808

The care of human life and happiness, and not their destruction, is the first and only legitimate object of good government.

—*THOMAS JEFFERSON*
Message to the citizens of Washington County, Maryland,
March 31, 1809

A free government with arbitrary means to administer it is a contradiction; a free government without adequate provision for personal security is an absurdity; a free government, with an uncontrolled power of military conscription, is a solecism, at once the most ridiculous and abominable that ever entered into the head of man.

—*DANIEL WEBSTER* (1782–1852)
Speech,
1811

The only orthodox object of the institution of government is to secure the greatest degree of happiness possible to the general mass of those associated under it.

—*THOMAS JEFFERSON*
To Francis A. Van Der Kemp,
March 22, 1812

I think we have more machinery of government than is necessary, too many parasites living on the labor of the industrious.

—*THOMAS JEFFERSON*
Letter to Charles Yancey,
1816

The principal support of free government is to be derived from the sound morals and intelligence of the people; and the more extensive means of education, the more confidently we may rely upon the preservation of our public liberties.

—*JAMES MONROE*
A Narrative of a Tour of Observation
1818

The government of the Union ... is emphatically, and truly, a government of the people. In form and in substance it emanates from them. Its powers are granted by them, and are to be exercised directly on them, and for their benefit.

—*JOHN MARSHALL*
McCulloch v. Maryland
1819

This government is acknowledged by all to be one of enumerated powers. ... But the question respecting the extent of the powers actually granted, is perpetually arising, and will probably continue to arise, so long as our system shall exist.

—*JOHN MARSHALL*
McCulloch v. Maryland
1819

The sword and the purse, all the external relations, and no inconsiderable portion of the industry of the nation, are entrusted to its government ... a government entrusted with such ample powers, on the

due execution of which the happiness and prosperity of the nation so vitally depends, must also be entrusted with ample means for their execution. The power being given, it is the interest of the nation to facilitate its execution. It can never be their interest, and cannot be presumed to have been their intention, to clog and embarrass its execution.
—*JOHN MARSHALL*
McCulloch v. Maryland
1819

The free system of government we have established is so congenial with reason, with common sense, and with a universal feeling, that it must produce approbation and a desire of imitation, as avenues may be found for truth to the knowledge of nations.
—*JAMES MADISON*
Letter to Pierre E. Duponceau,
January 23, 1826

GOVERNMENT SPENDING & PUBLIC DEBT

No nation ought to be without a debt. A national debt is a national bond.
—*THOMAS PAINE* (1737–1809)
Common Sense
1776

It is the highest impertinence and presumption, therefore, in kings and ministers to pretend to watch over the economy of private people, and to restrain their expense. ... They are themselves always, and without any exception, the greatest spendthrifts in the society.
—*ADAM SMITH* (1723–1790)
An Inquiry into the Nature and Causes of the Wealth of Nations
1776

A national debt, if it is not excessive, will be to us a national blessing.
—*ALEXANDER HAMILTON* (1755–1804)
Letter to Robert Morris,
April 30, 1781

The Federal Government should neither be independent nor too much dependent. It should neither be raised above responsibility or control, nor should it want the means of maintaining its own weight, authority, dignity, and credit. To this end, permanent funds are indispensable, but they ought to be of such a nature and so moderate in their amount as never to be inconvenient.
—*ALEXANDER HAMILTON*
"The Continentalist, No. 6."
July 4, 1782

The maxim of buying nothing without the money in our pocket to pay for it, would make of our country one of the happiest upon earth. Experience during the war proved this; as I think every man will remember that under all the privations it obliged him to submit to during that period he slept sounder, and awaked happier than he can do now. Desperate of finding relief from a free course of justice, I look forward to the abolition of all credit as the only other remedy which can take place.
—*THOMAS JEFFERSON* (1743–1826)
Letter to Alexander Donald,
July 28, 1787

I go on the principle that a public debt is a public curse.
—*JAMES MADISON* (1751–1836)
Letter to Henry Lee,
April 13, 1790

Public money ought to be touched with

the most scrupulous consciousness of honor.

—THOMAS PAINE
Rights of Man
1792

As a very important source of strength and security, cherish public credit. One method of preserving it is to use it as sparingly as possible.

—GEORGE WASHINGTON (1732–1799)
Farewell Address,
September 17, 1796

I wish it were possible to obtain a single amendment to our constitution. I would be willing to depend on that alone for the reduction of the administration of our government to the genuine principles of its constitution; I mean an additional article, taking from the federal government the power of borrowing.

—THOMAS JEFFERSON
Letter to John Taylor,
November 26, 1798

I am for a government rigorously frugal & simple, applying all the possible savings of the pubic revenue to the discharge of the national debt; and not for a multiplication of officers & salaries merely to make partisans, & for increasing, by every device, the public debt, on the principle of its being a public blessing.

—THOMAS JEFFERSON
Letter to Elbridge Gerry,
January 26, 1799

To contract new debts is not the way to pay old ones.

—GEORGE WASHINGTON
To James Welch,
April 7, 1799

What more is necessary to make us wise and happy people? Still one thing more, fellow citizens—a wise and frugal government, which shall restrain men from injuring one another, which shall leave them otherwise free to regulate their own pursuits of industry and improvement, and shall not take from the mouth of labor the bread it has earned. This is the sum of good government, and this is necessary to close the circle of our felicities.

—THOMAS JEFFERSON
First Inaugural Address,
March 4, 1801

If we can prevent the government from wasting the labors of the people, under the pretense of taking care of them, they must become happy.

—THOMAS JEFFERSON
To Thomas Cooper,
January 29, 1802

We are endeavoring, too, to reduce the government to the practice of a rigorous economy, to avoid burdening the people, and arming the magistrate with a patronage of money, which might be used to corrupt and undermine the principles of our government.

—THOMAS JEFFERSON
Letter to Mr. Pictet,
February 5, 1803

The same prudence which in private life would forbid our paying our own money for unexplained projects, forbids it in the dispensation of the public moneys.

—THOMAS JEFFERSON
Letter to Shelton Giliam,
June 19, 1808

I, however, place economy among the

first and most important of republican virtues, and public debt as the greatest of the dangers to be feared.

—*THOMAS JEFFERSON*
To William Plumer,
July 21, 1816

I sincerely believe that banking establishments are more dangerous than standing armies, and that the principle of spending money to be paid by posterity, under the name of funding, is but swindling futurity on a large scale.

—*THOMAS JEFFERSON*
Letter to John Taylor,
May 28, 1816

We must not let our rulers load us with perpetual debt.

—*THOMAS JEFFERSON*
Letter to Samuel Kercheval,
July 12, 1816

It is incumbent on every generation to pay its own debts as it goes—a principle which, if acted on, would save one-half the wars of the world.

—*THOMAS JEFFERSON*
Letter to Destutt Tracy,
1820

The multiplication of public offices, increase of expense beyond income, growth and entailment of a public debt, are indications soliciting the employment of the pruning-knife.

—*THOMAS JEFFERSON*
To Spencer Roane,
March 9, 1821

GREAT MEN & STATESMEN

We assemble parliaments and councils, to have the benefit of their collected wisdom; but we necessarily have, at the same time, the inconvenience of their collected passions, prejudices, and private interests. By the help of these, artful men overpower their wisdom, and dupe its possessors; and if we may judge by the acts, arrets, and edicts, all the world over, for regulating commerce, an assembly of great men is the greatest fool upon earth.

—*BENJAMIN FRANKLIN* (1706–1790)
Letter to Benjamin Vaughan,
July 26, 1784

Of all the memorable eras that have marked the progress of men from the savage state to the refinements of luxury, that which has combined them into society, under a wise system of government, and given form to a nation, has ever been recorded and celebrated as the most important. Legislators have ever been deemed the greatest benefactors of mankind—respected when living, and often deified after their death. Hence the fame of Fohi and Confucius—of Moses, Solon and Lycurgus—of Romulus and Numa—of Alfred, Peter the Great, and Mango Capac; whose names will be celebrated through all ages, for framing and improving constitutions of government, which introduced order into society and secured the benefits of law to millions of the human race.

—*NOAH WEBSTER* (1758–1843)
An Examination into the Leading Principles of the Federal Constitution
October 17, 1787

Did you ever see a portrait of a great man without perceiving strong traits of pain and anxiety?

—*JOHN ADAMS* (1735–1826)
Letter to Thomas Jefferson,
May 6, 1816

GREED

Be not tempted to presume by success: for many that have got largely, have lost all, by coveting to get more.
—*WILLIAM PENN* (1644–1718)
Some Fruits of Solitude
1693

If thou art clean and warm, it is sufficient, for more doth but rob the poor and please the wanton.
—*WILLIAM PENN*
Some Fruits of Solitude
1693

The generality are the worse for their plenty. The voluptuous consumes it, the miser hides it: it is the good man that uses it, and to good purposes. But such are hardly found among the prosperous.
—*WILLIAM PENN*
Some Fruits of Solitude
1693

If you desire many things, many things will seem but a few.
—*BENJAMIN FRANKLIN* (1706–1790)
Poor Richard's Almanack
c. 1732

To procure tranquility of mind we must avoid desire & fear, the two principal diseases of the mind.
—*THOMAS JEFFERSON* (1743–1826)
To William Short,
October 31, 1819

GUNS & WEAPONS

O sir, we should have fine times, indeed, if, to punish tyrants, it were only sufficient to assemble the people! Your arms, wherewith you could defend yourselves, are gone; and you have no longer an aristrocratical, no longer a democratical spirit. Did you ever read of any revolution in a nation, brought about by the punishment of those in power, inflicted by those who had no power at all?
—*PATRICK HENRY* (1736–1799)
Speech in the Virginia Ratifying Convention,
June 5, 1778

A well regulated militia, being necessary to the security of a free state, the right of the people to keep and bear arms, shall not be infringed.
—*CONSTITUTION OF THE UNITED STATES*
The Bill of Rights, Amendment 2
1787

Before a standing army can rule, the people must be disarmed; as they are in almost every kingdom of Europe. The supreme power in America cannot enforce unjust laws by the sword; because the whole body of the people are armed, and constitute a force superior to any band of regular troops that can be, on any pretence, raised in the United States.
—*NOAH WEBSTER* (1758–1843)
An Examination of the Leading Principles of the Federal Constitution
1787

H

ALEXANDER HAMILTON

Hamilton is really a colossus to the anti-republican party. Without numbers, he is a host within himself.
—*THOMAS JEFFERSON* (1743–1826)
Letter to James Madison,
September 21, 1795

The publication [of Hamilton's pamphlet] under all its characters is a curious specimen of the ingenious folly of its author. Next to the error of publishing at all, is that of forgetting that simplicity and candor are the only dress which prudence would put on innocence. Here we see every rhetorical artifice employed to excite the spirit of party to prop up his sinking reputation, and whilst the most exaggerated complaints are uttered against the unfair and virulent persecutions of himself, he deals out in every page the most malignant insinuations, against others. The one against you is a masterpiece of folly, because its impotence is in exact proportion to its venom.
—*JAMES MADISON* (1751–1836)
To Thomas Jefferson,
October 20, 1797

In this dark and insidious manner did this intriguer lay schemes in secret against me, and, like the worm at the root of the peach, did he labor for twelve years, underground and in darkness, to girdle the root, while all the axes of the Anti-Federalists, Democrats, Jacobins, Virginia debtors to English merchants, and French hirelings, chopping as they were for the whole time at the trunk, could not fell the tree.
—*JOHN ADAMS* (1735–1826)
July 20, 1807

HAPPINESS

If thou wouldst be happy, bring thy mind to thy condition, and have an indifferency for more than what is sufficient.
—*WILLIAM PENN* (1644–1718)
Some Fruits of Solitude
1693

Seek not to be rich, but happy. The one lies in bags, the other in content; which wealth can never give.
—*WILLIAM PENN*
Some Fruits of Solitude
1693

Roses grow upon briars, which is to signify that all temporal sweets are mixed with bitter. But what seems more especially to be meant by it is that pure happiness, the crown of glory, is to be come at in no other way than by bearing Christ's cross, by a life of mortifi-

cation, self-denial, and labor, and bearing all things for Christ.
—*JONATHAN EDWARDS* (1703–1758)
Images or Shadows of Divine Things
1748

My days have been so wondrous free,
  The little birds that fly
With careless ease from tree to tree,
  Were but as blest as I,
Were but as blest as I.
  Ask the gliding waters,
If a tear of mine
  Increased their stream,
And ask the breathing gales
  If ever I lent a sigh to them,
If I lent a sigh to them.
—*FRANCIS HOPKINSON* (1737–1791)
My Days Have Been So Wondrous Free
1759

Kings or parliaments could not *give* the rights essential to happiness. ... We claim them from a higher source— from the King of kings, and Lord of all the earth. They are not annexed to us by parchments and seals. They are created in us by the decrees of Providence ... It would be an insult on the divine Majesty to say, that he has given or allowed any man or body of men a right to make me miserable. If no man or body of men has such a right, I have a right to be happy. If there can be no happiness without freedom, I have a right to be free. If I cannot enjoy freedom without security of property, I have a *right to be thus secured.*
—*JOHN DICKINSON* (1732–1794)
Reply to a Committee in Barbados,
1766

That Mankind were intended to be happy, at least that God Almighty gave them power of being so, if they would

properly exert the means He has bestowed upon them.
—*JAMES IREDELL* (1751–1799)
Essay,
1775

For the first and great question, and that which involves every other in it, and from which every other will flow, is happiness.
—*THOMAS PAINE* (1737–1809)
The Forester's Letters
1776

Our greatest happiness ... does not depend on the condition of life in which chance has placed us, but is always the result of a good conscience, good health, occupation and freedom in all just pursuits.
—*THOMAS JEFFERSON* (1743–1826)
"Notes on Virginia"
1782

Happiness depends more upon the internal frame of a person's own mind than on the externals in the world.
—*GEORGE WASHINGTON* (1732–1799)
To Mary Washington,
February 15, 1787

A mind always employed is always happy. This is the true secret, the grand recipe for felicity.
—*THOMAS JEFFERSON*
To Martha Jefferson,
May 21, 1787

It is neither wealth nor splendor, but tranquility and occupation, which give happiness.
—*THOMAS JEFFERSON*
Letter to Mrs. A. S. Marks
1788

Human felicity is produced not so much by great pieces of good fortune that seldom happen, as by little advantages that occur every day.
—BENJAMIN FRANKLIN (1706–1790)
Autobiography
1791

Whatever the apparent cause of any riots may be, the real one is always want of happiness.
—THOMAS PAINE
Rights of Man, II
1792

HEALTH & MEDICINE

Have wholesome, but not costly food, and be rather cleanly than dainty in ordering it.
—WILLIAM PENN (1644–1718)
Some Fruits of Solitude
1693

Eat to live and not live to eat.
—BENJAMIN FRANKLIN (1706–1790)
Poor Richard's Almanack
1733

To lengthen thy life lessen thy meals.
—BENJAMIN FRANKLIN
Poor Richard's Almanack
1733

Early to bed and early to rise, makes a man healthy, wealthy, and wise.
—BENJAMIN FRANKLIN
Poor Richard's Almanack
1735

God heals and the doctor takes the fee.
—BENJAMIN FRANKLIN
Poor Richard's Almanack
1736

Health is man's best wealth.
—BENJAMIN FRANKLIN
Poor Richard's Almanack
1746

We are not so sensible of the greatest health as of the least sickness.
—BENJAMIN FRANKLIN
Poor Richard's Almanack
1747

Health must not be sacrificed to learning. A strong body makes the mind strong.
—THOMAS JEFFERSON (1743–1826)
To Peter Carr,
August 19, 1785

Knowledge indeed is desirable, a lovely possession, but I do not scruple to say that health is more so. It is of little consequence to store the mind with science if the body be permitted to become debilitated. If the body be feeble, the mind will not be strong.
—THOMAS JEFFERSON
To Thomas Mann Randolph, Jr.,
August 27, 1786

Of all exercises walking is best. ... No one knows, till he tries, how easily a habit of walking is acquired. A person who never walked three miles will in the course of a month become able to walk 15 or 20 without fatigue. I have known some great walkers & had particular accounts of many more; and I never knew or heard of one who was not healthy & long lived. This species of exercise therefore is much to be advised.
—THOMAS JEFFERSON
To Thomas Mann Randolph, Jr.,
August 27, 1786

The sovereign invigorator of the body is exercise, and of all the exercises, walking is best.

—THOMAS JEFFERSON
To Thomas Mann Randolph, Jr.,
August 27, 1786

With your talents and industry, with science, and that steadfast honesty which eternally pursues right, regardless of consequences, you may promise yourself every thing—but health, without which there is no happiness. An attention to health then should take place of every other object. The time necessary to secure this by active exercises, should be devoted to it in preference to every other pursuit.

—THOMAS JEFFERSON
To Thomas Mann Randolph, Jr.,
July 6, 1787

Let me recommend the best medicine in the world: a long journey, at a mild Season, thro' a pleasant Country, in easy stages.

—JAMES MADISON (1751–1836)
To Horatio Gates,
February 23, 1794

I have yet, I believe, some years in store, for I have a good state of health and a happy mind, and I take care of both by nourishing the first with temperance and the latter with abundance. This, I believe, you will allow to be the true philosophy of life.

—THOMAS PAINE (1737–1809)
To Samuel Adams,
January 1, 1803

The inexperienced and presumptuous band of medical tyros let loose upon the world destroys more of human life in one year than all the Robin Hoods, Cartouches, and Macheaths do in a century.

—THOMAS JEFFERSON
Letter to Dr. Caspar Wistar,
June 21, 1807

HISTORY

A too great inattention to past occurrences retards and bewilders our judgment in every thing; while, on the contrary, by comparing what is past with what is present, we frequently hit on the true character of both, and become wise with very little trouble. It is a kind of countermarch, by which we get into the rear of Time, and mark the movements and meanings of things as we make our return.

—THOMAS PAINE (1737–1809)
The Crisis
1777

The history of the earth! doth it present any thing but crimes of the most heinous nature, committed from one end of the world to the other? We observe avarice, rapine, and murder, equally prevailing in all parts. History perpetually tells us, of millions of people abandoned to the caprice of the maddest princes, and of whole nations devoted to the blind fury of tyrants. Countries destroyed; nations alternately buried in ruins by other nations; some parts of the world beautifully cultivated, returned again to the pristine state; the fruits of ages of industry, the toil of thousands in a short time destroyed by a few!

—MICHEL GUILLAUME JEAN DE
CRÈVECOEUR (1735–1813)
Letters From an American Farmer
1782

Wars & contentions indeed fill the pages of history with more matter. But more blest is that nation whose silent course of happiness furnishes nothing for history to say. This is what I ambition for my own country.
—THOMAS JEFFERSON (1743–1826)
To M. Le Comte Diodati,
March 29, 1807

History, in general, only informs us what bad government is.
—THOMAS JEFFERSON
Letter to John Norvell,
June 14, 1807

It is truly unfortunate that those engaged in public affairs so rarely make notes of transactions passing within their knowledge. Hence history becomes fable instead of fact. The great outlines may be true, but the incidents and colouring are according to the faith or fancy of the writer.
—THOMAS JEFFERSON
To William Writ,
August 14, 1814

A morsel of genuine history is a thing so rare as to be always valuable.
—THOMAS JEFFERSON
Letter to John Adams,
September 8, 1817

I feel a much greater interest in knowing what passed two or three thousand years ago, than in what is now passing.
—THOMAS JEFFERSON
To Nathaniel Macon
January 12, 1819

The infant periods of most nations are buried in silence or veiled in fable; and the world perhaps has lost but little which it needs regret. The origin and outset of the American Republic contain lessons of which posterity ought not to be deprived: and happy there never was a case in which every interesting incident could be so accurately preserved.
—JAMES MADISON (1751–1836)
To William Eustis,
July 8, 1819

History fades into fable; fact becomes clouded with doubt and controversy; the inscription molders from the tablet; the statue falls from the pedestal. Columns, arches, pyramids, what are they but heaps of sand; and their epitaphs, but characters written in the dust?
—WASHINGTON IRVING (1783–1859)
The Sketch Book
1820

I consider the true history of the American Revolution, and the establishments of our present Constitution, as lost forever; and nothing but misrepresentations, or partial accounts of it, will ever be recovered.
—JOHN ADAMS (1735–1826)
Quoted in Lt. Francis Hall, *Travels in Canada and the United States in 1816 and 1817*
1819

No studies seem so well calculated to give a proper expansion to the mind as Geography and history; and when not absorbing an undue portion of time, are as beneficial and becoming to the one sex as to the other.
—JAMES MADISON
To Reynolds Chapman,
January 25, 1821

The public history of all countries, and all ages, is but a sort of mask, richly colored. The interior working of the machinery must be foul.
—*JOHN QUINCY ADAMS* (1767–1848)
Diary entry,
November 9, 1822

History may distort truth, and will distort it for a time, by the superior efforts at justification of those who are conscious of needing it most. Nor will the opening scenes of our present government be seen in their true aspect until the letters of the day, now held in private hoards, shall be broken up and laid open to public view.
—*THOMAS JEFFERSON*
To William Johnson,
June 12, 1823

HONESTY

'Tis hard (but glorious) to be poor and honest. An empty sack can hardly stand upright; but if it does, 'tis a stout one.
—*BENJAMIN FRANKLIN* (1706–1790)
Poor Richard's Almanack
1750

Of more worth is one honest man to society, and in the eyes of God, than all the crowned ruffians that ever lived.
—*THOMAS PAINE* (1737–1809)
Common Sense
1776

The only way to make men honest is to prevent their being otherwise, by tying them firmly to the accomplishment of their contracts.
—*GEORGE WASHINGTON* (1732–1799)
To Lund Washington,
December 17, 1778

One great error is that we suppose mankind more honest than they are.
–*ALEXANDER HAMILTON* (1755–1804)
At the Constitutional Convention,
June 22, 1787

I hope I shall always possess firmness and virtue enough to maintain ... the character of an "Honest Man."
—*GEORGE WASHINGTON*
Letter to Alexander Hamilton,
August 28, 1788

I hold the maxim no less applicable to public than to private affairs, that honesty is always the best policy.
—*GEORGE WASHINGTON*
Farewell Address,
September 17, 1796

The first of qualities for a great statesman is to be honest. And if it were possible that this opinion were an error, I should rather carry it with me to my grave than to believe that a man cannot be a statesman without being dishonest.
—*JOHN ADAMS* (1735–1826)
Letter to William Eustis,
June 22, 1809

Men are disposed to live honestly, if the means of doing so are open to them.
—*THOMAS JEFFERSON* (1743–1826)
Letter to M. Barre de Marbois,
June 14, 1817

HONOR

I would lay down my life for America, but I cannot trifle with my honor.
—*JOHN PAUL JONES* (1747–1792)
Letter to A. Livingston,
September 4, 1777

National honor is national property of the highest value.
—*JAMES MONROE* (1758–1831)
First Inaugural Address,
March 4, 1817

HUMAN NATURE

We must … make the best of mankind as they are, since we cannot have them as we wish.
—*GEORGE WASHINGTON* (1732–1799)
To Philip Schuyler,
December 24, 1775

We must take human nature as we find it. Perfection falls not to the share of mortals.
—*GEORGE WASHINGTON*
To John Jay,
August 1, 1786

It is really a strange thing that there should not be room enough in the world for men to live without cutting one another's throats.
—*GEORGE WASHINGTON*
To Marquis de Lafayette,
June 19, 1788

HUMANITY

We should take mankind as they are, and not as they ought to be or would be if they were perfect in wisdom and virtue.
—*SAMUEL PHILLIPS PAYSON* (1736–1801)
From a sermon delivered in Boston,
1778

HUMILITY

Affect not to be seen, and men will less see thy weakness.

—*WILLIAM PENN* (1644–1718)
Some Fruits of Solitude
1693

Enquire often, but judge rarely, and thou wilt not often be mistaken.
—*WILLIAM PENN*
More Fruits of Solitude
1702

HYPOCRISY

We are apt to be very pert at censuring others, where we will not endure advice ourselves. And nothing shows our weakness more than to be so sharp-sighted at spying other men's faults, and so purblind about our own.
—*WILLIAM PENN* (1644–1718)
Some Fruits of Solitude
1693

Mankind are very odd creatures: one half censure what they practice, the other half practice what they censure; the rest always say and do as they ought.
—*BENJAMIN FRANKLIN* (1706–1790)
Poor Richard's Almanack
1752

How easy it is to persuade men to sign anything by which they can't be affected!
—*GEORGE MASON* (1725–1792)
To Zachariah Johnston,
1791

The prejudice of unfounded belief, often degenerates into the prejudice of custom, and becomes at last rank hypocrisy. When men, from custom or fashion or any worldly motive, profess or pretend to believe what they do not believe, nor can give any reason for believing, they unship the helm of their morality, and being no longer honest to their own minds they feel no moral difficulty in being unjust to others.

—*THOMAS PAINE* (1737–1809)
Examination of the Prophecies
1807

How easily we prescribe for others a cure for their difficulties, while we cannot cure our own.

—*THOMAS JEFFERSON* (1743–1826)
To John Adams,
January 22, 1821

I

IMMIGRATION

Every industrious European who transports himself here may be compared to a sprout growing at the foot of a great tree; it enjoys and draws but a little portion of sap; wrench it from the parent roots, transplant it, and it will become a tree bearing fruit also.
—*MICHEL GUILLAUME JEAN DE
CRÈVECOEUR* (1735–1813)
Letters from an American Farmer
1782

I do not mean that every one who comes will grow rich in a little time; no, but he may procure an easy, decent maintenance, by his industry. Instead of starving he will be fed, instead of being idle he will have employment; and these are riches enough for such men as come over here.
—*MICHEL GUILLAUME JEAN DE
CRÈVECOEUR*
Letters from an American Farmer
1782

The bosom of America is open to receive not only the Opulent, and respectable Strange, but the oppressed and persecuted of all Nations And Religions; whom we shall welcome to a participation of all our rights and privileges, if by decency and propriety of conduct they appear to merit the enjoyment.
—*GEORGE WASHINGTON* (1732–1799)
"Letter to the members of the
Volunteer Association and other
Inhabitants of the Kingdom of Ireland
who have lately arrived in the City of
New York"
December 2, 1783

Rather than quarrel about territory, let the poor, the needy, and oppressed of the earth, and those who want land, resort to the fertile plains of our western country, the *second land of promise*, and there dwell in peace, fulfilling the first and great commandment.
—*GEORGE WASHINGTON*
To David Humphreys,
July 25, 1785

I had always hoped that this land might become a safe and agreeable asylum to the virtuous and persecuted part of mankind, to whatever nation they might belong.
—*GEORGE WASHINGTON*
To Francis Adrian Van der Kemp,
May 28, 1788

When we are considering the advantages that may result from an easy mode of naturalization, we ought also to consider the cautions necessary to guard against abuses; it is no doubt very desirable, that we should hold out as many inducements as possible, for the worthy part of mankind to come and settle amongst us, and throw their fortunes into a common lot with ours. But, why is this desirable? Not merely to swell the catalogue of people. No, sir, 'tis to increase the wealth and strength of the community, and those who acquire the rights of citizenship, without adding to the strength or wealth of the community; are not the people we are in want of.

—JAMES MADISON (1751–1836)
Speech in Congress,
February 3, 1790

IMPEACHMENT

Our allegiance binds us not to the laws of England any longer than while we live in England, for the laws of the parliament of England reach no further, nor do the king's writs under the great seal go any further.

—JOHN WINTHROP (1588–1649)
The History of New England
from 1630 to 1649
1646

The President, Vice-President, and all civil officers of the United States, shall be removed from office on impeachment for, and conviction of, treason, bribery, or other high crimes and misdemeanors.

—CONSTITUTION OF THE UNITED STATES
Article II, Section 4
1787

The power of impeachment is given by this Constitution, to bring great offenders to punishment. It is calculated to bring them to punishment for crimes which it is not easy to describe, but which every one must be convinced is a high crime and misdemeanor against the government. This power is lodged in those who represent the great body of the people, because the occasion for its exercise will arise from acts of great injury to the community, and the objects of it may be such as cannot be easily reached by an ordinary tribunal. The trial belongs to the Senate, lest an inferior tribunal should be too much awed by so powerful an accuser.

—JAMES IREDELL (1751–1799)
Speech in North Carolina Ratifying
Convention,
July 28, 1788

INDEPENDENCE & NATIONAL FREEDOM

Reflect how you are to govern a people who think they ought to be free, and think they are not. Your scheme yields no revenue; it yields nothing but discontent, disorder, disobedience; and such is the state of America, that after wading up to your eyes in blood, you could only end just where you begun; that is, to tax where no revenue is to be found, to - my voice fails me; my inclination indeed carries me no farther - all is confusion beyond it.

—EDMUND BURKE (1729–1797)
First Speech on the Conciliation with
America, American Taxation,
April 19, 1774

The country shall be independent, and we will be satisfied with nothing short of it.

—SAMUEL ADAMS (1722–1803)
1774

Deny them [the colonies] this participation of freedom, and you break that sole bond, which originally made, and must still preserve the unity of the empire.

—EDMUND BURKE
Second Speech on Conciliation with America, The Thirteen Resolutions, March 22, 1775

If it was possible for men, who exercise their reason to believe, that the divine Author of our existence intended a part of the human race to hold an absolute property in, and an unbounded power over others, marked out by his infinite goodness and wisdom, as the objects of a legal domination never rightfully resistible, however severe and oppressive, the inhabitants of these colonies might at least require from the parliament of Great-Britain some evidence, that this dreadful authority over them, has been granted to that body. But a reverence for our Creator, principles of humanity, and the dictates of common sense, must convince all those who reflect upon the subject, that government was instituted to promote the welfare of mankind, and ought to be administered for the attainment of that end. The legislature of Great-Britain, however, stimulated by an inordinate passion for a power not only unjustifiable, but which they know to be peculiarly reprobated by the very constitution of that kingdom, and desperate of success in any mode of contest, where regard should be had to truth, law, or right, have at length, deserting those, attempted to effect their cruel and impolitic purpose of enslaving these colonies by violence, and have thereby rendered it necessary for us to close with

their last appeal from reason to arms. Yet, however blinded that assembly may be, by their intemperate rage for unlimited domination, so to sight justice and the opinion of mankind, we esteem ourselves bound by obligations of respect to the rest of the world, to make known the justice of our cause.

—THOMAS JEFFERSON (1743–1826) and JOHN DICKINSON (1732–1794)
"A Declaration by the Representatives of the United Colonies of North America, Now Met in Congress at Philadelphia, Setting Forth the Causes and Necessity of Their Taking Up Arms"
July 6, 1775

In our own native land, in defence of the freedom that is our birthright, and which we ever enjoyed till the late violation of it—for the protection of our property, acquired solely by the honest industry of our fore-fathers and ourselves, against violence actually offered, we have taken up arms. We shall lay them down when hostilities shall cease on the part of the aggressors, and all danger of their being renewed shall be removed, and not before.

—THOMAS JEFFERSON and JOHN DICKINSON
"A Declaration by the Representatives of the United Colonies of North America, Now Met in Congress at Philadelphia, Setting Forth the Causes and Necessity of Their Taking Up Arms" (Although the entire document is credited to Jefferson and Dickinson, this section follows Jefferson's draft.)
July 6, 1775

We for ten years incessantly and ineffectually besieged the throne as supplicants; we reasoned, we remonstrated with parliament, in the most mild and decent language.

Administration sensible that we should regard these oppressive measures as freemen ought to do, sent over fleets and armies to enforce them. The indignation of the Americans was roused, it is true; but it was the indignation of a virtuous, loyal, and affectionate people. A Congress of delegates from the United Colonies was assembled at Philadelphia, on the fifth day of last September. We resolved again to offer an humble and dutiful petition to the King, and also addressed our fellow-subjects of Great-Britain. We have pursued every temperate, every respectful measure; we have even proceeded to break off our commercial intercourse with our fellow-subjects, as the last peaceable admonition, that our attachment to no nation upon earth should supplant our attachment to liberty.

This, we flattered ourselves, was the ultimate step of the controversy: but subsequent events have shewn, how vain was this hope of finding moderation in our enemies.

—*THOMAS JEFFERSON and JOHN DICKINSON*
"A Declaration by the Representatives of the United Colonies of North America, Now Met in Congress at Philadelphia, Setting Forth the Causes and Necessity of Their Taking Up Arms"
July 6, 1775

Of this general spirit existing in the American *nation* ... of this spirit of independence, animating the *nation* of America, I have the most authentic information. It is not new among them;

it is, and ever has been their established principle, their confirmed persuasion; it is their nature and their doctrine. [Referring to an eminent and reliable informant] he assured me with a certainty which his judgment and opportunity gave him, that these were the prevalent and steady principles of America: That you might destroy their towns, and cut them off from the superfluities, perhaps the conveniences of life, but that they were prepared to despise your power, and would not lament their loss, whilst they had, what, my lords?—Their woods and liberty. ... [They] prefer poverty with liberty, to golden chains and sordid affluence; ... will die in defence of their rights, as men—as freemen. ... 'Tis liberty to liberty engaged, that they will defend themselves, their families and their country. In this great cause they are immovably allied. It is the alliance of God and nature—immutable, eternal, fixed as the firmament of Heaven!"

—*WILLIAM PITT, EARL OF CHATHAM* (1708–1778)
Speech in House of Lords, December 30, 1775

Don't Tread on Me

—*ANONYMOUS*
Colonel Christopher Gadsden submitted a design for a flag to the Provincial Congress in South Carolina, consisting of a coiled snake with the words "Don't tread on me." These flags became common among American troops during the Revolution.
c. 1775

Our unalterable resolution would be to be free. They have attempted to subdue us by force, but God be praised! in vain.

Their arts may be more dangerous than their arms. Let us then renounce all treaty with them upon any score but that of total separation, and under God trust our cause to our swords.

—SAMUEL ADAMS
To James Warren,
April 16, 1776

If representation and legislation are inseparably connected, it follows, that when great numbers have emigrated into a foreign land, and are so far removed from the parent state that they neither are or can be properly represented by the government from which they have emigrated, that then nature itself points out the necessity of their assuming to themselves the powers of legislation; and they have a right to consider themselves as a separate state from the other, and, as such, to form themselves into a body politic.

—SAMUEL WEST (1730–1807)
"On the Right to Rebel Against Governors"
May 29, 1776

It is not choice then, but necessity that calls for Independence as the only means by which foreign Alliances can be obtained; and a proper confederation by which internal peace and Union may be secured. Contrary to our earnest, early, and repeated petitions for peace, liberty and safety, our enemies press us with war, threaten us with danger and Slavery.

—RICHARD HENRY LEE (1732–1794)
To Landon Carter,
June 2, 1776

Resolved: That these colonies are, and of right ought to be, free and independent states, that they are absolved of all allegiance to the British Crown, and that all political connection between them and the state of Great Britain is, and ought to be, totally dissolved. That it is expedient forthwith to take the most effectual measures for forming foreign Alliances. That a plan of confederation be prepared and transmitted to the respective colonies for their consideration and approbation.

—RICHARD HENRY LEE
Resolution in Congress,
June 7, 1776

The second day of July, 1776, will be the most memorable Epocha, in the history of America. I am apt to believe that it will be celebrated, by succeeding generations, as the great anniversary festival. It ought to be commemorated as the day of deliverance, by solemn acts of devotion to God Almighty. It ought to be solemnized with pomp and parade, with shews, games, sports, guns, bells, bonfires, and illuminations from one end of this continent to the other from this time forward forevermore.

—JOHN ADAMS (1735–1826)
Letter to Abigail Adams,
July 3, 1776
(The Declaration of Independence was voted upon July 2, but signed on July 4.)

Yesterday the greatest question was decided which was ever debated in America; and a greater perhaps never was, nor will be, decided upon men. A resolution was passed without one dissenting colony, that those United Colonies are, and of right ought to be, free and independent states.

—JOHN ADAMS
Letter to Abigail Adams,
July 3, 1776

You will think me transported with enthusiasm, but I am not. I am well aware of the toil, and blood, and treasure, that it will cost us to maintain this declaration, and support and defend these States. Yet, through all the gloom, I can see the rays of ravishing light and glory. I can see that the end is more than worth all the means, and that posterity will triumph in that day's transaction, even although we should rue it, which I trust in God we shall not.
—*JOHN ADAMS*
Letter to Abigail Adams,
July 3, 1776

We must all hang together, or assuredly we shall all hang separately.
—*BENJAMIN FRANKLIN* (1706–1790)
At the signing of the Declaration of
Independence,
July 4, 1776

The die was now cast; I had passed the Rubicon. Sink or swim, live or die, survive or perish with my country, was my unalterable determination.
—*JOHN ADAMS*
To Jonathan Sewell, describing his
thoughts after making the decision to
vote for the adoption of the Declaration of Independence,
1776

Everything that is right or reasonable pleads for separation. The blood of the slain, the weeping voice of nature cries, 'tis time to part.
—*THOMAS PAINE* (1737–1809)
Common Sense
1776

I am not induced by motives of pride, party, or resentment to espouse the doctrine of separation and independence; I am clearly, positively, and conscientiously persuaded that it is the true interest of this continent to be so; that every thing short of that is mere patchwork, that it can afford no lasting felicity; that it is leaving the sword to our children, and shrinking back at a time, when, a little more, a little farther, would have rendered this continent the glory of the earth.
—*THOMAS PAINE*
Common Sense
1776

We have it in our power to begin the world over again.
—*THOMAS PAINE*
Common Sense
(1776)

The present time, likewise, is that peculiar time, which never happens to a nation but once, *viz.* the time of forming itself into a government. Most nations have let slip the opportunity, and by that means have been compelled to receive laws from their conquerors, instead of making laws for themselves. … but from the errors of other nations, let us learn wisdom, and lay hold of the present opportunity—*To begin government at the right end.*
—*THOMAS PAINE*
Common Sense
1776

Nothing short of independence, it appears to me, can possibly do. A peace on other terms would, if I may be allowed the expression, be a peace of war.
—*GEORGE WASHINGTON* (1732–1799)
Letter to John Banister,
April 21, 1778

The final superiority of America over every attempt which an island might make to conquer her, was as naturally marked in the constitution of things, as the future ability of a giant over a dwarf is delineated in his features while an infant.
—THOMAS PAINE
Common Sense on George III's Speech
1782

An original genius, unfettered with precedents, and exalted with just ideas of the rights of human nature, and the obligations of universal benevolence, might have struck out a middle line, which would have secured as much liberty to the colonies, and as great a degree of supremacy to the parent state, as their common good required: But the helm of Great Britain was not in such hands.
—DAVID RAMSAY (1749–1815)
The History of the American Revolution
1789

The declaration of independence confirmed in form what had existed before in substance. It announced to the world new States, possessing and exercising complete sovereignty, which they were resolved to maintain.
—JAMES MONROE (1758–1831)
Views on the subject of Internal Improvements, reasons for Veto of the Cumberland Road Bill
1822

May it [the Declaration of Independence] be to the world what I believe it will be (to some parts sooner, to others later, but finally to all): the signal for arousing men to burst the chains under which monkish ignorance and superstition have persuaded them to bind themselves and assume the blessings and security of self-government.
—THOMAS JEFFERSON
Letter to Roger C. Weightman,
June 24, 1826

Is it the Fourth?
—THOMAS JEFFERSON
Last words,
July 3, 1826

Independence forever!
—JOHN ADAMS
In response to a cannon firing in celebration of Independence Day,
July 4, 1826

It is my living sentiment, and by the blessing of God it shall be my dying sentiment—Independence now and Independence forever.
—DANIEL WEBSTER (1782–1852)
Eulogy on John Adams and Thomas Jefferson, Faneuil Hall, Boston,
August 2, 1826

INTELLIGENCE & KNOWLEDGE

It is admirable to consider how many millions of people come into, and go out of the world, ignorant of themselves, and of the world they have lived in.
—WILLIAM PENN (1644–1718)
Some Fruits of Solitude
1693

Neither despise, nor oppose, what thou dost not understand.
—WILLIAM PENN
Some Fruits of Solitude
1693

Refuse not to be informed: for that shows pride or stupidity.

—*WILLIAM PENN*
Some Fruits of Solitude
1693

No people will tamely surrender their Liberties, nor can any be easily subdued, when knowledge is diffused and Virtue is preserved. On the Contrary, when People are universally ignorant, and debauched in their Manners, they will sink under their own weight without the aid of foreign invaders.

—*SAMUEL ADAMS* (1722–1803)
To James Warren,
1775

The cunning of the fox is as murderous as the violence of the wolf.

—*THOMAS PAINE* (1737–1809)
The Crisis
1776

It is the faculty of the human mind to become what it contemplates, and to act in unison with its object.

—*THOMAS PAINE*
Rights of Man, I
1791

Ignorance is of a peculiar nature; once dispelled, it is impossible to re-establish it. It is not originally a thing of itself, but is only the absence of knowledge; and though man may be *kept* ignorant, he cannot be *made* ignorant.

—*THOMAS PAINE*
Rights of Man, I
1791

Experience, in all ages, and in all countries, has demonstrated, that it is impossible to control Nature in her distri-

bution of mental powers. She gives them as she pleases. Whatever is the rule by which she ... scatters them among mankind, that rule remains a secret to man. It would be as ridiculous to attempt to fix the hereditaryship of human beauty, as of wisdom. Whatever wisdom constituently is, it is like a seedless plant; it may be reared when it appears, but it cannot be voluntarily produced. There is always a sufficiency somewhere in the general mass of society for all purposes; but with respect to the parts of society, it is continually changing its place. It rises in one today, in another tomorrow, and has most probably visited in rotation every family of the earth, and again withdrawn.

—*THOMAS PAINE*
Rights of Man, II
1792

There is a natural aptness in man, and more so in society, because it embraces a greater variety of abilities and resource, to accommodate itself to whatever situation it is in.

—*THOMAS PAINE*
Rights of Man, II
1792

Knowledge ... can never be equally divided among mankind, any more than property, real or personal, any more than wives or women.

—*JOHN ADAMS* (1735–1826)
Letter to John Taylor,
April 15, 1814

A silly reason from a wise man is never the true one.

—*JAMES MADISON* (1751–1836)
To Richard Rush,
June 27, 1817

Knowledge is power ... knowledge is safety ... knowledge is happiness.

—*THOMAS JEFFERSON* (1743-1826)
Letter to George Ticknor,
November 25, 1817

A popular Government, without popular information, or the means of acquiring it, is but a Prologue to a Farce or a Tragedy; or, perhaps both. Knowledge will forever govern ignorance: And a people who mean to be their own Governors, must arm themselves with the power which knowledge gives.

—*JAMES MADISON*
Letter to W. T. Barry,
August 4, 1822

Knowledge ... is the great sun in the firmament. Life and power are scattered with all its beams.

—*DANIEL WEBSTER* (1782–1852)
Speech at the laying of the cornerstone
at the Bunker Hill Monument,
June 17, 1825

J

THOMAS JEFFERSON

Ambition is the subtlest Beast of the Intellectual and Moral Field. It is wonderfully adroit in concealing itself from its owner. ... Jefferson thinks he shall by this step get a Reputation of a humble, modest, meek man, wholly without ambition or vanity. He may even have deceived himself into this Belief. But if a Prospect opens, the World will see and he will see, that he is as ambitious as Oliver Cromwell though no soldier.
—*JOHN ADAMS* (1735–1826)
Letter to John Quincy Adams,
January 3, 1794

His genius is of the old French school. It conceives better than it combines.
—*JOHN QUINCY ADAMS* (1767–1848)
Diary entry,
November 23, 1804

You should remember that Jefferson was but a boy to me. I was at least ten years older than him in age and more than twenty years older than him in politics.
—*JOHN ADAMS*
Letter to Benjamin Rush,
October 25, 1809

I held levees once a week, that all my time might not be wasted by idle visits. Jefferson's whole eight years was a levee. ...

Jefferson and Rush were for liberty and straight hair. I thought curled hair was as republican as straight.
—*JOHN ADAMS*
Letter to Benjamin Rush,
December 25, 1811

You and I ought not to die, before We have explained ourselves to each other.
—*JOHN ADAMS*
Letter to Thomas Jefferson,
July 15, 1813

His talents were of the highest order, his ambition transcendent, and his disposition to intrigue irrepressible.
—*JOHN ADAMS*
Parties in the United States
c. January 1822

Mr. Jefferson came into Congress, in June, 1775, and brought with him a reputation for literature, science, and a happy talent of composition. Writings of his were handed about, remarkable for the peculiar felicity of expression.
—*JOHN ADAMS*
To Timothy Pickering,
August 6, 1822

The committee met, discussed the sub-

145

ject, [of the Declaration of Independence] and then appointed Mr. Jefferson and me to make the draught, I suppose because we were the two first on the list. The subcommittee met. Jefferson proposed to me to make the draught. Adams: I will not. Jefferson: You should do it. Adams: Oh! no. Jefferson: Why will you not? You ought to do it. Adams: I will not. Jefferson: Why? Adams: Reasons enough. Jefferson: What can be your reasons? Adams: Reason first—You are a Virginian, and a Virginian ought to appear at the head of this business. Reason second—I am obnoxious, suspected and unpopular. You are very much otherwise. Reason third—You can write ten times better than I can. Jefferson: Well if you are decided, I will do as well as I can. Adams: Very well. When you have drawn it up, we will have a meeting.

—*JOHN ADAMS*
To Timothy Pickering,
August 6, 1822

He lives and will live in memory and gratitude of the wise and good, as a luminary of science, as a votary of liberty, as a model of patriotism, and as a benefactor of human kind.

—*JAMES MADISON* (1751–1836)
In memory of Thomas Jefferson
1826

He saw the gross inconsistency between the principles of the Declaration of Independence and the fact of negro slavery, and he could not, or would not, prostitute the faculties of his mind to the vindication of that slavery which from his soul he abhorred. Mr. Jefferson had not the spirit of martyrdom. He would have introduced a flaming denunciation of slavery into the Declaration of Independence, but the discretion of his colleagues struck it out.

—*JOHN QUINCY ADAMS*
Diary entry,
January 27, 1831

JOHN PAUL JONES

It's of an American frigate the "Richard" by name
Mounted forty-four guns, and from New York she came.
A-cruising down the channel of Old England's fame
With a noble commander, Paul Jones was his name.
We had not cruised long before two sails we espies
A large forty-four and a twenty likewise,
Some fifty bright shipping, well loaded with store,
And the convoy stood in for the old Yorkshire shore.
'Bout the hour of twelve we came alongside
With a long speaking trumpet: Whence came you? he cried;
Come, answer me quickly, I'll hail you no more
Or else a broadside into you I will pour.
We fought them four glasses, four glasses so hot,
'Til forty bold seamen lay dead on the spot,
And fifty-five more lay bleeding in gore,
While the thundering loud cannons of Paul Jones did roar.
Our carpenter being frighten'd, to Paul Jones he came,
Our ship she leaks water and is likewise in flame,
Paul Jones he made answer, and to him replied,

If we can do no better, we'll sink along-
side.
Paul Jones he then turned to his men
and did say
Let every man stand the best of his play,
For broadside for broadside they fought
on the main
Like true buckskin heroes we return'd
it again.
The Serapis wore round our ship for
to rake,
And many proud hearts of the English
did ache;
The shot flew so hot, and so fierce and
so fast,
And the bold British colours were hauled
down at last.
Oh now, my brave boys, we have taken
a rich prize
A large forty-four and a twenty likewise;
To help the poor mothers that have reason to weep
For the loss of their sons in the
unfathomed deep.

—*Anonymous*
Paul Jones
c. 1779

JUDICIARY & THE COURTS

Judges must beware of hard construc-
tions and strained influence; for there
is no worse torture than the torture of
laws: specially in the case of laws pe-
nal, they ought to have care, that that
which was meant for terror be not
turned into right.

—*Francis Bacon*
"Of Judicature," Essays
1625

Honest Men often go to Law for their
Right; when Wise Men would sit down

with the Wrong, supposing the first
Loss least. In some Countries the Course
of the Courts is so tedious, and the Ex-
pence so high, that the Remedy, *Justice*, is worse than, *Injustice*, the Disease.
In my Travels I once saw a Sign call'd
The Two Men at Law; One of them was
painted on one Side, in a melancholy
Posture, all in Rags, with this Scroll, *I
have lost my Cause*. The other was
drawn capering for Joy, on the other Side,
with these Words, *I have gain'd my
Suit*; but he was stark naked.

—*Benjamin Franklin* (1706–1790)
Poor Richard's Almanack
1742

To such a height the expense of courts
is gone / That poor men are re-
dressed—till they're undone.

—*Benjamin Franklin*
Poor Richard's Almanack
1742

Every new tribunal, erected for the decision of facts, without the interven-
tion of a jury ... is a step towards establishing aristocracy, the most
oppressive of absolute governments.

Sir William Blackstone (1723–1780)
Commentaries on the Laws of England
1765–1769

[J]udges, therefore, should be always
men of learning and experience in the
laws, of exemplary morals, great patience, calmness, coolness, and attention. Their minds should not be dis-
tracted with jarring interests; they
should not be dependent upon any man,
or body of men.

—*John Adams* (1735–1826)
Thoughts on Government
1776

The dignity and stability of government in all its branches, the morals of the people, and every blessing of society depend so much upon an upright and skillful administration of justice, that the judicial power ought to be distinct from both the legislative and executive, and independent upon both, that so it may be a check upon both, and both should be checks upon that.

—*JOHN ADAMS*
Thoughts on Government
1776

It is better to toss up cross and pile in a cause than to refer it to a judge whose mind is warped by any motive whatever, in that particular case. But the common sense of twelve honest men gives a still better chance of just decision than the hazard of cross and pile.

—*THOMAS JEFFERSON* (1743–1826)
Notes on Virginia
1782

Laws are a dead letter without courts to expound and define their true meaning and operation.

—*ALEXANDER HAMILTON* (1712–1756)
The Federalist Papers
1788

Next to permanency in office, nothing can contribute more to the independence of the judges than a fixed provision for their support.

—*ALEXANDER HAMILTON*
The Federalist Papers
1788

To produce uniformity in these determinations, they ought to be submitted in the last resort, to one SUPREME TRIBUNAL. . . . If there is in each state

a court of final jurisdiction, there may be as many different final determinations on the same point, as there are courts. There are endless diversities in the opinions of men. We often see not only different courts, but the judges of the same court differing from each other. To avoid the confusion which would unavoidably result from the contradictory decisions of a number of independent judicatories, all nations have found it necessary to establish one court paramount to the rest, possessing a general superintendance, and authorised to settle and declare in the last resort an uniform rule of civil justice.

—*ALEXANDER HAMILTON*
The Federalist Papers
1788

We have considered the previous question stated in a letter written by your direction to us by the Secretary of State on the 18th of last month, [regarding] the lines of separation drawn by the Constitution between the three departments of the government. These being in certain respects checks upon each other, and our being judges of a court in the last resort, are considerations which afford strong arguments against the propriety of our extra-judicially deciding the questions alluded to, especially as the power given by the Constitution to the President, of calling on the heads of departments for opinions, seems to have been *purposely* as well as expressly united to the *executive* departments.

—*JOHN JAY* (1745–1829)
To George Washington,
August 8, 1793

The legislative authority of any country, can only be restrained by its own muncipal constitution. This is a principle that springs from the very nature of society; and the judicial authority can have no right to question the validity of a law, unless such a jurisdiction is expressly given by the constitution.

—*JOHN MARSHALL* (1755–1835)
Argument as counsel in *Ware v. Hilton*
1796

It is emphatically the province and duty of the judicial department to say what the law is. ... If two laws conflict with each other, the courts must decide on the operation of each. ... This is of the very essence of judicial duty.

—*JOHN MARSHALL*
Marbury v. Madison
1803

Where the heads of departments are the political or confidential agents of the executive, merely to execute the will of the President, or rather to act in cases in which the executive possesses a constitutional or legal discretion, nothing can be more perfectly clear than that their acts are only politically examinable. But where a specific duty is assigned by law, and individual rights depend upon the performance of that duty, it seems equally clear that the individual who considers himself injured, has a right to resort to the laws of this country for a remedy.

—*JOHN MARSHALL*
Marbury v. Madison
1803

However true the fact may be, that the tribunals of the states will administer justice as impartially as those of the nation, to parties of every description,

it is not less true that the Constitution itself either entertains apprehensions on this subject, or views with such indulgence the possible fears and apprehensions of suitors, that it has established national tribunals for the decision of controversies between aliens and a citizen, or between citizens of different states.

—*JOHN MARSHALL*
Bank of the United States v. Deveaux
1809

If the legislatures of the several states may, at will, annul the judgments of the courts of the United States, and destroy the rights acquired under those judgments, the Constitution itself becomes a solemn mockery; and the nation is deprived of the means of enforcing its laws by the instrumentality of its own tribunals.

—*JOHN MARSHALL*
United States v. Peters
1809

Knowing that religion does not furnish grosser bigots than law, I expect little from old judges.

—*THOMAS JEFFERSON*
Letter to Thomas Cooper,
1810

Whether a law be void for its repugnancy to the Constitution, is, at all times, a question of much delicacy, which out seldom, if ever, to be decided in the affirmative, in a doubtful case. ... But it is not on slight implication and vague conjecture that the legislature is to be pronounced to have transcended its powers, and its acts to be considered as void. The opposition between the Constitution and the law should be such that the judge feels a clear and strong conviction of their incompatibility with each other.

—JOHN MARSHALL
Fletcher v. Peck
1810

The judgment of a state court should have the same credit, validity, and effect, in every other court in the United States, which it had in the state where it was pronounced, and that whatever leas would be good toa suit thereon in such state, and none others, could be pleaded in any other court in the United States.

—JOHN MARSHALL
Hampton v. MConnel
1818

The constitution, on this hypothesis, is a mere thing of wax in the hands of the judiciary, which they may twist and shape into any form they please.

—THOMAS JEFFERSON
Letter to Judge Spencer Roane,
September 6, 1819

Should Congress, in the execution of its powers, adopt measures which are prohibited by the Constitution; or should Congress, under the pretext of executing its powers, pass laws for the accomplishment of objects not entrusted to the government; it would become the painful duty of this tribunal, should a case requiring such a decision come before it, to say that such an act was not the law of the land.

—JOHN MARSHALL
McCulloch v. Maryland
1819

The judiciary of the United States is the subtle corps of sappers and miners constantly working under ground to undermine the foundations of our confederated fabric. ... A judiciary independent of a king or executive alone, is a good thing; but independence of the will of the nation is a solecism, at least in a republican government.

—THOMAS JEFFERSON
Letter to Thomas Ritchie,
December 25, 1820

It is a very dangerous doctrine to consider the judges as the ultimate arbiters of all constitutional questions. It is one which would place us under the despotism of an oligarchy.

—THOMAS JEFFERSON
Letter to W. C. Jarvis,
1820

Our judges are as honest as other men, and not more so. They have, with others, the same passions for party, for power, and the privilege of their corps.

—THOMAS JEFFERSON
Letter to W. C. Jarvis,
1820

The legislative and executive branches may sometimes err, but elections and dependance will bring them to rights. The judiciary branch is the instrument which working, like gravity, without intermission, is to press us at last into one consolidated mass.

—THOMAS JEFFERSON
To Archibald Thweat,
January 19, 1821

The great object of my fear is the federal judiciary. That body, like gravity, ever acting, with noiseless foot, and unalarming advance, gaining ground step by step, and holding what it gains, is ingulfing insidiously the special governments into the jaws of that which feeds them.

—*THOMAS JEFFERSON*
Letter to Charles Hammon,
August 18, 1821

The most delicate and at the same time, the proudest attribute of American jurisprudence, is the right of its judicial tribunals to decide questions of constitutional law. In other governments these questions cannot be entertained or decided by courts of justice; and, therefore, whatever may be the theory of the constitution, the legislative authority is practically omnipotent, and there is no means of contesting the legality or justice of a law but by an appeal to arms. This can be done only when oppression weighs heavily and grivously on the whole people, and is then resisted by all because it is felt by all. But the oppression that strikes at a humble individual, though it robs him of character, or fortune, or life, is remediless; and, if it becomes the subject of judicial inquiry, judges may lament, but cannot resist, the mandates of the legislature.

—*JOSEPH STORY* (1779–1845)
Address before the Suffolk Bar,
September 4, 1821

At the establishment of our constitutions, the judiciary bodies were supposed to be the most helpless and harmless members of the government. Experience, however, soon showed in what way they were to become the most dangerous; that the insufficiency of the means provided for their removal gave them a free hold and irresponsibility in office, that their decisions, seeming to

concern individual suitors only, pass silent and unheeded by the public at large; that these decisions, nevertheless, become law by precedent, sapping, by little and little, the foundations of the constitution, and working its change by construction, before any one has perceived that that invisible and helpless worm has been busily employed in consuming its substance. In truth, man is not made to be trusted for life, if secured against all liability to account.

—*THOMAS JEFFERSON*
Letter to Monsieur A. Corray,
October 31, 1823

Courts are the mere instruments of the law, and can will nothing. ... Judicial power is never exercised for the purpose of giving effect to the will of the Judge; always for the purpose of giving effect to the will of the Legislature; or, in other words, to the will of the law.

—*JOHN MARSHALL*
Osborn v. Bank of the United States
1824

When they [the courts] are said to exercise a discretion, it is a mere legal discretion, a discretion to be exercised in discerning the course prescribed by law; and, when that is discerned, it is the duty of the Court to follow it.

—*JOHN MARSHALL*
Osborn v. Bank of the United States
1824

I am no votary of the infallibility of any human tribunal; but it is no more than a just tribute to truth and candour to acknowledge, that the Supreme Court of the *United States* has hitherto discharged its high duties with such ability, firmness, and moderation, as to command the respect, and retain the confidence of the nation. I have always been much impressed with the immensity of the weight and value of its trust, and with the severe and majestic simplicity of its character. It may be said of that Court, and certainly with as much propriety as it has been said in reference to the *Roman sages*, that justice has there unveiled her mysteries and erected her temple.

—*JAMES KENT* (1763–1847)
Lecture at Columbia College,
February 2, 1824

JURIES

All men are Republicans by nature and Royalists only by fashion. And this is fully proved by that passionate adoration, which all men show to that great and almost only remaining bulwark of natural rights, *trial by juries*, which is founded on a pure Republican basis. Here the power of Kings is shut out. No Royal negative can enter this Court. The Jury, which is here, supreme, is a *Republic*, a body of *Judges chosen from among the people*.

—*THOMAS PAINE* (1737–1809)
The Forester's Letters
1776

In suits at common law, where the value in controversy shall exceed twenty dollars, the rights of a trial by jury shall be preserved, and no fact tried by a jury, shall be otherwise re-examined in any court of the United States, than according to the rules of the common law.

—*CONSTITUTION OF THE UNITED STATES*
The Bill of Rights, Amendment 7
1787

JUSTICE

As justice is a preserver, so it is a better procurer of peace than war.

—*WILLIAM PENN* (1644–1718)
An Essay Towards the Present and Future Peace of Europe
1693

Justice is justly represented blind, because she sees no difference in the parties concerned. She has but one scale and weight, for rich and poor, great and small.

—*WILLIAM PENN*
Some Fruits of Solitude
1693

Our law says well, to delay justice is injustice.

—*WILLIAM PENN*
Some Fruits of Solitude
1693

Justice is a great support of society, because an insurance to all men of their property: this violated, there's no security, which throws all into confusion to recover it.

—*WILLIAM PENN*
More Fruits of Solitude
1702

Without justice, courage is weak.

—*BENJAMIN FRANKLIN* (1706–1790)
Poor Richard's Almanack
1734

Justice is due, even to an enemy.

—*THOMAS PAINE* (1737–1809)
"Common Sense on George III's Speech"
1782

We have now a National character to

establish, and it is of the utmost importance to stamp favorable impressions upon it; let justice be then one of its characteristics, and gratitude another.
—GEORGE WASHINGTON (1732–1799)
To Theodorick Bland,
April 4, 1783

A wise nation will never permit those who relieve the wants of their Country, or who rely most on its faith, its firmness and its resources, when either of them is distrusted, to suffer by the event.
—JAMES MADISON (1751–1836)
Address to the States,
April 25, 1783

Justice is the end of government. It is the end of society.
—JAMES MADISON
The Federalist Papers
1788

All the tranquility, the happiness & security of mankind rest on justice, on the obligation to respect the rights of others.
—THOMAS JEFFERSON (1743–1826)
Opinion on the French Treaties,
April 28, 1793

Justice is indiscriminately due to all, without regard to numbers, wealth, or rank.
—JOHN JAY (1745–1829)
Georgia v. Brailsford
1794

I believe that justice is instinct and innate, that the moral sense is as much a part of our constitution as that of feeling, seeing, or hearing.
—THOMAS JEFFERSON
Letter to John Adams,
1816

Kentucky

Ye gentlemen and ladies fair,
  Who grace this famous city,
Just listen if you've time to spare
  While I rehearse a ditty,
And for the opportunity
  Conceive yourself quite lucky,
For 'tis not often here you see
  A hunter from Kentucky.

Chorus
Oh, Kentucky, The hunters of Kentucky
Oh, Kentucky, The hunters of Kentucky

You've heard, I s'pose, how New Orleans
  Is famed for wealth and beauty,
There's girls of ev'ry hue it seems,
  From snowy white to sooty;
So Pakenham he made his brags,
  If he in fight was lucky,
He'd have their girls and cotton bags,
  In spite of old Kentucky.

Chorus

But Jackson, he was wide awake,
  And was not scared of trifles;
For well he knew what aim we take
  With our Kentucky rifles;
He led us down to Cypress Swamp,
  The ground was low and mucky;
There stood John Bull in pomp,
  And here was old Kentucky.

Chorus

A bank was rais'd to hide our breast,
  Not that we thought of dying,
But we always like to rest,
  Unless the game is flying;
Behind it stood our little force
  None wished it to be greater,
For ev'ry man was half a horse,
  And half an alligator.

Chorus

They found, at last, 'twas vain to fight,
  Where lead was all the booty,
And so they wisely took to flight,
  And left us all our beauty.
And now, if danger e'er annoys,
  Remember what our trade is,
Just send for us Kentucky boys,
  And we'll protect ye, ladies.

Chorus
  —SAMUEL WOODWORTH (1785–1842)
    The Hunters of Kentucky
                    c. 1815

Kings & Aristocrats

Happy that king who is great by justice, and that people who are free by obedience. Where the ruler is just, he may be strict; else it is two to one it turns upon him: and though he should

prevail, he can be no gainer, where his people are the losers.
—*WILLIAM PENN* (1644–1718)
Some Fruits of Solitude
1693

When kings the sword of justice first lay down,
They are no kings, though they possess the crown.
Titles are shadows, crowns are empty things,
The good of subjects is the end of kings.
—*DANIEL DEFOE* (1660–1731)
The True-Born Englishman
1701

That the king can do no wrong is a necessary and fundamental principle of the English constitution.
—*SIR WILLIAM BLACKSTONE* (1723–1780)
Commentaries
1765–1769

Breach of trust in a governor, or attempting to enlarge a limited power, effectually absolves subjects from every bond of covenant and peace; the crimes acted by a king against the people are the highest treason against the highest law among men.
—*BENJAMIN CHURCH* (1734–1778)
Boston Massacre Oration,
March 5, 1773

Nothing flatters vanity, or confirms obstinacy in Kings more than repeated petitioning.
—*THOMAS PAINE* (1737–1809)
Common Sense
1776

But where says some is the King of America? I'll tell you Friend, he reigns above, and doth not make havoc of mankind like the Royal Brute of Britain. ... let it be brought forth placed on the divine law, the word of God; let a crown be placed thereon, by which the world may know, that so far as we approve of monarchy, that in America THE LAW IS KING.
—*THOMAS PAINE*
Common Sense
1776

For all men being originally equals, no *one* by *birth* could have a right to set up his own family in perpetual preference to all others forever, and though himself might deserve *some* decent degree of honors of his contemporaries, yet his descendants might be far too unworthy to inherit them. One of the strongest *natural* proofs of the folly of hereditary right in kings, is that nature disapproves it, otherwise she would not so frequently turn it into ridicule by giving mankind an *ass for a lion*.
—*THOMAS PAINE*
Common Sense
1776

A Republican form of government is pointed out by nature—Kingly governments by an unequality of power. In Republican governments, the leaders of the people, if improper, are removable by vote; Kings only by arms; an unsuccessful vote in the first case, leaves the voter safe; but an unsuccessful attempt in the latter, is death.
—*THOMAS PAINE*
The Forester's Letters
1776

A Republican government hath more true grandeur in it than a Kingly one: On the

155

part of the public it is more consistent with freemen to appoint their rulers than to have them born; and on the part of those who preside, it is far nobler to be a ruler by the choice of the people, than a King by the chance of birth. Every honest Delegate is more than a Monarch.
—*THOMAS PAINE*
The Forester's Letters
1776

If anybody thinks that kings, nobles or priests are good conservators of the public happiness, send him here [to France]. ... He will see here ... that these descriptions of men are an abandoned confederacy against the happiness of the mass of the people. The omnipotence of their effect cannot be better proved than in this country particularly, where, notwithstanding the finest soil upon earth, the finest climate under heaven, and a people of the most benevolent, the most gay and amiable character of which the human form is susceptible; where such a people, I say, surrounded by so many blessings from nature, are loaded with misery, by kings, nobles and priests, and by them alone.
—*THOMAS JEFFERSON* (1743–1826)
To George Wythe,
1786

The more aristocracy appeared, the more it was despised; there was a visible imbecility and want of intellects in the majority, a sort of *je ne sais quoi*, that while it affected to be more than citizen, was less than man. It lost ground from contempt more than from

hatred; and it was rather jeered at as an ass, than dreaded as a lion. This is the general character of aristocracy, or what are called Nobles or Nobility, or rather No-ability, in all countries.
—*THOMAS PAINE*
Rights of Man, I
1791

All hereditary government is in its nature tyranny.
—*THOMAS PAINE*
Rights of Man, II
1792

To inherit a government, is to inherit the people, as if they were flocks and herds.
—*THOMAS PAINE*
Rights of Man, II
1792

The first aristocrats in all countries were brigands. Those of later times, sycophants.
—*THOMAS PAINE*
Dissertation on First Principles of Government
1795

We are teaching the world the great truth that Gov[ernments] do better without Kings and Nobles than with them. The merit will be doubled by the other lesson that Religion flourishes in greater purity, without than with the aid of Gov[ernment].
—*JAMES MADISON* (1751–1836)
Letter to Edward Livingston,
July 19, 1822

LABOR & WORK

Love labour: for if thou dost not want it for food, thou mayest for physic. It is wholesome for thy body, and good for thy mind. It prevents the fruits of idleness, which many times comes of nothing to do, and leads too many to do what is worse than nothing.
—*WILLIAM PENN* (1644–1718)
Some Fruits of Solitude
1693

When men are employed they are best contented.
—*BENJAMIN FRANKLIN* (1706–1790)
Autobiography
(Begun in 1771, published in full 1868)

It is here then that the idle may be employed, the useless become useful, and the poor become rich; but by riches I do not mean gold and silver, we have but little of those metals; I mean a better sort of wealth, cleared lands, cattle, good houses, good clothes, and an increase of people to enjoy them.
—*MICHEL GUILLAUME JEAN DE CRÈVECOEUR* (1735–1813)
Letters From an American Farmer
1782

Interesting occupations are essential to happiness: indeed the whole art of being happy consists in the art of finding employment.
—*THOMAS JEFFERSON* (1743–1826)
To Martha Jefferson Randolph,
April 26, 1790

My observation on every employment in life is that wherever and whenever one person is found adequate to the discharge of a duty by close application thereto, it is worse executed by two persons, and scarcely done at all if three or more are employed therein.
—*GEORGE WASHINGTON* (1732–1799)
To Henry Knox,
September 24, 1792

Workmen in most Countries I believe are necessary plagues—in this [country] where entreaties as well as money must be used to obtain their work and keep them to their duty they baffle all calculation in the accomplishment of any plan or repairs they are engaged in;—and require more attention to and looking after than can be well conceived.
—*GEORGE WASHINGTON*
To William Gordon,
October 15, 1797

To suggestions of the last kind, the adepts of the new school have a ready answer; Industry will succeed and

157

prosper in proportion as it is left to the exertions of individual enterprise. This favorite dogma, when taken as a general rule, is true; but as an exclusive one, it is false, and leads to error in the administration of public affairs. In matters of industry, human enterprise ought, doubtless, to be left free in the main; not fettered by too much regulation; but practical politicians know that it may be beneficially stimulated by prudent aids and encouragements on the part of the government.

—*ALEXANDER HAMILTON* (1755–1804)
"Lucius Crassus"
December 24, 1801

Labor in this country is independent and proud. It has not to ask the patronage of capital, but capital solicits the aid of labor. ... Labor is the great producer of wealth: it moves all other causes.

—*DANIEL WEBSTER* (1782–1852)
Speech in the House of
Representatives,
April 2, 1824

LANGUAGE & WRITING

Speak properly, and in as few words as you can, but always plainly; for the end of speech is not ostentation but to be understood.

—*WILLIAM PENN* (1644–1718)
More Fruits of Solitude
1702

If you would not be forgotten, as soon as you are dead and rotten, either write things worth reading, or do things worth the writing.

—*BENJAMIN FRANKLIN* (1706–1790)
Poor Richard's Almanack
1738

A Pen is certainly an excellent Instrument, to fix a Man's Attention and to inflame his Ambition.

—*JOHN ADAMS* (1735–1826)
Diary entry,
1760

Amidst your Ardour for Greek and Latin I hope you will not forget your mother Tongue. Read Somewhat in the English Poets every day. ...You will never be alone, with a Poet in your Pocket. You will never have an idle Hour.

—*JOHN ADAMS*
To John Quincy Adams,
May 14, 1781

We sometimes experience sensations to which language is not equal. The conception is too bulky to be born alive, and in the torture of thinking we stand dumb. Our feelings imprisoned by their magnitude, find no way out, and, in the struggle of expression, every finger tries to be a tongue.

—*THOMAS PAINE* (1737–1809)
The Crisis
1782

Style in writing or speaking is formed very early in life while the imagination is warm, & impressions are permanent.

—*THOMAS JEFFERSON* (1743–1826)
To John Bannister, Jr.,
October 15, 1785

I have often observed that by lending words for my thoughts I understand my thoughts the better. Thoughts are a kind of mental smoke, which require words to illuminate them.

—*THOMAS PAINE*
To Benjamin Franklin,
December 31, 1785

The use of words is to express ideas. Perspicuity therefore requires not only that the ideas should be distinctly formed, but that they should be expressed by words distinctly and exclusively appropriated to them. But no language is so copious as to supply words and phrases for every complex idea, or so correct as not to include many equivocally denoting different ideas. Hence it must happen, that however accurately objects may be discriminated in themselves, and however accurately the discrimination may be considered, the definition of them may be rendered inaccurate by the inaccuracy of the terms in which it is delivered. And this unavoidable inaccuracy must be greater or less, according to the complexity and novelty of the objects defined. When the Almighty himself condescends to address mankind in their own language, his meaning luminous as it must be, is rendered dim and doubtful, by the cloudy medium through which it is communicated.

—*JAMES MADISON* (1751–1836)
The Federalist Papers
1788

To know the affinity of tongues seems to be one step towards promoting the affinity of nations.

—*GEORGE WASHINGTON* (1732–1799)
To the Marquis de Lafayette,
January 10, 1788

Human language is local and changeable.

—*THOMAS PAINE*
Age of Reason, I
1794

A change has been long desired in English orthography, such as might render it an easy and true index of the pronunciation of words. The want of conformity between the combinations of letters, and the sounds they should represent, increases to foreigners the difficulty of acquiring the language, occasions great loss of time to children in learning to read, and renders correct spelling rare but in those who read much.

—*THOMAS JEFFERSON*
To John Wilson,
1813

The new circumstances under which we are placed call for new words, new phrases, and for the transfer of old words to new objects. An American dialect will therefore be formed.

—*THOMAS JEFFERSON*
Letter to John Waldo,
1813

Such is the character of human language, that no word conveys to the mind, in all situations, one single definite idea; and nothing is more common than to use words in a figurative sense. Almost all compositions contain words, which, taken in their rigorous sense, would convey a meaning different from that which is obviously intended. It is essential to just construction, that many words which import something excessive, should be understood in a more mitigated sense—in that sense which common usage justifies. The word "necessary" is of this description. It has not a fixed character peculiar to itself. It admits of all degrees of comparison; and it is often connected with other words, which increase or diminish the impression the mind receives of the urgency it imports.

—*JOHN MARSHALL* (1755–1835)
McCulloch v. Maryland
1819

To provide for the purity, the uniformity, and the stability of language, is of great importance under many aspects; and especially as an encouragement to genius and to literary labours by extending the prospect of just rewards. A universal and immortal language is among the wishes never likely to be gratified: But all languages are more or less susceptible of improvement and of preservation; and none can be better entitled to the means of perfecting and fixing it, than that common to this Country and Great Britain, since there is none that seems destined for a greater and freer portion of the human family.

—*James Madison*
To William S. Cardell,
March 1820

Dictionaries are but the depositories of words already legitimated by usage. Society is the work-shop in which new ones are elaborated. When an individual uses a new word, if ill-formed it is rejected in society, if well formed, adopted, and, after due time, laid up in the depository of dictionaries.

—*Thomas Jefferson*
To John Adams,
August 15, 1820

One-half the doubts in life arise from the defects of language.

—*William Johnson* (c. 1770–1848)
Gibbons v. Ogden
1824

All languages, written as well as oral, tho much less than oral, are liable to changes from causes, some of them inseparable from the nature of man, and the progress of society. A perfect remedy for the evil must therefore be unattainable. But as far as it may be attainable, the attempt is laudable; and next to compleat success is that of recording with admitted fidelity the state of a language at the epoch of the Record. In the exposition of laws, and even of Constitutions, how many important errors, may be produced by mere innovations in the use of words and phrases, if not controllable by a recurrence to the original, and authentic meaning attached to them.

—*James Madison*
To Sherman Converse,
March 10, 1826

Laws

Law is whatever is boldly asserted and plausibly maintained.

—*Aaron Burr* (1756—1836)
Quoted in James Parton's
The Life and Times of Aaron Burr
Date of quote unknown

Since multiplicity of comments, as well as of laws, have great inconveniencies, and serve only to obscure and perplex, all manner of comments and expositions on any part of these fundamental constitutions, or on any part of the common or statute laws of Carolina, are absolutely prohibited.

—*Anonymous*
"Fundamental Constitutions of
Carolina of 1669"
1669

Any government is free to the people under it where the laws rule and the people are a party to the laws.

—*William Penn* (1644–1718)
Frame of Government
1682

For in all the states of created beings, capable of laws, where there is no law there is no freedom.
—*JOHN LOCKE* (1632–1704)
Two Treatises on Civil Government
1690

Wherever Law ends, Tyranny begins.
—*JOHN LOCKE*
Second Treatise of Government
1690

The voice of nations and the course of things
Allow that laws superior are to kings.
—*DANIEL DEFOE* (1660–1731)
The True-Born Englishman
1701

Laws like to cobwebs catch small flies;
Great ones break through before your eyes.
—*BENJAMIN FRANKLIN* (1706–1790)
Poor Richard's Almanack
1734

Where carcasses are, eagles will gather,
And where good laws are, much people flock thither.
—*BENJAMIN FRANKLIN*
Poor Richard's Almanack
1734

Laws too gentle are seldom obeyed; too severe, seldom executed.
—*BENJAMIN FRANKLIN*
Poor Richard's Almanack
1756

To say the Parliament is absolute and arbitrary is a contradiction. The Parliament cannot make 2 and 2, 5: omnipotency cannot do it. The supreme power in a state is *jus dicere* only: *jus dare*, strictly speaking, belongs alone to GOD. Parliaments are in all cases to *declare* what is for the good of the whole; but it is not the *declaration* of Parliament that makes it so. There must be in every instance a higher authority, viz., GOD. Should an act of Parliament be against any of *his* natural laws, which are *immutably* true, *their* declaration would be contrary to eternal truth, equity, and justice, and consequently void: and so it would be adjudged by the Parliament itself when convinced of their mistake.
—*JAMES OTIS* (1725–1783)
*The Rights of the British Colonies
Asserted and Proved*
1764

The doctrine of the law then is this: that precedents and rules must be followed, unless flatly absurd or unjust; for though their reason be not obvious at first view, yet we owe such a deference to former times as wholly without consideration.
—*SIR WILLIAM BLACKSTONE* (1723–1780)
Commentaries on the Laws of England
1765–1769

There is one general Observation I would make; that the End of Government is the Happiness of every Individual, so far as is consistent with the Good of *the Whole*. To attain this End is impossible without Laws, and their due Execution. 'Tis necessary that Laws should be established, else Judges and Juries must go according to their Reason, that is, their Will; and this is in the strictest Sense arbitrary. On this Reason, I take to be grounded that well known Maxim, that *the Judge* should never be *the Legislator*: Because, then, the Will of the Judge would be the Law;

and this tends directly to a State of Slavery. The Rules and Orders of a State must be known, and must be certain, that People may know how to act; or else they are equally uncertain, as if the Law depended upon the arbitrary Opinion of Another.

—*THOMAS HUTCHINSON* (1711–1780)
"Charge to the Grand Jury," in
Quincy's Reports 232, 234
1767

The law no passion can disturb. ... On the one hand, it is inexorable to the cries and lamentations of the prisoner; on the other, it is deaf, deaf as an adder, to the clamours of the populace.

—*JOHN ADAMS* (1735–1826)
In defense of British soldiers on trial
after the Boston Massacre,
December 1770

If an assault was made to endanger their lives, the law is clear they [the British soldiers] had a right to kill in their own defense. If it was not so severe as to endanger their lives, yet if they were assaulted at all, struck and abused by blows of any sort, by snowballs, oyster shells, cinders, the law reduces the offense of killing down to manslaughter, in consideration of those passions of our nature which cannot be eradicated.

—*JOHN ADAMS*
Address to the jury during the trial of
the British soldiers involved in the
Boston Massacre,
December 7, 1770

A government of laws, and not of men.

—*JOHN ADAMS*
Essay in the *Boston Gazette*,
1774

As good government is an empire of laws, how shall your laws be made? In a large society, inhabiting an extensive country, it is impossible that the whole should assemble to make laws. The first necessary step, then, is to depute power from the many to a few of the most wise and good.

—*JOHN ADAMS*
Thoughts on Government
1776

A strict observance of the written laws is doubtless one of the high duties of a good citizen, but it is not the highest. The laws of necessity, of self preservation, of saving our country when in danger, are of a higher obligation. ... To lose our country by a scrupulous adherence to written law would be to lose the law itself, with life, liberty, property and all those who are enjoying them with us; thus absurdly sacrificing the ends to the means.

—*THOMAS JEFFERSON* (1743–1826)
Letter to J. B. Colvin,
September 20, 1780

Ignorance of the law is not excuse in any country. If it were, the laws would lose their effect, because it can always be pretended.

—*THOMAS JEFFERSON*
Letter to M. Limozin,
December 22, 1787

It will be of little avail to the people that the laws are made by men of their own choice, if the laws be so voluminous that they cannot be read, or so incoherent that they cannot be understood; if they be repealed or revised before they are promulgated, or undergo such incessant changes that no man who

162

knows what the law is today can guess what it will be to-morrow.
—*JAMES MADISON* (1751–1836)
The Federalist Papers
1788

It is essential to the idea of a law, that it be attended with a sanction; or, in other words, a penalty or punishment for disobedience. If there be no penalty annexed to disobedience, the resolutions or commands which pretend to be laws will, in fact, amount to nothing more than advice or recommendation.
—*ALEXANDER HAMILTON* (1755–1804)
The Federalist Papers
1787

The greatest calamity to which the United States can be subject, is a vicissitude of laws, and continual shifting and changing from one object to another, which must expose the people to various inconveniences. This has a certain effect, of which sagacious men always have, and always will make an advantage. From whom is advantage made? From the industrious farmers and tradesmen, who are ignorant of the means of making such advantages.
—*JAMES MADISON*
Virginia Ratifying Convention,
June 11, 1788

It would have been a truth, if Mr. Locke had not said it, that where there is no law, there can be no liberty, and nothing deserves the name of law but that which is certain, and universal in its operation upon all the members of the community.
—*BENJAMIN RUSH* (1745–1813)
To David Ramsay,
1788

The great object of a free people must be so to form their government and laws, and so to administer them, as to create a confidence in, and respect for, the laws; and thereby induce the sensible and virtuous part of the community to declare in favor of the laws and to support them without an expensive military force.
—*RICHARD HENRY LEE* (1732–1794)
Letters of the Federal Farmer
1788

The execution of the laws is more important than the making of them.
—*THOMAS JEFFERSON*
To M. L'Abbe Arnond,
July 19, 1789

Law and liberty cannot rationally become the objects of our love, unless they first become the objects of our knowledge.
—*JAMES WILSON* (1742–1798)
"Of the Study of the Law in the United States"
c. 1790

The first and governing maxim in the interpretation of a statute is to discover the meaning of those who made it.
—*JAMES WILSON*
"Of the Study of the Law in the United States"
c. 1790

Without liberty, law loses its nature and its name, and becomes oppression. Without law, liberty also loses its nature and its name, and becomes licentiousness.
—*JAMES WILSON*
"Of the Study of the Law in the United States"
c. 1790

In planning, forming, and arranging laws, deliberation is always becoming, and always useful.

—*JAMES WILSON*
Lectures on Law
1791

I have always held it an opinion (making it also my practice) that it is better to obey a bad law, making use at the same time of every argument to show its errors and procedure its repeal, than forcibly to violate it; because the precedent of breaking a bad law might weaken the force, and lead to a discretionary violation, of those which are good.

—*THOMAS PAINE* (1737–1809)
Rights of Man, II
1792

The law should be equal for all, whether it rewards or punishes, whether it protects or restrains.

—*THOMAS PAINE*
Plan of a Declaration of Rights
1792

If the laws are to be so trampled upon with impunity, and a minority (a small one too) is to dictate to the majority, there is an end put ... to republican government; and nothing but anarchy and confusion is to be expected hereafter. Some other man or society may dislike another law, and oppose it with equal propriety, until all laws are prostrate, and every one (the strongest I presume) will carve for himself.

—*GEORGE WASHINGTON* (1732–1799)
To Charles M. Thurston,
August 10, 1794

A good government is a system of restraints on the actions and passions of its subjects. All good citizens will rank these restraints among their rights, and not among their grievances. A spirit of national liberty exults in submission to the controul of just and salutary laws.

—*JONATHAN MAXCY* (1768–1820)
An oration,
1799

Every man in the uncivil state claims a right to be the judge of his own cause, and the avenger of his own wrongs. He relinquishes both these rights when he enters into society. He now has a claim to assistance and protection from the aggregate wisdom and force of the community. Every right which he now possesses, rests on the social compact. He cannot now conduct himself in any way that is repugnant to established laws and constitutions. These prescribe the rights of every individual, and these alone secure genuine civil liberty.

—*JONATHAN MAXCY*
An oration,
1799

If it be understood that the common law is established by the constitution, it follows that no part of the law can be altered by the legislature ... and the whole code with all its incongruities, barbarisms, and bloody maxims would be inviolably saddled on the good people of the United States.

—*JAMES MADISON*
The Report of 1800,
January 7, 1800

A nation which appeals to law, rather [than] to force, is particularly bound to understand the use of the instrument [a treatise on international law] by which it wishes to maintain its rights, as well as of those which, against its wishes, it may be called on to employ. Where the Sword alone is the law, there is less inconsistency, if not more propriety in neglecting those Teachers of right and duty.

—*JAMES MADISON*
To Peter S. DuPonceau,
December 8, 1810

By the law of the land is most clearly intended the general law[;] a law which hears, before it condemns; which proceeds upon inquiry, & renders judgme[nt] only after trial. The meaning is, that every citizen shall hold his life, liberty, property, & immunities, under the protection of the general rules which govern society.

—*DANIEL WEBSTER* (1782–1852)
*Trustees of Dartmouth College
v. Woodward*
March 10, 1818

The mass of the law is, to be sure, accumulating with an almost incredible rapidity. ... It is impossible not to look without some discouragement upon the ponderous volumes, which the next half century will add to the groaning shelves of our jurists.

—*JOSEPH STORY* (1779–1845)
Address before Suffolk Bar,
September 4, 1821

Laws are made for men of ordinary understanding, and should therefore be construed by the ordinary rules of common sense. Their meaning is not to be sought for in metaphysical subtleties, which may make anything mean everything or nothing, at pleasure.

—*THOMAS JEFFERSON*
Letter to William Johnson,
1823

Society cannot exist without wholesome restraints. Those restraints cannot be inflicted, without security and respect to the persons who administer them. ... try to remember, Elizabeth, that the laws alone remove us from the condition of the savages.

—*JAMES FENIMORE COOPER*
(1789–1851)
The Pioneers
1823

LAWYERS

Of Lawyers and Physicians I shall say nothing, because this Countrey is very Peaceable and Healthy; long may it so continue and never have occasion for the Tongue of the one, nor the Pen of the other, both equally destructive of Men's Estates and Lives.

—*GABRIEL THOMAS* (fl. 1690s)
Pennsylvania and West Germany
1698

God works wonders now and then/ Behold a lawyer an honest man.

—*BENJAMIN FRANKLIN* (1706–1790)
Poor Richard's Almanack
1733

I know you lawyers can, with ease/ Twist words and meanings as you please.

—*BENJAMIN FRANKLIN*
Poor Richard's Almanack
1740

All associations are dangerous to good Government ... and associations of Lawyers the most dangerous of any next to the Military.

—*CADWALLADER COLDEN* (1688–1776)
To the Earl of Halifax,
February 22, 1765

A lawyer without books would be like a workman without tools.
—THOMAS JEFFERSON (1743–1826)
To Thomas Turpin,
February 5, 1769

It [law] alone can bring into use many parts of knowledge you have acquired and will still have a taste for, and pay you for cultivating the Arts of Eloquence. It is a sort of General Lover that wooes all the Muses and Graces. ... I greatly commend your determined adherence to probity and Truth in the Character of a Lawyer but fear it would be impracticable.
—JAMES MADISON (1751–1836)
To William Bradford,
September 25, 1773

In no country, perhaps, in the world is the law so general a study. The profession itself is numerous and powerful, and in most provinces [in America] it takes the lead.
—EDMUND BURKE (1729–1797)
Speech in Parliament for conciliation with the colonies,
March 22, 1775

It would be a blessing to mankind if God would never give a genius without principle; and in like manner would be a happiness to society if none but honest men would be suffered to be lawyers. The wretch who will write on any subject for bread, or in any service for pay, and he who will plead in *any case* for a *fee*, stands equally in rank with the prostitute who lets out her person.
—THOMAS PAINE (1737–1809)
A Serious Address to the People of Pennsylvania
1778

Law ... is a field which is uninteresting and boundless ... so encumbered with voluminous rubbish and the baggage of folios that it requires uncommon assiduity and patience to manage so unwieldy a work.
—JAMES KENT (1763–1847)
To Simeon Baldwin,
October 10, 1782

[Lawyers] are plants that will grow in any soil that is cultivated by the hands of others; and when once they have taken root they will extinguish every other vegetable that grows around them. ... The most ignorant, the most bungling member of that profession, will, if placed in the most obscure part of the country, promote litigiousness, and amass more wealth without labour, than the most opulent farmer, with all his toils.
—MICHEL GUILLAUME JEAN DE CRÈVECOEUR (1735–1813)
Letters From an American Farmer
1782

The order [of lawyers] is becoming continually more and more powerful. ... There is danger of lawyers becoming powerful as a combined body. The people should be guarded against it as it might subvert every principle of law and establish a perfect aristocracy. ... This order of men should be annihilated.
—BENJAMIN AUSTIN (1733–1819)
Observations on the Pernicious Practice of the Law
1786

They have a proverb here [in London], which I do not know how to account for;—in speaking of a difficult point, they say, *it would puzzle a Philadelphia lawyer.*

—ANONYMOUS
A Humorous Description of the Manners and Fashions of London; in a Letter from a Citizen of America to his Correspondent in Philadelphia
This is the earliest known usage of the phrase "Philadelphia lawyer" to mean "a shrewd lawyer expert in legal technicalities."
1788

The law—a profession whose general principles enlighten and enlarge, but whose minutiae contract and distract the mind.

—JOSEPH STORY (1779–1845)
To Samuel P. P. Fay,
September 6, 1798

A man can never gallop over the fields of law on Pegasus, nor fly across them on the wing of oratory. If he would stand on *terra firma* he must descend; if he would be a great lawyer, he must first consent to be only a great drudge.

—DANIEL WEBSTER (1782–1852)
To Thomas Merrill,
November 11, 1803

Accuracy and diligence are much more necessary to a lawyer than great comprehension of mind or brilliancy of talent.

—DANIEL WEBSTER
To Thomas Merrill,
November 11, 1803

Study is *truly* the grand requisite for a lawyer. Men may be born poets, and leap from their cradle painters; nature may have made them musicians, and called on them only to exercise, and not to acquire, ability. But law is artificial.

It is a human science to be learnt, not inspired.

—DANIEL WEBSTER
To James Hervey Bingham,
January 19, 1806

The practice of the law, it is said, tends to brutalize the feelings, to subvert the judgment, and to annihilate every virtuous principle of the human heart. ... A lawyer, from the first moment he enters into business, becomes habituated to scenes of injustice and oppression; from which, if he possesses the smallest particle of sensibility, he turns at first with disgust and abhorrence; but custom soon renders them familiar, and in process of time he can view them with the utmost coolness and indifference. This lamentable consequence is the frequent practice of the law. For, it is evident, that a perpetual fellowship with dishonesty, and a constant intercourse with villainy, will in time, destroy every tender emotion and sap by degrees the foundation of the most rigid virtue.

—GEORGE WATTERSON (1783–1854)
The Lawyer, or Man as he ought not to be
1808

He who is always his own counsellor will often have a fool for a client.

—ANONYMOUS
Port Folio (Philadelphia),
August 1809

The discussion of constitutional questions throws a lustre round the bar, and gives a dignity to its functions, which can rarely belong to the profession in any other country. Lawyers are here emphatically placed as sentinels upon the outposts of the constitution; and no nobler end can be proposed for their ambition or patriotism, than to stand as faithful guardians of the constitution, ready to defend its legitimate powers, and to stay the arm of legislative, executive, or popular oppression.

—*JOSEPH STORY*
Address before the Suffolk Bar,
September 4, 1821

The New England folks have a saying, that three Philadelphia lawyers are a match for the very devil himself.

—*ANONYMOUS*
Salem Observer,
March 14, 1824

LAZINESS & SLOTH

O Lazy-bones! Dost think God would have given thee arms and legs if he had not designed thou shouldst use them.

—*BENJAMIN FRANKLIN* (1706–1790)
Poor Richard's Almanack,
1739

Up, sluggard, and waste not life; in the grave will be sleeping enough.

—*BENJAMIN FRANKLIN*
Poor Richard's Almanack
1741

Serving God is doing good to man, but praying is thought an easier service and therefore is more generally chosen.

—*BENJAMIN FRANKLIN*
Poor Richard's Almanack
1753

He that never eats too much will never be lazy.

—*BENJAMIN FRANKLIN*
Poor Richard's Almanack
1756

Idleness begets ennui, ennui the hypochondriac, and that a diseased body. No laborious person was ever yet hysterical.

—*THOMAS JEFFERSON* (1743–1826)
To Martha Jefferson,
March 28, 1787

A mind always employed is always happy. This is the true secret, the grand recipe, for felicity. The idle are the only wretched.

—*THOMAS JEFFERSON*
To Martha Jefferson,
May 21, 1787

LIBERTY

Ubi lierartas ibi patria. [Where liberty is, there is my country]

—*JAMES OTIS* (1725–1783)
His motto,
Date Unknown

Where liberty dwells, there is my country.

—*ATTRIBUTED TO BENJAMIN FRANKLIN*
(1706–1790)
Date Unknown

Do thou, great liberty, inspire our souls,
And make our lives in thy possession happy
Or our deaths glorious in thy just defense.

—*JOSEPH ADDISON* (1672–1719)
Motto of the *Massachusetts Spy,*
November 22 to April 6, 1713

Man's original liberty after it is resigned (yet under due restrictions) ought to be cherished in all wise governments; or otherwise a man in making himself a subject, he alters himself from a free-

man into a slave, which to do is repugnant to the law of nature. Also the natural equality of men amongst men must be duly favored; in that government was never established by God or nature to give one man a prerogative to insult over another; therefore in a civil as well as in a natural state of being, a just equality is to be indulged so far as that every man is bound to honor every man, which is agreeable both with nature and religion (I Pet. ii. 17): *Honor all men.*
—*JOHN WISE* (1652–1725)
A Vindication of the Government of New England Churches
1717

The second great immunity of man is an original liberty enstamped upon his rational nature. He that intrudes upon this liberty violates the law of nature.
—*JOHN WISE*
A Vindication of the Government of New England Churches
1717

Those who would give up essential liberty to purchase a little temporary safety deserve neither liberty nor safety.
—*BENJAMIN FRANKLIN* (1706–1790)
Speech to the Pennsylvania Assembly,
November 11, 1755

[L]iberty must at all hazards be supported. We have a right to it, derived from our Maker. But if we had not, our fathers have earned and bought it for us, at the expense of their ease, their estates, their pleasure, and their blood.
—*JOHN ADAMS* (1735–1826)
A Dissertation on the Canon and Feudal Law
1765

A perpetual jealousy, respecting liberty, is absolutely requisite in all free states.
—*JOHN DICKINSON* (1732–1794)
Letters from a Farmer in Pennsylvania
1768

Come, join hand in hand, brave Americans all,
And rouse your bold hearts at fair Liberty's call;
No tyrannous acts shall suppress your just claim,
Or stain with dishonor America's name.

Chorus:
In Freedom we're born and in Freedom we'll live.
Our purses are ready. Steady, friends, steady;
Not as slaves, but as Freemen our money we'll give.

Our worthy forefathers, let's give them a cheer,
To climates unknown did courageously steer;
Thro' oceans to deserts for Freedom they came,
And dying, bequeath'd us their freedom and fame.

Chorus

The tree their own hands had to Liberty rear'd,
They lived to behold growing strong and revered;
With transport they cried, Now our wishes we gain,
For our children shall gather the fruits of our pain.

Chorus

Then join hand in hand, brave Americans all,
By uniting we stand, by dividing we fall;
In so righteous a cause let us hope to
succeed,
For heaven approves of each generous
deed.

Chorus

In Freedom we're born and in Freedom we'll live.
Our purses are ready. Steady, friends,
steady;
Not as slaves, but as Freemen our
money we'll give
—*JOHN DICKINSON*
"The Liberty Song"
1768

That no man should scruple, or hesitate a moment to use arms in defence
of so valuable a blessing [as liberty],
on which all the good and evil of life
depends, is clearly my opinion. Yet arms
… should be the last resort.
—*GEORGE WASHINGTON* (1732–1799)
To George Mason,
April 5, 1769

What are all the Riches, the Luxuries,
and even the Conveniences of Life compared with that Liberty where with God
and Nature have set us free, with that
inestimable Jewel which is the Basis of
all other Enjoyments?
—*ALEXANDER MCDOUGAL* (1731–1786)
To the Free and Loyal Inhabitants of
the City and Colony of New York,
May 16, 1770

When any one's liberty is attacked or
threatened, he is first to try gentle methods for his safety; to reason with, and

persuade the adversary to desist, if there
be opportunity for it; or get out of his
way, if he can; and if by such means
he can prevent the injury, he is to use
no other.

But the experience of all ages has
shewn that those, who are so unreasonable as to form designs of injuring
others, are seldom to be diverted from
their purpose by argument and persuasion alone; Notwithstanding all that can
be said to shew the injustice and inhumanity of their attempt, they persist in
they have gratified the unruly passion
which set them to work. And in this
case, what is to be done by the sufferer! Is he to use no other means for
his safety, but remonstrance or flight,
when these will not secure him? Is he
patiently to take the injury and suffer
himself to be robbed of his liberty or
his life, if the adversary sees fit to take
it? Nature certainly forbids this tame
submission, and loudly calls to a more
vigorous defence. Self-preservation is
one of the strongest, and a universal
principle of the human mind:

And this principle allows of every
thing necessary to self-defence, opposing force to force, and violence to violence. This is so universally allowed
that I need not attempt to prove it.

But since it has been supposed by
some that Christianity forbids all violent resisting of evil, or defending ourselves against injuries in such a manner as will hurt, or endanger those who
attack us; it may not be amiss to enquire briefly, Whether defensive war be
not allowed by the gospel of Christ, the
Prince of peace.

And there are, if I mistake not, several passages in the new testament,
which shew, that, it was not the design

of this divine institution to take away from mankind the natural right of defending their liberty, even by the sword.

—*SIMEON HOWARD* (?–c. 1804)
Sermon preached to the Ancient and Honorable Artillery Company in Boston,
June 7, 1773

If liberty is such a thing, and so great a blessing as it has been represented, it is, certainly, a rich talent that Heaven has been pleased to entrust with every man, and it undoubtedly becomes all to be constantly, and thoroughly awake to a sense of their duty respecting it. We are too ready to fancy, that when once we have appointed legislators, and given them charge of this inestimable treasure, we need give ourselves no farther concern about it. But this is not our whole duty. We are all stewards, to whom the God of nature has committed this talent. The design of appointing a few individuals to government, is not to free the rest from their obligations but to assist them in the discharge of their duty, in the same manner that ministers of the gospel are to assist their hearers in those duties that respect the care of their souls. Communities ought therefore to keep an impartial and watchful eye on government. They are urged to do so, by a consideration of the avaricious, and aspiring dispositions of mankind in general, and the peculiar opportunities and temptations that Governors have to indulge them. In these latter ages of the world, after it has been found by several thousands years experience, that such as have been made the guardians of liberty, have in almost every instance, where it was thought practicable, endeavoured to make themselves masters, instead of continuing stewards of the community; in these days, I say, we are more distinctly, sensible, and frequently called on to watch the conduct of government. Liberty is not an absolute right of our own, if it were, we might support, and guard, or neglect it at pleasure. It is a loan of heaven, for which we must account with the great God. It is therefore, as unreasonable for us to place an unlimited confidence in any earthly ruler, as to place such a confidence in our spiritual ministers and depend wholly on them to settle our final account with the holy judge of the universe.

—*NATHANIEL NILES* (1741–1828)
Two discourses on liberty, delivered at the North Church, in Newbury-port,
June 5, 1774

That civil liberty is of great worth, may be inferred from the conduct of God towards the Jewish nation. He promised them freedom from the oppression of their enemies as a testimony of his favour in case of their obedience; and as a chastisement for their disobedience, he threatened them with a state of servitude. From this it is certain that the omnicient God himself, esteems liberty a great blessing.

—*NATHANIEL NILES*
Two discourses on liberty, delivered at the North Church, in Newbury-port,
June 5, 1774

We your majesty's faithful subjects … [beg] to lay our grievances before the throne. …

The apprehension of being degraded into a state of servitude, from the pre-eminent rank of English freemen, while our minds retain the strongest love of liberty, and clearly foresee the miseries preparing for us and our posterity, excites emotions in our breasts, which, though we cannot describe, we should not wish to conceal. Feeling as men, and thinking as subjects in the manner we do, silence would be disloyalty. By giving this faithful information, we do all in our power to promote the great objects of your royal cares, the tranquility of your government, and the welfare of your people...

—ANONYMOUS
Petition from the General Congress in
America to the King,
October 26, 1774

Give me the steady, uniform, unshaken security of constitutional freedom. Give me the right of trial by jury of my own neighbors, and to be taxed by my own representatives only. What will become of the law and courts of justice without this? I would die to preserve the law upon a solid foundation; but take away liberty, and the foundation is destroyed.

—ALEXANDER HAMILTON (1755–1804)
"A Full Vindication of the Measures of
Congress"
December 15, 1774

There is a certain enthusiasm in liberty, that makes human nature rise above itself in acts of bravery and heroism.

—ALEXANDER HAMILTON
"A Full Vindication of the Measures of
Congress"
December 15, 1774

Honour, justice and humanity call upon us to hold, and to transmit to our posterity, that liberty, which we received from our ancestors. It is not our duty to leave wealth to our children: but it is our duty, to leave liberty to them. No infamy, iniquity, or cruelty, can exceed our own, if we, born and educated in a country of freedom, intitled to its blessings, and knowing their value, pusillanimously deserting the post assigned to us by Divine Providence, surrender succeeding generations to a condition of wretchedness, from which no human efforts, in all probability, will be sufficient to extricate them; the experience of all states mournfully demonstrating to us, that when arbitrary power has been established over them, even the wisest and bravest nations that ever flourished, have, in a few years, degenerated into abject and wretched vassals.

—JOHN DICKINSON
Resolutions of Committee for the
Providence of Pennsylvania,
1774

Our forefathers passed the vast Atlantic, spent their blood and treasure, that they might enjoy their liberties, both civil and religious, and transmit them to their posterity. Their children have waded through seas of difficulty, to leave us free and happy in the enjoyment of English privileges. Now if we should give them up, can our children give up and call us blessed? ... Let us all be of one heart, and stand fast in the liberty wherewith Christ has made us free. And may He, of His infinite mercy, grant us deliverance out of all our troubles.

—WILLIAM PRESCOTT (1726–1795)
Source Unknown
1774

Is life so dear, or peaceful so sweet, as

to be purchased at the price of chains and slavery? Forbid it, Almighty God! I know not what course others may take, but as for me, give me liberty or give me death!

—PATRICK HENRY (1736–1799)
Speech at the Virginia Convention
(There is some question whether Henry ever used these words, which were first reported five decades later by his biographer William Wirt.)
March 23, 1775

It is natural to man to indulge in the illusions of hope. We are apt to shut our eyes against a painful truth—and listen to the song of that syren, till she transforms us into beasts. Is this the part of wise men, engaged in a great and arduous struggle for liberty? Are we disposed to be of the number of those, who having eyes, see not, and having ears, hear not, the things which so nearly concern their temporal salvation? For my part, whatever anguish of spirit it might cost, I am willing to know the whole truth; to know the worst, and to provide for it.

—PATRICK HENRY
Speech at the Virginia Convention,
March 23, 1775

Liberty may be defined in general, a *power of action*, or a certain suitableness or preparedness for exertion, and a freedom from force, or hindrance from any external cause. *Liberty* when predicated of man as a moral agent, and accountable creature, is that suitableness or preparedness to be the subject of volitions, or exercises of will, with reference to moral objects; by the influence of motives, which we find belongeth to all men of common ca-

pacity, and who are come to the years of understanding.

—LEVI HART (1738–1808)
*Liberty Described and Recommended:
A Sermon Preached to the
Corporation of Freemen in Farmington
(Connecticut)*
1775

But a Constitution of Government once changed from Freedom, can never be restored. Liberty once lost is lost forever.

—JOHN ADAMS
To Abigail Adams,
1775

Liberty has been planted here; and the more it is attacked, the more it grows and flourishes.

—SAMUEL SHERWOOD (Dates unknown)
"The Church's Flight into the Wilderness, An Address On The Times"
January 17, 1776

But while we are nobly opposing with our lives and estates the tyranny of the British Parliament, let us not forget the duty which we owe to our lawful magistrates; let us never mistake licentiousness for liberty. The more we understand the principles of liberty, the more readily shall we yield obedience to lawful authority; for no man can oppose good government but he that is a stranger to true liberty.

—SAMUEL WEST (1730–1807)
On the Right to Rebel Against Governors
May 29, 1776

There is not a single instance in history in which civil liberty was lost, and religious liberty preserved entire. If therefore we yield up our temporal property, we at the same time deliver the conscience into bondage.

—*JOHN WITHERSPOON* (1723–1794)
The Dominion of Providence Over the Passions of Men
1776

Though the flame of liberty may sometimes cease to shine, the coal never can expire.

—*THOMAS PAINE* (1737–1809)
The Crisis
1776

It is a common observation here [Paris] that our cause is *the cause of all mankind*, and that we are fighting for their liberty in defending our own.

—*BENJAMIN FRANKLIN*
Letter to Samuel Cooper,
1777

If justice, good faith, honor, gratitude and all the other Qualities which enoble the character of a nation, and fulfill the ends of Government, be the fruits of our establishments, the cause of liberty will acquire a dignity and lustre, which it has never yet enjoyed; and an example will be set which can not but have the most favorable influence on the rights of mankind.

—*JAMES MADISON* (1751–1836)
Address to the States
April 25, 1783

The establishment of Civil and Religious Liberty was the Motive which induced me to the Field—the object is attained— and it now remains to be my earnest wish & prayer, that the Citizens of the United States could make a wise and virtuous use of the blessings placed before them.

—*GEORGE WASHINGTON*
To the Reformed German Congregation of New York City,
November 27, 1783

The people never give up their liberties but under some delusion.

—*EDMUND BURKE* (1729–1797)
Speech at Country Meeting of Buckinghamshire,
1784

Real liberty is neither found in despotism or the extremes of democracy, but in moderate governments.

—*ALEXANDER HAMILTON*
Constitutional Convention,
June 26, 1787

Is the relinquishment of the trial by jury and the liberty of the press necessary for your liberty? Will the abandonment of your most sacred rights tend to the security of your liberty? Liberty, the greatest of all earthy blessings—give us the precious jewel, and you may take every thing else! ... Guard with jealous attention the public liberty. ... Unfortunately, nothing will preserve it but downright force. Whenever you give up that force, you are inevitably ruined.

—*PATRICK HENRY*
Speech at the Virginia Convention,
June 5, 1788

Experience has proved that the real danger to America and to liberty lies in the defect of *energy* and *stability* in the present establishments of the United States.

—*JAMES MADISON* (1751–1836)
To Philip Mazzei,
October 8, 1788

Liberty may be endangered by the abuses of liberty as well as the abuses of power.

—JAMES MADISON
The Federalist Papers
1788

God grant, that not only the Love of Liberty, but a thorough Knowledge of the Rights of Man, may pervade all the Nations of the Earth, so that a Philosopher may set his Foot anywhere on its Surface, and say, "This is my Country."

—BENJAMIN FRANKLIN
Letter to David Hartley,
December 4, 1789

The numbers of men in all ages have preferred ease, slumber, and good cheer to liberty, when they have been in competition.

—JOHN ADAMS
To Samuel Adams,
October 18, 1790

Whatever facilitates a general intercourse of sentiments, as good roads, domestic commerce, a free press, and particularly a *circulation of newspapers through the entire body of the people*, and *Representatives going from, and returning among every part of them*, is equivalent to a contraction of territorial limits, and is favorable to liberty, where these may be too extensive.

—JAMES MADISON
"On Public Opinion"
December 19, 1791

Liberty and order will never be *perfectly* safe, until a trespass on the constitutional provisions for either, shall be felt with the same keenness that resents an invasion of the dearest rights, until every citizen shall be an Argus to espy, and an Aegeon to avenge, the unhallowed deed.

—JAMES MADISON
Speech to Congress,
1792

Liberty cannot be purchased by a wish.

—THOMAS PAINE
Letter to the People of France,
1792

Liberty is the power to do everything that does not interfere with the rights of others: thus, the exercise of the natural rights of every individual has no limits save those that assure to other members of society the enjoyment of the same rights.

—THOMAS PAINE
Plan of a Declaration of Rights
1792

The pretext of propagating liberty can make no difference. Every nation has a right to carve out its own happiness in its own way, and it is the height of presumption in another to attempt to fashion its political creed.

—ALEXANDER HAMILTON
To George Washington,
May 2, 1793

He that would make his own liberty secure, must guard even his enemy from oppression; for if he violates this duty, he establishes a precedent that will reach to himself.

—THOMAS PAINE
From *The Writings of Thomas Paine*,
edited by Moncure D. Conway
Originally published in 1795

Timid men ... prefer the calm of

despotism to the boisterous sea of liberty.

—*THOMAS JEFFERSON* (1743–1826)
To Philip Mazzei,
April 24, 1796

The distinction between liberty and licentiousness is ... a repetition of the Protean doctrine of implication, which is ever ready to work its ends by varying its shape.

—*JAMES MADISON*
To the General Assembly of Virginia,
January 23, 1799

Perhaps it is a universal truth that the loss of liberty at home is to be charged to provisions against danger, real or pretended, from abroad.

—*JAMES MADISON*
To Thomas Jefferson,
May 13, 1799

It behooves every man who values liberty of conscience for himself, to resist invasions of it in the case of others; or their case may, by change of circumstances, become his own.

—*THOMAS JEFFERSON*
Letter to Benjamin Rush,
April 21, 1803

I would define liberty to be a power to do as we would be done by.

—*JOHN ADAMS*
To J. H. Tiffany,
March 31, 1819

Straight is the gate and narrow is the way that leads to liberty, and few nations, if any, have found it.

—*JOHN ADAMS*
To Richard Rush,
May 14, 1821

If the true spark of religious and civil liberty be kindled, it will burn. Human agency cannot extinguish it. Like the earth's central fire, it may be smothered for a time; the ocean may overwhelm it; mountains may press it down; but its inherent and unconquerable force will heave both the ocean and the land, and at some time or other, in some place or other, the volcano will break out and flame up to heaven.

—*DANIEL WEBSTER* (1782–1852)
Address at Bunker Hill Monument
Cornerstone laying,
June 17, 1825

LIES & FALSEHOODS

Where thou art obliged to speak, be sure to speak the truth: for equivocation is half way to lying; as lying, the whole way to hell.

—*WILLIAM PENN* (1644–1718)
Some Fruits of Solitude
1693

Man's tongue is soft and bone doth lack; / Yet a stroke therewith may break a man's back.

—*BENJAMIN FRANKLIN* (1706–1790)
Poor Richard's Almanack
1740

A continual circulation of lies among those who are not much in the way of hearing them contradicted, will in time pass for truth; and the crime lies not in the believer but the inventor.

—*THOMAS PAINE* (1737–1809)
The Crisis
1777

He who permits himself to tell a lie once, finds it much easier to do a second and third time, till at length it becomes habitual; he tells lies without attending to it, and truths without the world's believing him. This falsehood of the tongue leads to that of the heart, and in time depraves all its good dispositions.

—*Thomas Jefferson* (1743–1826)
Notes on the State of Virginia
1781–1785

An insinuation, which a man who makes it does not believe himself, is equal to lying. It is the cowardice of lying. It unites the barest part of that vice with the meanest of all others. An open liar is a highwayman in his profession, but an insinuating liar is a thief skulking in the night.

—*Thomas Paine*
To the Opposers of the Bank
1787

It is an easy thing to tell a lie, but it is difficult to support the lie after it is told.

—*Thomas Paine*
Age of Reason
1795

The man who never looks into a newspaper is better informed than he who reads them, inasmuch as he who knows nothing is nearer the truth than he whose minds filled with falsehoods and errors.

—*Thomas Jefferson*
Letter to John Norvell,
June 11, 1807

LOVE

If ever two were one, then surely we.
If ever man were loved by wife, then thee;
If ever wife was happy in a man,
Compare with me, ye women, if you can.
I prize thy love more than whole mines of gold
Or all the riches that the East doth hold.
My love is such that rivers cannot quench,
Nor ought but love from thee, give recompense.
Thy love is such I can no way repay,
The heavens reward thee manifold, I pray.
Then while we live, in love let's so persevere
That when we live no more, we may live ever.

—*Anne Bradstreet* (c. 1612–1672)
"To My Dear and Loving Husband"
1678

My head, my heart, mine eyes, my life, nay, more,
My joy, my magazine of earthly store,
If two be one, as surely thou and I,
How stayest thou there, whilst I at Ipswich lie?
So many steps, head from the heart to sever,
If but a neck, soon should we be together.
I, like the Earth this season, mourn in black,
My Sun is gone so far in's zodiac,
Whom whilst I 'joyed, nor storms, nor frost I felt,
His warmth such frigid colds did cause to melt.
My chilled limbs now numbed lie forlorn;
Return, return, sweet Sol, from Capricorn;
In this dead time, alas, what can I more
Than view those fruits which through thy heat I bore?

Which sweet contentment yield me for
a space,
True living pictures of their father's
face.
O strange effect! now thou art south-
ward gone,
I weary grow the tedious day so long;
But when thou northward to me shalt
return,
I wish my Sun may never set, but burn
Within the Cancer of my glowing
breast,
The welcome house of him my dearest
guest.
Where ever, ever stay, and go not
thence,
Till nature's sad decree shall call thee
hence;
Flesh of thy flesh, bone of thy bone,
I here, thou there, yet both but one.
—*ANNE BRADSTREET*
"A Letter to Her Husband, Absent
upon Public Employment"
1678

Never marry but for love; but see that
thou lovest what is lovely.
—*WILLIAM PENN* (1644–1718)
Some Fruits of Solitude
1693

He that falls in love with himself will
have no rivals.
—*BENJAMIN FRANKLIN* (1706–1790)
Poor Richard's Almanack
1739

If you would be loved, love and be
loveable.
—*BENJAMIN FRANKLIN*
Poor Richard's Almanack
1755

You bid me burn your letters, but I must
forget you first.
—*JOHN ADAMS* (1735–1826)
Letter to Abigail Adams,
April 28, 1776

Divided love is never happy.
—*THOMAS PAINE* (1737–1809)
Age of Reason, II
1795

'Tis that delight some transport we can
feel
Which painters cannot paint, nor words
reveal
Nor any art we know of can conceal.
—*THOMAS PAINE*
What is Love?
1800

LUCK & GOOD FORTUNE

Poets say fortune's blind and cannot
see, / But certainly they must deceived
be; / Else could it not most commonly
fall out / That fools should have and
wise men go without.
—*BENJAMIN FRANKLIN* (1706–1790)
Poor Richard's Almanack
1734

M

JAMES MADISON

Mr. Madison is wholly unfit for the storms of War. Nature has cast him in too benevolent a mould. Admirably adapted to the tranquil scenes of peace—blending all the mild amiable virtues, he is not fit for the rough and rude blasts which the conflicts of nations generate.

—*HENRY CLAY* (1777–1852)
Letter to Caesar Rodney,
December 29, 1812

… stimulating everything in the manner worthy of a little commander-in-chief, with his little round hat and huge cockade.

—*RICHARD RUSH* (1780–1859)
Letter to Benjamin Rush,
June 20, 1812

MAJORITIES & MINORITIES

But in every distinct house of these states, the members are equal in their vote; the most ayes make the affirmative vote, and most no's the negative: They don't weigh the intellectual furniture, or other distinguishing qualifications of the several voters in the scales of the golden rule of fellowship; they only add up the ayes, and the no's, and so determine the suffrage of the house.

—*JOHN WISE* (1652–1725)
A Vindication of the Government of New-England Churches
1717

There is no maxim, in my opinion, which is more liable to be misapplied, and which, therefore, more needs elucidation, than the current one, that the interest of the majority is the political standard of right and wrong.

—*JAMES MADISON* (1751–1836)
To James Monroe,
October 5, 1786

Monopolies … are justly classed among the greatest nuisances in Government. … Monopolies are sacrifices of the many to the few. Where the power is in the few it is natural for them to sacrifice the many to their own partialities and corruptions. Where the power as with us is in the many not in the few the danger cannot be very great that the few will be thus favored. It is much more to be dreaded that the few will be unnecessarily sacrificed to the many.

—*JAMES MADISON*
To Thomas Jefferson,
October 17, 1788

179

Wherever the real power in a Government lies, there is the danger of oppression. In our Governments, the real power lies in the majority of the Community, and the invasion of private rights is chiefly to be apprehended, not from the acts of Government contrary to the sense of its constituents, but from acts in which the Government is the mere instrument of the major number of the constituents.

—*James Madison*
To Thomas Jefferson,
October 17, 1788

On a candid examination of history, we shall find that turbulence, violence, and abuse of power, by the majority trampling on the rights of the minority, have produced factions and commotions which, in republics, have, more frequently than any other cause, produced despotism.

—*James Madison*
To Thomas Jefferson,
February 4, 1790

Such is the nature of representative government, that it quietly decides all matters by majority.

—*Thomas Paine* (1737–1809)
Rights of Man, II
1792

All, too, will bear in mind this sacred principle, that though the will of the majority is in all cases to prevail, that will to be rightful must be reasonable; that the minority possess their equal rights, which equal law must protect, and to violate would be oppression.

—*Thomas Jefferson* (1743–1826)
First inaugural address,
March 4, 1801

Where the Law of the majority ceases to be acknowledged, there government ends, the Law of the strongest takes its place, & life & property are his who can take them.

—*Thomas Jefferson*
To James Gassway,
February 17, 1809

In governments, where the will of the people prevails, the danger of injustice arises from the interest, real or supposed, which a majority may have in trespassing on that of the minority.

—*James Madison*
To Thomas Cooper,
March 23, 1824

Manners

If thou thinkest twice, before thou speakest once, thou wilt speak twice the better for it.

—*William Penn* (1644–1718)
Some Fruits of Solitude
1693

Return the civilities thou receivest, and be ever grateful for favours.

—*William Penn*
Some Fruits of Solitude
1693

Visits should be short like a winter's day
Lest you're too troublesome, hasten away.

—*Benjamin Franklin* (1706–1790)
Poor Richard's Almanack
1733

None but the well-bred man knows how to confess a fault or acknowledge

himself in error.
—*BENJAMIN FRANKLIN*
Poor Richard's Almanack
1738

Tart words make no friends. A spoonful of honey will catch more flies than a gallon of vinegar.
—*BENJAMIN FRANKLIN*
Poor Richard's Almanack
1744

Contradict not at every turn what others have to say.
—*GEORGE WASHINGTON* (1732–1799)
Rules of Civility
1745

It is absurd to act the same with a clown and a prince.
—*GEORGE WASHINGTON*
Rules of Civility
1745

In company of those of higher quality than yourself, speak not till you are asked a question.
—*GEORGE WASHINGTON*
Rules of Civility
1745

A good example is the best sermon.
—*BENJAMIN FRANKLIN*
Poor Richard's Almanack

It is ill-manners to silence a fool, and cruelty to let him go on.
—*BENJAMIN FRANKLIN*
Poor Richard's Almanack
1757

Nothing is more certain than that a general profligacy and corruption of manners make a people ripe for destruction. A good form of government may hold the rotten materials together for some time, but beyond a certain pitch, even the best constitution will be ineffectual, and slavery must ensue.
—*JOHN WITHERSPOON* (1723–1794)
The Dominion of Providence Over the Passions of Men
1776

The domestic tranquility of a nation, depends greatly, on the *chastity* of what may properly be called *national manners*.
—*THOMAS PAINE* (1737–1809)
Common Sense
1776

Benevolence is due from one to another, not as a return of advantage received, but as an essential mark of humanity, demanded of our Creator. And the omission to indifferent persons, is reproachable; to relations, allies and friends, infamous.
—*ANONYMOUS*
Rudiments of Law and Government Deduced from the Law of Nature
1783

It takes three generations to make a gentleman.
—*JAMES FENIMORE COOPER*
(1789–1851)
Pioneers
1823

MARRIAGE

An husband and wife that love and value one another, show their children and servants, that they should do so too. Others visibly lose their authority in their families, by their contempt of one an-

other: and teach their children to be unnatural by their own examples.
—WILLIAM PENN (1644–1718)
Some Fruits of Solitude
1693

If love be not thy chiefest motive, thou wilt soon grow weary of a married state, and stray from thy promise, to search out thy pleasures in forbidden places.
—WILLIAM PENN
Some Fruits of Solitude
1693

They that marry for money, cannot have the true satisfaction of marriage; the requisite means being wanting.
—WILLIAM PENN
Some Fruits of Solitude
1693

Grief often treads upon the heels of pleasure; / Married in haste we oft repent at leisure; / Some by experience find the words misplaced; / Married at leisure, they repent in haste.
—BENJAMIN FRANKLIN (1706–1790)
Poor Richard's Almanack
1734

Marriage, as old men note, hath likened been / Unto a public crowd or common rout, / Where those that are without would fain get in, / And those that are within would fain get out.
—BENJAMIN FRANKLIN
Poor Richard's Almanack
1734

Where there's marriage without love, there will be love without marriage.
—BENJAMIN FRANKLIN
Poor Richard's Almanack
1734

You cannot pluck roses without fear of thorns, / Nor enjoy a fair wife without danger of horns.
—BENJAMIN FRANKLIN
Poor Richard's Almanack
1734

Keep your eyes wide open before marriage, half shut afterwards.
—BENJAMIN FRANKLIN
Poor Richard's Almanack
1738

One good husband is worth two good wives, for the scarcer things are, the more they're valued.
—BENJAMIN FRANKLIN
Poor Richard's Almanack
1742

I know of no Medicine fit to diminish the violent natural Inclinations you mention; and if I did, I think I should not communicate it to you. Marriage is the proper Remedy. It is the most natural State of Man, and therefore the State in which you are most likely to find solid Happiness. Your Reasons against entering into it at present, appear to me not well-founded. The circumstantial Advantages you have in View by postponing it, are not only uncertain, but they are small in comparison with that of the Thing itself, the being married and settled. It is the Man and Woman united that make the compleat human Being. Separate, she wants his Force of Body and Strength of Reason; he, her Softness, Sensibility and acute Discernment. Together they are more likely to succeed in the World. A single Man has not nearly the Value he would have in that State of Union. He is an incomplete Animal. He resembles the odd half of a Pair of Scissors. If you get a prudent healthy Wife, your Industry in your Profession, with her good economy, will be a Fortune sufficient.

—BENJAMIN FRANKLIN
Letter to a young man,
June 25, 1745

I have always considered marriage as the most interesting event of one's life, the foundation of happiness or misery.

—GEORGE WASHINGTON (1732–1799)
To Burwell Bassett,
May 23, 1785

[M]ore permanent and genuine happiness is to be found in the sequestered walks of connubial life than in the giddy rounds of promiscuous pleasure.

—GEORGE WASHINGTON
To Marquis de la Rourie,
August 10, 1786

Though I appear a sort of wanderer, the married state has not a sincerer friend than I am. It is the harbor of human life, and is, with respect to the things of this world, what the next world is to this. It is home; and that one word conveys more than any other word can express. For a few years we may glide along the tide of youthful single life and be wonderfully delighted; but it is a tide that flows but once, and what is still worse, it ebbs faster than it flows, and leaves many a hapless voyager aground. I am one, you see, that have experienced the fate I am describing.

—THOMAS PAINE (1737–1809)
To Kitty Nicholson Few,
January 6, 1789

When I see my female friends drop off by matrimony I am sensible of something that affects me like a loss in spite of all the appearances of joy: I cannot help mixing the sincere compliment of regret with that of congratulation. It appears as if I had outlived or lost a friend. It seems to me as if the original was no more, and that which she is changed to forsakes the circle and forgets the scenes of former society. Felicities are cares superior to those she formerly cared for, create to her a new landscape of life that excludes the little friendships of the past. It is not every lady's mind that is sufficiently capacious to prevent those greater objects crowding out the less, or that can spare a thought to former friendships after she has given her hand and heart to the man who loves her.

—THOMAS PAINE
To Kitty Nicholson Few,
January 6, 1789

When divorces can be summoned to the aid of levity, or vanity, or of avarice, a state of marriage frequently becomes a state of war or strategem.

—JAMES WILSON (1742–1798)
Lectures on Law
1791

Seven hundred wives, and three hundred concubines, are worse than none; and however it may carry with it the appearance of heightened enjoyment, it defeats all the felicity of affection, by leaving it no point to fix upon.

—THOMAS PAINE
Age of Reason, II
1795

MASSACHUSETTS

The land to me seemed a paradise. ...
[I]f this land be not rich, then the whole
world is poor.
—*THOMAS MORTON*(c. 1590–1647)
New English Canaan
1637

The first public love of my heart is the
Commonwealth of Massachusetts.
—*JOSIAH QUINCY, JR.* (1772–1864)
Speech directed at the U.S. House of
Representatives,
January 14, 1811

MEANS & ENDS

A good end cannot sanctify evil means;
nor must we ever do evil, that good
may come of it.
—*WILLIAM PENN*(1644–1718)
Some Fruits of Solitude
1693

It is too common an error, to invert the
order of things; by making an end of
that which is a means, and a means of
that which is an end.
—*WILLIAM PENN*
Some Fruits of Solitude
1693

MEMORY

In the progress of politics, as in the
common occurrences of life, we are
not only apt to forget the ground we
have travelled over, but frequently neglect to gather up experience as we
go.
We expend, if I may so say, the
knowledge of every day on the circumstances that produce it, and journey on
in search of new matter and new refinements: But as it is pleasant, and
sometimes useful, to look back, even
to the first periods of infancy, and trace
the turns and windings through which
we have passed, so we may likewise
derive many advantages by halting a
while in our political career, and taking
a review of the wonderous complicated labyrinth of little more than yesterday.
—*THOMAS PAINE* (1737–1809)
The Crisis
1777

Were a man to be totally deprived of
memory, he would be incapable of
forming any just opinion; every thing
about him would seem a chaos; he
would have even his own history to ask
from every one; and by not knowing
how the world went on in his absence,
he would be at a loss to know how it
ought to be on when he recovered, or
rather, returned to it again.
—*THOMAS PAINE*
The Crisis
1777

MERCY & COMPASSION

Justice, that in the rigid paths of law,
would still some drops from Pity's
fountain draw.
—*JOHN LANGHORNE* (1735–1779)
The Country Justice
c. 1766

It is the madness of folly to expect
mercy from those who have refused
to do justice.
—*THOMAS PAINE* (1737–1809)
The Crisis
1776

There is a kind of bastard generosity, which, by being extended to all men, is as fatal to society, on one hand, as the want of true generosity is on the other. A lax manner of administering justice, falsely termed moderation, has a tendency both to dispirit public virtue and promote the growth of public evils.

—THOMAS PAINE
The Crisis
1776

We hold that the moral obligation of providing for old age, helpless infancy, and poverty, is far superior to that of supplying the invented wants of courtly extravagance, ambition and intrigue.

—THOMAS PAINE
Address and Declaration of the
Friends of Universal Peace and Liberty,
1791

When it shall be said in any country in the world, my poor are happy, neither ignorance nor distress is to be found among them; my jails are empty of prisoners, my streets of beggars; the aged are not in want, the taxes are not oppressive; the rational world is my friend, because I am the friend of its happiness: when these things can be said, then may that country boast its constitution and its government.

—THOMAS PAINE
Rights of Man, II
1792

My compassion for the unfortunate, whether friend or enemy, is ... lively and sincere.

—THOMAS PAINE
To the French National Convention,
January 15, 1793

MILITARY & WAR

Establish the eternal truth that acquiescence under insult is not the way to escape war.

—THOMAS JEFFERSON (1743–1826)
Date unknown

Noe ffreeman shall be compelled to receive any Marriners or Souldiers into his house and there suffer them to Sojourne, against their willes provided Always it be not in time of Actuall Warr within this province.

—ANONYMOUS
New York Charter of Libertyes of 1683,
1683

It is a great mark of the corruption of our natures, and what ought to humble us extremely, and excite the exercise of our reason to a nobler and juster sense, that we cannot see the use and pleasure of our comforts but by the want of them. As if we could not taste the benefit of health, but by the help of sickness; nor understand the satisfaction of fullness without the instruction of want; not, finally, know the comfort of peace but by the smart and penance of the vices of war: And without dispute that is not the lest reason that God is pleased to chastise us so frequently with it.

—WILLIAM PENN (1644–1718)
*An Essay Towards the Present and
Future Peace of Europe*
1693

I heard the bullets whistle; and believe me, there is something charming in the sound.

—GEORGE WASHINGTON (1732–1799)
Letter to his mother,
May 3, 1754

How stands the glass around?
For shame you take no care, my boys,
How stands the glass around?
Let wine and mirth abound;
The trumpet sound,
The colors they do fly my boys;
To fight, kill or wound;
As you would be found,
Contented with hard fare, my boys
On the cold ground

O why, soldiers why?
O why should we be melancholy boys,
O why soldiers why?
Whose bus'ness is to die;
What? sighing? Fye!
Drink on, drown fear, be jolly boys;
'Tis he, you or I, wet, hot, cold or dry;
We're always bound to follow boys,
And scorn to fly.

'Tis but vain;
I mean not to upbraid you boys,
'Tis but vain;
For a soldier to complain;
Should next campaign,
Send us to him that made us boys;
We're free from pain,
But should we remain,
A bottle and kind landlady
Cures all again.

—ANONYMOUS
"Why, Soldiers, Why; Wolfe's Song"
c. 1759

But whatever may be the design of this military appearance; whatever use some persons may intend and expect to make of it: This we all know, and *every child in the street is taught to know it*; that while a people retain a just sense of Liberty, blessed by God, as this people yet do, the insolence of power will for ever be despised.

—SAMUEL ADAMS (1722–1803)
Essay in the *Boston Gazette* about
British forces in Boston,
1768

A people who would stand fast in their liberty, should furnish themselves with weapons proper for their defence, and learn the use of them.

It is indeed an hard case, that those who are happy in the blessings of providence, and disposed to live peaceably with all men, should be obliged to keep up the idea of blood and slaughter, and expend their time and treasure to acquire the arts and instruments of death. But this is a necessity which the depravity of human nature has laid upon every state. Nor was there ever a people that continued, for any considerable time, in the enjoyment of liberty, who were not in a capacity to defend themselves against invaders, unless they were too poor and inconsiderable to tempt an enemy.

—SIMEON HOWARD (?–c. 1804)
To the Ancient and Honorable
Artillery Company in Boston,
June 7, 1773

Men are also bound, individuals and societies, to take care of their temporal happiness, and do all they lawfully can, to promote it. But what can be more inconsistent with this duty, than submitting to great encroachments upon our liberty? Such submission tends to slavery; and compleat slavery implies every evil that the malice of man and devils can inflict.

—SIMEON HOWARD
To the Ancient and Honorable
Artillery Company in Boston,
June 7, 1773

We want not courage; it is discipline alone in which we are exceeded by the most formidable troops that ever trod the earth. Surely our hearts flutter no more at the sound of war than did those of the immortal band of Persia, the Macedonian phalanx, the invincible Roman legions, the Turkish janissaries, the *gens d'armes* of France, or the well-known grenadiers of Britain. A well-disciplined militia is a safe, an honorable guard to a community like this, whose inhabitants are by nature brave, and are laudably tenacious of that freedom in which they were born. From a well-regulated militia we have nothing to fear; their interest is the same with that of the State. When a country is invaded, the militia are ready to appear in its defense; they march into the field with that fortitude which a consciousness of the justice of their cause inspires; they do not jeopardize their lives for a master who considers them only as the instruments of his ambition, and whom they regard only as the daily dispenser of the scanty pittance of bread and water. No; they fight for their houses, their lands, for their wives, their children; for all who claim the tenderest names, and are held dearest in their hearts; they fight *pro aris et focis*, for their liberty, and for themselves, and for their God.

—*JOHN HANCOCK* (1737–1793)
Boston Massacre Oration,
March 5, 1774

Don't fire until you see the whites of their eyes.

—*WILLIAM PRESCOTT* (1726–1795)
Order given to soldiers at the Battle of Bunker Hill. The quotation is sometimes attributed to Israel Putnam.
June 17, 1775

[Cowardice is a] crime of all others the most infamous in a soldier, the most injurious to an army, and the last to be forgiven.

—*GEORGE WASHINGTON*
General Orders,
July 7, 1775

I too am almost sick of the parade/ Of honours purchas'd at the price of peace.

—*MERCY OTIS WARREN* (1728–1814)
The Group, Act. I, Sc. 1
1775

There is a time for all things, a time to preach and a time to pray, but those times have passed away. There is a time to fight, and that time has now come.

—*PETER MUHLENBERG* (Dates unknown)
Sermon,
January 1776

Three things prompt men to a regular discharge of their duty in time of action—natural bravery, hope of reward, and fear of punishment.

—*GEORGE WASHINGTON*
To John Hancock,
February 9, 1776

Without a respectable navy—alas America!

—*JOHN PAUL JONES* (1747–1792)
Letter to Robert Morris,
October 17, 1776

The distinction between a well-regulated army and a mob is the good order and discipline of the first and the licentious and disorderly behavior of the latter.

—*GEORGE WASHINGTON*
To Israel Putnam,
1776

That the people have a right to bear arms for the defence of themselves and the state; and as standing armies in the time of peace are dangerous to liberty, they ought not to be kept up; And that the military should be kept under strict subordination to, and governed by, the civil power.

—ANONYMOUS
Pennsylvania Constitution
1776

I'll sell my clock, I'll sell my reel,
I'll sell my flax and spinning wheel,
To buy my true love a sword of steel,
Johnny has gone for a soldier.

—ANONYMOUS
"Johnny Has Gone For a Soldier"
c. 1776

It is not a field of a few acres of ground, but a cause, that we are defending, and whether we defeat the enemy in one battle, or by degrees, the consequences will be the same.

—THOMAS PAINE (1737–1809)
The Crisis
1777

But in war we may be certain of these two things, viz. that cruelty in an enemy, and motions made with more than usual parade, are alays signs of weakness. He that can conquer, finds his mind too free and pleasant to be brutish; and he that intends to conquer, never makes too much show of his strength.

—THOMAS PAINE
The Crisis
1777

I wish to have no connection with any ship that does not sail *fast*; for

I intend to go *in harm's way*.

—JOHN PAUL JONES
Letter to unknown person,
November 16, 1778

If the Americans are servilely kept to the European Plan [of fighting], they will make an awkward figure, be laughed at as a bad army by their enemy, and defeated in every encounter which depends upon maneuvers.

—GENERAL CHARLES LEE (1731–1782)
Speech to Congress,
1778

He who is the author of a war lets loose the whole contagion of hell and opens a vein that bleeds a nation to death.

—THOMAS PAINE
The Crisis
1778

It is the object only of war that makes it honorable.

—THOMAS PAINE
The Crisis
1778

If there is a sin superior to every other it is that of willful and offensive war. Most other sins are circumscribed within narrow limits, that is, the power of *one* man cannot give them a very general extension, and many kind of sins have only a mental existence from which no infection arises; but he who is the author of a war lets loose the whole contagion of Hell ...

—THOMAS PAINE
The Crisis
1778

In a general view there are very few conquests that repay the charge of making them, and mankind are pretty well convinced that it can never be worth their while to go to war for profit sake. If they are made war upon, their country invaded, or their existence at stake, it is their duty to defend and preserve themselves, but in every other light and from every other cause is war inglorious and detestable.

—THOMAS PAINE
The Crisis
1778

When men ... have the incitements of military honor to engage their ambition and pride, they will cheerfully submit to inconveniences which in a state of tranquility would appear insupportable.

—GEORGE WASHINGTON
To Continental Congress,
January 20, 1779

I have not yet begun to fight.

—JOHN PAUL JONES
Reply to the call for surrender during the battle between the American ship *Bonhomme Richard* and the British ship *Serapis,*
September 23, 1779

The seeds of almost every former war have been sown in the injudicious or defective terms of the preceding peace.

—THOMAS PAINE
Peace, and the Newfoundland Fisheries
1779

There is nothing so likely to produce peace as to be well prepared to meet an enemy.

—GEORGE WASHINGTON
Letter to Elbridge Gerry,
January 29, 1780

A change in Generals, like a change of physicians, served only to keep the flattery alive, and furnish new pretenses for new extravagance.

—THOMAS PAINE
The Crisis
1780

When will men be convinced, that even successful wars at length become misfortunes to those who unjustly commenc'd them, and who triumph'd blindly in their success, not seeing all the consequences.

—BENJAMIN FRANKLIN (1706–1790)
Source unknown
1780

An honorable Peace is and always was my first wish! I can take no delight in the effusion of human Blood; but, if this War should continue, I wish to have the most active part in it.

—JOHN PAUL JONES
To Gouverneur Morris,
September 2, 1782

The army ... is a dangerous instrument to play with.

—GEORGE WASHINGTON
To Alexander Hamilton,
April 4, 1783

There never was a good war or a bad peace.

—BENJAMIN FRANKLIN
Letter to Josiah Quincy,
September 11, 1783

Weakness provokes insult & injury, while a condition to punish it often prevents it.

—THOMAS JEFFERSON
To John Jay,
August 23, 1785

Then rushed to meet the insulting foe;
They took the spear—but left the shield.
—PHILIP FRENEAU (1752–1832)
"To the Memory of the Brave Americans Who Fell at Eutaw Springs, S.C.,
September 8th, 1781"
1786

A standing military force, with an overgrown Executive will not long be safe companions to liberty. The means of defence against foreign danger, have been always the instruments of tyranny at home. Among the Romans it was a standing maxim to excite a war, whenever a revolt was apprehended. Throughout all Europe, the armies kept up under the pretext of defending, have enslaved the people.
—JAMES MADISON (1751–1836)
Speech at the Constitutional
Convention,
June 29, 1787

A country invaded is in the condition of a house broke into, and on no other principle than this, can a reflective mind at least such as mine, justify war to itself.
—THOMAS PAINE
To the Marquis of Lansdowne,
September 21, 1787

A standing army is one of the greatest mischiefs that can possibly happen.
—JAMES MADISON
Debates, Virginia Convention
1787

Flames once kindled are not always easily extinguished.
—THOMAS PAINE
Prospects on the Rubicon
1787

War involves in its progress such a train of unforeseen and unsupposed circumstances ... that no human wisdom can calculate the end. It has but one thing certain, and that is to increase taxes.
—THOMAS PAINE
Prospects on the Rubicon
1787

Standing armies are dangerous to liberty.
—ALEXANDER HAMILTON (1755–1804)
The Federalist Papers
1787

No soldier shall, in time of peace be quartered in any house, without the consent of the owner, nor in time of war, but in a manner to be prescribed by law.
—CONSTITUTION OF THE UNITED STATES
Amendment 3, The Bill of Rights
1787

With regard to the militia, it must be observed, that though he [the President] has the command of them when called into the actual service of the United States, yet he has not the power of calling them out.
—JAMES IREDELL (1751–1799)
Speech in North Carolina Ratifying
Convention,
July 28, 1788

To judge from the history of mankind, we shall be compelled to conclude that the fiery and destructive passions of war reign in the human breast with much more powerful sway than the mild and beneficent sentiments of peace; and that to model our political systems upon speculations of lasting tranquillity would be to calculate on the weaker springs of human character.

—ALEXANDER HAMILTON
The Federalist Papers
1788

To be prepared for war is one of the most effectual means of preserving peace.

—GEORGE WASHINGTON
First Annual Address to Congress,
January 8, 1790

Whatever enables us to go to war, secures our peace.

—THOMAS JEFFERSON
Letter to James Monroe,
July 11, 1790

Whilst war is to depend on those whose ambition, whose revenge, whose avidity, or whose caprice may contradict the sentiment of the community, and yet be uncontrolled by it; whilst war is to be declared by those who are to spend the public money, not by those who are to pay it; by those who are to direct the public forces, not by those who are to support them; by those whose power is to be raised, not by those whose chains may be riveted, the disease must continue to be *hereditary* like the government of which it is the offspring. As the first step towards a cure, the government itself must be regenerated. Its will must be made subordinate to, or rather the same with, the will of the community.

—JAMES MADISON
Essay in the *National Gazette*,
January 31, 1792

Each generation should be made to bear

the burden of its own wars, instead of carrying them on, at the expense of other generations.

—JAMES MADISON
Essay in the *National Gazette*,
February 2, 1792

War contains so much folly, as well as wickedness, that much is to be hoped from the progress of reason; and if any thing is to be hoped, every thing ought to be tried.

—JAMES MADISON
Essay in the *National Gazette*,
February 2, 1792

Those who are to *conduct a war* cannot in the nature of things, be proper or safe judges, whether *a war ought* to be *commenced, continued*, or *concluded*. They are barred from the latter functions by a great principle in free government, analogous to that which separates the sword from the purse, or the power of executing from the power of enacting laws.

—JAMES MADISON
Helvidius No. 1,
August 24, 1793

War is in fact the true nurse of executive aggrandizement. In war a physical force is to be created, and it is the executive will which is to direct it. In war the public treasures are to be unlocked, and it is the executive hand which is to dispense them. In wars the honors and emoluments of office are to be multiplied; and it is the executive patronage under which they are to be enjoyed. It is in war, finally, that laurels are to be gathered, and it is the executive brow they are to encircle. The strongest passions, and the most dangerous weaknesses of the human breast; ambition, avarice, vanity, the honorable or venal love of fame, are all in conspiracy against the desire and duty of peace.

—JAMES MADISON
Helvidius No. 4,
September 14, 1793

If we desire to avoid insult, we must be able to repel it; if we desire to secure peace, one of the most powerful instruments of our rising prosperity, it must be known, that we are at all times ready for War.

—GEORGE WASHINGTON
Fifth Annual Address to Congress,
December 13, 1793

I am, against every invitation to war, an advocate of peace. The insults of Spain, Britain, or any others. ... I deem no more worthy of our notice as a nation than those of a lunatic to a man in health—for I consider them as desperate and raving mad.

—JAMES MONROE (1758–1831)
To Thomas Jefferson,
1793

Of all the enemies to public liberty war is, perhaps, the most to be dreaded, because it comprises and develops the germ of every other. War is the parent of armies; from these proceed debts and taxes; and armies, and debts, and taxes are the known instruments for bringing the many under the domination of the few. In war, too, the discretionary power of the Executive is extended; its influence in dealing out offices, honors, and emoluments is multiplied; and all the means of seducing the minds, are added to those

of subduing the force, of the people. The same malignant aspect in republicanism may be traced in the inequality of fortunes, and the opportunities of fraud, growing out of a state of war, and in the degeneracy of manners and of morals, engendered by both. No nation could preserve its freedom in the midst of continual warfare.

—JAMES MADISON
"Political Observations"
April 20, 1795

[United under one government, we] will avoid the necessity of those overgrown military establishments, which, under any form of government, are inauspicious to liberty, and which are to be regarded as particularly hostile to republican liberty.

—GEORGE WASHINGTON
Farewell Address,
September 17, 1796

The most sincere neutrality is not a sufficient guard against the depredations of nations at war. To secure a respect to a neutral flag requires a naval force organized and ready to vindicate it from insult or aggression.

—GEORGE WASHINGTON
Address to Congress,
December 7, 1796

The constitution supposes, what the History of all Governments demonstrates, that the Executive is the branch of power most interested in war, & most prone to it. It has accordingly with studied care, vested the question of war in the Legislature. But the Doctrines lately advanced strike at the root of all these provisions, and will deposit the peace of the Country in that Department which the Constitution distrusts as most ready without cause to renounce it. For if the opinion of the President, not the facts & proofs themselves are to sway the judgment of Congress, in declaring war, and if the President in the recess of Congress create a foreign mission, appoint the minister, & negotiate a War Treaty, without the possibility of a check even from the Senate, until the measures present alternatives overruling the freedom of its judgment; if again a Treaty when made obliges the Legislature to declare war contrary to its judgment, and in pursuance of the same doctrine, a law declaring war, imposes a like moral obligation, to grant the requisite supplies until it be formally repealed with the consent of the President & Senate, it is evident that the people are cheated out of the best ingredients in their Government, the safeguards of peace which is the greatest of their blessings.

—JAMES MADISON
Letter to Thomas Jefferson,
April 2, 1797

I abhor war and view it as the greatest scourge of mankind.

—THOMAS JEFFERSON
To Eldridge Gerry,
1797

Whatever diversity of opinion there may be with regard to military and naval preparations, for the defence and security of the country, there are some things in which all well-informed and reflecting men unite.

—ALEXANDER HAMILTON
"Lucius Crassus"
December 24, 1801

None but an armed nation can dispense with a standing army.

—THOMAS JEFFERSON
Letter to unknown recipient,
February 25, 1803

A military government may make a nation great, but it cannot make them free.

—FISHER AMES (1758–1808)
The Dangers of American Liberty
1805

The surest way to prevent war is not to fear it.

—JOHN RANDOLPH (1773–1833)
Speech before Committee of Whole in
the United States House of
Representatives,
March 5, 1806

Were armies to be raised whenever a speck of war is visible in our horizon, we never should have been without them. Our resources would have been exhausted on dangers which have never happened, instead of being reserved for what is really to take place.

—THOMAS JEFFERSON
Sixth Annual Message to Congress,
December 2, 1806

Whensoever hostile aggressions ... require resort to war, we must meet our duty and convince the world that we are just friends and brave enemies.

—THOMAS JEFFERSON
To Andrew Jackson,
December 3, 1806

The spirit of this country is totally adverse to a large military force.

—THOMAS JEFFERSON
Letter to Chandler Price,
February 28, 1807

It is a nice task to speak of war, so as to impress our own people with a dislike of it, and not impress foreign Governments with the idea that they may take advantage of the dislike.

—JAMES MADISON
To Thomas Jefferson,
September 7, 1808

For a people who are free, and who mean to remain so, a well-organized and armed militia is their best security.

—JAMES MADISON
Message to Congress,
November 8, 1808

Always remember[ing] that an armed and trained militia is the firmest bulwark of republics—that without standing armies their liberty can never be in danger, nor with large ones safe.

—JAMES MADISON
First Inaugural Address,
March 4, 1809

If you wish to avoid foreign collision, you had better abandon the ocean—surrender your commerce, give up all your prosperity.

—HENRY CLAY (1777–1852)
Speech to the U.S. House of Representatives about harassment of American ships by British ships,
January 22, 1812

For the hotter the war, boys, the quicker the peace.

—ANONYMOUS
Republican broadside just after the declaration of the war against Great Britain,
1812

The creator has not thought proper to mark those in the forehead who are of stuff to make good generals. We are first, therefore, to seek them blindfold, and let them learn the trade at the expense of great losses.

—THOMAS JEFFERSON
Letter to General Baily,
February 1813

Tell the men to fire faster and not to give up the ship; fight her till she sinks.

—JAMES LAWRENCE (1781–1813)
On board the U.S. frigate *Chesapeake*,
June 1, 1813

We have met the enemy and they are ours—two ships, two brigs, one schooner and a sloop.

—OLIVER HAZARD PERRY (1758–1819)
Message to General William Henry Harrison after Battle of Lake Eire,
September 10, 1813

And although among our blessings we cannot number an exemption from the evils of war; yet these will never be regarded as the greatest of evils by the friends of liberty and of the rights of nations. Our country has before preferred them to the degraded condition which was the alternative, when the sword was drawn in the cause which gave birth to our national Independence, and none who contemplate the magnitude, and feel the value of that glorious event, will shrink from a struggle to maintain the high and happy ground on which it placed the American people.

—JAMES MADISON
Annual Message to Congress,
December 7, 1813

Every citizen [should] be a soldier. This was the case with the Greeks and the

Romans, and must be that of every free state.

—*THOMAS JEFFERSON*
Letter to James Monroe,
1813

The insulated state in which nature has placed the American continent should so far avail it that no spark of war kindled in the other quarters of the globe should be wafted across the wide oceans which separate us from them.

—*THOMAS JEFFERSON*
To Baron Humboldt,
1813

We must train and classify the whole of our male citizens, and make military instruction a regular part of collegiate education. We can never be sage until this is done.

—*THOMAS JEFFERSON*
Letter to James Monroe,
1813

Long may she ride, our Navy's pride,
  And spur to resolution:
And seaman boast, and landsmen toast,
  The Frigate Constitution.

—*ANONYMOUS*
"The Frigate Constitution"
c. 1813

The enemy says that Americans are good at a long shot, but cannot stand the cold iron. I call upon you instantly to give a lie to the slander. Charge!

—*WINFIELD SCOTT* (1786–1866)
Address to the 11th Infantry Regiment, Chippewa, Canada,
June 5, 1814

The individual who refuses to defend his rights when called by his Govern-
ment, deserves to be a slave, and must be punished as an enemy of his country and friend to her foe.

—*ANDREW JACKSON* (1767–1845)
Proclamation to the people of
Louisiana from Mobile,
September 21, 1814

Where is it written in the Constitution, in what article or section is it contained, that you may take children from their parents, and parents from their children, and compel them to fight the battles of any way in which the folly or the wickedness of government may engage it?

—*DANIEL WEBSTER* (1782–1852)
Remarks in the House of
Representatives,
December 9, 1814

By the Eternal, they shall not sleep on our soil!

—*ANDREW JACKSON*
Referring to the British,
December 23, 1814

Experience has taught us that neither the pacific dispositions of the American people nor the pacific character of their political institutions can altogether exempt them from that strife which appears beyond the ordinary lot of nations to be incident to the actual period of the world, and the same faithful monitor demonstrates that a certain degree of preparation for war is not only indispensable to avert disasters in the onset, but afford also the best security for the continuance of peace.

—*JAMES MADISON*
Speech to the Senate and the House of
Representatives,
February 18, 1815

The safety of these States and everything dear to a free people must depend in an eminent degree on the militia. ... This arrangement should be formed, too, in time of peace, to be the better prepared for war.
—*JAMES MADISON*
First Inaugural Address,
March 4, 1817

The right of self-defense never ceases. It is among the most sacred, and alike necessary to nations and to individuals.
—*JAMES MONROE*
Second annual message to Congress,
November 16, 1818

If a system of universal and permanent peace would be established, or if in war, the belligerent parties would respect the rights of neutral powers, we should have no occasion for a navy or an army. ... The history of all ages proves that this cannot be presumed; on the contrary, that at least one half of every century, in ancient as well as modern times, has been consumed in wars, and often of the most general and desolating character.
—*JAMES MONROE*
Speech to the House of Representatives,
January 30, 1824

MODESTY

He is happiest of whom the world says least, good or bad.
—*THOMAS JEFFERSON* (1743–1826)
To John Adams,
August 27, 1786

My great wish is to go on in a strict but silent performance of my duty; to avoid attracting notice, and to keep my name out of the newspapers.
—*THOMAS JEFFERSON*
Letter to Francis Hopkinson,
January 11, 1789

MONEY

A penny saved is a penny earned.
—Anonymous, though often attributed to Benjamin Franklin,
Date Unknown

Lend not beyond thy ability, nor refuse to lend out of thy ability; especially when it will help others more than it can hurt thee.
—*WILLIAM PENN* (1644–1718)
Some Fruits of Solitude
1693

Nothing but money
Is sweeter than honey.
—*BENJAMIN FRANKLIN* (1706–1790)
Poor Richard's Almanack
1735

If you know how to spend less than you get, you have the philosopher's stone.
—*BENJAMIN FRANKLIN*
Poor Richard's Almanack
1736

There are three faithful friends—an old wife, an old dog, and ready money.
—*BENJAMIN FRANKLIN*
Poor Richard's Almanack
1738

He who multiplies riches multiplies cares.
—*BENJAMIN FRANKLIN*
Poor Richard's Almanack
1744

Beware of little expenses; a small leak will sink a great ship.
—*BENJAMIN FRANKLIN*
Poor Richard's Almanack
1745

If you would know the value of money, go and try to borrow some.
—*BENJAMIN FRANKLIN*
Poor Richard's Almanack
1758

Paper credit never was long supported in any country, on a national scale, where it was not founded on a joint basis of public and private credit. ... The only certain manner to obtain a permanent paper credit is to engage the moneyed interest immediately in it, by making them contribute the whole or part of the stock, and giving them the whole or part of the profits.
—*ALEXANDER HAMILTON* (1755–1804)
To James Duane,
September 3, 1780

Whether Virginia is to remain exempt from the epidemic malady [paper currency] will depend on the ensuing Assembly. My hopes rest chiefly on the exertions of Col. Mason and the failure of the experiments elsewhere. That these must fail is morally certain; for besides the proofs of it already visible in some States, and the intrinsic defect of the paper in all, this ficticious money will rather feed than cure the spirit of extravagance which sends away the coin to pay the unfavorable balance, and will therefore soon be carried to market to buy up coin for that purpose. From that moment depreciation is inevitable. The value of money consists in the uses it will serve. Specie will serve all the uses of paper. Paper will not serve one of the essential uses of specie. The paper therefore will be less valuable than specie.
—*JAMES MADISON* (1751–1836)
To Thomas Jefferson,
August 12, 1786

I am not tired of working for nothing but I cannot afford it.
—*THOMAS PAINE* (1737–1809)
To Thomas Jefferson,
October 4, 1800

JAMES MONROE

He is a man whose soul might be turned wrong side outwards, without discovering a blemish to the world.
—*THOMAS JEFFERSON* (1743–1826)
Letter to W. T. Franklin,
1786

... is one of the most improper and incompetent that could be selected. Naturally dull and stupid; extremely illiterate; indecisive to a degree that would be incredible to one who did not know him; pusillanimous, and of course hypocritical; has no opinion on any subject and will always be under the government of the worst men.
—*AARON BURR* (1756–1836)
Letter to his son-in-law commenting on James Monroe as a presidential candidate,
1816

I have known many much more rapid in reaching a conclusion, but few with a certainty so unerring.
—*JOHN CALDWELL CALHOUN* (1782–1850)
Letter to S. L. Governeur,
August 8, 1818

MORALITY & MORALISTS

The powers of the human mind appear to be arranged in a certain order like the strata of earth. They are thrown out of their order by the fall of man. The moral powers appear to have occupied the highest and first place. They recover it in solitude, and after sleep, hence the advantage of solitary punishments, and of consulting our morning pillow in cases where there is a doubt of what is right, or duty. The first thoughts in a morning if followed seldom deceive or mislead us. They are generally seasoned by the moral powers.

In Macbeth a lady is restrained from the murder of a king by his resemblance of her father as he slept. Should not all men be restrained from acts of violence and even of unkindness against their fellow men by observing in them something which resembles the Saviour of the World? If nothing else certainly, a human figure?

—*BENJAMIN RUSH* (1745–1813)
Commonplace Book
1790

My country is the world, and my religion is to do good.

—*THOMAS PAINE* (1737–1809)
The Rights of Man
1791

With respect to Aesop, though the moral is in general just, the fable is often cruel; and the cruelty of the fable does more injury to the heart, especially in a child, than the moral does good to the judgment.

—*THOMAS PAINE*
Age of Reason, II
1795

'Tis substantially true, that virtue or morality is a necessary spring of popular government. The rule indeed extends with more or less force to every species of free Government.

—*GEORGE WASHINGTON* (1732–1799)
Farewell Address,
September 17, 1796

Without morals a republic cannot subsist any length of time; they therefore who are decrying the Christian religion, whose morality is so sublime and pure (and) which insures to be good eternal happiness, are undermining the solid foundation of morals, the best security for the duration of free governments.

—*CHARLES CARROLL* (1737–1832)
Letter to James McHenry,
November 4, 1800

The man who is a *good* public character from *craft*, and not from moral principle, if such a character can be called *good*, is not much to be depended on.

—*THOMAS PAINE*
To John Fellows,
July 31, 1805

We had all rather associate with a good humored, light-principled man than with an ill tempered rigorist in morality.

—*THOMAS JEFFERSON* (1743–1826)
To Benjamin Rush,
January 3, 1808

I sincerely then believe with you in the general existence of a moral instinct. I think it the brightest gem with which the human character is studded; and the want of it as more degrading than the most hideous of the bodily deformities.

—*THOMAS JEFFERSON*
To Thomas Law,
June 13, 1814

I fear, from the experience of the last 25 years that morals do not, of necessity, advance hand in hand with the sciences.

—*THOMAS JEFFERSON*
To J. Correa de Serra,
June 28, 1815

Whatever makes men good Christians, makes them good citizens.

—*DANIEL WEBSTER* (1782–1852)
Speech at Plymouth,
December 22, 1820

MOTIVES & INTENTIONS

The views of men can only be known, or guessed at, by their words or actions.

—*GEORGE WASHINGTON* (1732–1799)
To Patrick Henry,
January 15, 1799

N

NATIVE AMERICANS

In respect of us, they are a poor people, and for want of skill and judgment in the knowledge and use of our things, do esteem our trifles before things of great value. Notwithstanding [this,] in their proper manner (considering the want of such means as we have), they seem very ingenious, for although they have no such tools, nor any such crafts, sciences, and arts as we, yet in those things they do, they show excellence of wit.

—THOMAS HARRIOT (1560–1621)
*A Brief and True Report of the New
Found Land of Virginia*
1588

According to human reason, guided only by the light of nature, these people lead the more happy and freer life, being void of care, which torments so many minds of so many Christians; they are not delighted in baubles, but in useful things.

—THOMAS MORTON (c. 1590–1647)
*Manners and Customs of the Indians
(of New England)*
1637

I have observed that they will not be troubled with superfluous commodities. Such things as they find they are taught by necessity to make use of, they will make choice of, and seek to purchase with industry. So that, in respect that their life is so void of care, and they are so loving also that they make use of those things they enjoy (the wife of one excepted), as common goods, and are therein so compassionate that, rather than one should starve through want, they would starve all. Thus do they pass away the time merrily, not regarding our pomp (which they feel daily before their faces), but are better content with their own, which some men esteem so meanly of.

—THOMAS MORTON
*Manners and Customs of the Indians
(of New England)*
1637

All this while the Indians came skulking about them, and would sometimes show themselves aloof off, but when any approached near them, they would run away. ... But about the 16th of March, a certain Indian came boldly amongst them and spoke to them in broken English, which they could well understand but marveled at it. At length they understood by discourse with him, that he was not of these parts, but belonged to the eastern parts where some English ships came to fish, with whom he was acquainted and could name sundry of them by their names, amongst whom he had got his language. He became profitable to them in acquainting them with many things concerning the state of the country in the east parts where he lived, which was afterwards profitable unto them; as also of the people here, of their names, number and strength, of their situation and distance from this place, and who was chief amongst them. His name was Samoset. He told them also of another Indian whose name was Squanto, a native of this place, who had been in England and could speak better English than himself.

—WILLIAM BRADFORD (1590–1657)
Of Plymouth Plantation
c. 1650

I had often before this said, that if the Indians should come, I should chuse rather to be killed by them then taken alive but when it came to the tryal my mind changed; their glittering weapons so daunted my spirit, that I chose rather to go along with those (as I may say) ravenous Bears, then that moment to end my dayes.

—MARY ROWLANDSON (c. 1636–1711)
The Soveraignty & Goodness of God,
Together, with the Faithfulness of His
Promises Displayed; Being a Narrative
of the Captivity and Restauration of
Mrs. Mary Rowlandson
1682

Every king hath his council, and that consists of all the old and wise men of his nation, which perhaps is two hundred people: nothing of moment is undertaken, be it war, peace, selling of land or traffic, without advising with them; and which is more, with the young men too. It is admirable to consider how powerful the kings are, and yet how they move by the breath of their people.

—WILLIAM PENN (1644–1718)
A Letter from William Penn
1683

Since the Europeans came into these parts, they are grown great lovers of strong liquors, rum especially, and for it exchange the richest of their skins and furs.

—WILLIAM PENN
A Letter from William Penn
1683

They care for little, because they want but little, and the reason is, a little contents them in this they are sufficiently revenged on us; if they are ignorant of our pleasures, they are also free from our pains. They are not disquieted with bills of lading and exchange, nor perplexed with Chancery suits and Exchequer-reckonings. We sweat and toil to live; their pleasure feeds them; I mean, their hunting, fishing and fowling, and this table is spread every where: they eat twice a day, morning and evening; their seats and table are the ground.

—WILLIAM PENN
A Letter from William Penn
1683

These poor people are under a dark night in things relating to religion, to be sure, the tradition of it; yet they believe in God and immortality, without the help of metaphysics; for they say there is a great king that made them, who dwells in a glorious country to the southward of them, and that the souls of the good

201

shall go thither, where they shall live again.

—WILLIAM PENN
A Letter from William Penn
1683

They had now made peace with the Indians, but there was one thing wanting to make that peace lasting. The natives could by no means persuade themselves that the English were heartily their friends so long as they disdained to intermarry with them. And, in earnest, had the English consulted their own security and the good of the colony, had they intended either to civilize or convert these gentiles, they would have brought their stomachs to embrace this prudent alliance.

—WILLIAM BYRD, II (1674–1744)
History of the Dividing Line
(Byrd is speaking about Jamestown, Virginia)
1728

I appeal to any white man to say if he ever entered Logan's cabin hungry and he gave him not meat; if ever he came cold and naked and he clothed him not?

—LOGAN (1725–1780)
Message to Lord Dunmore, governor of Virginia,
November 11, 1774

Besides the small pox and the use of spiritous liquors, the two greatest curses they have received from us, there is a sort of physical antipathy, which is equally powerful from one end of the continent to the other. Wherever they happen to be mixed, or even to live in the neighbourhood of the Europeans, they become exposed to a variety of accidents and misfortunes to which they always fall victims: such are particular fevers, to which they were strangers before, and sinking into a singular sort of indolence and sloth.

—MICHEL GUILLAUME JEAN DE
CRÈVECOEUR (1735–1813)
Letters From an American Farmer
1782

Savages we call them, because their Manners differ from ours, which we think the Perfection of Civility; they think the same of theirs. Perhaps, if we could examine the Manners of different Nations with Impartiality, we should find no People so rude, as to be without any Rules of Politness; nor any so polite, as not to have some Remains of Rudeness.

—BENJAMIN FRANKLIN (1706–1790)
Remarks Concerning the Savages of North America
1784

I believe the Indian to be in body and mind equal to the white man.

—THOMAS JEFFERSON (1743–1826)
Letter to François Jean de Beauvoir, Chevalier de Chastellux,
June 7, 1785

The two principles on which our conduct towards the Indians should be founded are justice & fear. After the injuries we have done them, they cannot love us, which leaves us no alternative but that of fear to keep them from attacking us. But justice is what we should never lose sight of, & in time it may recover their esteem.

—THOMAS JEFFERSON
To Benjamin Hawkins,
August 13, 1786

Religion, Morality and knowledge being necessary to good government and the happiness of mankind, Schools and the means of education shall forever be encouraged. The utmost good faith shall always be observed towards the Indians, their lands and property shall never be taken from them without their consent; and in their property, rights and liberty, they never shall be invaded or disturbed, unless in just and lawful wars authorized by Congress; but laws founded in justice and humanity shall from time to time be made, for preventing wrongs being done to them, and for preserving peace and friendship with them.
—ANONYMOUS
Northwest Ordinance,
1787

Humanity and good policy must make it the wish of every good citizen of the United States, that husbandry, and consequently civilization, should be introduced among the Indians. So strongly am I impressed with the beneficial effects ... that I shall always take a singular pleasure in promoting ... every measure which may tend to ensure it.
—GEORGE WASHINGTON (1732–1799)
To Timothy Pickering,
January 20, 1791

I must confess I cannot see much prospect of living in tranquility with them [Indians], so long as a spirit of land-jobbing prevails, and our frontier settlers entertain the opinion, that there is not the same crime (or indeed no crime at all) in killing an Indian as in killing a white man.
—GEORGE WASHINGTON
To David Humphreys,
July 20, 1791

We first knew you a feeble plant which wanted a little earth whereon to grow. We gave it to you; and afterward, when we could have trod you under our feet, we watered and protected you; and now you have grown to be a mighty tree, whose top reaches the clouds, and whose branches overspread the whole land, whilst we, who were the tall pine of the forest, have become a feeble plant and need your protection.
—RED JACKET (SAGOYEWATHA), Chief of the Seneca (c. 1758–1830)
Source unknown
c. 1792

In leading them [the Indians] to agriculture, to manufactures & civilization, in bringing together their & our settlements, & in preparing them ultimately to participate in the benefits of our government, I trust and believe we are acting for their greatest good.
—THOMAS JEFFERSON
Letter to Congress,
1803

Sell a country! Why not sell the air, the clouds and the great sea, as well as the earth? Did not the Great Spirit make them all for the use of his children?
—TECUMSEH (1768–1813)
Council at Vincennes, Indiana Territory,
August 14, 1810

My father! The Great Spirit is my father! The earth is my mother—and on her bosom I will recline.
—TECUMSEH
Council at Vincennes, Indiana Territory; Answer to request to sit at "his father's" (Governor William Henry Harrison's) side,
August 14, 1810

I am a Shawnee. My forefathers were warriors. Their son is a warrior. From them I take only my existence. From my tribe I take nothing. I am the maker of my own fortune. And oh, that I might make the fortunes of my red people, and of my country, as great as the conceptions of my mind, when I think of the Great Spirit that rules this universe.

—TECUMSEH
Council at Vincennes, Indiana Territory, August 14, 1810

The way, and the only way, to stop this evil [encroachment of Indian land by whites], is for all the red men to unite in claiming a common and equal right in the land, as it was at first, and should be yet, for it was never divided, but belongs to all for the use of each.

—TECUMSEH
To Governor William Henry Harrison at Vincennes, Indiana
1810

These lands are ours. No one has a right to remove us, because we were the first owners. The Great Spirit above has appointed this place for us, on which to light our fires, and here we will remain. As to boundaries, the Great Spirit knows no boundaries, nor will his red children acknowledge any.

—TECUMSEH
To Joseph Barron, messenger of President James Madison,
1810

[American Indian tribes'] rights to complete sovereignty, as independent nations, were necessarily diminished, and their power to dispose of the soil at their own will, to whomsoever they pleased, was denied by the original fundamental principle, that discovery gave exclusive title to those who made it.

—JOHN MARSHALL (1755–1835)
Johnson v. McIntosh
1823

On the discovery of this immense continent, the great nations of Europe were eager to appropriate to themselves so much of it as they could respectively acquire. Its vast extent offered an ample field to the ambition and enterprise of all; and the character and religion of its inhabitants afforded an apology for considering them as a people over whom the superior genius of Europe might claim an ascendency. ... But, as they were all in pursuit of nearly the same object, it was necessary, in order to avoid conflicting settlements, and consequent war with each other, to establish a principle, which all should acknolwedge as the law by which the right of acquisition, which they all asserted, should be regulated as between themselves. This principle was, that discovery gave title to the government by whose subjects, or by whose authority, it was made, against all other European governments, which title might be consummated by possession.

—JOHN MARSHALL
Johnson v. McIntosh
1823

[The tribes'] relation [to the United States] was that of a nation claiming and receiving the protection of one more powerful; not that of individuals abandoning their national character, and submitting as subjects to the laws of a master.

—JOHN MARSHALL
Johnson v. McIntosh
1823

NATURAL LAW

There are in nature certain foundations of justice, whence all civil laws are derived but as streams.
—*FRANCIS BACON* (1561–1626)
The Advancement of Learning
1605

The first and fundamental law of Nature ... is "to seek peace and follow it." The second, the sum of the right of Nature ... is, "by all means we can to defend ourselves."
—*THOMAS HOBBES* (1588–1679)
Leviathan
1651

Among the natural rights of the colonists are these: first, a right to *life*; secondly, to *liberty*; thirdly to *property*; together with the right to support and defend them in the best manner they can. Those are evident branches of, rather than deductions from, the duty of self-preservation, commonly called the first law of nature.
—*SAMUEL ADAMS* (1722–1803)
The Rights of the Colonists
1772

Now all acts of legislature apparently contrary to natural right and justice, are, in our laws, and must be in the nature of things considered as void. The laws of nature are the laws of God; whose authority can be superseded by no power on earth. A legislature must not obstruct our obedience to him from whose punishments they cannot protect us.
—*GEORGE MASON* (1725–1792)
Robin v. Hardaway
1772

When the first principles of civil society are violated, and the rights of a whole people are invaded, the common forms of municipal law are not to be regarded. Men may then betake themselves to the law of nature; and if they but conform their actions to that standard, all cavils against them betray either ignorance or dishonesty. There are some events in society to which human laws can not extend; but when applied to them, lose all their force and efficacy. In short, when human laws contradict or discountenance the means which are necessary to preserve the essential rights of any society, they defeat the proper ends of all laws, and so become null and void.
—*ALEXANDER HAMILTON* (1755–1804)
"A Full Vindication of the Measures of Congress"
December 15, 1774

The all wise Creator of man imprest certain laws on his nature. A desire of happiness, and of society, are two of those laws. They were not intended to destroy, but to support each other. Man has therefore a right to *promote* the *best* union of both, in order to enjoy both in the *highest* degree. Thus, while this right is properly exercised, desires, that seem *selfish*, by a happy combination, produce the welfare of *others*.
—*JOHN DICKINSON* (1732–1794)
Political Writings
1774

Human nature itself is evermore an advocate for liberty. There is also in human nature a resentment of injury, and indignation against wrong. A love of truth and a veneration of virtue. These amiable passions, are the "latent spark." ... If the people are capable of understanding, seeing and feeling the differences between true and false, right and wrong, virtue and vice, to what better principle can the friends of mankind apply than to the sense of this difference.

—*JOHN ADAMS* (1735–1826)
The Novanglus
1775

The fundamental source of all your errors, sophisms and false reasonings is a total ignorance of the natural rights of mankind. Were you once to become acquainted with these, you could never entertain a thought, that all men are not, by nature, entitled to a parity of privileges. You would be convinced, that natural liberty is a gift of the beneficent Creator to the whole human race, and that civil liberty is founded in that; and cannot be wrested from any people, without the most manifest violation of justice.

—*ALEXANDER HAMILTON*
The Farmer Refuted
1775

To grant that there is a supreme intelligence who rules the world and has established laws to regulate the actions of his creatures; and still to assert that man, in a state of nature, may be considered as perfectly free from all restraints of law and government, appears to a common understanding altogether irreconcilable. Good and wise men, in all ages, have embraced a very dissimilar theory. They have supposed that the deity, from the relations we stand in to himself and to each other, has constituted an eternal and immutable law, which is indispensably obligatory upon all mankind, prior to any human institution whatever. This is what is called

the law of nature. ... Upon this law depend the natural rights of mankind.

—*ALEXANDER HAMILTON*
The Farmer Refuted
1775

He who takes nature for his guide is not easily beaten out of his argument.

—*THOMAS PAINE* (1737–1809)
Common Sense
1776

It is not only vain, but wicked, in a legislator to frame laws in opposition to the laws of nature, and to arm them with the terrors of death. This is truly creating crimes in order to punish them.

—*THOMAS JEFFERSON* (1743–1826)
"Notes on the Crimes Bill"
1779

The transcendent law of nature and of nature's God ... declares that the safety and happiness of society are the objects at which all political institutions aim, and to which all institutions must be sacrificed.

—*JAMES MADISON* (1751–1836)
The Federalist Papers
1788

All the great laws of society are laws of nature.

—*THOMAS PAINE*
Rights of Man, II
1792

Man cannot make principles; he can only discover them.

—*THOMAS PAINE*
The Age of Reason
1794

The law of nature and the law of revela-

NATATURE & WILDLIFE

tion are both Divine; they flow, though in different channels, from the same adorable source. It is indeed preposterous to separate them from each other.
—JAMES WILSON (1742–1798)
Of the Law of Nature
1804

No man has a natural right to commit aggression on the equal rights of another, and this is all from which the laws ought to restrict him; every man is under the natural duty of contributing to the necessities of society, and this is all the laws should enforce on him and no man having a natural right to be the judge between himself and another, it is his natural duty to submit to the umpirage of an impartial third.
—THOMAS JEFFERSON
Letter to F. W. Gilmor
1816

America, with the same voice which spoke herself into existence as a nation, proclaimed to mankind the inextinguishable rights of human nature, and the only lawful foundations of government.
—JOHN QUINCY ADAMS (1767–1848)
July 4 Address,
July 4, 1821

All eyes are opened or opening to the rights of man. The general spread of the lights of science has already opened to every view the palpable truth, that the mass of mankind has not been born with saddles on their backs, nor a favored few booted and spurred, ready to ride them legitimately, by the grace of God.
—THOMAS JEFFERSON
Letter to R. C. Weightman,
June 24, 1826

NATURE & WILDLIFE

In the beginning all the world was America.
—JOHN LOCKE (1632–1704)
Two Treatises of Government
1690

It were happy if we studied nature more in natural things, and acted according to nature, whose rules are few, plain, and most reasonable.
—WILLIAM PENN (1644–1718)
Some Fruits of Solitude
1693

The country life is to be preferred; for there we see the works of God; but in cities little else but the works of men: and the one makes a better subject for our contemplation than the other.
—WILLIAM PENN
Some Fruits of Solitude
1693

There are but two natural sources of wealth and strength—the earth and the ocean.
—THOMAS PAINE (1737–1809)
Peace, and the Newfoundland Fisheries
1779

I wish the bald eagle had not been chosen as the representative of our country, he is a bird of bad moral character … like those among men who live by sharpening and robbing, he is generally poor, and often very lousy. … The turkey … is a much more respectable bird, and withal a true original native of America.
—BENJAMIN FRANKLIN (1706–1790)
Letter to Sarah Bache,
January 26, 1784

A world of this extent may, at first thought, appear to us to be great; but if we compare it with the immensity of space in which it is suspended, like a bubble or a balloon in the air, it is infinitely less in proportion than the smallest grain of sand is to the size of the world, or the finest particle of dew to the whole ocean; and is therefore but small; and ... is only *one* of a system of worlds, of which the universal creation is composed.
—THOMAS PAINE
Age of Reason, I
1794

Every thing we behold is, in one sense, a mystery to us. Our own existence is a mystery: the whole vegetable world is a mystery. We cannot account how it is that an acorn, when put into the ground, is made to develop itself, and become an oak. We know not how it is that the seed we sow unfolds and multiplies itself, and returns to us such an abundant interest for so small a capital.
—THOMAS PAINE
Age of Reason, I
1794

It is difficult beyond description to conceive that space can have no end; but it is more difficult to conceive an end.
—THOMAS PAINE
Age of Reason, I
1794

Look on this beautiful world, and read the truth / In her fair pages.
—WILLIAM CULLEN BRYANT (1794–1878)
The Ages
1821

The melancholy days are come, the saddest of the year, of wailing winds, and naked woods, and meadows brown and sere.
—WILLIAM CULLEN BRYANT
The Death of the Flowers
1825

The groves were God's first temples.
—WILLIAM CULLEN BRYANT
A Forest Hymn
1825

NECESSITY

Necessity never made a good bargain.
—BENJAMIN FRANKLIN (1706–1790)
Poor Richard's Almanack
1735

Great necessities call out great virtues.
—ABIGAIL ADAMS (1744–1818)
Letter to John Quincy Adams,
January 19, 1780

Whatever is necessary or proper to be done, must be done immediately. We must rise vigorously upon the evil, or it will rise upon us. A show of spirit will grow into real spirit.
—THOMAS PAINE (1737–1809)
To Joseph Reed,
June 4, 1780

Necessity is the plea for every infringement of human freedom. It is the argument of tyrants; it is the creed of slaves.
—WILLIAM PITT, EARL OF CHATHAM
(1708–1778)
Speech in the House of Commons,
November 18, 1783

NEW ENGLAND

A sup of New England's air is better

than a whole draft of old England's ale.
—*REV. FRANCIS HIGGINSON*
(1586–1630)
New England's Plantation
1630

In the month of June, *Anno Salutis* 1622, it was my chance to arrive in the parts of New England with 30 servants and provision of all sorts fit for a plantation; and while our houses were building, I did endeavor to take a survey of the country. The more I looked, the more I liked it. And when I had more seriously considered of the beauty of the place, with all her fair endowments, I did not think that in all the known world it could be paralleled for so many goodly groves of trees, dainty fine round rising hillocks, delicate fair large plains, sweet crystal fountains, and clear running streams that twine in fine meanders through the meads, making so sweet a murmuring noise to hear as would even lull the senses with delight asleep, so pleasantly do they glide upon the pebble stones.
—*THOMAS MORTON* (c. 1590–1647)
New English Canaan
1637

I have lived in a country seven years, and all that time I never heard one profane oath, and all that time I never did see a man drunk in that land. Where was that country? It was New England.
—*GILES FIRMIN* (Dates unknown)
Sermon to the Lords and Commons,
c. 1675

The New Englanders are a people of God, settled in those which were once the devil's territories.
—*COTTON MATHER* (1663–1728)
Wonders of the Invisible World
1693

The sway of the clergy in New England is indeed formidable. No mind beyond mediocrity dares there to develop itself.
—*THOMAS JEFFERSON* (1743–1826)
Letter to Horatio Gates Spafford,
1816

NORTH CAROLINA

Surely there is no place in the world where the inhabitants live with less labor than in North Carolina.
—*WILLIAM BYRD, II* (1674–1744)
A Journey to the Land of Eden in 1733
1733

In North Carolina, everyone does what seems best in his own eyes.
—*WILLIAM BYRD, II*
History of the Dividing Line and Other Tracts
1866

To speak the truth, 'tis a thorough aversion to labor that makes people file off to North Carolina, where plenty and a warm sun confirm them in their disposition to laziness for their whole lives.
—*WILLIAM BYRD, II*
History of the Dividing Line and Other Tracts
1866

P

Thomas Paine

There never was a man less beloved in a place than Paine in this, having at different times disputed with everybody. The most rational thing he could have done would have been to have died the instant he had finished his Common Sense, for he never again will have it in his power to leave the world with so much credit.

—*Sarah Franklin Bache*
Letter to Benjamin Franklin,
January 14, 1781

Can nothing be done in our Assembly for poor Paine? Must the merits of "Common Sense" continue to glide down the stream of time unrewarded by this country? His writings ... have had a powerful effect upon the public mind. Ought they not, then, to meet an adequate reward?

—*George Washington* (1732–1799)
Letter to James Madison,
June 12, 1784

He seems cocksure of bringing about a revolution in Great Britain and I think it quite as likely he will be promoted to the pillory.

—*Gouverneur Morris* (1752–1816)
Diary entry,
February 16, 1792

In the best of times, he had a larger share of every other sense than of common sense, and lately the intemperate use of ardent spirits has I am told, considerably impaired the small stock, which he originally possessed.

—*Gouverneur Morris*
Letter to Thomas Jefferson,
March 6, 1794

I know not whether any man in the world has had more influence on its inhabitants or affairs for the last thirty years than Tom Paine. There can be no severer satyr on the age. For such a mongrel between pig and puppy, begotten by a wild boar on a bitch wolf, never before in any age of the world was suffered by the poltroonery of mankind, to run through such a career of mischief. Call it then the Age of Paine.

—*John Adams* (1735–1826)
Letter to Benjamin Waterhouse,
October 29, 1805

His private life disgraced his public character, certain immoralities, and low and vulgar habits, which are apt to follow in the train of almost habitual drunkenness, rendered him a disgusting object for many of the latter years of his life, though his mental faculties retained much of their former luster.

—JOEL BARLOW (1754–1812)
An open letter to the *Raleigh Register*,
October 18, 1809

Paine thought more than he read.

—THOMAS JEFFERSON (1743–1826)
Letter to J. Cartwright,
1824

PASSION

I have oftentime thought that a passionate man is like a weak spring that cannot stand long locked.

—WILLIAM PENN (1644–1718)
Some Fruits of Solitude
1693

It has more of wantonness than wisdom, and resembles those that eat to please their palate, rather than their appetite.

—WILLIAM PENN
Some Fruits of Solitude
1693

Passion is a sort of fever in the mind, which ever leaves us weaker than it found us.

—WILLIAM PENN
Some Fruits of Solitude
1693

A man in a passion rides a wild horse.

—BENJAMIN FRANKLIN (1706–1790)
Poor Richard's Almanack
1749

The end of passion is the beginning of repentance.

—BENJAMIN FRANKLIN
Poor Richard's Almanack
1749

Where men have not public spirit to render themselves serviceable, it ought to be the study of government to draw the best use possible from their vices. When the governing passion of any man or set of men is once known, the method of managing them is easy; for even misers, whom no public virtue can impress, would become generous, could a heavy tax be laid upon covetousness.

—THOMAS PAINE (1737–1809)
The Crisis
1777

Men are often false to their country and their honor, false to duty and even to their interest, but multitudes of men are never long false or deaf to their passions.

—FISHER AMES (1758–1808)
Speech given in Boston,
February 8, 1800

PATRIOTISM

To a generous mind, the public good, as it is the end of government, so it is also such a noble and excellent one, that the prospect of attaining it will animate the pursuit, and being attained, it will reward the pains. The very name of patriotism is indeed become a jest with some men; which would be much stranger than it is, had not so many others made a jest of the thing, serving their own base and wicked ends, under the pretext and colour of it. But there will be hypocrites in politicks, as well as in religion. Nor ought so sacred a name to fall into contempt, however it may have been prostituted & profaned, to varnish over crimes. And those times are *perilous* indeed, wherein *men shall be* only *lovers of their own selves*, hav-

211

ing no concern for the good of the public. Shall we go to the pagans to learn this god-like virtue? Even they can teach it ... [A Christian lacking patriotism] ... would be a reproach not only to his religion, a religion of charity and beneficence, but even to our own common nature, as corrupt and depraved as it is. But how much more infamous were this, in persons of public character? in those, on whom the welfare of their country, under providence, immediately depends?

—REV. JONATHAN MAYHEW (1720–1776)
Election sermon,
1754

The only [worthy] principles of public conduct ... are to sacrifice estate, ease, health, and applause, and even life, to the sacred calls of his country. These manly sentiments, in private life, make the good citizen in public life, the patriot and the hero.

—JAMES OTIS (1725–1783)
Statement in court opposing "Writs of Assistance,"
1761

Where is the man who owes nothing to the land in which he lives? Whatever that land may be, he owes to it the most precious thing possessed by man, the morality of his actions and the love of virtue.

—JEAN JACQUES ROUSSEAU (1712–1778)
Emile; or, On Education
1762

The *true patriot* therefore, will enquire into the causes of the *fears* and *jealousies* of his countrymen; and if he finds they are not *groundless*, he will be far from endeavoring to allay or stifle them:

On the contrary, constrain'd by the *Amor Patriae* and from *public* views, he will by all proper means in his power *foment* and *cherish* them: He will, as far as he is able, keep the attention of his fellow citizens awake to their grievances; and not suffer them to be at rest, till the causes of their just complaints are removed.—At such a time Philanthrop's Patriot [a King's man] may be "very cautious of charging the want of ability or integrity to those with whom any of the powers of government are entrusted": But the true patriot, will constantly be jealous of those very men: Knowing that power, especially in times of corruption, makes men wanton; that it intoxicates the mind; and unless those with whom it is entrusted, are carefully watched, such is the weakness or the perverseness of human nature, they will be apt to domineer over the people, instead of governing them, according to the known laws of the state, to which alone they have submitted. If he finds, upon the best enquiry, the want of ability or integrity; that is, an ignorance of, or a disposition to depart from, the constitution, which is the measure and rule of government & submission, he will point them out, and loudly proclaim them: He will stir up the people, incessantly to complain of such men, till they are either reform'd, or remov'd from that sacred trust, which it is dangerous for them any longer to hold.

—SAMUEL ADAMS (1722–1803)
Essay in the *Boston Gazette*,
1771

Patriotism is as much a virtue as justice, and is as necessary for the support of societies as natural affection is for the support of families. The Amor Patriae is both a moral and a religious duty. It comprehends not only the love of our neighbors but of millions of our fellow creatures, not only of the present but of future generations. This virtue we find constitutes a part of the first characters of history.

—*BENJAMIN RUSH* (1745–1813)
Untitled essay,
1773

Men must be ready, they must pride themselves and be happy to sacrifice their private pleasures, passions and interests, nay, their private friendships and dearest connections, when they stand in competition with the rights of society.

—*JOHN QUINCY ADAMS* (1767–1848)
To Mercy Warren,
April 16, 1776

Our affairs are hastening fast to a Crisis; and the approaching Campaign will, in all probability, determine forever the fate of America. ... The Militia of the United Colonies are a Body of Troops that may be depended upon. To their Virtue, their Delegates in Congress now make the most solemn Appeal. They are called upon to say, whether they will live Slaves, or die Freemen. They are requested to step forth in Defense of their Wives, their Children, their Liberty, and every Thing they hold dear. The Cause is certainly a most glorious one; and I hope every Man in the Colony of Maryland is determined to see it gloriously ended, or to perish in the Ruins of it.

—*JOHN HANCOCK* (1737–1793)
To the Convention of Maryland,
June 4, 1776

Our own Country's Honor, all call upon us for a vigorous and manly exertion, and if we now shamefully fail, we shall become infamous to the whole world. Let us therefore rely upon the goodness of the Cause, and the aid of the supreme Being, in whose hands Victory is, to animate and encourage us to great and noble Actions.

—*GEORGE WASHINGTON* (1732–1799)
General Orders,
July 2, 1776

The hour is fast approaching, on which the Honor and Success of this army, and the safety of our bleeding Country depend.

Remember officers and Soldiers, that you are Freemen, fighting for the blessings of Liberty—that slavery will be your portion, and that of your posterity, if you do not acquit yourselves like men.

—*GEORGE WASHINGTON*
General Orders,
August 23, 1776

I only regret that I have but one life to lose for my country.

—*NATHAN HALE* (1755–1776)
Speech before the gallows in New York where he was to be hanged for spying against the British,
September 22, 1776

These are the times that try men's souls. The summer solider and the sunshine patriot will, in this crisis, shrink from the services of their country, but he that stands it NOW deserves the love and thanks of man and woman.

—*THOMAS PAINE* (1737–1809)
The Crisis
1776

The Sun never shined on a cause of greater worth.

—*THOMAS PAINE*
Common Sense
1776

There must be a positive passion for the public good, the public interest, honour, power and glory, established in the minds of people, or there can be no republication government nor any real liberty: and this public passion must be superior to all private passions. Men must be ready, they must pride themselves and be happy to sacrifice their private pleasures, passions, and interests, nay, their private friendships and dearest connections, when they stand in competition with the rights of society.

—*JOHN ADAMS* (1735–1826)
To Mercy Warren,
1776

Banish unmanly fear, acquit yourselves like men, and with firm confidence trust the event with that Almighty and benevolent Being who hath commanded you to hold fast the liberty with which he has made you free; and who is able as well as willing to support you in performing his orders.

—*JOHN JAY* (1745–1829)
To the General Committee of Tryon County,
July 22, 1777

What reason is there to expect that Heaven will help those who refuse to help themselves; or that Providence will grant liberty to those who want courage to defend it. ... Let not the history of the present glorious contest declare to future generations that the people of your country, after making the highest professions of zeal for the American cause, fled at the first appearance of danger, and behaved like women. ... Instead of supplicating the protection of your enemies, meet them with arms in your hands—make good your professions, and let not your attachment to freedom be manifested only in your words.

—*JOHN JAY*
To the General Committee of Tryon County,
July 22, 1777

The approbation of my country is what I wish; and, as far as my abilities and opportunities will permit, I hope I shall endeavor to deserve it. It is the highest reward to a feeling mind; and happy are they, who so conduct themselves to merit it.

—*GEORGE WASHINGTON*
To Patrick Henry,
March 28, 1778

I will venture to assert, that a great and lasting war can never be supported on this principle [patriotism] alone. It must be aided by a prospect of interest or some reward.

—*GEORGE WASHINGTON*
To John Banister,
April 21, 1778

It is not difficult to regard men of every nation as members of the same family; but when placed in that point of view, my fellow citizens appear to me as my brethren, and the others as related to me only in the more distant and adventitious degrees.

—*JOHN JAY*
To Gouverneur Morris,
1783

My affections are deeply rooted in America, and are of too long standing to admit of transplantation. In short, my friend, I can never become so far a citizen of the world as to view every part of it with equal regard; and perhaps nature is wiser in tying our hearts to our native soil, than they are who think they divest themselves of foibles in proportion as they wear away those bonds.

—JOHN JAY
To Gouverneur Morris,
1783

I would go to hell for my country.
—THOMAS JEFFERSON (1743–1826)
Upon being appointed commissioner
to France,
1785

It is unquestionably true, that the great body of the people love their country, and wish it prosperity; and this observation is particularly applicable to the people of a free country, for they have more and stronger reasons for loving it than others.

—JOHN JAY
Address to the People of New York,
1787

The consciousness of having discharged that duty which we owe to our country is superior to all other considerations.

—GEORGE WASHINGTON
To James Madison,
March 2, 1788

Delightful are the prospects that will open to the view of United America— her sons well prepared to defend their own happiness, and ready to relieve the misery of others—her fleets formidable, but only to the unjust—her revenue sufficient, yet unoppressive—her commerce affluent, without debasing— peace and plenty within her borders— and the glory that arises from a proper use of power, encircling them.

—JOHN DICKINSON (1732–1794)
Letters of Fabius #8,
1788

I was summoned by my country, whose voice I can never hear but with veneration and love.

—GEORGE WASHINGTON
First Inaugural Address,
April 30, 1789

Guard against the postures of pretended patriotism.

—GEORGE WASHINGTON
Farewell Address,
September 17, 1796

God in his great goodness grant, in the future vicissitudes of the world, that our countrymen, whenever their essential rights shall be attacked, will divest themselves of all party prejudice, and devote their lives and properties in defence of the sacred liberties of their country, without any view to emolument, but that which springs from glorious and honorable actions.

—JOHN JOSEPH HENRY (1759–1811)
Journal
1811

Enemies beware, keep a proper distance,
Else we'll make you stare at our firm resistance;
Let alone the lads who are freedom tasting,

Don't forget our dads gave you once a
basting.
To protect our rights 'gainst your flint
and triggers
See on yonder heights our patriotic diggers.
Men of ev'ry age, color, rank, profession,
Ardently engaged, labor in succession.
Pick-axe, shovel, spade, crow-bar, hoe
and barrow
Better not invade, Yankees have the
marrow.

Scholars leave their schools with patriotic teachers
Farmers seize their tools, headed by
their preachers,
How they break the soil—brewers,
butchers, bakers—
Here the doctors toil, there the under-
takers.
Bright Apollo's sons leave their pipe and
tabor,
Mid the roar of guns join the martial
labor,
Round the embattled plain in sweet concord rally,
And in freedom's strain sing the foes
finale.
Pick-axe, shovel, spade, crow-bar, hoe
and barrow
Better not invade, Yankees have the
marrow.

Better not invade, don't forget the spirit
Which our dads displayed and their sons
inherit.
If you still advance, friendly caution
slighting,
You may get by chance a bellyful of
fighting!
Plumbers, founders, dyers, tinmen,
turners, shavers,

Sweepers, clerks, and criers, jewelers
and engravers,
Clothiers, drapers, players, cartmen,
hatters, tailors,
Gaugers, sealers, weighers, carpenters
and sailors!
Pick-axe, shovel, spade, crow-bar, hoe
and barrow
Better not invade, Yankees have the
marrow.
—SAMUEL WOODWORTH (1785–1842)
"The Patriotic Diggers"
1812

Our country! In her intercourse with
foreign nations, may she always be in
the right; but our country, right or
wrong.
—STEPHEN DECATUR (1779–1820)
Toast at dinner in his honor,
April 1816

The individual owes the exercise of all
his faculties to the service of his coun-
try.
—JOHN QUINCY ADAMS
Letter to Francis Calley Gray,
August 3, 1818

When a whole nation is roaring Patriotism at the top of its voice, I am fain to
explore the cleanliness of its hands and
the purity of its heart.
—RALPH WALDO EMERSON (1803–1882)
Journal
1824

Let our object be, Our Country, our
whole Country, and nothing but our
Country.
—DANIEL WEBSTER (1782–1852)
Speech at the setting of the corner-
stone for the Bunker Hill monument,
June 17, 1825

PATRONAGE & APPOINTMENTS

The appointment to offices is, of all the functions of Republican and perhaps every other form of Government, the most difficult to guard against abuse. Give it to a numerous body, and you at once destroy all responsibility, and create a perpetual source of faction and corruption. Give it to the Executive wholly, and it may be made an engine of improper influence and favoritism.

—JAMES MADISON (1751–1836)
Observations on Jefferson's Draft
Constitution,
October 15, 1788

I think it absolutely necessary that the President should have the power of removing [his subordinates] from office; it will make him, in a peculiar manner, responsible for their conduct, and subject him to impeachment himself, if he suffers them to perpetrate with impunity high crimes or misdemeanors against the United States, or neglects to superintend their conduct, so as to check their excesses.

—JAMES MADISON
Remarks in the House of
Representatives,
May 19, 1789

My political conduct in nominations, even if I was influenced by principle, must be exceedingly circumspect and proof against lust criticism, for the eyes of Argus are upon me, and no slip will pass unnoticed that can be improved into a supposed partiality for friends or relatives.

—GEORGE WASHINGTON (1732–1799)
Letter to Bushrod Washington,
July 27, 1789

If due participation of office is a matter of right, how are vacancies to be obtained? Those by death are few; by resignation, none.

—THOMAS JEFFERSON (1743–1826)
Letter to Elias Simpson et al.,
July 12, 1801

On the appointment to office, I have been forc'd either to distribute the offices among the friends of the candidates, to guard myself against the imputation of favoritism, or to take my own course, and appoint those whom I knew & confided in, without regard to them. Had I pursued the former, the office in my hands, for two or three years of the latter term, would have sunk to nothing. I therefore adopted the latter, and have steadily pursued it, believing that I had given sufficient proof of respect for, and confidence in each of the members of the administration, by appointing & continuing him in his place.

—JAMES MONROE (1758–1831)
Letter to Thomas Jefferson,
March 22, 1824

PEACE

To preserve peace will no doubt be difficult, but by accomplishing it we can show our wisdom and magnanimity, and secure to our people the enjoyment of a dignified repose by indulging which they will be prosperous and happy.

—JAMES MONROE (1758–1831)
Letter to *Cocked Hats*,
Date unknown

*Cedant arma togae** is a glorious sentence; the voice of the dove; the olive branch of peace. A blessing so great, that when it pleases God to chastise us severely for our sins, it is with the rod of war, that, for the most part, He whips us: and experience tells us none leaves deeper marks behind it.

—*WILLIAM PENN* (1644–1718)
"An Essay Towards the Present and Future Peace of Europe"
1693
*May arms yield to the gown; let violence give place to law.

There appears to me but three things upon which peace is broken, viz. to keep, to recover, or to add.

—*WILLIAM PENN*
"An Essay Towards the Present and Future Peace of Europe"
1693

What can we desire better than peace, but the grace to use it? Peace preserves our possessions; we are in no danger of invasions: our trade is free and safe, and we rise and lie down without anxiety. The rich bring out their hoards, and employ the poor manufacturers: buildings and diverse projections, for profit and pleasure, go on: it excites industry, which brings wealth, as that gives the means of charity and hospitality, not the lowest ornaments of a kingdom or commonwealth. But war ... seizes all these comforts at once, and stops the civil channel of society. The rich draw in their stock, the poor turn soldiers, or thieves, or starve: no industry, no building, no manufactury, little hospitality or charity; but what the peace gave, the war devours.

—*WILLIAM PENN*
"An Essay Towards the Present and Future Peace of Europe"
1693

Knowing to what violent resentments and incurable animosities civil discords are apt to exasperate and inflame the contending parties, we think ourselves required by indispensable obligations to Almighty God, to your Majesty, to our fellow-subjects, and to ourselves, immediately to use all the means in our power, not incompatible with our safety, for stopping the further effusion of blood, and for averting the impending calamities that threaten the British Empire.

—*ANONYMOUS*
Olive Branch Petition, a last attempt by moderate colonists to avoid war with Great Britain,
July 8, 1775

Our plan is peace forever.

—*THOMAS PAINE* (1737–1809)
Common Sense
1776

The love and desire of peace is not confined to Quakerism, it is the *natural*, as well as the religious wish of all denominations of man.

—*THOMAS PAINE*
Common Sense
1776

I have never known a peace made, even the most advantageous, that was not censured as inadequate, and the makers condemned as injudicious or corrupt. "Blessed are the peacemakers" is, I suppose, to be understood in the other world; for in this they are frequently cursed.

—*BENJAMIN FRANKLIN* (1706–1790)
To John Adams,
October 12, 1781

A universal and perpetual peace, it is to

be feared, is in the catalogue of events, which will never exist but in the imaginations of visionary philosophers, or in the breasts of benevolent enthusiasts. It is still however true, that war contains so much folly, as well as wickedness, that much is to be hoped from the progress of reason; and if any thing is to be hoped, every thing ought to be tried.
—JAMES MADISON (1751–1836)
Article in *The National Gazette*,
February 2, 1792

As to myself, I love peace, and I am anxious that we should give the world still another useful lesson, by showing to them other modes of punishing injuries than by war, which is as much a punishment to the punisher as to the sufferer.
—THOMAS JEFFERSON (1743–1826)
To Tench Coxe,
May 1, 1794

Peace is the best time for improvement and preparation of every kind; it is in peace that our commerce flourishes most, that taxes are most easily paid, and that the revenue is most productive.
—JAMES MONROE
First Inaugural Address,
March 4, 1817

Great calamities make appeals to the benevolence of mankind, which ought not to be resisted. Good offices in such emergencies exalt the character of the party rendering them. By exciting grateful feelings, they soften the intercourse between nations, and tend to prevent war.
—JAMES MONROE
Message to Congress,
May 4, 1822

PENNSYLVANIA

But if I have been unkindly used by some I left behind me, I found love and respect enough where I came: an universal kind welcome, every sort in their way.
—WILLIAM PENN (1644–1718)
"A Letter from William Penn"
1683

The air is sweet and clear, the heavens serene.
—WILLIAM PENN
"A Letter from William Penn"
1683

The woods are adorned with lovely flowers, for colour, greatness, figure and variety: I have seen the gardens of London best stored with that sort of beauty, but think they may be improved by our woods.
—WILLIAM PENN
"A Letter from William Penn"
1683

Pennsylvania is the Keystone of the Democratic arch.
—PENNSYLVANIA DEMOCRATIC COMMITTEE
1803

PERSEVERANCE & DETERMINATION

Patience and diligence, like faith, remove mountains.
—WILLIAM PENN (1644–1718)
Some Fruits of Solitude
1693

Without Steadiness or Perseverance no Virtue can long subsist; and however honest and well-meaning a Man's Principles may be, the Want of this is suffi-

219

cient to render them ineffectual, and useless to himself or others.
—BENJAMIN FRANKLIN (1706–1790)
"On Constancy," in the
Pennsylvania Gazette,
April 4, 1734

An indifferent measure carried through with perseverance is better than a good one taken up only at intervals.
—THOMAS JEFFERSON (1743–1826)
To Timothy Pickering,
September 6, 1780

A progressive state is necessary to the happiness and perfection of man. Whatever attainments are already reached, attainments still higher should be pursued. Let us, therefore, strive with noble emulation. Let us suppose we have done nothing, while any thing yet remains to be done. Let us, with fervent zeal, press forward, and make unceasing advances in every thing that can support, improve, refine, or embellish society. ... The commencement of our government has been eminently glorious: let our progress in every excellence be proportionably great. It will—it must be so.
—JAMES WILSON (1741–1798)
Oration,
July 4, 1788

PESSIMISM & OPTIMISM

It is incumbent upon us, and contributes also to our own tranquility, that we put the best construction upon a thing it will bear.
—THOMAS PAINE (1737–1809)
Age of Reason, II
1795

I think with you, that it is a good world

on the whole; that it has been framed on a principle of benevolence, and more pleasure than pain dealt out to us. There are, indeed, (who might say nay) gloomy and hypochondriac minds, inhabitants of diseased bodies, disgusted with the present, and despairing of the future; always counting that the worst will happen, because it may happen. To these I say, how much pain have cost us the evils which have never happened! My temperament is sanguine. I steer my bark with Hope in the head, leaving Fear in the stern. My hopes, indeed, sometimes fail; but not oftener than the forebodings of the gloomy. There are, I acknowledge, even in the happiest life, some terrible convulsions, heavy setoffs against the opposite page of the account.
—THOMAS JEFFERSON (1743–1826)
To John Adams,
April 1816

PHILOSOPHY & ETHICS

A little philosophy inclineth man's mind to atheism, but depth in philosophy bringeth men's minds about to religion.
—FRANCIS BACON (1561–1626)
Of Atheism
c. 1625

Philosophy as well as foppery often changes fashion.
—BENJAMIN FRANKLIN (1706–1790)
Poor Richard's Almanack
1753

The skeptical philosophers claim and exercise the privilege of assuming, without proof, the very first principles of their philosophy; and yet they require, from others, a proof of everything by reasoning. They are unreasonable in both points.

—JAMES WILSON (1741–1798)
Lectures,
1790–1791

There is ... only a single categorical imperative and it is this: Act only on that maxim through which you can at the same time will that it should become a universal law.

—IMMANUEL KANT (1724–1804)
The Metaphysic of Morals
1797

PLEASURE & PAIN

Pain wastes the body, pleasure the understanding.

—BENJAMIN FRANKLIN (1706–1790)
Poor Richard's Almanack
1735

There is no truth more certain than that all our enjoyments fall short of our expectations.

—GEORGE WASHINGTON (1732–1799)
To Elizabeth Parke Custis,
September 14, 1794

I do not agree that an age of pleasure is no compensation for a moment of pain. I think, with you, that life is a fair matter of account, and the balance often, nay generally, in its favor. It is not indeed easy, by calculation of intensity and time, to apply a common measure, or to fix the par between pleasure and pain; yet it exists, and is measurable.

—THOMAS JEFFERSON (1743–1826)
To John Adams,
August 1816

POLITICAL PARTIES & FACTIONS

The little wranglings and indecent contentions of personal party, are as dishonorable to our characters, as they are injurious to our repose.

—THOMAS PAINE (1737–1809)
The Crisis
1783

A zeal for different opinions concerning religion, concerning government, and many other points, as well of speculation as of practice; an attachment of different leaders ambitiously contending for preeminence and power; or to persons of other descriptions whose fortunes have been interesting to the human passions, have, in turn, divided mankind into parties, inflamed them with mutual animosity, and rendered them much more disposed to vex and oppress each other than to cooperate for their common good. ... But the most common and durable source of factions has been the various and unequal distribution of property.

—JAMES MADISON (1751–1836)
The Federalist Papers
1787

To secure the public good, and private rights, against the danger of ... faction, and at the same time to preserve the spirit and form of popular government, is then the great object to which our inquiries are directed.

—JAMES MADISON
The Federalist Papers
1787

By a faction, understand a number of citizens, whether amounting to a majority or minority of the whole, who are united and actuated by some common impulse of passion, or of interest, adverse to the rights of other citizens, or to the permanent and aggregate interests of the community.

—*JAMES MADISON*
The Federalist Papers
1787

[On factionalism—the tendency to form special interest groups]: Liberty is to faction what air is to fire, an element without which it instantly expires. But it could not be less folly to abolish liberty, which is essential to political life, because it nourishes faction, than it would be to wish the annihilation of air, which is essential to animal life, because it imparts to fire its destructive agency.

—*JAMES MADISON*
The Federalist Papers
1787

No free Country has ever been without parties, which are a natural offspring of Freedom.

—*JAMES MADISON*
Note on his suffrage speech at the Constitutional Convention of 1787, 1787

Party knows no impulse but spirit, no prize but victory. It is blind to truth, and hardened against conviction. It seeks to justify error by perseverance, and denies to its own mind the operation of its own judgment. A man under the tyranny of party spirit is the greatest slave upon earth, for none but himself can deprive him of the freedom of thought.

—*THOMAS PAINE*
"To the Opposers of the Bank"
1787

I am not a Federalist, because I never submitted the whole system of my opinions to the creed of any party of men whatever in religion, in philosophy, in politics, or in any thing else where I was capable of thinking for myself. Such an addiction is the last degradation of a free and moral agent. If I could not go to heaven but with a party, I would not go there at all.

—*THOMAS JEFFERSON* (1743–1826)
To Francis Hopkinson,
March 13, 1789

In all political societies, different interests and parties arise out of the nature of things, and the great art of politicians lies in making them checks and balances to each other.

—*JAMES MADISON*
Article in the *National Gazette*,
January 23, 1792

A little matter will move a party, but it must be something great that moves a nation.

—*THOMAS PAINE*
Rights of Man
1792

It is the nature and intention of a constitution to *prevent governing by party*, by establishing a common principle that shall limit and control the power and impulse of party, and that says to all parties, *thus far shalt thou go and no further*. But in the absence of a constitution, men look entirely to party; and instead of principle governing party, party governs principle.

—*THOMAS PAINE*
Dissertation on the First Principles of Government
1795

Let me now ... warn you in the most solemn manner against the baneful effects of the spirit of party. ... It serves always to distract the public councils and enfeebles the public administration. It agitates the community with ill-founded jealousies and false alarms; kindles the animosity of one party against another; foments occasionally riot and insurrection. It opens the door to foreign influence and corruption. ... A fire not to be quenched, it demands a uniform vigilance to prevent its bursting into flame, lest, instead of warming, it should consume.

—*GEORGE WASHINGTON* (1732–1799)
Farewell Address,
September 17, 1796

I have already observed the danger to be apprehended from founding our parties on geographical discrimination.

—*ALEXANDER HAMILTON* (1755–1804)
From the original draft in Hamilton's
hand of Washington's
Farewell Address,
c. 1796

Every difference of opinion is not a difference of principle. We have called by different names brethren of the same principle. We are all Republicans, we are all Federalists. If there be any among us who would wish to dissolve this Union or to change its republican form, let them stand undisturbed as monuments of the safety with which error of opinion may be tolerated where reason is left free to combat it.

—*THOMAS JEFFERSON*
First Inaugural Address,
March 4, 1801

In the history of parties and the names

they assume, it often happens, that they finish by the direct contrary principles with which they profess to begin.

—*THOMAS PAINE*
To the Citizens of the United States
1802

I could never do anything but was ascribed to sinister motives.

—*JOHN ADAMS* (1735–1826)
Letter to Benjamin Rush,
August 28, 1811

Within the local limits, parties generally exist, founded on the different sorts of property, even sometimes on divisions by streets or little streams; frequently on political and religious differences. Attachments to rival individuals, are not seldom a source of the same divisions. In all these cases, the party animosities are the more violent as the compass of the Society may more easily admit of the contagion and collision of the passions; and according to that violence is the danger of oppression by one party on the other; by the majority on the minority.

—*JAMES MADISON*
Detached Memoranda,
1817

POSTERITY

If we would amend the world, we should mend ourselves; and teach our children to be, not what we are, but what they should be.

—*WILLIAM PENN* (1644–1718)
Some Fruits of Solitude
1693

We are too careless of posterity, not

considering that as they are, so the next generation will be.
—*WILLIAM PENN*
Some Fruits of Solitude
1693

If there must be trouble let it be in my day, that my child may have peace.
—*THOMAS PAINE* (1737-1809)
The Crisis
1776

Posterity! You will never know how much it cost the present generation to preserve your freedom! I hope you will make good use of it! If you do not, I shall repent it in heaven that I ever took half the pains to preserve it!
—*JOHN ADAMS* (1735–1826)
To Abigail Adams,
1777

It should be the highest ambition of every American to extend his views beyond himself, and to bear in mind that his conduct will not only affect himself, his country, and his immediate posterity; but that its influence may be co-extensive with the world, and stamp political happiness or misery on ages yet unborn.
—*GEORGE WASHINGTON* (1732–1799)
To the legislature of Pennsylvania,
September 5, 1789

The little spice of ambition which I had in my younger days has long since evaporated, and I set still less store by a posthumous than a present name.
—*THOMAS JEFFERSON* (1743–1826)
Letter to James Madison,
1795

Let us develop the resources of our land,
call forth its powers, build up its institutions, promote all its great interests, and see whether we also, in our day and generation, may not perform something worthy to be remembered.
—*DANIEL WEBSTER* (1782–1852)
Address (These words are also incised in marble on the wall of the U.S. House of Representatives chamber),
June 17, 1825

POVERTY & ECONOMIC INEQUALITY

It is a reproach to religion and government to suffer so much poverty and excess.
—*WILLIAM PENN* (1644–1718)
Some Fruits of Solitude
1693

Were the superfluities of a nation valued, and made a perpetual tax or benevolence, there would be more alms-houses than poor; schools than scholars; and enough to spare for government besides.
—*WILLIAM PENN*
Some Fruits of Solitude
1693

One half of the world does not know how the other half lives.
—*BENJAMIN FRANKLIN* (1706–1790)
Poor Richard's Almanack
1755

I have no doubt but that the misery of the lower classes will be found to abate wherever the Government assumes a freer aspect, & the laws favor a subdivision of property.
—*JAMES MADISON* (1751–1836)
Letter to Thomas Jefferson,
June 19, 1786

If equality is as I contend the leading feature of the U. States, where then are the riches and wealth whose representation and protection is the peculiar province of this permanent body. Are they in the hands of the few who may be called rich; in the possession of less than a hundred citizens? Certainly not. They are in the great body of the people, among whom there are no men of wealth, and very few of real poverty.

—*CHARLES PINCKNEY* (1757–1824)
"Plan of a Government for America"
June 25, 1787

All communities divide themselves into the few and the many. The first are the rich and well-born, the other the mass of the people.

—*ALEXANDER HAMILTON* (1755–1804)
To the Constitutional Convention,
1787

It is only in civilized nations where extremes are to be found in the human species—it is here where wealthy and dignified mortals roll along the streets in all the parade and trappings of royalty, while the lower class are not half so well fed as the horses of the former. It is this cruel inequality which has given rise to the epithets of nobility, vulgar, mob, canaille, etc. and the degrading, but common observation— Man differs more from man, than man from beast—The difference is purely artificial. Thus do men create an artificial inequality among themselves and then cry out it is all natural.

—*ROBERT CORAM* (1761–1796)
"Political Inquiries, to which is added a plan for the establishment of schools throughout the United States"
1791

That property will ever be unequal is certain. Industry, superiority of talents, dexterity of management, extreme frugality, fortunate opportunities, or the opposite, or the means of those things, will ever produce that effect, without having recourse to the harsh, ill-sounding names of avarice and oppression.

—*THOMAS PAINE* (1737–1809)
Dissertation on First Principles of Government
1795

It is the practice of what has unjustly obtained the name of civilization (and the practice merits not to be called either charity or policy) to make some provision for persons becoming poor and wretched, only at the time they become so. Would it not, even as a matter of economy, be far better, to devise means to prevent their becoming poor.

—*THOMAS PAINE*
Agrarian Justice
1797

Poverty ... is a thing created by that which is called civilized life. It exists not in the natural state.

—*THOMAS PAINE*
Agrarian Justice
1797

I care not how affluent some may be, provided that none be miserable in consequence of it. But it is impossible to enjoy affluence with the felicity it is capable of being enjoyed, while so much misery is mingled in the scene. The sight of the misery, and the unpleasant sensations it suggests, which, though they may be suffocated cannot be extinguished, are a greater drawback upon the felicity of affluence than the proposed 10 percent [inheritance tax] upon property is worth. He that would not give the one to get rid of the other, has no charity, even for himself.

—THOMAS PAINE
Agrarian Justice
1797

The great mass of the poor, in all countries, are become an hereditary race, and it is next to impossible for them to get out of that state of themselves. It ought also to be observed, that this mass increases in all the countries that are called civilized. More persons fall annually into it, than get out of it.

—THOMAS PAINE
Agrarian Justice
1797

I have not observed men's honesty to increase with their riches.

—THOMAS JEFFERSON (1743–1826)
Letter to Jeremiah Moore,
1800

The freest government, if it could exist, would be not be long acceptable, if the tendency of the laws were to create a rapid accumulation of property in few hands, and to render the great mass of the population dependent and penniless. In such a case, the popular power would be likely to break in upon the rights of property, or else the influence of property to limit and control the exercise of popular power. ... In the nature of things, those who have not property, and see their neighbors possess much more than they think them to need, cannot be favorable to laws made for the protection of property. When this class becomes numerous, it grows clamorous. It looks on property as its prey and plunder, and is naturally ready, at all times, for violence and revolution.

—DANIEL WEBSTER (1782–1852)
"First Settlement of New England,"
speech delivered at Plymouth, Massachusetts, to commemorate the 200th anniversary of the landing of the Pilgrims,
December 22, 1820

To provide employment for the poor and support for the indigent is among the primary, and at the same time not least difficult cares of the public authority. In very populous Countries the task is particularly arduous. In our favored Country where employment and food are much less subject to failures or deficiencies the interposition of the public guardianship is required in a far more limited degree. Some degree of interposition nevertheless, is at all times and every where called for.

—JAMES MADISON
To Frederick C. Schaeffer,
January 8, 1820

In general, the great can protect themselves, but the poor and humble require the arm and shield of the law.

—ANDREW JACKSON (1767–1845)
Letter to John Quincy Adams,
August 26, 1821

POWER

We ought at the same time to be upon our guard against Power, wherever we apprehend that it may affect ourselves or our Fellow-Subjects. ... Power may be justly compared to a great river which, while kept within its due bounds is both beautiful and useful; but when it overflows its banks, is then too impetuous to be stemmed, it bears down all before it and brings destruction and desolation wherever it goes. If this then is the nature of power, let us at least do our duty, and likewise men use our utmost care to support liberty, the only bulwark against lawless power.

—ANDREW HAMILTON(?–1741)
Defense of Peter Zenger,
1735

For one person alone to have the Government of a people in his hands, would be too great a Temptation. It tends to excite and draw forth the Pride of man, to make him unsufferably haughty; it gives him too much liberty to exert his corruptions and it encourages him to become a Tyrant and an oppressor, to dispense with Laws and break the most solemn oaths.

—JOHN BARNARD (1681–1770)
The Presence of Great God in the
Assembly of Political Rulers
1746

The jaws of power are always open to devour, and her arm is always stretched out, if possible, to destroy the freedom of thinking, speaking, and writing.

—JOHN ADAMS (1735–1826)
"Dissertation on the Canon and
Feudal Law"
1765

Although unrestrained power in one person may have been the first and most natural recourse of mankind from rapine and disorder; yet all restrictions of power, made by laws, or participation of sovereignty, are apparent improvements upon what began in unlimited power.

—BENJAMIN CHURCH (1734–1778)
Boston Massacre Oration,
March 5, 1773

Nip the shoots of arbitrary power in the bud, is the only maxim which can ever preserve the liberties of any people.

—JOHN ADAMS
In the Boston Gazette,
February 6, 1775

I am more and more convinced that man is a dangerous creature and that power, whether vested in many or a few, is ever grasping, and like the grave cries, "Give, Give."

—ABIGAIL ADAMS (1744–1818)
Letter to John Adams,
November 27, 1775

A fondness for power is implanted, in most men, and it is natural to abuse it, when acquired.

—ALEXANDER HAMILTON (1755–1804)
The Farmer Refuted
1775

It is a maxim that in every government, there must exist, somewhere, a supreme, sovereign, absolute, and uncontrollable power; but this power resides always in the body of the people; and it never was, or can be delegated to one man, or a few; the great Creator has never given to men a right to vest others with authority over them, unlimited either in duration or degree.

—ANONYMOUS
General Court of Massachusetts,
Proclamation,
January 23, 1776

[A]s all Men of Delicacy and Sentiment are averse to Exercising the power they possess, yet as there is a natural propensity in Human Nature to domination, I thought the most generous plan was to put it out of the power of the Arbitrary and Tyranick to injure us with impunity by Establishing some Laws in our favour upon just and Liberal principles.

—ABIGAIL ADAMS
Letter to Mercy Otis Warren,
April 27, 1776

A long and violent abuse of power, is generally the Means of calling the right of it in question.

—THOMAS PAINE (1737–1809)
Common Sense
1776

We repose an unwise confidence in any government, or in any men, when we invest them officially with too much, or an unnecessary quantity of, discretionary power; for though we might clearly confide in almost any man of the present age, yet we ought ever to remember that virtue is not hereditary either in the office or in the persons.

—THOMAS PAINE
"A Serious Address to the People of Pennsylvania"
1778

Uncontrolled power, in the hands of an incensed, imperious and rapacious conqueror, is an engine of dreadful execution; and woe be to that country over which it can be exercised.

—THOMAS PAINE
The Crisis Extraordinary
1780

Benignity, moderation, and justice, are virtues adapted only to the humble paths of life: we love to talk of virtue and to admire its beauty, while in the shade of solitude, and retirement; but when we step forth into active life, if it happen to be in competition with any passion or desire, do we observe it to prevail? Hence so many religious impostors have triumphed over the credulity of mankind, and have rendered their frauds the creeds of succeeding generations, during the course of many ages; until worne away by time, they have been replaced by new ones. Hence the most unjust war, if supported by the greatest force, always succeeds; hence the most just ones, when supported only by their justice, as often fail. Such is the ascendancy of power; the supreme arbiter of all the revolutions which we observe in this planet: so irresistible is power, that it often thwarts the tendency of the most forcible causes, and prevents their subsequent salutary effects, though ordained for the good of man by the Governor of the universe.

—MICHEL GUILLAUME JEAN DE
CRÈVECOEUR (1735–1813)
Letters From an American Farmer
1782

The abuse of any power always operates to call the right of that power in question.

—THOMAS PAINE
Attack on Paper Money Laws
1786

Men always love power.

—ALEXANDER HAMILTON
(1755–1804)
Constitutional Convention,
June 18, 1787

228

All men having power ought to be distrusted to a certain degree.

—JAMES MADISON (1751–1836)
Speech to the Constitutional
Convention,
July 11, 1787

The substantial basis of the power of a nation arises out of its population, its wealth and its revenues. To these may be added the disposition of the people.

—THOMAS PAINE
Prospects on the Rubicon
1787

In the general course of human nature, a power over a man's subsistence amounts to a power over his will.

—ALEXANDER HAMILTON
The Federalist Papers
1787–1788

It is weakness rather than wickedness which renders men unfit to be trusted with unlimited power.

—JOHN ADAMS
"A Defense of the Constitution of
Government of the United States of
America"
1787–1788

Wherever there is an interest and power to do wrong, wrong will generally be done, and not less readily by a powerful & interested party than by a powerful and interested prince.

—JAMES MADISON
Letter to Thomas Jefferson,
October 20, 1788

It cannot have escaped those who have attended with candour to the arguments employed against the extensive powers of the government, that the authors of them have very little considered how far these powers were necessary means of attaining a necessary end. They have chosen rather to dwell on the inconveniences which must be unavoidably blended with all political advantages; and on the possible abuses which must be incident to every power or trust of which a beneficial use can be made. This method of handling the subject cannot impose on the good sense of the people of America. It may display the subtlety of the writer; it may open a boundless field for rhetoric and declamation; it may inflame the passions of the unthinking, and may confirm the prejudices of the misthinking. But cool and candid people will at once reflect, that the purest of human blessings must have a portion of alloy in them; that the choice must always be made, if not of the lesser evil, at least of the GREATER, not the PERFECT good; and that in every political institution, a power to advance the public happiness involves a discretion which may be misapplied and abused.

—JAMES MADISON
The Federalist Papers
1788

No axiom is more clearly established in law, or in reason, than that wherever the end is required, the means are authorised; whenever a general power to do a thing is given, every particular power necessary for doing it, is included.

—JAMES MADISON
The Federalist Papers
1788

The accumulation of all power, legislative, executive, and judiciary, in the same hands, whether of one, a few, or many, and whether hereditary, self-appointed, or elective, may justly be pronounced the very definition of tyranny.

—JAMES MADISON
The Federalist Papers
1788

It will not be denied that power is of an encroaching nature, and that it ought to be effectually restrained from passing the limits assigned to it.

—JAMES MADISON
The Federalist Papers
1788

Power naturally grows. Why? Because human passions are insatiable.

—JOHN ADAMS
Letter to Roger Sherman,
July 18, 1789

Few men are contented with less power than they have a right to exercise.

—SAMUEL ADAMS (1722–1803)
To Richard Henry Lee,
1789

Immortal power is not a human right.

—THOMAS PAINE
Rights of Man, I
1791

Where an excess of power prevails, property of no sort is duly respected. No man is safe in his opinions, his person, his faculties or his possessions.

—JAMES MADISON
In the *National Gazette*,
March 29, 1792

All power exercised over a nation, must have some beginning. It must be either delegated, or assumed. There are no other sources. All delegated power is trust, and all assumed power is usurpation. Time does not alter the nature and quality of either.

—THOMAS PAINE
Rights of Man, II
1792

Those who abuse liberty when they possess it would abuse power could they obtain it.

—THOMAS PAINE
To the Citizens of the United States
1802

He is certainly a political novice or a hypocrite, who will pretend that the antifederal opposition to the government is to be ascribed to the concern of the people for their liberties, rather than to the profligate ambition of their demagogues, eager for power, and suddenly alarmed by the imminent danger of losing it; demagogues, who leading lives like Clodius, and with the maxims of Cato in their mouths, cherishing principles like Catiline, have acted steadily on a plan of usurpation like Caesar.

—FISHER AMES (1758–1808)
The Dangers of American Liberty
1805

An honest man can feel no pleasure in the exercise of power over his fellow citizens.

—THOMAS JEFFERSON (1743–1826)
Letter to John Melish,
January 13, 1813

The fundamental article of my political creed is that despotism, or unlimited sovereignty, or absolute power, is the same in a majority or a popular

PRESIDENCY

assembly, an aristocratical council, an oligarchical junta, and a single emperor.

—JOHN ADAMS
Letter to Thomas Jefferson,
November 13, 1815

Power must never be trusted without a check.

—JOHN ADAMS
Letter to Thomas Jefferson,
February 2, 1816

All power in human hands is liable to be abused. In Governments independent of the people, the rights and interests of the whole may be sacrificed to the views of the Government. In Republics, where ... the majority govern, a danger to the minority arises from ... a sacrifice of their rights to the interests ... of the majority. No form of government, therefore, can be a perfect guard against the abuse of power.

—JAMES MADISON
Letter to Thomas Ritchie,
December 18, 1825

PRESIDENCY

You are apprehensive of monarchy; I, of aristocracy. I would therefore have given more power to the President and less to the Senate.

—JOHN ADAMS (1735–1826)
Letter to Thomas Jefferson,
November 16, 1787

The history of human conduct does not warrant that exalted opinion of human virtue which would make it wise in a nation to commit interests of so delicate and momentous a kind as those which concern its intercourse with the rest of the world to the sole disposal of a magistrate, created and circumstanced, as would be a President of the United States.

—ALEXANDER HAMILTON
(1755–1804)
The Federalist Papers
1787

The process of election affords a moral certainty, that the office of President will never fall to the lot of any man who is not in an eminent degree endowed with the requisite qualifications. Talents for low intrigue, and the little arts of popularity, may alone suffice to elevate man to the first honors in a single State; but it will require other talents, and a different kind of merit, to establish him in the esteem and confidence of the whole Union ... so as to make him a successful candidate for the distinguished office of President of the United States.

—ALEXANDER HAMILTON
The Federalist Papers
1787

I must heartily wish the choice to which you allude [his election to the presidency] may not fall on me. ... If I should conceive myself in a manner constrained to accept, I call Heaven to witness that this very act would be the greatest sacrifice of my personal feelings and wishes that I ever have been called upon to make.

—GEORGE WASHINGTON (1732–1799)
Letter to Benjamin Lincoln,
October 26, 1788

My movements to the chair of government will be accompanied by feelings

231

not unlike those of a culprit who is going to the place of his execution.
—GEORGE WASHINGTON
Letter to Henry Knox,
April 1, 1789

I bade adieu to Mount Vernon, to private life, and to domestic felicity, and with a mind oppressed with more anxious and painful sensations than I have words to express, set out for New York … with the best disposition to render service to my country in obedience to its calls, but with less hope of answering its expectations.
—GEORGE WASHINGTON
Diaries of George Washington,
April 16, 1789

[The President] is the dignified, but accountable magistrate of a free and great people. The tenure of his office, it is true, is not hereditary; nor is it for life: but still it is a tenure of the noblest kind: by being the man of the people, he is invested; by continuing to be the man of the people, his investiture will be voluntarily, and cheerfully, and honourably renewed.
—JAMES WILSON (1742–1798)
Lectures on Law
1791

The powers of the Executive of the U. States are more definite, and better understood perhaps than those of almost any other Country; and my aim has been, and will continue to be, neither to stretch, nor relax from them in any instance whatever, unless imperious circumstances shd. render the measure indispensable.
—GEORGE WASHINGTON
Letter to Alexander Hamilton,
July 2, 1794

I have no ambition to govern men. It is a painful and thankless office.
—THOMAS JEFFERSON (1743–1826)
Letter to John Adams,
1796

No man will ever bring out of the Presidency the reputation which carries him into it.
—THOMAS JEFFERSON
Letter to Edward Rutledge,
1796

I have no idea that I shall be chosen President a second time; though this is not to be talked of. The business of the office is so oppressive that I shall hardly support it two years longer.
—JOHN ADAMS
Letter to Abigail Adams,
February 22, 1799

The President is the sole organ of the nation in its external relations, and its sole representative with foreign nations.
—JOHN MARSHALL (1755–1835)
Annals of Congress
1800

I have learned to expect that it will rarely fall to the lot of imperfect man to retire from this station with the reputation and the favor which bring him into it.
—THOMAS JEFFERSON
First Inaugural Address,
1801

The intimate political relation, subsisting between the president of the United States and the heads of departments, necessarily renders any legal investigation of the acts of one of those high officers peculiarly irksome, as well as delicate; and excites some hesitation with respect to the propriety of entering into such investigation.

—JOHN MARSHALL
Marbury v. Madison
1803

The province of the court is solely, to decide on the rights of individuals, not to enquire how the executive, or executive officers, perform duties in which they have a discretion. Questions, in their nature political, or which are, by the Constitution and laws, submitted to the executive, can never be made in this court.

—JOHN MARSHALL
Marbury v. Madison
1803

I am tired of an office where I can do no more good than many others, who would be glad to be employed in it. To myself, personally, it brings nothing but unceasing drudgery and daily loss of friends.

—THOMAS JEFFERSON
Letter to John Dickinson,
January 13, 1807

The President has, or ought to have, the whole nation before him, and he ought to select the men best qualified and most meritorious for offices at this own responsibility, without being shackled by any check by law, constitution, or institution. Without this unrestrained liberty, he is not a check upon the legislative power nor either branch of it. Indeed, he must be the slave of the party that brought him in.

—JOHN ADAMS
Letter to John Quincy Adams,
February 18, 1811

No man who ever held the office of President would congratulate a friend on obtaining it. He will make one man ungrateful, and a hundred men his enemies, for every office he can bestow.

—JOHN ADAMS
Letter to Josiah Quincy,
February 14, 1825

PRIDE & VANITY

There is a troublesome humour some men have, that if they may not lead, they will not follow, but had rather a thing were never done, than not done their own way, though otherwise very desirable.

—WILLIAM PENN (1644–1718)
Some Fruits of Solitude
1693

Pride breakfasted with Plenty, dined with Poverty, and supped with Infamy.

—BENJAMIN FRANKLIN (1706–1790)
Poor Richard's Almanack
c. 1732–1757

Pride is said to be the last vice the good man gets clear of.

—BENJAMIN FRANKLIN
Poor Richard's Almanack
c. 1732–1757

Success has ruined many a man.

—BENJAMIN FRANKLIN
Poor Richard's Almanack
1752

Oh! that I could wear out of my mind every mean and base affectation, conquer my natural Pride and Self Conceit, expect no more deference from my fellows than I deserve, acquire that meekness, and humility, which are the

sure marks and Characters of a great and generous Soul, and subdue every unworthy Passion and treat all men as I wish to be treated by all. How happy should I then be, in the favour and good will of all honest men, and the sure prospect of a happy immortality!
—JOHN ADAMS (1735–1826)
Diary entry,
February 16, 1756

Pride costs us more than hunger, thirst, and cold.
—THOMAS JEFFERSON (1743–1826)
Letter to Thomas Jefferson Smith,
February 21, 1825

PRIVACY

For a man's house is his castle.
—SIR EDWARD COKE (1552–1634)
The Institutes of the Lawes of England,
Vol. 1
1628–1641

So long as a man rides his hobby-horse, peaceably and quietly along the King's highway, and neither compels you or me to get up behind him,— pray, Sir, what have either you or I to do with it?
—LAURENCE STERNE (1713–1768)
Tristram Shandy, Book I, Chapter 7
1759

PROGRESS

Man advances from idea to idea, from thought to thought, and all the time he is unaware of his marvelous progress.
—THOMAS PAINE (1737–1809)
Answers to Four Questions on Legislative and Executive Powers
1791

PROPERTY

And as Reason tells us, all are born thus *naturally equal*, i.e., with an *equal Right* to their *Persons*; so also with an equal Right to their *Preservation*; and therefore to *such Things* as Nature affords for their *Subsistence*. ... [Each Man entitled to the fruits of his labor] ... Thus *every Man* having a *natural Right* to (or being the Proprietor of) his own *Person* and his own *Actions* and *Labour* and to what he can honestly acquire by his Labour, which we call *Property*; it certainly follows, that no Man can have a Right to the *Person* or *Property* of *another* ... [and a Man has a right to defend his property].
—REV. ELISHA WILLIAMS (1694–1755)
A Seasonable Plea
1744

The first man who, having fenced in a piece of land, said, "This is mine," and found people naive enough to believe him, that man was the true founder of the civil society.
—JEAN JACQUES ROUSSEAU (1712–1778)
Discourse upon the Origin and Foundation of the Inequality Among Mankind
1754

It is essentially a natural right, that a man shall quietly enjoy, and have the sole disposal of his own property. ... The security of right and property, is the great end of government. Surely, then, such measures as tend to render right and property precarious, tend to destroy both property and government, for these must stand or fall together. Property is admitted to have an existence in the savage state of nature; and if it is necessary for the support of sav-

age life, it by no means becomes less so in civil society.
—ANONYMOUS
House of Representatives of Massachusetts statement to the king's representative, 1768

Great Britain claims a right to take away nine-tenths of our estates—have we a right to the remaining tenth? No—To say we have, is a "traiterous" position, denying her supreme legislature. So far from *having* property, according to these late found novels, *we are ourselves a property.*
—JOHN DICKINSON (1732–1794)
Speech in Pennsylvania Provincial Convention, 1774

Each individual of the society has a right to be protected by it in the enjoyment of his life, liberty, and property, according to standing laws. He is obliged, consequently, to contribute his share to the expense of this protection; and to give his personal service, or an equivalent, when necessary. But no part of the property of any individual can, with justice, be taken from him, or applied to public uses, without his own consent, or that of the representative body of the people. In fine, the people of this commonwealth are not controllable by any other laws than those to which their constitutional representative body have given their consent.
—JOHN ADAMS (1735–1826)
Thoughts on Government 1776

So great moreover is the regard of the law for private property, that it will not authorize the least violation of it; no, not even for the general good of the whole community.
—SIR WILLIAM BLACKSTONE (1723–1780)
Commentaries of the Laws of England 1783

Whenever there is, in any country, uncultivated land and unemployed poor, it is clear that the laws of property have been so far expended as to violate natural right.
—THOMAS JEFFERSON (1743–1826)
Letter to James Madison, 1785

In what then does *real* power consist? The answer is short and plain—in *property.*
—NOAH WEBSTER (1758–1843)
"An Examination into the Leading Principles of the Federal Constitution" October 17, 1787

The liberty of the press, trial by jury, the Habeas Corpus writ, even Magna Carta itself, although justly deemed the palladia of freedom, are all inferior considerations, when compared with a general distribution of real property among every class of people. The power of entailing estates is more dangerous to liberty and republican government, than all the constitutions that can be written on paper, or even than a standing army. Let the people have property, and they *will* have power—a power that will for ever be exerted to prevent a restriction of the press, an abolition of trial by jury, or the abridgement of any other privilege.
—NOAH WEBSTER
"An Examination into the Leading Principles of the Federal Constitution" October 17, 1787

235

The moment the idea is admitted into society that property is not as sacred as the laws of God, and that there is not a force of law and public justice to protect it, anarchy and tyranny commence. If "Thou shalt not covet" and "Thou shalt not steal" were not commandments of Heaven, they must be made inviolable precepts in every society before it can be civilized or made free.

—JOHN ADAMS
A Defense of the American
Constitutions
1787

Those who hold and those who are without property have ever formed distinct interests in society. Those who are creditors, and those who are debtors, fall under a like discrimination. A landed interest, a manufacturing interest, a mercantile interest, a moneyed interest, with many lesser interests, grow up of necessity in civilization and divide them into different classes, actuated by different sentiments and views.

—JAMES MADISON (1751–1836)
The Federalist Papers
1787

If all power be suffered to slide into hands not interested in the rights of property which must be the case whenever a majority fall under that description, one of two things cannot fail to happen; either they will unite against the other description and become the dupes and instruments of ambition, or their poverty and independence will render them the mercenary instruments of wealth. In either case liberty will be subverted; in the first by a despotism growing out of anarchy, in the second, by an oligarchy founded on corruption.

—JAMES MADISON
"Observations on Jefferson's Draft
Constitution"
October 15, 1788

Private Property therefore is a Creature of Society, and is subject to the Calls of that Society, whenever its Necessities shall require it, even to its last Farthing.

—BENJAMIN FRANKLIN (1706–1790)
"On the Legislative Branch"
1789

Government is instituted to protect property of every sort. ... This being the end of government, that alone is a just government, which impartially secures to every man, whatever is his own.

—JAMES MADISON
Article in the National Gazette,
March 29, 1792

As a man is said to have a right to his property, he may be equally said to have a property in his rights.

—JAMES MADISON
Article in the National Gazette,
March 29, 1792

It is ... natural for man to wish to be the absolute lord and master of what he holds in occupancy.

—GEORGE WASHINGTON (1732–1799)
To William Grickland,
July 15, 1797

There could be no such thing as landed property originally. Man did not make the earth, and, though he had a natural right to occupy it, he had no right to

236

locate as *his property* in perpetuity on any part of it.

—THOMAS PAINE (1737–1809)
Agrarian Justice
1797

A representative form of government rests no more on political contributions than on those laws which regulate the descent and transmission of property.

—DANIEL WEBSTER (1782–1852)
Address to the Massachusetts
Convention,
1820

It would seem, then, to be the part of political wisdom to found government on property; and to establish such distribution of property, by the laws which regulate its transmission and alienation, as to interest the great majority of society in the protection of government.

—DANIEL WEBSTER
Address to the Massachusetts
Convention,
1820

Power *naturally* and *necessarily* follows property.

—DANIEL WEBSTER
Address to the Massachusetts
Convention,
1820

There is not a more dangerous experiment than to place property in the hands of one class, and political power in those of another. ...If property cannot retain the political power, the political power will draw after it the property.

—DANIEL WEBSTER
Address to the Massachusetts
Convention,
1820

PUBLIC OFFICE

When a man assumes a public trust, he should consider himself as public property.

—THOMAS JEFFERSON (1743–1826)
Remark to Baron von Humboldt,
Date unknown

Governments can never be well administered, but where those entrusted make conscience of well discharging their places.

—WILLIAM PENN (1644–1718)
Some Fruits of Solitude
1693

I have accepted a seat in the [Massachusetts] House of Representatives, and thereby have consented to my own ruin, to your ruin, and the ruin of our children. I give you this warning, that you may prepare your mind for your fate.

—JOHN ADAMS (1735–1826)
To Abigail Adams,
1770

Public life is a situation of power and energy; he trespasses against his duty who sleeps upon his watch, as well as he that goes over the enemy.

—EDMUND BURKE (1729–1797)
Thoughts on the Cause of the Present Discontents
1770

Rulers, surely, even the most dignified and powerful of them, should not be so elevated with the thoughts of their power, as to forget from whom it comes; for what purposes it is delegated to them.

—REV. JONATHAN MAYHEW (1720–1776)
Election Sermon,
1774

Every post is honorable in which a man can serve his country.
—GEORGE WASHINGTON (1732–1799)
To Benedict Arnold,
September 14, 1775

Every man who acts beyond the lien of private life, must expect to pass through two severe examinations. First, as to his motives; secondly, as to his conduct. On the former of these depends his character for honesty; on the latter for wisdom.
—THOMAS PAINE (1737–1809)
Four Letters on Interesting Subjects
1776

On my first entrance into public life, I formed a resolution from which I never departed, to abstain, whilst in that situation from dealing in any way, in public property or transactions of any kind; and I am satisfied that during my respites, and since my retirement, from the public Service, I never became possessed of any Stock that could give me a title to the derelict in question.
—JAMES MADISON (1751–1836)
"Vices of the Political System"
April 1787

In a Republic personal merit alone could be the ground of political exaltation, but it would rarely happen that this merit would be so pre-eminent as to produce universal acquiesence.
—JAMES MADISON
Speech in the Constitutional Convention,
June 6, 1787

The term, sir, for which the senate is chosen, is a grievance—it is too long to trust any body of men with power:

It is impossible but that such men will be tenacious of their places; they are to be raised to a lofty eminence, and they will be loth to come down; and in the course of six years, may by management, have it in their power to create officers, and obtain influence enough, to get in again, and so for life. When we felt the hand of British oppression upon us, we were so jealous of rulers, as to declare them eligible but for three years in six. In this Constitution we forget this principle. I, sir, think that rulers ought at short periods, to return to private life, that they may know how to feel for, and regard their fellow creatures. In six years, sir, and at a great distance, they will quite forget them.
"For time and absence cure the purest love."
We are apt to forget our friends, except when we are conversing with them.
—SAMUEL NASSON (1744–1800)
Speech at Massachusetts Ratifying Convention,
February 1, 1788

The aim for every political constitution is, or ought to be, first, to obtain for rulers men who possess most wisdom to discern, and most virtue to pursue the common good of the society; and in the next place, to take the most effectual precautions for keeping them virtuous, whilst they continue to hold their public trust.
—JAMES MADISON
The Federalist Papers
1788

Nothing so strongly impels a man to regard the interest of his constituents,

as the certainty of returning to the general mass of the people, from whence he was taken, where he must participate in their burdens.
—GEORGE MASON (1725—1792)
Speech in the Virginia Ratifying Convention,
June 17, 1788

It is a truth sufficiently illustrated by experience, that when the people act by their representatives, they are commonly irresistible.
—ALEXANDER HAMILTON (1755–1804)
New York Ratification Convention,
June 25, 1788

I have learned too much of the vanity of human affairs to expect felicity from the scenes of public life.
—MARTHA WASHINGTON (1731–1802)
Letter to Mrs. Warren,
December 26, 1789

We are not to consider ourselves, while here, as at church or school, to listen to the harangues of speculative piety; we are here to talk of the political interests committed to our charge.
—FISHER AMES (1758–1808)
Speech in the U.S. House of Representatives,
1789

In no case ought the eyes of the people to be shut on the conduct of those entrusted with power; nor their tongues tied from a just wholesome censure on it, any more than from merited commendations. If neither gratitude for the honor of the trust, nor responsibility for the use of it, be sufficient to curb the unruly passions of public functionaries, add new bits to the bridle rather

than to take it off altogether. This is the precept of common sense illustrated and enforced by experience—uncontrolled power, ever has been, and ever will be administered by the passions more than by reason.
—JAMES MADISON
"Political Reflections"
February 23, 1799

The ordinary affairs of a nation offer little difficulty to a person of any experience.
—THOMAS JEFFERSON
Letter to James Sullivan,
1808

PUBLIC OPINION & PREJUDICE

The public must and will be served.
—WILLIAM PENN (1644–1718)
Some Fruits of Solitude
1693

If what men most admire they would despise,
'Twould look as if mankind were growing wise.
—BENJAMIN FRANKLIN (1706–1790)
Poor Richard's Almanack
1735

Your representative owes you, not his industry only, but his judgment; and he betrays instead of serving you if he sacrifices it to your opinion.
—EDMUND BURKE (1729–1797)
Speech to the Electors of Bristol,
November 3, 1774

We are never in a proper condition of doing justice to others, while we continue under the influence of some leading partiality, so neither are we capable

of doing it to ourselves while we remain fettered by any obstinate prejudice.
—*THOMAS PAINE* (1737–1809)
Common Sense
1776

I am sensible that he who means to do mankind a real service must set down with the determination of putting up, and bearing with all their faults, follies, prejudices and mistakes until he can convince them that he is right, and that his object is a general good.
—*THOMAS PAINE*
To Robert Morris,
February 20, 1782

As he rose like a rocket, he would fall like the stick.
—*THOMAS PAINE*
Common Sense on Financing the War,
referring to Edmund Burke
1782

I have never yet made, and I hope I never shall make, it the least point of consideration, whether a thing is *popular* or *unpopular*, but whether it is *right* or *wrong*. That which is right will become popular, and that which is wrong will soon lose its temporary popularity, and sink into disgrace.
—*THOMAS PAINE*
A Friend to Rhode-Island and the Union
1783

When occasions present themselves, in which the interests of the people are at variance with their inclinations, it is the duty of the person whom they have appointed to be the guardians of those interests, to withstand the temporary delusion, in order to give them time and opportunity for more cool and sedate reflection.
—*ALEXANDER HAMILTON* (1755–1804)
The Federalist Papers
1787

Of those men who have overturned the liberties of republics, the greatest number have begun their career by paying an obsequious court to the people, commencing demagogues and ending tyrants.
—*ALEXANDER HAMILTON*
The Federalist Papers
1787

I would not have the first wish, the momentary impulse of the public mind, become law. For it is not always the sense of the people, with whom, I admit, that all power resides. On great questions, we first hear the loud clamors of passion, artifice, and faction. I consider biennial elections as a security that the sober, second thought of the people shall be law.
—*FISHER AMES* (1758–1808)
Speech in Massachusetts Convention,
January 1788

All governments, even the most despotic, depend, in a great degree, on opinion. In free republics it is most peculiarly the case. In these the will of the people makes the essential principle of the government, and the laws which control the community receive their tone and spirit from the public wishes. It is the fortunate situation of our country, that the minds of the people are exceedingly enlightened and refined.
—*ALEXANDER HAMILTON*
Speech in the New York Assembly,
June 17, 1788

It is an unquestionable truth, that the body of the people in every country desire sincerely its prosperity. But it is equally unquestionable that they do not possess the discernment and stability necessary for systematic government. To deny that they are frequently led into the grossest of errors, by misinformation and passion, would be a flattery which their own good sense must despise.

—ALEXANDER HAMILTON
Speech in the New York Assembly,
June 1788

If we are to take for the criterion of truth the majority of suffrages, they ought to be gathered from those philosophical and patriotic citizens who cultivate their reason, apart from the scenes which distract its operations, and expose it to the influence of the passions. The advantage enjoyed by public bodies in the light struck out by the collision of arguments, is but too often overbalanced by the heat proceeding from the same source. Many other sources of involuntary error might be added. It is no reflection on Congress to admit for one, the united voice of the place, where they may happen to deliberate. Nothing is more contagious than opinion, especially on questions, which being susceptible of very different glosses, beget in the mind a distrust of itself. It is extremely difficult also to avoid confounding the local with the public opinion, and to withhold the respect due to the latter, from the fallacious specimens exhibited by the former.

—JAMES MADISON (1751–1836)
To Benjamin Rush,
March 7, 1790

The larger a country, the less easy for its real opinion to be ascertained, and the less difficult to be counterfeited; when ascertained or presumed, the more respectable it is in the eyes of individuals. This is favorable to the authority of government. For the same reason, the more extensive a country, the more insignificant is each individual in his own eyes. This may be unfavorable to liberty.

—JAMES MADISON
Essay in the National Gazette,
December 19, 1791

Public opinion sets bounds to every government, and is the real sovereign in every free one. As there are cases where the public opinion must be obeyed by the government; so there are cases, where not being fixed, it may be influenced by the government. This distinction, if kept in view, would prevent or decide many debates on the respect due from the governemnt on the sentiments of the people.

—JAMES MADISON
Essay in the National Gazette,
December 19, 1791

I shall so far take the sense of the public for my guide.

—THOMAS PAINE
Rights of Man, II
1792

I have learned to hold popular opinion of no value.

—ALEXANDER HAMILTON
Letter to George Washington,
1794

It is on great occasions only, and after time has been given for cool and delib-

erate reflection, that the real voice of the people can be known.
—*GEORGE WASHINGTON* (1732–1799)
Letter to Edward Carrington,
May 1, 1796

The first thing in all great operations of such a government as ours is to secure the opinion of the people.
—*ALEXANDER HAMILTON*
To Theodore Sedgwick,
February 2, 1799

In the formation of laws and constitutions of civil government, public opinion is the capital director. To conform these to the humors, habits, and opinions of a people, is deemed an important part of legislative wisdom. Legislators ever have been and ever will be influenced by the public mind. For a legislative body to act in opposition to that, is an Herculean task, which has seldom been attempted, and, when attempted in elective governments, has never been followed with success.
—*ZEPHANIAH SWIFT MOORE*
(1770–1820)
"An Oration on the Anniversary of the Independence of the United States of America"
1802

No nation, however powerful, any more than an individual, can be unjust with impunity. Sooner or later public opinion, an instrument merely moral in the beginning, will find occasion physi-

cally to inflict its sentences on the unjust.
—*THOMAS JEFFERSON* (1743–1826)
To James Madison,
1804

[T]rue to their nature, the people, or rabble, rather always think the greatest fool the wisest man. They have proved it in this instance, by their selecting him [a local politician] to make laws for them. Alas, for my country! all your citizens want is rope.
—*ANNE NEWPORT ROYALL* (1769–1854)
Letters from Alabama,
June 2, 1821

PURITANISM

What from the Church at Boston? I know no such church, neither will I own it. Call it the whore and strumpet of Boston, no Church of Christ!
—*ANNE HUTCHINSON* (1591–1643)
From *Antinomianism in the Colony of Massachusetts Bay, 1636-1638*, edited by Charles Francis Adams
c. 1638

The character of the inhabitants of this province [Mass.] is much improved in comparison of what it was—but Puritanism and a spirit of persecution is not yet totally extinguished.
—*ANDREW BURNABY* (Dates unknown)
Travels Through the Middle Settlements of North America
1775

R

REASON

The satisfaction of our senses is low, short, and transient. But the mind gives a more raised and extended pleasure, and is capable of an happiness founded upon reason; not bounded and limited by the circumstances that bodies are confined to.
—*WILLIAM PENN* (1644–1718)
Some Fruits of Solitude
1693

The present is an age of philosophy, and America the empire of reason. Here, neither the pageantry of courts, nor the glooms of superstition, have dazzled or beclouded the mind. Our duty calls us to act worthy of the age and the country that gave us birth.
—*JOEL BARLOW* (1754–1812)
July 4th Oration delivered in
Hartford, Connecticut,
July 4, 1787

Your own reason is the only oracle given you by heaven, and you are answerable not for the rightness but uprightness of the decision.
—*THOMAS JEFFERSON* (1743–1826)
To Peter Carr,
August 10, 1787

In disquisitions of every kind there are certain primary truths, or first principles, upon which all subsequent reasoning must depend.
—*ALEXANDER HAMILTON* (1755–1804)
The Federalist Papers
1788

So convenient a thing it is to be a reasonable creature, since it enables one to find or make a reason for everything one has a mind to do.
—*BENJAMIN FRANKLIN* (1706–1790)
Autobiography
1791

Reason and Ignorance, the opposites of each other, influence the great bulk of mankind. If either of these can be rendered sufficiently extensive in a country, the machinery of Government goes easily on. Reason obeys itself; and Ignorance submits to whatever is dictated to it.
—*THOMAS PAINE* (1737–1809)
Rights of Man, I
1791

It would not only be wrong, but bad policy, to attempt by force what ought to be accomplished by reason.
—*THOMAS PAINE*
Rights of Man, II
1792

Reason and discussion will soon bring

things right, however wrong they may begin.
—THOMAS PAINE
Rights of Man, II
1792

Reason, like time, will make its own way, and prejudice will fall in a combat with interest.
—THOMAS PAINE
Rights of Man, II
1792

The greatest forces that can be brought into the field of revolutions, are reason and common interest. Where these can have the opportunity of acting, opposition dies with fear, or crumbles away by conviction.
—THOMAS PAINE
Age of Reason, I
1794

The most formidable weapon against errors of every kind is Reason. I have never used any other, and I trust I never shall.
—THOMAS PAINE
Age of Reason, I
1794

There is no rule without exceptions: but it is false reasoning which converts exceptions into the general rule.
—THOMAS JEFFERSON
To Thomas Law,
June 13, 1814

The art of reasoning becomes of first importance. In this line antiquity has left us the finest models for imitation; ... I should consider the speeches of Livy, Sallust, and Tacitus, as pre-eminent specimens of logic, taste, and that sen-

tentious brevity which, using not a word to spare, leaves not a moment for inattention to the hearer. Amplification is the vice of modern oratory.
—THOMAS JEFFERSON
Letter to David Harding,
April 20, 1824

RELIGION

In God we trust.
—U.S. MOTTO
"In God is our trust" was the original phrase stated by Francis Scott Key in 1814. The above motto, more popular and more familiar, appeared on U.S. coins beginning in 1864.

Columbus did not find out America by chance, but God directed him at that time to discover it; it was contingent to him, but necessary to God.
—ROBERT BURTON (1577–1640)
The Anatomy of Melancholy
1621

An oath, sir, is an end of all strife, and it is God's ordinance.
—ANNE HUTCHINSON (1591–1643)
Spoken at her trial in Boston,
November 1, 1637

There goes many a ship to sea, with many hundred souls in one ship, whose weal and woe is common, and is a true picture of a commonwealth or a human combination or society. It hath fallen out sometimes that both Papists and Protestants, Jews and Turks may be embarked in one ship; upon which supposal I affirm that all the liberty of conscience that ever I pleaded for turns upon these two hinges—that none of the papists, Protestants, Jews or Turks be forced to come to the ship's prayers or worship, nor compelled from their own particular prayers or worship, if they practice any.

—ROGER WILLIAMS (c. 1603–1683)
Letter to the Town of Providence,
January 1655

Therefore, if any of these said persons (Quakers, Jews, Turks and Egyptians) come in love unto us, we cannot, in conscience, lay hands upon them, but give them free egresse and regresse into our town and houses, as God shall persuade our consciences. And in this we are true subjects both of Church and State, for we are bounde by the law of God and men to doe good unto all men and evil to noe one.

—ANONYMOUS
"The Flushing Remonstrance," to
Governor Stuyvesant,
December 27, 1657

All men are truly said to be tenants at will, and it may as truly be said that all have a lease of their lives, some longer, some shorter, as it pleases our great Landlord to let. All have their bounds set, over which they cannot pass, and till the expiration of that time, no dangers, no sickness, no pains, nor troubles shall put a period to our days. The certainty that that time will come, together with the uncertainty, how, where, and when, should make us so to number our days as to apply our hearts to wisdom, that when we are put out of these houses of clay we may be sure of an everlasting habitation that fades not away.

—ANNE BRADSTREET (c. 1612–1672)
Meditations Divine and Moral
c. 1660

Noe person within the said colonye at any tyme hereafter shall bee any wise molested, punished, disquieted or called in question for any difference in opinions in matters of religion which doe not actually disturb the civil peace of our sayd colonye; but that all ... freely and fullye have and enjoy his and their own judgments and consciences in matters of religious concernments.

—CHARTER OF THE COLONY OF
RHODE ISLAND
1663

In short, what religious, what wise, what prudent, what good natured person would be a persecutor; certainly it's an office only fit for those who being void of all reason, to evidence the verity of their own religion, fancy it to be true, from that strong propensity and greedy inclination they find in themselves to persecute the contrary; a weakness of so ill a consequence to all civil societies, that the admission of it ever was, and ever will prove their utter ruin, as well as their great infelicity who pursue it.

—WILLIAM PENN (1644–1718)
The Great Case of Liberty and
Conscience
1670

Toleration (for these ten years past) has not been more the cry of some, than persecution has been the practice of others, though not on grounds equally rational.

—WILLIAM PENN
The Great Case of Liberty and
Conscience
1670

God is better served in resisting a temptation to evil, than in many formal prayers.

—WILLIAM PENN
Some Fruits of Solitude
1693

It is a sad reflection that many men hardly have any religion at all; and most men have none of their own: for that which is the religion of their education, and not of their judgment, is the religion of another, and not theirs.

—WILLIAM PENN
Some Fruits of Solitude
1693

Thou wouldst take much pains to save thy body: take some, prithee, to save thy soul.

—WILLIAM PENN
Some Fruits of Solitude
1693

And of all plagues with which mankind are curs'd,
Ecclesiastic tyranny's the worst.

—DANIEL DEFOE (1660–1731)
The True-Born Englishman
1701

Because no People can be truly happy, though under the greatest Enjoyment of Civil Liberties, if abridged of the Freedom of their Consciences, ... I do hereby grant and declare, That no Person or Persons, inhabiting in this Province or Territories, who shall confess and acknowledge *One* almighty God, the Creator, Upholder and Ruler of the World; and profess him or themselves obliged to live quietly under the Civil Government, shall be in any Case molested or prejudiced, in his or their Person or Estate, because of his or their

conscientious Persuasion or Practice, nor be compelled to frequent or maintain any religious Worship, Place or Ministry, contrary to his or their Mind, or to do or suffer any other Act or Thing, contrary to their religous Persuasion.

—WILLIAM PENN
Pennsylvania Charter of Privileges,
1701

Because the Happiness of Mankind depends so much upon the Enjoying of Liberty of their Consciences as aforesaid, I do hereby solemnly declare, promise and grant, for me, my Heirs and Assigns, That the *First* Article of this Charter relating to Liberty of Conscience, and every Part and Clause therein, according to the true Intent and Meaning thereof, shall be kept and remain, without any Alteration, inviolably for ever.

—WILLIAM PENN
Pennsylvania Charter of Privileges,
1701

I write the wonders of the Christian religion, flying from the depravations of Europe to the American strand; and, assisted by the holy author of that religion, I do, with all conscience of truth, required therein by Him who is the truth itself, report the wonderful displays of His infinite power, wisdom, goodness, and faithfulness, wherewith His divine providence hath irradiated an Indian wilderness.

—COTTON MATHER (1663–1728)
Magnalia Christi Americana
1702

To be like Christ is to be a Christian.

—WILLIAM PENN
Last words,
1718

How many observe Christ's birthday! How few, his precepts! O! 'tis easier to keep holidays than commandments.
—BENJAMIN FRANKLIN (1706–1790)
Poor Richard's Almanack
c. 1732

Talking against religion is unchaining a tiger; the beast let loose may worry his deliverer.
—BENJAMIN FRANKLIN
Poor Richard's Almanack
1751

What is the proper Business of Mankind in this Life? We came into the World naked and destitute of all the Conveniences and necessaries of Life. And if we were not provided for, and nourished by our Parents or others should inevitably perish as soon as born. We increase in strength of Body and mind by slow and insensible Degrees. 1/3 of our Time is consumed in sleep, and 3/4 of the remainder, is spent in procuring a mere animal sustenance. And if we live to the Age of three score and Ten and then set down to make an estimate in our minds of the Happiness we have enjoyed and the Misery we have suffered, We shall find I am apt to think, that the overbalance of Happiness is quite inconsiderable. We shall find that we have been through the greatest Part of our Lives pursuing Shadows, and empty but glittering Phantoms rather than substances. We shall find that we have applied our whole Vigour, all our Faculties, in the Pursuit of Honour, or Wealth, or Learning or some other such delusive Trifle, instead of the real and everlasting Excellences of Piety and Virtue. Habits of Contemplating the Deity and his transcendent

Excellences, and correspondent Habits of complacency in and Dependence upon him, Habits of Reverence and Gratitude, to God, and Habits of Love and Compassion to our fellow men and Habits of Temperance, Recollection and self Government will afford us a real and substantial Pleasure. We may then exult in a Consciousness of the Favour of God, and the Prospect of everlasting Felicity.
—JOHN ADAMS (1735–1826)
Diary entry,
May 1756

The frightful engines of ecclesiastical councils, of diabolical malice, and Calvinistical good-nature never failed to terrify me exceedingly whenever I thought of preaching.
—JOHN ADAMS
To Richard Cranch,
October 18, 1756

Let the pulpit resound with the doctrine and sentiments of religious liberty. Let us hear of the dignity of man's nature, and the noble rank he holds among the works of God. ... Let it be known that British liberties are not the grants of princes and parliaments.
—JOHN ADAMS
"Dissertation on the Canon and Feudal Law"
1765

A watchful eye must be kept on ourselves, lest while we are building ideal monuments of renown and bliss here, we neglect to have our names enrolled in the annals of Heaven.
—JAMES MADISON (1751–1836)
To William Bradford,
November 9, 1772

In regard to religion, mutual toleration in the different professions thereof is what all good and candid minds in all ages have ever practiced ... The only sects which he [Locke] thinks ought to be and which by all wise laws are excluded from such toleration are those who teach doctrines subversive of the civil government under which they live. The Roman Catholics or Papists are excluded by reason of such doctrines as these: that princes excommunicated may be deposed, and those they call heretics may be destroyed without mercy; besides their recognizing the pope in so absolute a manner, in subversion of government, by introducing as far as possible into the states under whose protection they enjoy life, liberty, and property that solecism in politics, *Imperium in imperio*, leading directly to the worst anarchy and confusion, civil discord, war and bloodshed.
—*SAMUEL ADAMS* (1722–1803)
"The Rights of Colonists"
1772

Union of Religious Sentiments begets a surprizing confidence and Ecclesiastical Establishments tend to great ignorance and Corruption all of which facilitate the Execution of Mischievous Projects.
—*JAMES MADISON*
To William Bradford,
January 23, 1774

That diabolical, hell-conceived principle of persecution rages among some, and to their eternal infamy the clergy can furnish their quota of imps for such a business.
—*JAMES MADISON*
To William Bradford,
January 23, 1774

A thousand things may intercept our petitions on their way to an earthly monarch; but a combination of all our enemies in earth and hell cannot prevent a pious wish in its flight to Heaven.
—*NATHANIEL NILES* (1741–1828)
Two discourses on liberty; delivered at the North Church, in Newbury-port,
June 5, 1774

Spiritual freedom is the root of political liberty. ... As the union between spiritual freedom and political liberty seems nearly inseparable, it is our duty to defend both.
—*THOMAS PAINE* (1737–1809)
Thoughts on Defensive War
1775

The God who gave us life, gave us liberty at the same time.
—*THOMAS JEFFERSON* (1743–1826)
Summary View of the Rights of British America
1775

As to religion, I hold it to be the indispensable duty of all government, to protect all conscientious professors thereof, and I know of no other business which government hath to do therewith.
—*THOMAS PAINE*
Common Sense
1776

To God, and not to man, are all men accountable on the score of religion.
—*THOMAS PAINE*
Common Sense
1776

It is the will of the Almighty, that there should be diversity of religious opinions among us: It affords a larger field for our Christian kindness. Were we all of one way of thinking, our religious dispositions would want matter for probation; and on this liberal principle, I look on the various denominations among us, to be like children of the same family, differing only, in what is called, their Christian names.

—THOMAS PAINE
Common Sense
1776

He is the best friend to American liberty, who is most sincere and active in promoting true and undefiled religion, and who sets himself with the greatest firmness to bear down on profanity and immorality of every kind. Whoever is an avowed enemy of God, I scruple not to call him an enemy to his country.

—JOHN WITHERSPOON (1723–1794)
1776

That religion, or the duty which we owe to our CREATOR, and the manner of discharging it, can be directed only by reason and conviction, not by force or violence; and therefore, all men are equally entitled to the free exercise of religion, according to the dictates of conscience; and that it is the mutual duty of all to practise Christian forbearance, love, and charity; towards each other.

—JAMES MADISON
(Also attributed to George Mason)
Virginia Declaration of Rights,
1776

The opinions of men are not the object of civil government, nor under its jurisdiction.

—THOMAS JEFFERSON
Virginia Statute of Religious Freedom,
1779

[T]he happiness of a people and the good order and preservation of civil government essentially depend upon piety, religion, and morality.

—ANONYMOUS
Massachusetts Bill of Rights
1780

Is uniformity obtainable? Millions of innocent men, women, and children, since the introduction of Christianity, have been burnt, tortured, fined, imprisoned, yet we have not advanced an inch toward uniformity. What has been the effect of coercion? To make one half the world fools, and the other half hypocrites. To support roguery and error all over the earth.

—THOMAS JEFFERSON
Notes on the State of Virginia,
1782

It does me no injury for my neighbor to say there are twenty gods, or no God.

—THOMAS JEFFERSON
Notes on the State of Virginia,
1782

Without religion, I believe that learning does real mischief to the morals and principles of mankind.

—BENJAMIN RUSH (1745–1813)
To John Armstrong,
March 19, 1783

In the circle of my acquaintance (which has not been small), I have generally been denominated a Deist, the reality of which I never disputed, being conscious I am no Christian, except mere infant baptism make me one; and as to being a Deist, I know not, strictly speaking, whether I am one or not, for I have never

249

read their writings; mine will therefore determine the matter; for I have not in the least disguised my sentiments, but have written freely without any conscious knowledge of prejudice for, or against any man, sectary or party whatever; but wish that good sense, truth and virtue may be promoted and flourish in the world, to the detection of delusion, superstition, and false religion; and therefore my errors in the succeeding treatise, which may be rationally pointed out, will be readily rescinded.

—ETHAN ALLEN (1738–1789)
Reason the Only Oracle of Man
1784

Nothing is more evident to the understanding part of mankind, than that in those parts of the world where learning and science has prevailed, miracles have ceased; but in such parts of it as are barbarous and ignorant, miracles are still in vogue; which is of itself a strong presumption that in the infancy of letters, learning and science, or in the world's non-age, those who confided in miracles, as a proof of the divine mission of the first promulgators of revelation, were imposed upon by fictitious appearances instead of miracles.

Furthermore, the author of Christianity warns us against the impositions of false teachers, and ascribes the signs of the true believers, saying, "And these signs shall follow them that believe, in my name shall they cast out devils, they shall speak with new tongues, they shall take up serpents, and if they drink any deadly thing it shall not hurt them, they shall lay hands on the sick and they shall recover." These are the express words of the founder of Christianity, and are contained in the very commission, which he gave to his eleven Apostles, who were to promulgate his gospel in the world; so that from their very institution it appears that when the miraculous signs, therein spoken of, failed, they were considered as unbelievers, and consequently no faith or trust to be any longer reposed in them or their successors. For these signs were those which were to perpetuate their mission, and were to be continued as the only evidences of the validity and authenticity of it, and as long as these signs followed, mankind could not be deceived in adhering to the doctrines which the Apostles and their successors taught; but when these signs failed, their divine authority ended. Now if any of them will drink a dose of deadly poison, which I could prepare, and it does not "hurt them," I will subscribe to their divine author and end the dispute; not that I have a disposition to poison any one, nor do I suppose that they would dare to take such a dose as I could prepare for them, which, if so, would evince that they were unbelievers themselves, though they are extremely apt to censure others for unbelief, which according to their scheme is a damnable sin.

—ETHAN ALLEN
Reason the Only Oracle of Man
1784

We should begin by setting conscience free. When all men of all religions ... shall enjoy equal liberty, property, and an equal chance for honors and power ... we may expect that improvements will be made in the human character and the state of society.

—JOHN ADAMS
To Dr. Price,
April 8, 1785

250

It gives me much pleasure to observe by 2 printed reports sent me by Col. Grayson that in the latter Congress had expunged a clause contained in the first for setting apart a district of land in each Township, for supporting the Religion of the Majority of inhabitants. How a regulation, so unjust in itself, so foreign to the Authority of Congress so hurtful to the sale of the public land, and smelling so strongly of an antiquated Bigotry, could have received the countenance of a Committee is truly matter of astonishment.
—JAMES MADISON
To James Monroe,
May 29, 1785

[E]xperience witnesseth that ecclesiastical establishments, instead of maintaining the purity and efficacy of Religion, have had a contrary operation. During almost fifteen centuries has the legal establishment of Christianity been on trial. What have been its fruits? More or less in all places, pride and indolence in the Clergy, ignorance and servility in the laity, in both, superstition, bigotry and persecution.
—JAMES MONROE
Address to the Virginia General Assembly,
June 20, 1785

Who does not see that the same authority which can establish Christianity, in exclusion of all other Religions, may establish with the same ease any particular sect of Christians, in exclusion of all other Sects?
—JAMES MONROE
Address to the Virginia General Assembly,
June 20, 1785

Rulers who wished to subvert the public liberty, may have found an established Clergy convenient auxiliaries. A just Government instituted to secure & perpetuate it needs them not.
—JAMES MONROE
Address to the Virginia General Assembly,
June 20, 1785

Torrents of blood have been spilt in the old world, by vain attempts of the secular arm, to extinguish Religious discord, by proscribing all difference in Religious opinion. Time has at length revealed the true remedy. Every relaxation of narrow and rigorous policy, whenever it has been tried, has been found to assuage the disease. The American Theatre has exhibited proofs that equal and compleat liberty, if it does not wholly eradicate it, sufficiently destroys its malignant influence on the health and prosperity of the State.
—JAMES MONROE
Address to the Virginia General Assembly,
June 20, 1785

We hold it for a fundamental and inalienable truth that religion and the manner of discharging it can be directed only by reason and conviction not by force and violence. The religion, then, of every man must be left to the conviction and conscience of every man; and it is the right of every man to exercise it as these may dictate.
—JAMES MONROE
Address to the Virginia General Assembly,
June 20, 1785

You yourself may find it easy to live a

virtuous life, without the assistance afforded by religion; you having a clear perception of the advantage of virtue, and the disadvantages of vice, and possessing a strength of resolution sufficient to enable you to resist common temptations. But think how great a portion of mankind consists of weak and ignorant men and women, and of inexperienced, inconsiderate youth of both sexes, who have need of the motives of religion to restrain them from vice, to support their virtue, and retain them in the practice of it till it becomes habitual, which is the great point for its security. And perhaps you are indebted to her originally, that is to your religious education, for the habits of virtue upon which you now justly value yourself. You might easily display your excellent talents of reasoning upon a less hazardous subject, and thereby obtain a rank with our most distinguished authors. For among us it is not necessary, as among the Hottentots, that a youth, to be raised into the company of men, should prove his manhood by beating his mother.

—*BENJAMIN FRANKLIN*
To Thomas Paine (Franklin's response
to *The Age of Reason*),
1785

We, the General Assembly of Virginia, do enact that no man shall be compelled to frequent or support any religious worship, place, or ministry whatsoever, nor shall be enforced, restrained, molested, or burthened in his body or goods, or shall otherwise suffer, on account of his religious opinions of belief; but that all men shall be free to profess, and by argument to maintain, their opinions in matters of religion, and that the same shall in no wise diminish, enlarge, or affect their civil capabilities.

—*THOMAS JEFFERSON*
Virginia Act for Religious Freedom,
1786

I have lived, Sir, a long time, and the longer I live, the more convincing proof I see of this truth—that God governs in the affairs of men. And if a sparrow cannot fall to the ground without his notice, is it probable that an empire can rise without his aid?

—*BENJAMIN FRANKLIN*
Debates in the Constitutional
Convention,
June 28, 1787

No person demeaning himself in a peaceable and orderly manner shall ever be molested on account of his mode of worship or religious sentiments in the said territory.

—*ANONYMOUS*
Northwest Ordinance, art. 1,
July 13, 1787

The business of civil government is to protect the citizen in his rights, to defend the community from hostile powers, and to promote the general welfare. Civil government has no business to meddle with the private opinions of the people. If I demean myself as a good citizen, I am accountable, not to man, but to God, for the religious opinions which I embrace, and the manner in which I worship the supreme being. ... But while I assert the right of religious liberty, I would not deny that the civil power has a right, in some cases, to interfere with religion. It has a right to prohibit and punish gross immoralities and impieties; because the open prac-

tice of these is of evil example and public detriment. For this reason, I heartily approve of our laws against drunkeness, profane swearing, blasphemy, and professed atheism.
—*OLIVER ELLSWORTH* (1745–1807)
Speech at the Connecticut Ratifying Convention,
1787

The United States of America have exhibited, perhaps, the first example of governments erected on the simple principles of nature; and if men are now sufficiently enlightened to disabuse themselves of artifice, imposture, hypocrisy, and superstition, they will consider this event as an era in their history. Although the detail of the formation of the American governments is at present little known or regarded either in Europe or in America, it may hereafter become an object of curiosity. It will never be pretended that any persons employed in that service had interviews with the gods, or were in any degree under the influence of Heaven, more than those at work upon ships or houses, or laboring in merchandise or agriculture; it will forever be acknowledged that these governments were contrived merely by the use of reason and the senses.
—*JOHN ADAMS*
"A Defence of the Constitutions of Government of the United States of America"
1787–1788

Religious persecution may shield itself under the guise of a mistaken and overzealous piety.
—*EDMUND BURKE* (1729–1797)
Impeachment of Warren Hastings,
February 7, 1788

Happily for the states, they enjoy the utmost freedom of religion. This freedom arises from that multiplicity of sects, which pervades America, and which is the best and only security for religious liberty in any society. For where there is such a variety of sects, there cannot be a majority of any one sect to oppress and persecute the rest. Fortunately for this commonwealth [Virginia], a majority of the people are decidedly against any exclusive establishment—I believe it to be so in the other states. There is not a shadow of right in the general government to intermeddle with religion. Its least interference with it would be a most flagrant usurpation.
—*JAMES MADISON*
Speech in the Virginia Ratifying Convention,
June 12, 1788

It is true, we are not disposed to differ much, at present, about religion; but when we are making a constitution, it is to be hoped, for ages and millions yet unborn, why not establish the free exercise of religion as a part of the national compact.
—*RICHARD HENRY LEE* (1732–1794)
Letters of the Federal Farmer
1788

There seems to be a disposition in men to find fault, rather than to act as they ought. The works of creation itself have been objected to: and one learned prince declared, that if he had been consulted, they would have been improved. With what book has so much fault been found, as with the Bible? Perhaps, principally, because it so clearly and strongly enjoins men to do right. How many, how plausible objections have been made against it, with how much ardor, with how much pains? Yet, the book has done more good than all the books in the world; would do much more, if duly regarded; and might lead the objectors against it to happiness, if they would value it as they should.

—JOHN DICKINSON (1732–1794)
"Letters of Fabius" #4,
1788

Every man, conducting himself as a good citizen, and being accountable, to God alone for his religious opinions, ought to be protected in worshiping the Deity according to the dictates of his own conscience.

—GEORGE WASHINGTON (1732–1799)
Letter to the United Baptist Church of Virginia,
May 1789

Congress should not establish a religion, and enforce the legal observation of it by law, nor compel men to worship God in any Manner contrary to their conscience.

—JAMES MADISON
Annals of Congress 730,
August 15, 1789

As to those employed in teaching and inculcating the duties of religion, there may be some indelicacy in singling them out [as a category in a census], as the general government is proscribed from interfering, in any manner whatever, in matters respecting religion; and it may be thought to do this, in ascertaining who, and who are not, ministers of the gospel.

—JAMES MADISON
Speech in Congress,
February 2, 1790

As to Jesus of Nazareth, my Opinion of whom you particularly desire, I think the System of Morals and his Religion, as he left them to us, the best the World ever saw or is likely to see; but I apprehend it has received various corrupting Changes, and I have, with most of the present Dissenters in England, some Doubts as to his Divinity; tho' it is a question I do not dogmatize upon, having never studied it, and think it needless to busy myself with it now, when I expect soon an Opportunity of knowing the Truth with less Trouble.

—BENJAMIN FRANKLIN
To Ezra Stiles,
March 9, 1790

For happily the government of the United States, which gives to bigotry no sanction, to persecution no assistance, requires only that they who live under its protection should demean themselves as good citizens, in giving it on all occasions their effectual support. ... May the children of the Stock of Abraham, who dwell in this land, continue to merit and enjoy the good will of the other inhabitants, while every one shall sit in safety under his own vine and fig-tree, and there shall be none to make him afraid.

—GEORGE WASHINGTON
Letter to the Hebrew congregation of Newport, Rhode Island,
August 17, 1790

All religions are in their nature mild and benign, and united with principles of morality. They could not have made proselites at first, by professing anything that was vicious, cruel, persecuting, or immoral. Like everything else, they had their beginning; and they proceeded by persuasion, exhortation, and example. How then is it that they lose their native mildness, and become morose and intolerant?

It proceeds from the connection which Mr. Burke recommends. By engendering the church with the state, a sort of mule animal, capable only of destroying, and not of breeding up, is produced, called *The Church established by Law*. It is a stranger, even from its birth, to any parent mother on which it is begotten, and whom in time it kicks out and destroys.

—THOMAS PAINE
Rights of Man, I
1791

Persecution is not an original feature in *any* religion; but it is always the strongly-marked feature of all law-religions, or religions established by law. Take away the law-establishment, and every religion reassumes its original benignity.

—THOMAS PAINE
Rights of Man, I
1791

Every religion is good, that teaches man to be good.

—THOMAS PAINE
Rights of Man, II
1792

I do not believe that any two men, on what are called doctrinal points, think alike who think at all. It is only those who have not thought that appear to agree.

—THOMAS PAINE
Rights of Man, II
1792

If we suppose a large family of children, who, on any particular day, or particular circumstance, made it a custom to present to their parents some token of their affection and gratitude, each of them would make a different offering, and most probably in a different manner. Some would pay their congratulations in themes of verse or prose, by some little devices, as their genius dictated, or according to what they thought would please; and, perhaps, the least of all, not able to do any of those things, would ramble into the garden, or the field, and gather what it thought the prettiest flower it could find, though, perhaps, it might be but a simple weed. The parents would be more gratified by such variety, than if the whole of them had acted on a concerted plan, and each had made exactly the same offering. This would have the cold appearance of contrivance, or the harsh one of control. But of all unwelcome things, nothing could more afflict the parent than to know, that the whole of them had afterwards gotten together by the ears, boys and girls, fighting, scratching, reviling, and abusing each other about which was the best or the worst present.

Why may we not suppose, that the great Father of all is pleased with variety of devotion; and that the greatest offense we can act, is that by which we seek to torment and render each other miserable.

—THOMAS PAINE
Rights of Man, II
1792

Religion is very improperly made a political machine.

—THOMAS PAINE
Rights of Man, II
1792

Adam, if ever there were such a man, was created a Deist; but in the mean time let every man follow, as he has a right to do, the religion and the worship he prefers.

—THOMAS PAINE
Age of Reason, I
1794

All national institutions of churches, whether Jewish, Christian, or Turkish, appear to me no other than human inventions set up to terrify and enslave mankind, and monopolize power and profit.

—THOMAS PAINE
Age of Reason, I
1794

Any system of religion that has anything in it that shocks the mind of a child cannot be a true system.

—THOMAS PAINE
Age of Reason, I
1794

Every national church or religion has established itself by pretending some special mission from God communicated to certain individuals. The Jews have their Moses; the Christians their Jesus Christ, their apostles, and saints; and the Turks their Mahomet; as if the way to God was not open to every man alike.

—THOMAS PAINE
Age of Reason, I
1794

I believe in one God and no more, and I hope for happiness beyond this life. I believe in the equality of man; and I believe that religious duties consist in doing justice, loving mercy, and endeav-

oring to make our fellow creatures happy.

—THOMAS PAINE
Age of Reason, I
1794

It is only in the CREATION that all our ideas and conceptions of a *word of God* can unite.

—THOMAS PAINE
Age of Reason, I
1794

Jesus Christ founded no new system. He called men to the practice of moral virtues, and the belief of one God. The great trait in his character is philanthropy.

—THOMAS PAINE
Age of Reason, I
1794

Man does not learn religion as he learns the secrets and mysteries of a trade. He learns the theory of religion by reflection. It arises out of the action of his own mind upon the things which he sees, or upon what he may happen to hear or to read, and the practice joins itself thereto.

—THOMAS PAINE
Age of Reason, I
1794

Priests and conjurors are of the same trade.

—THOMAS PAINE
Age of Reason, I
1794

When I see throughout the greatest part of this book, [i.e., the Bible] scarcely any thing but a history of the grossest vices, and a collection of the most paltry and contemptible tales, I cannot dishonor my Creator by calling it by his name.

—*THOMAS PAINE*
Age of Reason, I
1794

Religious duties consist in doing justice, loving mercy, and endeavoring to make our fellow creatures happy.

—*THOMAS PAINE*
Age of Reason, I
1794

The word of God is the creation we behold. And it is in *this word*, which no human invention can counterfeit or alter, that God speaketh universally to man.

—*THOMAS PAINE*
Age of Reason, I
1794

When we contemplate the immensity of that Being, who directs and governs the incomprehensible WHOLE, of which the utmost ken of human sight can discover but a part, we ought to feel shame at calling such paltry stories [i.e., the Bible] the word of God.

—*THOMAS PAINE*
Age of Reason, I
1794

Whenever we read the obscene stories, the volumptuous debaucheries, the cruel and turturous executions, the unrelenting vindictiveness with which more than half the BIble is filled, it would be more consistent that we called it the word of a demon than the word of God. It is a history of wickedness, that has served to corrupt and brutalize mankind; and,

for my own part, I sincerely detest it, as I detest everything that is cruel.

—*THOMAS PAINE*
Age of Reason, I
1794

It is a duty incumbent on every true deist, that he vindicates the moral justice of God against the calumnies of the Bible.

—*THOMAS PAINE*
Age of Reason, II
1795

People in general know not what wickedness there is in this pretended word of God. Brought up in habits of superstition, they take it for granted, that the bible is true, and that it is good. They permit themselves not to doubt of it; and they carry the ideas they form of the benevolence of the Almighty to the book which they have been taught to believe was written by his authority. Good heavens, it is quite another thing! It is a book of lies, wickedness, and blasphemy; for what can be greater blasphemy than to ascribe the wickedness of man to the orders of the Almighty.

—*THOMAS PAINE*
Age of Reason, II
1795

The only sect that has not persecuted, are the Quakers, and the only reason that can be given for it is, that they are rather Deists than Christians. They do not believe much about Jesus Christ, and they call the scriptures a dead letter.

—*THOMAS PAINE*
Age of Reason, II
1795

One great advantage of the Christian religion is that it brings the great principle of the law of nature and nations—Love your neighbor as yourself, and do to others as you would that others should do to you,—to the knowledge, belief, and veneration of the whole people.

—*JOHN ADAMS*
Diary entry,
August 14, 1796

Amongst other strange things said of me, I hear it is said by the deists that I am one of their number; and, indeed, that some good people think I am no Christian. This thought gives me much more pain than the appellation of Tory, because I think religion of infinitely higher importance than politics; and I find much cause to reproach myself that I have lived so long, and have given no decided and public proofs of my being a Christian.

—*PATRICK HENRY* (1736–1799)
To his daughter,
1796

Of all the tyrannies that afflict mankind, tyranny in religion is the worst. Every other species of tyranny is limited to the world we live in, but this attempts a stride beyond the grave and seeks to pursue us into eternity. It is there and not here, it is to God and not to man, it is to a heavenly and not an earthly tribunal that we are to account for our belief.

—*THOMAS PAINE*
Letter to a Mr. Erskine,
1797

Religion is a private affair between every man and his Maker, and no tribunal or third party has a right to interfere between them. It is not properly a thing of this world; it is only practiced in this world; but its object is in a future world; and it is not otherwise an object of just laws than for the purpose of protecting the equal rights of all, however various their belief may be.

—*THOMAS PAINE*
Letter to a Mr. Erskine,
1797

Practical religion consists in doing good; and the only way of serving God is, that of endeavoring to make his creation happy. All preaching that has not this for its object is nonsense and hypocrisy.

—*THOMAS PAINE*
Agrarian Justice
1797

Religion does not unite itself to show and noise. True religion is without either. Where there is both there is no true religion.

—*THOMAS PAINE*
To Camille Jordan,
1797

The intellectual part of religion is a private affair between every man and his Maker, and in which no third party has any right to interfere. The practical part consists in our doing good to each other.

—*THOMAS PAINE*
To Camille Jordan,
1797

The modes of worship are as various as the sects are numerous; and amidst all this variety and multiplicity there is but one article of belief in which every religion in the world agrees. That article has universal sanction. It is the belief of a God, or what the Greeks described by the word *Theism*, and the Latins by that of *Deism*.

—*THOMAS PAINE*
To Camille Jordan,
1797

The safety and prosperity of nations ultimately and essentially depend on the protection and blessing of Almighty God; and the national acknowledgment of this truth is not only an indispensable duty, which the people owe to him, but a duty whose natural influence is favorable to the promotion of that morality and piety, without which social happiness cannot exist, nor the blessings of a free government be enjoyed.

—*JOHN ADAMS*
"Proclamation for a National Fast"
1798

Believing with you that religion is a matter which lies solely between Man & his God, that he owes account to none other for his faith or his worship, that the legitimate powers of government reach actions only, & not opinions, I contemplate with sovereign reverence that act of the whole American people which declared that their legislature should "make no law respecting an establishment of religion, or prohibiting the free exercise thereof," thus building a wall of separation between Church & State. Adhering to this expression of the supreme will of the nation in behalf of the rights of conscience, I shall see with sincere satisfaction the progress of those sentiments which tend to restore to man all his natural rights, convinced he has no natural right in opposition to his social duties.

—*THOMAS JEFFERSON*
To the Baptist Association of
Danbury, Connecticut,
January 1, 1802

The key to heaven is not in the keeping of any sect, nor ought the road to it be obstructed by any. Our relation to each other in this world is as men, and the man who is a friend to man and to his rights, let his religious opinions be what they may, is a good citizen.

—*THOMAS PAINE*
To Samuel Adams,
January 1, 1803

It behooves every man who values liberty of conscience for himself, to resist invasions of it in the case of others.

—*THOMAS JEFFERSON*
Letter to Dr. Benjamin Rush,
1803

The only foundation for a useful education in a republic is to be laid in religion. Without this there can be no virtue, and without virtue there can be no liberty, and liberty is the object and life of all republican governments.

—*BENJAMIN RUSH*
On the Mode of Education Proper in a Republic
1806

What has preserved this race of Adamses in all their ramifications, in such numbers, health, peace, comfort, and mediocrity? I believe it is religion, without which they would have been rakes, fops, sots, gamblers, starved with hunger, frozen with cold, scalped by Indians, &c., &c., &c., been melted away and disappeared.

—*JOHN ADAMS*
To Benjamin Rush,
July 19, 1812

Every man's own reason must be his oracle.

—*THOMAS JEFFERSON*
Letter to Dr. Benjamin Rush,
March 6, 1813

The subject of religion, a subject on which I have ever been most scrupulously reserved, I have considered it as a matter between every man and his maker, in which no other, & far less the public had a right to intermeddle.

—*THOMAS JEFFERSON*
To Richard Rush,
May 31, 1813

The Bible is the best book in the world. It contains more of my little philosophy than all the libraries I have seen; and such parts of it as I cannot reconcile to my little philosophy, I postpone for further investigation.

—*JOHN ADAMS*
To Thomas Jefferson,
December 25, 1813

I am really mortified to be told that, in the United States of America, a fact like this can become a subject to inquiry, and of criminal inquiry, too, as an offence against religion; that a question about the sale of a book can be carried before the civil magistrate. Is this then our freedom of religion?

—*THOMAS JEFFERSON*
To N. G. Dufief,
April 19, 1814

Cabalistic Christianity, which is Catholic Christianity, and which has prevailed for 1,500 years, has received a mortal wound, of which the monster must finally die. Yet so strong is his constitution, that he may endure for centuries before he expires.

—*JOHN ADAMS*
To Thomas Jefferson,
July 16, 1814

Then conquer we must, for our cause it is just,
And this be our motto,—"In God is our trust!"

—*FRANCIS SCOTT KEY* (1779–1843)
"The Star-Spangled Banner"
1814

The question before the human race is, whether the God of nature shall govern the world by his own laws, or whether priests and kings shall rule it by fictitious miracles?

—*JOHN ADAMS*
To Thomas Jefferson,
June 20, 1815

I do not like the late resurrection of the Jesuits. ... If ever any congregation of men could merit eternal perdition on earth, and in hell, according to these historians, though, like Pascal, true Catholics, it is this company of Loyolas.

—*JOHN ADAMS*
To Thomas Jefferson,
May 5, 1816

I have ever thought religion a concern purely between our God and our consciences, for which we were accountable to him, and not to the priests. I never told my own religion, nor scrutinised that of another. I never attempted to make a convert, nor wished to changed another's creed ... it is in our lives, and not from our words, that our religion must be read.

—THOMAS JEFFERSON
To Mrs. M. Harrison Smith,
August 6, 1816

As I understand the Christian religion, it was, and is, a revelation. But how has it happened that millions of fables, tales, legends, have been blended with both Jewish and Christian revelation that have made them the most bloody religion that ever existed?

—JOHN ADAMS
To F. A. Van der Kamp,
December 27, 1816

Is the appointment of Chaplains to the two Houses of Congress consistent with the Constitution, and with the pure principle of religious freedom? In strictness the answer on both points must be in the negative. The Constitution of the U.S. forbids every thing like an establishment of a national religion. The law appointing Chaplains establishes a religious worship for the national representatives, to be performed by Ministers of religion, elected by a majority of them; and these are to be paid out of the national taxes. Does not this involve the principle of a national establishment, applicable to a provision for a religious worship for the Constituent as well as of the representative Body, approved by the majority, and conducted by Ministers of religion paid by the entire nation. The establishment of the chaplainship to Congress is a palpable violation of equal rights, as well as of Constitutional principles. The tenets of the Chaplains elected shut the door of wor-

ship against the members whose creeds and consciences forbid a participation in that of the majority.

—JAMES MADISON
Detached Memoranda,
post 1817

There is an evil which ought to be guarded against in the indefinite accumulation of property from the capacity of holding it in perpetuity by ecclesiastical corporations. The power of all corporations, ought to be limited in this respect. The growing wealth acquired by them never fails to be a source of abuses.

—JAMES MADISON
Detached Memoranda,
post 1817

All religions united with government are more or less inimical to liberty. All separated from government, are compatible with liberty.

—HENRY CLAY (1777–1852)
Speech in the House of
Representatives,
March 24, 1818

I have ever regarded the freedom of religious opinions and worship as equally belonging to every sect.

—JAMES MADISON
To Mordecai Noah,
May 15, 1818

I have received your letter of the 6th with the eloquent discourse delivered at the Consecration of the Jewish Synagogue. Having ever regarded the freedom of religious opinions and worship as equally belonging to every sect, and the secure enjoyment of it as the best human provision for bringing all either into the same way of thinking, or into that mutual charity which is the only proper substitute, I observe with pleasure the view you give of the spirit in which your Sect partake of the common blessings afforded by our Government and Laws.

—JAMES MADISON
To Mordecai M. Noah,
May 15, 1818

I wish your nation may be admitted to all the privileges of citizens in every country of the world. This country has done much. I wish it may do more; and annul every narrow idea in religion, government and commerce. Let the wits joke; the philosophers sneer; what then? It has pleased the Providence of the "first cause," the universal cause, that Abraham should give religion, not only to the Hebrews, but to Christians and Mohemetans, the greatest part of the civilized world.

—JOHN ADAMS
To Mordecai M. Noah,
July 31, 1818

It was the universal opinion of the Century preceding the last, that civil Government could not stand without the prop of a religious establishment, and that the Christian religion itself, would perish if not supported by a legal provision for its Clergy. The experience of Virginia conspicuously corroborates the disproof of both opinions. The Civil Government tho' bereft of everything like an anointed hierarchy possesses the requisite Stability and performs its functions with complete success: Whilst the number, the industry, and the morality of the priesthood and the devotion of the people have been manifestly in-

creased by the total separation of the Church from the State.

—JAMES MADISON
To Robert Walsh, Jr.,
March 2, 1819

Can a free government possibly exist with the Roman Catholic religion?

—JOHN ADAMS
To Thomas Jefferson,
May 19, 1821

From the day of the Declaration. ... They [the American people] were bound by the laws of God, which they all, and by the laws of the Gospel, which they nearly all, acknowledged as the rules of their conduct.

—JOHN ADAMS
Oration celebrating July 4,
July 4, 1821

The experience of the U.S. is a happy disproof of the error so long rooted in the unenlightened minds of well meaning Christians, as well as in the corrupt hearts of persecuting Usurpers, that without a legal incorporation of religious and civil polity, neither could be supported. A mutual independence is found most friendly to practical Religion, to social harmony, and to political prosperity.

—JAMES MADISON
To Frederick L. Schaeffer,
December 3, 1821

Notwithstanding the general progress made within the two last centuries in favour of this branch of Liberty, and the full establishment of it in some part of our Country, there remains in others a strong bias toward the old error, that without some sort of alliance or coalition between Government and Religion neither can be duly supported. Such indeed is the tendency to such a coalition, and such its corrupting influence on both the parties, that the danger can not be too guarded against and in a government of opinion, like ours, the only effectual guard, must be found in the soundness and Stability of the general opinion on the subject. Every new and successful example therefore of a perfect separation between ecclesiastical and Civil matters, is of importance, and I have no doubt that every new example will succeed, as every past one has done in showing that religion and Government will both exist in greater purity, the less they are mixed together.

—*James Madison*
To Edward Livingston,
July 10, 1822

The difficulty of reconciling the Christian mind to the absence of religious Tuition from a University, established by Law and at the common expense, is probably less with us [in Virginia] than with you [in Massachusetts]. The settled opinion here is that religion is essentially distinct from Civil Government and exempt from its cognizance; that a connection between them is injurious to both; that there are causes in the human breast, which ensure the perpetuity of religion without the aid of the law; that rival sects with equal rights, exercise mutual censorships in favor of good morals; that if new sects arise with absurd opinions or overheated imaginations, the proper remedies lie in time, forbearance, and example: that a legal establishment of Religion without a toleration, could not be thought of, and with a toleration, is no security for public quiet and harmony, but rather a

source itself of discord and animosity: and, finally, that these opinions are supported by experience, which has shewn that every relaxation of the Alliance between Law and Religion, from the partial example of Holland, to its consummation in Pennsylvania, New Jersey &c. has been found as safe in practice as it is sound in Theory.

—*James Madison*
To Edward Everett,
March 19, 1823

Revolution & Rebellion

And yet I think it may be presumed, a free-born People can never become so servile as to regard them [obey tyrants' edicts], while they have Eyes to see that such Rulers [who violate basic Law] have gone out of the Line of their Power.— There is no Reason they should be Fools because their Rulers are so.

—*Elisha Williams* (1694–1755)
A Seasonable Plea
1744

A PEOPLE really oppressed to a great degree by their sovereign cannot well be insensible when they are so oppressed. And such a people (if I may allude to an ancient *fable*) have, like the Hesperian fruit, a DRAGON for their *protector* and *guardian*; nor would they have any reason to mourn if some HERCULES should appear to dispatch him. For a nation thus abused to arise unanimously and to resist their prince, even to the dethroning him, is not criminal, but a reasonable way of vindicating their liberties and just rights; it is making use of the means, and the only means, which God has put into their power for mutual and self-defense. And it would be highly criminal in them not to make use of this means.

—*JONATHAN MAYHEW* (1720–1766)
"A Discourse Concerning Unlimited Submission and Nonresistance to the Higher Powers"
1750

For, please to observe, that if the end of all civil government be the good of society, if this be the thing that is aimed at in constituting civil rulers, and if the motive and argument for submission to government be taken from the apparent usefulness of civil authority, it follows that when no such good end can be answered by submission there remains no argument or motive to enforce it; and if instead of this good end's being brought about by submission, a *contrary end* is brought about and the ruin and misery of society effected by it, here is a plain and positive reason against submission in all such cases, should they ever happen. And therefore, in such cases a regard to the public welfare ought to make us withhold from our rulers that obedience and subjection which it would, otherwise, be our duty to render to them.

—*JONATHAN MAYHEW*
"A Discourse Concerning Unlimited Submission and Nonresistance to the Higher Powers"
1750

And he that would palm the doctrine of unlimited passive obedience and nonresistance upon mankind ... is not only a fool and a knave, but a rebel against common sense, as well as the laws of God, of Nature, and his Country.

—*JAMES OTIS* (1725–1783)
The Rights of the British Colonies
1764

They planted by your care? No! Your oppression planted 'em in America. They fled from your tyranny to a then uncultivated and unhospitable country where they exposed themselves to almost all the hardships to which human nature is liable, and among others to the cruelties of a savage foe, the most subtle, and I take upon me to say, the most formidable of any people upon the face of God's earth. And yet, actuated by principles of true English liberty, they met all these hardships with pleasure, compared with those they suffered in their own country, from the hands of those who should have been their friends.

They nourished by your indulgence? They grew by your neglect of 'em. As soon as you began to care about 'em, that care was exercised in sending persons to rule over 'em, in one department and another, who were perhaps the deputies of deputies to some member of this house, sent to spy out their liberty, to misrepresent their actions and to prey upon 'em; men whose behaviour on many occasions has caused the blood of those sons of liberty to recoil within them: men promoted to the highest seats of justice; some who to my knowledge were glad by going to a foreign country to escape being brought to the bar of a court of justice in their own.

They protected by your arms? They have nobly taken up arms in your defence, have exerted a valour amidst their constant and laborious industry for the defence of a country whose frontier while drenched in blood, its interior parts have yielded all its little savings to your emolument. And believe me, remember I this day told you so, that

264

same spirit of freedom which actuated that people at first, will accompany them still. But prudence forbids me to explain myself further. God knows I do not at this time speak from motives of party heat; what I deliver are the genuine sentiments of my heart; however superior to me in general knowledge and experience the reputable body of this House may be, yet I claim to know more of America than most of you, having seen and been conversant in that country. The people I believe are as truly loyal as any subjects the king has, but a people jealous of their liberties and who will vindicate them if ever they should be violated; but the subject is too delicate and I will say no more.

—ISAAC BARRE (1726–1802)
Speech in British Parliament,
February 11, 1765

Goody Bull and her daughter together fell out,*
Both squabbled and wrangled and made a great rout.
But the cause of the quarrel remains to be told,
Then lend both your ears and a tale I'll unfold.
Derry down, down, hey derry down,
Then lend both your ears and a tale I'll unfold.
The old lady, it seems, took a freak in her head,
That her daughter, grown woman, might earn her own bread,
Self-applauding her scheme, she was ready to dance,
But we're often too sanguine in what we advance.

Derry down, down, hey derry down,

But we're often too sanguine in what we advance.
For mark the event, thus for fortune we're cross,
Nor should people reckon without their good host,
The daughter was sulky and wouldn't come to,
And pray what in this case could the old woman do?

Derry down, down, hey derry down,
And pray what in this case could the old woman do?
Zounds, neighbor, quoth Pitt, what the devil's the matter?
A man cannot rest in his home for your clatter
Alas, cries the daughter, Here's dainty fine work,
The old woman grows harder than Jew or than Turk
Derry down, down, hey derry down,
The old woman grows harder than Jew or than Turk.
She be damned, says the farmer, and to her he goes
First roars in her ears, then tweaks her old nose,
Hello Goody, what ails you? Wake woman, I say,
I am come to make peace in this desperate fray.

Derry down, down, hey derry down,
I am come to make peace in this desperate fray.
Alas, cries the old woman, And must I comply?
I'd rather submit than the hussy should die.
Pooh, prithee, be quiet, be friends and agree,
You must surely be right if you're

guided by me,
Derry down, down, hey derry down,
You must surely be right if you're
guided by me.

—ANONYMOUS
"The World Turned Upside Down, or
The Old Woman Taught Wisdom"
(1766)
(*Goody Bull and her daughter =
Great Britain and America)

I rejoice that America has resisted.
Three millions of people, so dead to all
the feelings of liberty, as voluntarily to
submit to be slaves, would have been
fit instruments to make slaves of the
rest.

—WILLIAM PITT, EARL OF CHATHAM
(1708–1778)
Speech in the House of Commons,
January 14, 1766

Charity begins at home, and we ought
primarily to consult our own interest;
and besides, a little distress might bring
the people of that country [England] to
a better temper, and a sense of their
injustice towards us. No nation or
people in the world ever made any figure, who were dependent on any other
country for their food or clothing. Let
us then in justice to ourselves and our
children, break off a trade so pernicious
to our interest, and which is likely to
swallow up both our estates and liberties. ... We cannot, we will not, betray
the trust reposed in us by our ancestors, by giving up the least of our liberties. ... We will be freemen, or we will
die.

—SILAS DOWNER (1729–1785)
"A Discourse at the Dedication of the
Tree of Liberty"
1768

Since the Men from a Party, on fear of
a Frown,
Are kept by a Sugar-Plumb, quietly
down.
Supinely asleep, & depriv'd of their
Sight
Are strip'd of their Freedom, and rob'd
of their Right.
If the Sons (so degenerate) the Bless-
ing despise,
Let the Daughters of Liberty, nobly
arise,
And tho' we've no Voice, but a nega-
tive here.
The use of the Taxables, let us fore-
bear,
(Then Merchants import till yr. Stores
are all full
May the Buyers be few & yr. Traffick
be dull.)
Stand firmly resolved & bid Grenville
to see
That rather than Freedom, we'll part
with our Tea
And well as we love the dear Draught
when a dry,
As American Patriots,—our Taste we
deny,
Sylvania's, gay Meadows, can richly
afford,
To pamper our Fancy, or furnish our
Board,
And Paper sufficient (at home) still we
have,
To assure the Wise-acre, we will not
sign Slave.
When this Homespun shall fail, to re-
monstrate our Grief
We can speak with the Tongue or
scratch on a Leaf.
Refuse all their Colours, the richest of
Dye,
The juice of a Berry—our Paint can
supply,

To humour our Fancy—& as for our Houses,
They'll do without painting as well as our Spouses,
While to keep out the Cold of a keen winter Morn
We can screen the Northwest, with a well polish'd Horn,
And trust me a Woman by honest Invention
Might give this State Doctor a Dose of Prevention.
Join mutual in this, & but small as it seems
We may Jostle a Grenville & puzzle his Schemes
But a motive more worthy our patriot Pen,
Thus acting—we point out their Duty to Men,
And should the bound Pensioners, tell us to hush
We can throw back the Satire by biding them blush.

—*HANNAH GRIFFITTS* (1727–1817)
"The Female Patriots"
1768

Young ladies in town, and those that live 'round
Wear none but your own country linen;
Of economy boast, let your pride be the most
To show clothes of your own make and spinnin'.
What if homespun, they say, be not quite as gay
As brocades. Be not in a passion
For once it is known 'tis much worn in town
One and all will cry out 'tis the fashion!
And as one all agree, that you'll not married be,

To such as will wear London factory;
But at first sight refuse, tell 'em you will choose,
As encourage our own manufactory.
No more ribbons wear, nor in rich silks appear,
Love your country much better than fine things,
Begin without passion, 'twill soon be the fashion,
To grace your smooth locks with a twine string.
Throw away your bohea, and your green hyson tea,
And all things of a new fashioned duty;
Get in a good store of the choice Labrador,
There'll soon he enough here to suit ye.
These do without fear and to all you'll appear,
Fair charming, true, lovely and clever,
Though the times remain darkish,
Young men will be sparkish,
And love you much stronger than ever.

—*ANONYMOUS*
"Young Ladies in Town"
1768

That seat of science Athens,
    And earth's proud mistress, Rome,
Where now are all their glories
    We scarce can find a tomb.
Then guard your rights, Americans,
    Nor stoop to lawless sway,
Oppose, oppose, oppose, oppose
    For North America.

Proud Albion bow'd to Caesar,
    And numerous lords before,
To Picts, to Danes, to Normans,
    And many masters more;
But we can boast Americans
    Have never fall'n a prey,

Huzza, huzza, huzza, huzza
 For Free America.

We led fair Freedom hither,
 And lo, the desert smiled,
A paradise of pleasure
 New opened in the wild;
Your harvest, bold Americans,
 No power shall snatch away,
Preserve, preserve, preserve your rights
 In Free America.

Torn from a world of tyrants
 Beneath this western sky
We formed a new dominion,
 A land of liberty;
The world shall own we're freemen
 here,
 And such will ever be,
Huzza, huzza, huzza, huzza
 For love and liberty.

God bless this maiden climate,
 And through her vast domain
May hosts of heroes cluster
 That scorn to wear a chain.
And blast the venal sycophants
 Who dare our rights betray;
Assert yourselves, yourselves, your-
 selves
 For brave America,

Lift up your hearts, my heroes,
 And swear with proud disdain,
The wretch that would ensnare you
 Shall spread his net in vain;
Should Europe empty all her force,
 We'd meet them in array,
And shout huzza, huzza, huzza
 For brave America.

The land where freedom reigns shall
 still
 Be masters of the main,

In giving laws and freedom
 To subject France and Spain;
And all the isles o'er ocean spread
 Shall tremble and obey,
The prince who rules by Freedom's
 laws
 In North America.
 —*JOSEPH WARREN* (1741–1775)
 "Free America"
 c. 1770

Let us contemplate our forefathers and posterity; and resolve to maintain the rights bequeath'd to us from the former, for the sake of the latter. Instead of sitting down satisfied with the efforts we have already made, *which is the wish of the enemy* the necessity of the times, more than ever, calls for our utmost circumspection, deliberation, fortitude and perseverance. Let us remember that "if we suffer tamely a lawless attack upon our liberty, we encourage it, and involve others in our doom." It is a very serious consideration, which should deeply impress our minds, that *millions yet unborn may be the miserable sharers of the event.*
 —*SAMUEL ADAMS* (1722–1803)
 Speech,
 1771

If you, with united zeal and fortitude, oppose the torrent of oppression; if you feel the true fire of patriotism burning in your breasts; if you, from your souls, despise the most gaudy dress that slavery can wear; if you really prefer the lonely cottage (whilst blest with liberty) to gilded palaces, surrounded with the ensigns of slavery, you may have the fullest assurance that tyranny, with her accursed train, will hide their hideous heads in confusion, shame and despair;

if you perform your part, you must have the strongest confidence that THE SAME ALMIGHTY BEING who protected your pious and venerable forefathers, who enabled them to turn a barren wilderness into a fruitful field, who so often made bare his arms for their salvation, will still be mindful of you their offspring.

—JOSEPH WARREN
Boston Massacre Oration,
March 5, 1772

The voice of your fathers' blood cries to you from the ground; MY SONS SCORN TO BE SLAVES! in vain we met the frowns of tyrants; in vain, we crossed the boisterous ocean, found a new world, and prepared it for the happy residence of LIBERTY; in vain, we toiled; in vain, we fought; we bled in vain, if you, our offspring, want valour to repel the assaults of her invaders! Stain not the glory of your worthy ancestors; but like them resolve, never to part with your birthright; be wise in your deliberations, and determined in your exertions for the preservation of your liberties. Follow not the dictates of passion, but enlist yourselves under the sacred banner of reason; use every method in your power to secure your rights; at least prevent the curses of posterity from being heaped upon your memories.

—JOSEPH WARREN
Boston Massacre Oration,
March 5, 1772

Reason, humanity and religion, all conspire to teach us, that we ought in the best manner we can, to provide for the happiness of posterity. We are allied to them by the common tie of nature: They are not here to act their part: A concern for them is a debt which we owe for the care which our progenitors took for us: Heaven has made us their guardians, and intrusted to our care their liberty, honour, and happiness: For when they come upon the stage, they will be deeply affected by the transactions of their fathers, especially by their public transactions. If the present inhabitants of a country submit to slavery, slavery is the inheritance which they will leave to their children. And who that has the bowels of a father, or even the common feelings of humanity, can think without horror, of being the means of subjecting unborn millions to the iron scepter of tyranny?

—SIMEON HOWARD (?–c. 1804)
Sermon preached to the Ancient and
Honorable Artillery Company in
Boston,
June 7, 1773

And though the murderers may escape the just resentment of an enraged people; though drowsy justice, intoxicated by the poisonous draught prepared for her cup, still nods upon her rotten seat, yet be assured such complicated crimes will meet their due reward. Tell me, ye bloody butchers! ye villains high and low! ye wretches who contrived, as well as you who executed the inhuman deed! do you not feel the goads and stings of conscious guilt pierce through your savage bosoms?

—JOHN HANCOCK (1737–1793)
Boston Massacre Oration,
March 5, 1774

Here suffer me to ask (and would to heaven there could be an answer!) what tenderness, what regard, respect, or consideration has Great Britain shown, in their late transactions, for the security of the persons or properties of the inhabitants of the Colonies? Or rather what have they omitted doing to destroy that security? They have declared that they have ever had, and of right ought ever to have, full power to make laws of sufficient validity to bind the Colonies in all cases whatever. They have exercised this pretended right by imposing a tax upon us without our consent; and lest we should show some reluctance at parting with our property, her fleets and armies are sent to enforce their mad pretensions. The town of Boston, ever faithful to the British Crown, has been invested by a British fleet; the troops of George III have crossed the wide Atlantic, not to engage an enemy, but to assist a band of traitors in trampling on the rights and liberties of his most loyal subjects in America—those rights and liberties which, as a father, he ought ever to regard, and as a king, he is bound, in honor, to defend from violation, even at the risk of his own life.

—*JOHN HANCOCK*
Boston Massacre Oration,
March 5, 1774

I have the most animating confidence that the present noble struggle for liberty will terminate gloriously for America. And let us play the man for our God, and for the cities of our God; while we are using the means in our power, let us humbly commit our righteous cause to the great Lord of the Universe, who loveth righteousness and hateth iniquity. And having secured the approbation of our hearts, by a faithful and unwearied discharge of our duty

to our country, let us joyfully leave our concerns in the hands of him who raiseth up and pulleth down the empires and kingdoms of the world.

—*JOHN HANCOCK*
Boston Massacre Oration,
March 5, 1774

Blandishments will not fascinate us, nor will threats of a "halter" intimidate. For, under God, we are determined that wheresoever, whensoever, or howsoever we shall be called to make our exit, we will die free men.

—*JOSIAH QUINCY* (1744–1775)
Observations on the Boston Port Bill,
1774

On the fortitude, on the wisdom and on the exertions of this important day, is suspended the fate of this new world, and of unborn millions. If a boundless extent of continent, swarming with millions, will tamely submit to live, move and have their being at the arbitrary will of a licentious minister, they basely yield to voluntary slavery, and future generations shall load their memories with incessant execrations.— On the other hand, if we arrest the hand which would ransack our pockets, if we disarm the parricide which points the dagger to our bosoms, if we nobly defeat that fatal edict which proclaims a power to frame laws for us in all cases whatsoever, thereby entailing the endless and numberless curses of slavery upon us, our heirs and their heirs forever; if we successfully resist that unparalleled usurpation of unconstitutional power, whereby our capital is robbed of the means of life; whereby the streets of Boston are thronged with military executioners; whereby our coasts are lined and harbours crowded with ships of war; whereby the charter of the colony, that sacred barrier against the encroachments of tyranny, is mutilated and, in effect, annihilated; whereby a murderous law is framed to shelter villains from the hands of justice; whereby the unalienable and inestimable inheritance, which we derived from nature, the constitution of Britain, and the privileges warranted to us in the charter of the province, is totally wrecked, annulled, and vacated, posterity will acknowledge that virtue which preserved them free and happy; and while we enjoy the rewards and blessings of the faithful, the torrent of panegyrists will roll our reputations to that latest period, when the streams of time shall be absorbed in the abyss of eternity.

—JOSEPH WARREN
The Suffolk Resolves,
1774

There was a rich lady lived over the
  sea,
And she was an island queen,
Her daughter lived off in the new coun-
  try,
With an ocean of water between.
With an ocean of water between.
  With an ocean of water between.

The old lady's pockets were filled with
  gold,
Yet never contented was she,
So she ordered her daughter to pay her
  a tax,
Of thruppence a pound on the tea.
Of thruppence a pound on the tea.
  Of thruppence a pound on the tea.

Oh mother, dear mother, the daughter
  replied,

I'll not do the thing that you ask,
I'm willing to pay fair price on the tea,
But never the thruppenney tax.
But never the thruppenney tax.
But never the thruppenney tax.

You shall, cried the mother, and red-
  dened with rage,
For you're my own daughter, you see,
And it's only proper that daughter should
  pay
Her mother's a tax on the tea.
Her mother's a tax on the tea.
Her mother's a tax on the tea.

She ordered her servant to come up to
  her,
And to wrap up a package of tea.
And eager for thruppence a pound she
  put in
Enough for a large family.
Enough for a large family.
Enough for a large family.

The tea was conveyed to her daughter's
  own door,
All down by the oceanside,
But the bouncing girl poured out ever
  pound
On the dark and the boiling tide.
On the dark and the boiling tide.
On the dark and the boiling tide.

And then she called out to the island
  queen,
Oh mother, dear mother, called she,
Your tea you may have when 'tis
  steeped enough,
But never a tax from me!
But never a tax from me!
But never a tax from me!

—ANONYMOUS
"The Rich Lady Over the Sea"
c. 1774

Stand your ground. Don't fire unless fired upon, but if they mean to have a war, let it begin here!
—CAPT. JOHN PARKER (1729–1775)
Order to the Lexington Minutemen,
April 19, 1775

What a glorious morning for America!
—SAMUEL ADAMS
Upon hearing the sound of gunfire at
Lexington, Massachusetts,
April 19, 1775

Our cause is just. Our union is perfect. Our internal resources are great, and, if necessary, foreign assistance is undoubtedly attainable. ... The arms we have been compelled by our enemies to assume we will, in defiance of every hazard, with unabating firmness and perseverance, employ for the preservation of our liberties; being with one mind resolved to die free men rather than live slaves.
—JOHN DICKINSON (1732–1794)
(This document was written with
Thomas Jefferson)
"A Declaration by the Representatives of the United Colonies of North-America, Now Met in Congress at Philadelphia, Setting Forth the Causes and Necessity of Their Taking Up Arms"
July 6, 1775

[A]s to trade, it hangs so uncertain, that we may in a few months trade with all the world on our own risk, or it may return to its former channel. It seems now to depend on the reception of our last Petition from the Congress to the King; if that should be so considered as to lay a foundation for negotiation, we may be again reconciled—if not, I imagine WE SHALL DECLARE FOR INDEPENDENCE, and exert our utmost to defend ourselves. This proposition would have alarmed almost every person on the Continent a twelvemonth ago, but now the general voice is, if the Ministry and Nation will drive us to it, we must do it, rather than submit, after so many public resolutions to the contrary.
—ESTHER REED (1746–1780)
To Dennis De Berdt,
October 28, 1775

When your lordships look at the papers transmitted us from America, when you consider their decency, firmness and wisdom, you cannot but respect their cause, and wish to make it your own—for myself I must declare and avow that, in all my reading and observation, and it has been my favorite study—I have read Thucydides, and have studied and admired the master statesmen of the world—that for solidity and reasoning, force of sagacity, and widom of conclusion, under such a compilation of different circumstances, no nation or body of men can stand in preference to the general congress at Philadelphia.—I trust it is obvious to your lordships, that all attempts to impose servitude on such men, to establish despotism over such a mighty continental nation—must be vain—must be futile.
—WILLIAM PITT, Earl of Chatham
Statement in House of Lords,
December 20, 1775

If we wish to be free—if we mean to preserve inviolate those inestimable privileges for which we have been so long contending—if we mean not basely to abandon the noble struggle in which we have been so long engaged, and

which we have pledged ourselves never to abandon until the glorious object of our contest shall be obtained—we must fight!—I repeat it, sir, we must fight! An appeal to arms and to the God of Hosts is all that is left us!
—PATRICK HENRY (1736–1799)
Second Virginia Convention, 1775

It looks to me to be narrow and pedantic to apply the ordinary ideas of criminal justice to this great public contest. I do not know the method of drawing up an indictment against a whole people.
—EDMUND BURKE (1729–1797)
Speech on moving his resolutions for conciliation with the Colonies, 1775

Three millions of people, armed in the holy cause of liberty, and in such a country as that which we possess, are invincible by any force which our enemy can send against us. Besides, sir, we shall not fight our battles alone. There is a just God who presides over the destinies of nations; and who will raise up friends to fight our battles for us.
—PATRICK HENRY
Second Virginia Convention, 1775

It is an indispensable duty, my brethren, which we owe to God and our country, to rouse up and bestir ourselves, and, being animated with a noble zeal for the sacred cause of liberty, to defend our lives and fortunes, even to the shedding the last drop of blood. The love of our country, the tender affection that we have for our wives and children, the regard we ought to have for unborn posterity, yea, every-

thing that is dear and sacred, do now loudly call upon us to use our best endeavours to save our country. We must beat our ploughshares into swords, and our pruning-hooks into spears, and learn the art of self-defence against our enemies.
—SAMUEL WEST (1730–1807)
"On the Right to Rebel Against Governors"
May 29, 1776

Objects of the most stupendous magnitude, and measure in which the lives and liberties of millions yet unborn are intimately interested, are now before us. We are in the very midst of a revolution the most complete, unexpected and remarkable of any in the history of nations.
—JOHN ADAMS (1735–1826)
To William Cushing, June 9, 1776

The time is now near at hand which must probably determine whether Americans are to be freemen or slaves; whether they are to have any property they can call their own; whether their houses and farms are to be pillaged and destroyed, and themselves consigned to a state of wretchedness from which no human efforts will deliver them. The fate of unborn millions will now depend, under God, on the courage and conduct of this army. ... We have, therefore, to resolve to conquer or die.
—GEORGE WASHINGTON (1732–1799)
General Orders to American troops shortly before the Battle of Long Island, July 1776

He [her son] is wanted and must go.

You [her daughter] and I, Kate, have also service to do. Food must be prepared for the hungry; for before tomorrow night, hundreds, I hope thousands, will be on their way to join the continental forces.

—MARY DRAPER (c. 1718–1810)
Response to a call to arms,
1776

I have as little superstition in me as any man living, but my secret opinion has ever been, and still is, that God Almighty will not give up a people to military destruction, or leave them unsupportedly to perish, who have so earnestly and so repeatedly sought to avoid the calamities of war, by every decent method which wisdom could invent. Neither have I so much of the infidel in me, as to suppose that He has relinquished the government of the world, and given us up to the care of devils; and as I do not, I cannot see on what grounds the king of Britain can look up to heaven for help against us: a common murderer, a highwayman, or a house-breaker, has as good a pretence as he.

—THOMAS PAINE (1737–1809)
The Crisis
1776

Small islands not capable of protecting themselves, are the proper objects for kingdoms to take under their care; but there is something very absurd, in supposing a continent to be perpetually governed by an island. In no instance hath nature made the satellite larger than its primary planet, and as England and America, with respect to each other, reverses the common order of nature, it is evident they belong to different systems: England to Europe, America to itself.

—THOMAS PAINE
Common Sense
1776

The sun never shined on a cause of greater worth. 'Tis not the affair of a city, a country, a province, or a kingdom, but of a continent—of at least one eighth part of the habitable globe. 'Tis not the concern of a day, a year, or an age; posterity are virtually involved in the contest, and will be more or less affected, even to the end of time, by the proceedings now. Now is the seed time of continental union, faith and honor. The least fracture now will be like a name engraved with the point of a pin on the tender rind of a young oak; the wound will enlarge with the tree, and posterity read it in full grown characters.

—THOMAS PAINE
Common Sense
1776

'Twas on December's fifteenth day,
When we set sail for America;
'Twas on that dark and dismal day,
When we set sail for America.
'Twas on that dark and dismal time,
When we set sail for the Northern
    clime,
Where drums to beat and trumpets
    sound,
And unto Boston we were bound.
And when to Boston we did come,
We thought by the aid of our British
    guns,
To drive the rebels from that place,
To fill their hearts with sore disgrace.
But to our sorrow and surprise,
We saw men like grasshoppers rise;

They fought like heroes much enraged,
Which did affright old General Gage.
Like lions roaring of their prey,
They feared no danger or dismay;
Bold British blood runs through their
    veins,
And still with courage they sustain.
We saw those bold Columbia's sons
Spread death and slaughter from their
    guns:
Freedom or death! these heroes cry,
They did not seem afraid to die.
We said to York, as you've been told,
With the loss of many a Briton bold,
For to make those rebels own our King,
And daily tribute to him bring.
They said it was a garden place,
And that our armies could, with ease,
Pull down their town, lay waste their
    lands,
In spite of all their boasted bands.
A garden place it was indeed,
And in it grew many a bitter weed,
Which will pull down our highest hopes
And sorely wound our British troops.
'Tis now September the seventeenth day,
I wish I'd never come to America;
Full fifteen thousand has been slain,
Bold British heroes every one.
Now I've received my mortal wound,
I bid farewell to Old England's ground;
My wife and children will mourn for
    me,
Whilst I lie cold in America.
Fight on America's noble sons,
Fear not Britannia's thundering guns;
Maintain your cause from year to year,
God's on your side, you need not fear.
    —*ANONYMOUS*
    "The Dying Redcoat"
    c. 1776

The voice of fame, ere this reaches you,
will tell how greatly fortunate we have
been in this department. Burgoyne and
his whole army have laid down their arms,
and surrendered themselves to me and
my Yankees. Thanks to the Giver of all
victory for this triumphant success. ...

Major-General Phillips, who wrote me
that saucy note last year from St.
John's, is now my prisoner. ...

If Old England is not by this lesson
taught humility, then she is an obstinate old slut, bent upon her ruin.
    —*HORATIO GATES* (1728–1806)
    To his wife,
    October 17, 1777

If I were an American, as I am an Englishman, while a foreign troop was
landed in my country I never would lay
down my arms—never! never! never!
    —*WILLIAM PITT, EARL OF CHATHAM*
    Speech,
    November 18, 1777

We fight not to enslave, but to set a
country free, and to make room upon
the earth for honest men to live in.
    —*THOMAS PAINE*
    The Crisis
    1777

He that rebels against reason is a real
rebel, but he that in defence of reason,
rebels against tyranny, has a better title
to "Defender of the Faith" than George
the Third.
    —*THOMAS PAINE*
    The Crisis
    1777

Our cause is noble; it is the cause of
mankind!
    —*GEORGE WASHINGTON*
    To James Warren,
    March 31, 1779

Shall we hesitate to wear a clothing more simple; hair dressed less elegant, while at the price of this small privation, we shall deserve your benedictions. Who, amongst us, will not renounce with the highest pleasure, those vain ornaments, when she shall consider that the valiant defenders of America will be able to draw some advantage from the money which she may have laid out in these; that they will be better defended from the rigours of the seasons, that after their painful toils, they will receive some extraordinary and unexpected relief; that these presents will perhaps be valued by them at a greater price, when they will have it in their power to say: This is the offering of the Ladies. The time is arrived to display the same sentiments which animated us at the beginning of the Revolution, when we renounced the use of teas ... rather than receive them from our persecutors; when we made it appear to them that we placed former necessaries in the rank of superfluities, when our liberty was interested; when our republican and laborious hands spun the flax, prepared the linen intended for the use of our soldiers; when exiles and fugitives we supported with courage all the evils which are the concomitants of war. Let us not lose a moment; let us be engaged to offer the homage of our gratitude at the altar of military valour.

—ESTHER REED
"Sentiments of an American Woman"
1780

The greater the chaos, the greater will be your merit in bringing forth order.
—GEORGE WASHINGTON
To Philip Schuyler,
February 20, 1781

It will not be believed that such a force as Great Britain has employed for eight years in this country could be baffled in their plan of subjugating it by numbers infinitely less, composed of men oftentimes half starved, always in rags, without pay, and experiencing, at times, every species of distress which human nature is capable of undergoing.

—GEORGE WASHINGTON
To Nathanael Greene,
February 6, 1783

The foundation of our empire was not laid in the gloomy age of ignorance or superstition, but at an epoch when the rights of mankind were better understood and more clearly defined than at any former period.

—GEORGE WASHINGTON
Circular to the States,
June 8, 1783

With a heart full of love and gratitude, I now take my leave of you. I most devoutly wish that your latter days may be as prosperous and happy as your former ones have been glorious and honorable.

—GEORGE WASHINGTON
Farewell to his officers at Fraunces Tavern in New York City,
December 4, 1783

"The times that tried men's souls," are over—and the greatest and completest revolution the world ever knew is gloriously and happily accomplished.

—THOMAS PAINE
The Crisis
1783

The republican form and principle leaves no room for insurrection, because it provides and establishes a rightful means in its stead.

—THOMAS PAINE
"Dissertations on Government"
1786

A little rebellion, now and then, is a good thing, and as necessary in the political world as storms in the physical. ... It is a medicine necessary for the sound health of government.

—THOMAS JEFFERSON (1743–1823)
Letter to James Madison,
January 30, 1787

The spirit of resistance to government is so valuable on certain occasions that I wish it to be always kept alive. It will often be exercised when wrong, but better so than not to be exercised at all.

—THOMAS JEFFERSON
To Abigail Adams,
February 22, 1787

The tree of liberty must be refreshed from time to time with the blood of patriots and tyrants. It is its natural manure.

—THOMAS JEFFERSON
Letter to William Stevens Smith,
November 13, 1787

And what country can preserve its liberties, if its rulers are not warned from time to time, that this people preserve the spirit of resistance? Let them take arms. The remedy is to set them right as to facts, pardon and pacify them. What signify a few lives lost in a century or two?

—THOMAS JEFFERSON
Letter to Colonel William S. Smith,
1787

No form of government can always either avoid or control them [revolutions]. it is in vain to hope to guard against events too mighty for human foresign or precaution, and it would be idle to object to a government because it could not perform impossibilities.

—ALEXANDER HAMILTON (1755–1804)
The Federalist Papers
1787

There is nothing more common, than to confound the terms of *American Revolution* with those of *the late American war*. The American war is over but this is far from being the case with the American revolution. On the contrary, nothing but the first act of the great drama is closed. It remains yet to establish and perfect our new forms of government; and to prepare the principles, morals, and manners of our citizens, for these forms of government, after they are established and brought to perfection. ... Patriots of 1774, 1775, 1776—heroes of 1778, 1779, 1780! come forward! your country demands your services!—Philosophers and friends to mankind, come forward! your country demands your studies and speculations! Lovers of peace and order, who declined taking part in the late war, come forward! your country forgives your timidity and demands your influence and advice! Hear her proclaiming, in sighs and groans, in her governments, in her finances, in her trade, in her manufacturers, in her morals, and in her manners, 'The Revolution is not over.'

—BENJAMIN RUSH (1745–1813)
Address to the American people,
1787

The American Revolution, or the peculiar light of the age, seems to have opened the eyes of almost every nation in Europe, and a spirit of equal liberty appears fast to be gaining ground everywhere.

—GEORGE WASHINGTON
To Hector St. John de Crevecoeur,
April 10, 1789

Revolutions have for their object, a change in the moral condition of governments.

—THOMAS PAINE
Rights of Man, II
1792

The independence of America, considered merely as a separation from England, would have been a matter of but little importance, had it not been accompanied by a revolution in the principles and practices of government. She made a stand, not for herself only, but for the world.

—THOMAS PAINE
Rights of Man, II
1792

The revolution of America presented in politics what was only theory in mechanics.

—THOMAS PAINE
Rights of Man, II
1792

If there be a principle that ought not to be questioned within the United States, it is, that every nation has a right to abolish an old government and establish a new one. This principle is not only recorded in every public archive, written in every American heart, and sealed with the blood of a host of American martyrs; but is the only lawful tenure by which the United Sates hold their existence as a nation.

—JAMES MADISON (1751–1836)
Helvidius No. 3,
September 7, 1793

It is never to be expected in a revolution, that every man is to change his opinion at the same moment. There never yet was any truth or any principle so irresistibly obvious, that all men believed it at once. Time and reason must co-operate with each other to the final establishment of any principle; and, therefore, those who may happen to be first convinced have not a right to persecute others, on whom conviction operates more slowly. The moral principle of revolution is to instruct, not to destroy.

—THOMAS PAINE
"Dissertation on First Principles of Government"
1795

When all other rights are taken away the right of rebellion is made perfect.

—THOMAS PAINE
"Dissertation on First Principles of Government"
1795

Our revolution was so distinguished for moderation, virtue, and humanity as to merit the eulogium ... of being unsullied with a crime.

—GEORGE WASHINGTON
To John Hawkins Stone,
December 23, 1796

I agreed with a Colonel Conant and some other gentlemen that if the British went out by water, we should show two lanthorns in the North

Church steeple; and if by land, one, as a signal.

—PAUL REVERE (1734–1818)
To Jeremy Belknap,
1798

The assertion by Great Britain of a power to make laws for the other members of the Empire *in all cases whatsoever*, ended in the discovery, that she had a right to make laws for them, *in no cases whatsoever*.

—JAMES MADISON
The Report of 1800,
January 7, 1800

The fundamental principle of the revolution was, that the colonies were co-ordinate members with each other, and with Great-Britain; of an Empire, united by a common Executive Sovereign, but not united by any common Legislative Sovereign. The Legislative power was maintained to be as complete in each American Parliament, as in the British Parliament. And the royal prerogative was in force in each colony, by virtue of its acknowledging the King for its Executive Magistrate, as it was in Great Britain, by virtue of a like acknowledgment there. A denial of these principles by Great-Britain, and the assertion of them by America, produced the revolution.

—JAMES MADISON
The Report of 1800,
January 7, 1800

Soon after the action at Lexington, a number of enterprising young men, principally from Connecticut [including Benedict Arnold], proposed to each other a sudden march towards the lakes, and a bold attempt to surprise Ticonderoga, garrisoned by the king's troops ... so secretly, judiciously, and rapidly was the expedition conducted, that they entered the garrison and saluted the principal officer as their prisoner, before he had any reason to apprehend an enemy was near ... the commanding officer there inquired by whose authority this was done? Colonel [Ethan] Allen replied, "I demand your surrender in the name of the great Jehovah and of the Continental Congress."

—MERCY OTIS WARREN (1728–1814)
History of the Rise, Progress and Termination of the American Revolution
1805

If ever there was a holy war, it was that which saved our liberties and gave us independence.

—THOMAS JEFFERSON
Letter to J. W. Eppes,
1813

As to the history of the revolution, my ideas may be peculiar, perhaps singular. What do we mean by the revolution? The war? That was no part of the revolution; it was only an effect and consequences of it. The revolution was in the minds of the people, and this was effected from 1760–1775, in the course of fifteen years, before a drop of blood was shed at Lexington.

—JOHN ADAMS
Letter to Thomas Jefferson,
August 24, 1815

An oppressed people are authorized whenever they can to rise and break their fetters.

—HENRY CLAY (1777–1852)
Speech to the House of Representatives,
March 4, 1818

But what do we mean by the American Revolution? Do we mean the American war? The Revolution was effected before the war commenced. The Revolution was in the minds and hearts of the people; a change in their religious sentiments of their duties and obligations.
—JOHN ADAMS
Letter to Hezekiah Niles,
February 13, 1818

The great wheel of political revolution began to move in America.
—DANIEL WEBSTER (1782–1852)
Speech for the laying of the cornerstone for the Bunker Hill Monument,
June 17, 1825

RHODE ISLAND

Aquethneck shall henceforth be called the Ile of Rhods or Rhod-Island.
—RHODE ISLAND COLONIAL ASSEMBLY
March 13, 1694

The country people in the island, in general, are very unpolished and rude.
—ALEXANDER HAMILTON (1712–1756)
Itinerarium
August 18, 1744

RIGHTS OF THE PEOPLE

The first human subject and original of civil power is the people. For as they have a power every man over himself in a natural state, so upon a combination they can and do bequeath this power unto others, and settle it according as their united discretions shall determine. For that this is very plain, that when the subject of sovereign power is quite extinct, that power returns to the people again. And when they are free, they may set up what species of government they please; or if they rather incline to it, they may subside into a state of natural being if it be plainly for the best.
—JOHN WISE (1652–1725)
"A Vindication of the Government of New England Churches"
1717

[T]he great end of government ... [after the glory of God, is] ... the good of man, the common benefit of society ... instituted for the preservation of mens persons, properties & various rights.
—REV. JONATHAN MAYHEW (1720–1776)
Election Sermon,
1754

I have waited years in hopes to see some one friend of the colonies pleading in public for them. I have waited in vain. One privilege is taken away after another, and where we shall be landed God knows, and I trust will protect and provide for us even should we be driven and persecuted into a more western wilderness on the score of liberty, civil and religious, as many of our ancestors were to these once inhospitable shores of America. ...There has been a most profound and I think shameful silence, till it seems almost too late to assert our indisputable rights as men and as citizens. What must posterity think of us? The trade of the whole continent taxed by Parliament, stamps and other internal duties and taxes as they are called, talked of, and not one petition to the King and Parliament for relief.
—JAMES OTIS (1725–1783)
"Rights of the British Colonies Asserted and Proved"
1764

Now can there be any liberty where property is taken away without consent? Can it with any color of truth, justice, or equity be affirmed that the northern colonies are represented in Parliament? Has this whole continent of near three thousand miles in length, and in which and his other American dominions His Majesty has or very soon will have some millions of as good, loyal, and useful subjects, white and black, as any in the three kingdoms, the election of one member of the House of Commons?

—JAMES OTIS
"Rights of the British Colonies
Asserted and Proved"
1764

We may learn from the train of impositions received from the mother country the folly in glorying in the roast beef of Old England, since we are so notoriously flogged with the spit. A little soup-mauger with contentment is preferable to roast beef and plum pudding, since we are like to pay so dear for the roast.

For being called Englishmen without having the privileges of Englishmen is like unto a man in a gibbet with dainties set before him which would refresh him and satisfy his craving appetite if he could come at them, but being debarred of that privilege, they only serve for an aggravation to his hunger.

—BENJAMIN CHURCH (1734–1778)
Liberty and Property Vindicated
1765

I thank God we live in an age of rational inquisition, when the unfettered mind dares to expatiate freely on every object worthy its attention, when the privileges of mankind are thoroughly comprehended, and the rights of distinct societies are objects of liberal enquiry. The rod of the tyrant no longer excites our apprehensions, and to the frown of the despot which made the darker ages tremble, we dare oppose demands of right, and appeal to that constitution, which holds even kings in fetters.

—BENJAMIN CHURCH
Boston Massacre Oration,
March 5, 1773

That all power is vested in, and consequently derived from, the people; that magistrates are their trustees and servants, and at all times amenable to them.
—GEORGE MASON (1725–1792)
Virginia Bill of Rights,
June 12, 1776

Government is instituted for the common good; for the protection, safety, prosperity, and happiness of the people; and not for profit, honor, or private interest of any one man, family, or class of men; therefore, the people alone have an incontestable, unalienable, and indefeasible right to institute government; and to reform, alter, or totally change the same, when their protection, safety, prosperity, and happiness require it.
—JOHN ADAMS (1735–1826)
Thoughts on Government
1776

Accordingly it may be Observed, That it appears to Us That in emerging from a State of Nature, into a State of well regulated Society, Mankind gave up some of their natural Rights, in order that others of Greater Importance to their Well-being Safety & Happiness

both as Societies and Individuals might
be better Secured & defended.
—*ANONYMOUS*
Resolution of Town of Lexington,
Massachusetts,
1778

Government and the people do not in
America constitute distinct bodies. They
are one, and their interest the same. Members
of Congress, members of assembly,
or council, or by any other name
they may be called, are only a selected
part of the people. They are the representatives
of majesty, but not majesty
itself. The dignity exists inherently in
the universal multitude, and though it
may be delegated, cannot be alienated.
—*THOMAS PAINE* (1737–1809)
The Necessity of Taxation
1782

It is an axiom in my mind that our liberty
can never be safe but in the hands
of the people themselves, & that too of
the people wit a certain degree of instruction.
—*THOMAS JEFFERSON* (1743–1826)
To George Washington,
January 4, 1786

The definition of civil liberty is, briefly,
that portion of natural liberty which
men resign to the government, and
which then produces more happiness,
than it would have produced if retained
by the individuals who resign it—still
however leaving to the human mind,
the full enjoyment of every privilege that
is not incompatible with the peace and
order of society.
—*JAMES WILSON* (1742–1798)
Pennsylvania Ratifying Convention,
November 24, 1787

The truth is, that, in our governments,
the supreme, absolute, and uncontrollable
power *remains* in the people. As
our constitutions are superior to our
legislatures, so the people are superior
to our constitutions. Indeed, the superiority,
in this last instance, is much
greater; for the people possess over our
constitutions control in *act*, as well as
right. The consequence is, that the
people may change the constitutions
whenever and however they please.
This is a right of which no positive institution
can ever deprive them.
—*JAMES WILSON*
Pennsylvania Ratifying Convention,
November 24, 1787

A bill of rights is what the people are
entitled to against every government on
earth, general or particular, & what no
just government should refuse or rest
on inferences.
—*THOMAS JEFFERSON*
To James Madison,
December 20, 1787

The fabric of American empire ought
to rest on the solid basis of THE CONSENT
OF THE PEOPLE. The streams
of national power ought to flow from
that pure, original fountain of all legitimate
authority.
—*ALEXANDER HAMILTON* (1755–1804)
The Federalist Papers
1787

The enumeration in the Constitution, of
certain rights, shall not be construed to
deny or disparage others retained by the
people.
—*CONSTITUTION OF THE UNITED STATES*
Amendment 9, The Bill of Rights,
1787

The people are the only censors of their governors, and even their errors will tend to keep these to the true principles of their institutions. To punish these errors too severely would be to suppress the only safeguards of the public liberty.
—THOMAS JEFFERSON
Letter to Edward Carrington, 1787

The people are the only sure reliance for the preservation of our liberty.
—THOMAS JEFFERSON
Letter to James Madison, 1787

There are certain unalienable and fundamental rights, which informing the social compact, ought to be explicitly ascertained and fixed—a free and enlightened people, in forming this compact, will not resign all their rights to those who govern, and they will fix limits to their legislators and rulers, which will soon be plainly seen by those who are governed, as well as by those who govern: and the latter will know they cannot be passed unperceived by the former, and without giving a general alarm.
—RICHARD HENRY LEE (1732–1794)
Letters of a Federal Farmer
1787

The worthy Gentleman tells us, we have no reason to fear; but I always fear for the rights of the people…
—GEORGE MASON
Speech in Virginia Ratifying Convention, June 4, 1788

Since the general civilization of mankind, I believe there are more instances of abridgment of the freedom of the people, by gradual and silent encroachments of those in power, than by violent and sudden usurpations.
—JAMES MADISON (1751–1836)
Speech in the Virginia Convention, June 6, 1788

Rulers are the servants and agents of the people; the people are their masters.
—PATRICK HENRY (1736–1799)
Virginia Ratifying Convention, 1788

The trial by jury in the judicial department, and the collection of the people by their representatives in the legislature, are those fortunate inventions which have procured for them, in this country, their true proportion of influence and the wisest and most fit means of protecting themselves in the community. Their situation, as jurors and representatives, enables them to acquire information and knowledge in the affairs and government of the society; and to come forward, in turn, as the sentinels and guardians of each other.
—RICHARD HENRY LEE
Letters of the Federal Farmer
1788

The right of altering the government was a natural right, and not a right of government.
—THOMAS PAINE
Rights of Man, I
1791

To the Constitution … the term sovereign, is totally unknown. There is but one place where it could have been used with propriety. But, even in that place it would not, perhaps, have comported with the delicacy of those, who ordained and es-

tablished the Constitution. They *might* have announced themselves "SOVEREIGN" people of the *United States*: But serenely conscious of the *fact*, they avoided the *ostentatious declaration*.

—*JAMES WILSON*
Opinion in *Chisholm v. Georgia*
1793

Rights are not *gifts* from one man to another, nor from one class of men to another; for who is he who could be the first giver, or by what principle, or on what authority could he possess the right of giving?

—*THOMAS PAINE*
Dissertation on First Principles of Government
1795

The natural, civil and political *rights of man* are liberty, equality, security, property, social guarantees, and resistance to oppression.

—*THOMAS PAINE*
Dissertation on First Principles of Government
1795

Where the rights of men are equal, every man must finally see the necessity of protecting the rights of others as the most effectual security for his own.

—*THOMAS PAINE*
Dissertation on First Principles of Government
1795

We must support our rights or lose our character, and with it, perhaps, our liberties.

—*JAMES MADISON*
First Inaugural Address,
March 4, 1798

It is not denied that there may be cases in which a respect to the general principles of liberty, the essential rights of the people, or the overruling sentiments of humanity, might require a government, whether new or old, to be treated as an illegitimate despotism.

—*JAMES MADISON*
First Inaugural Address,
March 4, 1798

The will of the people is the only legitimate foundation of government, and to protect its free expression should be our first object.

—*THOMAS JEFFERSON*
Letter to Benjamin Waring,
March 1801

Nothing then is unchangeable but the inherent and unalienable rights of man.

—*THOMAS JEFFERSON*
To John Cartwright,
June 5, 1824

All power is inherent in the people.

—*THOMAS JEFFERSON*
To John Cartwright,
June 5, 1824

S

SEARCH & SEIZURE

And I take this opportunity to declare, that … I will to my dying day oppose, with all the powers and faculties God has given me, all such instruments of slavery on the one hand, and villainy on the other, as this writ of assistance is. It appears to me … the worst instrument of arbitrary power, the most destructive of English liberty, and the fundamental principles of the constitution, that ever was found in an English law-book.

—JAMES OTIS (1725–1783)
Argument against the writs of assistance,
February 1761

One of the most essential branches of English liberty is the freedom of one's house. A man's house is his castle; and whilst he is quiet, he is as well guarded as a prince in his castle.

—JAMES OTIS
Argument against the writs of assistance,
February 1761

Your Honours will find in the old book, concerning the office of a justice of peace, precedents of general warrants to search suspected houses. But in more modern books you will find only special warrants to search such and such houses specially named, in which the complainant has before sworn he suspects his goods are concealed; and you will find it adjudged *that special warrants only are legal*. In the same manner I rely on it, that the writ prayed for in this petition being general is illegal. It is a power that places the liberty of every man in the hands of every petty officer.

—JAMES OTIS
Argument against the writs of assistance,
February 1761

The poorest man may in his cottage bid defiance to all the force of the Crown. It may be frail; its roof may shake; the wind may blow through it; the storms may enter, the rain may enter, but the King of England cannot enter; all his forces dare not cross the threshold of the ruined tenement!

—WILLIAM PITT, EARL OF CHATHAM
(1708–1778)
Speech on the Excise Bill in House of Commons,
1763

That general warrants, whereby an officer or messenger may be commanded to search suspected places without evidence of a fact committed, or to seize any person or persons not named, or whose offense is not particularly described and supported by evidence, are grievous and oppressive, and ought not to be granted.

—ANONYMOUS
Virginia Declaration of Rights,
1776

Every subject has a right to be secure from all unreasonable searches, and seizures, of his person, his houses, his papers, and all his possessions. All warrants, therefore, are contrary to this right, if the cause or foundation of them be not previously supported by oath or affirmation, and if the order in the warrant to a civil officer, to make search in suspected places, or to arrest one or more suspected persons, or to seize their property, be not accompanied with a special designation of the persons or objects of search, arrest, or seizure; and no warrant ought to be issued but in cases, and with the formalities prescribed by the laws.

—ANONYMOUS
Massachusetts Constitution,
1780

The right of the people to be secure in their persons, houses, papers, and effects against unreasonable searches and seizures, shall not be violated, and no warrants shall issue, but upon probable cause, supported by oath or affirmation, and particularly describing the place to be searched, and the persons or things to be seized.

—CONSTITUTION OF THE UNITED STATES
Amendment 4, The Bill of Rights,
1787

It may be added, that the term "prob-

able cause," according to its usual acceptation, means less than evidence which would justify condemnation. ... It imports a seizure made under circumstances which warrant suspicion.

—JOHN MARSHALL (1755–1835)
Locke v. United States
1813

SECRECY & DISCRETION

It is wise not to seek a secret, and honest not to reveal one.

—WILLIAM PENN (1644–1718)
Some Fruits of Solitude
1693

Only trust thyself, and another shall not betray thee.

—WILLIAM PENN
Some Fruits of Solitude
1693

Three may keep a secret, if two of them are dead.

—BENJAMIN FRANKLIN (1706–1790)
Poor Richard's Almanack
1735

Where information is withheld, ignorance becomes a reasonable excuse. ... They see not, therefore they feel not.

—THOMAS PAINE (1737–1809)
The Crisis
1778

A government or an administration, who means and acts honestly, has nothing to fear, and consequently has nothing to conceal.

—THOMAS PAINE
Common Sense on Financing the War
1782

There are cases in which silence is a loud language.
—THOMAS PAINE
To George Washington,
August 3, 1796

Remember that we often repent of what we have said, but never of that which we have not.
—THOMAS JEFFERSON (1743–1826)
To Gideon Granger,
March 9, 1814

SELF-DISCIPLINE

Against diseases here the strongest fence / Is the defensive virtue, abstinence.
—BENJAMIN FRANKLIN (1706–1790)
Poor Richard's Almanack
1742

He is a governor that governs his passions, and is a servant that serves them.
—BENJAMIN FRANKLIN
Poor Richard's Almanack
1750

Rise early, that by habit it may become familiar, agreeable, healthy, and profitable. It may for a while be irksome to do this, but that will wear off and the practice will produce a rich harvest.
—GEORGE WASHINGTON (1732–1799)
To George Washington Parke Custis,
January 7, 1798

Sometimes it is said that man cannot be trusted with the government of himself. Can he then be trusted with the government of others?
—THOMAS JEFFERSON (1743–1826)
First Inaugural Address,
March 4, 1801

SELF-INTEREST

It is not the public, but private interest, which influences the generality of mankind, nor can the Americans any longer boast an exception.
—GEORGE WASHINGTON (1732–1799)
To John Laurens,
July 10, 1782

The most common and durable source of faction has been the various and unequal distribution of property. ... Where overmastering self-interests ... are involved, neither religious nor moral scruples can be depended upon to hold them in check. The establishment of government becomes necessary as the only alternative.
—JAMES MADISON (1751–1836)
The Federalist Papers
1787

Which is most blameworthy, those who see and will steadily pursue their interest, or those who cannot see, or seeing will not act wisely?
—GEORGE WASHINGTON
To David Stuart,
March 28, 1790

SELF-RELIANCE

It is an old and wise caution—That when your neighbour's house is on fire, we ought to take care of our own.
—ANDREW HAMILTON (?–1741)
Defense of Peter Zenger,
1735

God helps them that help themselves.
—BENJAMIN FRANKLIN (1706–1790)
Poor Richard's Almanack
1736

In things of moment on thyself depend,
Nor trust too far thy servant or a friend.
—BENJAMIN FRANKLIN
Poor Richard's Almanack
1749

SEPARATION OF POWERS

The preservation of a free Government requires not merely, that the me tes and bounds which separate each department of power be invariably maintained; but more especially that neither of them be suffered to overleap the great Barrier which defends the rights of the people.
—JAMES MADISON (1751–1836)
"Memorial and Remonstrance"
June 20, 1785

Every person, moderately acquainted with human nature, knows that public bodies, as well as individuals, are liable to the influence of sudden and violent passions, under the operation of which, the voice of reason is silenced. Instances of such influence are not so frequent, as in individuals; but its effects are extensive in proportion to the numbers that compose the public body. This fact suggests the expediency of dividing the powers of legislation between two bodies of men, whose debates shall be separate and not dependent on each other; that, if at any time, one part should appear to be under any undue influence, either from passion, obstinacy, jealousy of particular men, attachment to a popular speaker, or other extraordinary causes, there might be a power in the legislature sufficient to check every pernicious measure. Even in a small republic, composed of men, equal in property and abilities, and all meeting for the purpose

of making laws, like the old Romans in the field of Mars, a division of the body into two independent branches, would be a necessary step to prevent the disorders, which arise from the pride, irritability and stubbornness of mankind. This will ever be the case, while men possess passions, easily inflamed, which may bias eithier reason and lead them to erroneous conclusions.
—NOAH WEBSTER (1758–1843)
"An Examination into the Leading Principles of the Federal Constitution"
October 17, 1787

The separation of the legislature, divides the power—checks—restrains—amends the proceedings—at the same time, it creates no division of interest, that can tempt either branch to encroach upon the other, or upon the people. In turbulent times, such restraint is our greatest safety—in calm times, and in measures obviously calculated for the general good, both branches must always be unanimous.
—NOAH WEBSTER
"An Examination into the Leading Principles of the Federal Constitution"
October 17, 1787

The history of every government on earth affords proof of the utility of different branches in a legislature. But I appeal only to our own experience in America. To what cause can we ascribe the absurd measures of Congress, in times past, and the speedy recision of those measures, but to the want of some check? I feel the most profound deference for that honorable body, and perfect respect for their opinions; but some of their steps betray a great want of consideration—a defect, which perhaps nothing can remedy, but a division of their deliberations.

—NOAH WEBSTER
"An Examination into the Leading Principles of the Federal Constitution"
October 17, 1787

Many plausible things may be said in favor of pure democracy—many in favor of uniting the representatives of the people in a single house—but uniform experience proves both to be inconsistent with the peace of society; and the rights of freemen.

—NOAH WEBSTER
"An Examination into the Leading Principles of the Federal Constitution"
October 17, 1787

No man is a warmer advocate for proper restraints and wholesome checks in every department of government than I am; but I have never yet been able to discover the propriety of placing it absolutely out of the power of men to render essential services because a possibility remains of their doing ill.

—GEORGE WASHINGTON (1732–1799)
To Bushrod Washington,
November 10, 1787

One of the best securities against the creation of unnecessary offices or tyrannical powers, is an exclusion of the authors from all share in filling the one, or influence in the execution of the others.

—JAMES MADISON
Observations on Jefferson's Draft Constitution,
October 15, 1788

But the great security against a gradual concentration of the several powers in the same department, consists in giving to those who administer each department, the necessary constitutional means, and personal motives, to resist encroachments of the others. The provision for defence must in this, as in all other cases, be made commensurate to the danger of attack. Ambition must be made to counteract ambition. The interest of the man must be connected with the constitutional rights of the place. It may be a reflection on human nature, that such devices should be necessary to control the abuses of government.

—JAMES MADISON
The Federalist Papers
1788

The spirit of encroachment tends to consolidate the powers of all the departments in one, and thus to create whatever the form of government, a real despotism. A just estimate of that love of power, and proneness to abuse it, which predominates in the human heart is sufficient to satisfy us of the truth of this position.

—GEORGE WASHINGTON
Farewell Address,
1796

That distinction, between a government with limited and unlimited powers, is abolished, if those limits do not confine the persons on whom they are imposed, and if acts prohibited and acts allowed, are of equal obligation. It is a proposition too plain to be contested, that the Constitution controls any legislative act repugnant to it; or, that the legislature may alter the Constitution by an ordinary act.

—JOHN MARSHALL (1755–1835)
Marbury v. Madison
1803

The difference between the departments undoubtedly is, that the legislature makes, the executive executes, and the judiciary construes the law; but the maker of the law may commit something to the discretion of the other departments, and the precise boundary of this power is a subject of delicate and difficult inquiry, into which a Court will not enter unnecessarily.

—JOHN MARSHALL
Wayman v. Southard
1825

SLAVERY & RACE RELATIONS

The Numerousness of Slaves at this day in the Province, and the Uneasiness of them under their Slavery, hath put many upon thinking whether the Foundation of it be firmly and well laid; so as to sustain the Vast Weight that is built upon it. It is most certain that all Men, as they are the Sons of Adam, are; and have equal Right unto Liberty, and all other outward Comforts of Life. God hat the Earth [with all its Commodities] unto the Sons of Adam, Pal 115.16. And hat made of One Blood, all Nations of Men, for to dwell on all the face of the earth, and hat determined the Times before appointed, and the bounds of their habitation: That they should seek the Lord. Forasmuch then as we are the Offspring of GOD &c. Act 17.26, 27, 29. Now although the Title given by the last ADAM, doth infinitely better Mens Estates, respecting GOD and themselves; and grants them a most beneficial and inviolable Lease under the Broad Seal of Heaven, who were before only Tenants at Will: Yet through the Indulgence of GOD to our First Parents after the Fall, the outward Estate of all and every of the children, remains the same, as to one another. So that Originally, and Naturally, there is no such thing as Slavery. Joseph was rightfully no more a Slave to his Brethren, then they were to him: and they had no more Authority to Sell him, than they had to Slay him. And if they had nothing to do to Sell him; the Ishmaelites bargaining with them, and paying down Twenty pieces of Silver, could not make a Title. Neither could Potiphar have any better Interest in him than the Ishmaelites had, Gen. 37, 20, 27, 28. For he that shall in this case plead Alteration of Property, seems to have forfeited a great part of his own claim to Humanity. There is no proportion between Twenty Pieces of Silver, and LIBERTY.

—SAMUEL SEWALL (1652–1730)
The Selling of Joseph
1700

Which leads me to add one Remark: That the Number of purely white People in the World is proportionally very small. All Africa is black or tawny. Asia chiefly tawny. America (exclusive of the new Comers) wholly so. And in Europe, the Spaniards, Italians, French, Russians and Swedes, are generally of what we call a swarthy Complexion; as are the Germans also, the Saxons only excepted, who with the English, make the principal Body of White People on the Face of the Earth.

I could wish their Numbers were increased. And while we are, as I may call it, Scouring our Planet, by clearing America of Woods, and so making this Side of our Globe reflect a brighter Light to the Eyes of Inhabitants in Mars or Venus, why should we in the Sight of Superior Beings, darken its People?

Why increase the Sons of Africa, by Planting them in America, where we have so fair an Opportunity, by excluding all Blacks and Tawneys, of increasing the lovely White and Red? But perhaps I am partial to the complexion of my Country, for such Kind of Partiality is natural to Mankind.

—BENJAMIN FRANKLIN (1706–1790)
"Observations Concerning the
Increase of Mankind,
People of Countries"
1755

After some further conversation I said, that men who have power too often misapplied it; that though we made slaves of the Negroes, and the Turks made slaves of the Christian, I believed that liberty was the natural right of all men equally. This he did not deny, but said the lives of the Negroes were so wretched in their own country that many of them lived better here than there. I replied, "There is great odds in regard to us on what principle we act"; and so the conversation on that subject ended. I may here add that another person, some time afterwards, mentiond the wretchedness of the Negroes, occasioned by their intestine wars, as an argument in favor of our fetching them away for slaves. To which I replied, if compassion for the Africans, on account of their domestic troubles, was the real motive of our purchasing them, that spirit of tenderness being attended to, would incite us to use them kindly, that, as strangers brought out of affliction, their lives might be happy among us.

—JOHN WOOLMAN (1720–1772)
Journal entry,
May 9, 1757

The colonists are by the law of nature freeborn, as indeed all men are, white or black. No better reasons can be given for enslaving those of any color than such as Baron Montesquieu has humorously given as the foundation of that cruel slavery exercised over the poor Ethiopians, which threatens one day to reduce both Europe and America to the ignorance and barbarity of the darkest ages. Does it follow that 'tis right to enslave a man because he is black? Will short curled hair like wool instead of Christian hair, as 'tis called by those whose hearts are as hard as the nether millstone, help the argument? Can any logical inference in favor of slavery be drawn from a flat nose, a long or a short face? Nothing better can be said in favor of a trade that is the most shocking violation of the law of nature, has a direct tendency to diminish the idea of the inestimable value of liberty, and makes every dealer in it a tyrant, from the director of an African company to the petty chapman in needles and pins on the unhappy coast. It is a clear truth that those who every day barter away other men's liberty will soon care little for their own.

—JAMES OTIS (1725–1783)
"The Rights of the British Colonies
Asserted and Proved"
1764

Some view our sable race with scornful eye,
"Their colour is a diabolic dye."
Remember, Christians, Negroes black as Cain,
May be refin'd, and join th'angelic train.

—PHYLLIS WHEATLEY (c 1753–1784)
"On Being Brought From Africa to
America"
c. 1768

That execrable sum of all villainies, commonly called the Slave Trade.
—*JOHN WESLEY* (1703–1791)
Journal entry,
February 12, 1772

I believe a time will come when an opportunity will be offered to abolish this lamentable evil.
—*PATRICK HENRY* (1736–1799)
To Robert Pleasants,
January 18, 1773

If we cannot reduce this wished-for reformation [abolition of slavery] to practice, let us treat the unhappy victims with lenity. It is the furthest advance we can make toward justice. It is a debt we owe to the purity of our religion, to show that it is at variance with that law which warrants slavery.
—*PATRICK HENRY*
To Robert Pleasants,
January 18, 1773

Is it not amazing that at a time when the rights of humanity are defined and understood with precision, in a country, above all others, fond of liberty, that in such an age and in such a country we find men professing a religion the most humane, mild, gentle and generous, adopting a principle as repugnant to humanity as it is inconsistent with the Bible, and destructive to liberty? Every thinking, honest man rejects it in speculation; how few in practice from conscientious motives!
Would anyone believe I am the master of slaves of my own purchase! I am drawn along by the general inconvenience of living here without them. I will not, I cannot justify it. However

culpable my conduct, I will so far pay my devoir to virtue as to own the excellence and rectitude of her precepts, and lament my want of conformity to them.
—*PATRICK HENRY*
To Robert Pleasants,
January 18, 1773

[L]et us transmit to our descendants, together with our slaves, a pity for their unhappy lot and an abhorrence of slavery.
—*PATRICK HENRY*
To Robert Pleasants,
January 18, 1773

Slavery is an Hydra sin, and includes in it every violation of the precepts of the Law and the Gospel.
—*BENJAMIN RUSH* (1745–1813)
"On Slavekeeping"
1773

Ye men of sense and virtue—Ye advocates for American liberty, rouse up and espouse the cause of humanity and general liberty. Bear a testimony against a vice which degrades human nature, and dissolves that universal tie of benevolence which should connect all the children of men together in one great family—The plant of liberty is of so tender a nature, that it cannot thrive long in the neighbourhood of slavery.
—*BENJAMIN RUSH*
"On Slavekeeping"
1773

Could it be thought then that such a palpable violation of the law of nature, and of the fundamental principles of society, would be practiced by individuals and connived at, and tolerated by the public in British America! this land of liberty where the spirit of freedom glows with such ardor.—Did not obstinate incontestible facts compel me, I could never believe that British Americans would be guilty of such a crime.— I mean that of the *horrible slave trade*, carried on by numbers and tolerated by authority in this country.

—LEVI HART (1738–1808)
"Liberty Described and Recommended" Sermon Preached to the Corporation of Freemen in Farmington,
1775

How is it that we hear the loudest *yelps* for liberty among the drivers of negroes?

—SAMUEL JOHNSON (1709–1784)
"Taxation No Tyranny"
1775

He [George III] has waged cruel war against human nature itself, violating its most sacred rights of life and liberty in the persons of a distant people who never offended him, captivating & carrying them into slavery in another hemisphere, or to incur miserable death in their transportation thither. This piratical warfare, the opprobrium of INFIDEL powers, is the warefare of the CHRISTIAN king of Great Britain. Determined to keep open a market where MEN should be bought & sold, he has prostituted his negative for suppressing every legislative attempt to prohibit or to restrain this execrable commerce. And that this assemblage of horrors might want no fact of distinguished die, he is now exciting those very people to rise in arms among us, and to purchase that liberty of which

he has deprived them, by murdering the people on whom he also obtruded them: thus paying off former crimes committed against the LIBERTIES of one people, with crimes which he urges them to commit against the LIVES of another.

—THOMAS JEFFERSON (1743–1826)
Draft of Declaration of Independence
(This passage regarding slavery was not included in the final Declaration of Independence because the Southern states protested it.)
1776

The contempt we have been taught to entertain for the blacks, makes us fancy many things that are founded neither in reason nor experience; and an unwillingness to part with property of so valuable a kind will furnish a thousand arguments to show the impracticability or pernicious tendency of a scheme which requires such a sacrifice.

—ALEXANDER HAMILTON (1755–1804)
To John Jay,
March 14, 1779

WHEN we contemplate our abhorrence of that condition to which the arms and tyranny of Great Britain were exerted to reduce us; when we look back on the variety of dangers to which we have been exposed, and how miraculously our wants in many instances have been supplied, and our deliverances wrought, when even hope and human fortitude have become unequal to the conflict; we are unavoidably led to a ferious and grateful fence of the manifold blessings which we have undeservedly received from the hand of that Being from whom every good and perfect gift cometh. Impressed with there ideas, we conceive that it is our duty, and we rejoice that it is in our power to extend a portion of that freedom to others, which hath been extended to us; and a release from that state of thraldom to which we ourselves were tyrannically doomed, and from which we have now every prospect of being delivered.

—ANONYMOUS
"An Act for the Gradual Abolition of Slavery"
March 1, 1780

It is not for us to enquire why, in the creation of mankind, the inhabitants of the several parts of the earth were distinguished by a difference in feature or complexion. It is sufficient to know that all are the work of an Almighty Hand. We find in the distribution of the human species, that the most fertile as well as the most barren parts of the earth are inhabited by men of complexions different from ours, and from each other; from whence we may reasonably, as well as religiously, infer, that He who placed them in their various situations, hath extended equally his care and protection to all, and that it becometh not us to counteract his mercies. We esteem it a peculiar blessing granted to us, that we are enabled this day to add one more step to universal civilization, by removing as much as possible the sorrows of those who have lived in undeserved bondage, and from which, by the assumed authority of the kings of Great Britain, no effectual, legal relief could be obtained. Weaned by a long course of experience from those narrower prejudices and partialities we had imbibed, we find our hearts enlarged with kindness and benevolence towards men of all conditions and na-

tions; and we conceive ourselves at this particular period extraordinarily called upon, by the blessings which we have received, to manifest the sincerity of our profession, and to give a Substantial proof of our gratitude.

—ANONYMOUS
"An Act for the Gradual Abolition of Slavery"
March 1, 1780

I am glad to find the legislature persist in their resolution to recruit their line of the army for the war, though without deciding on the expediency of the mode under their consideration, would it not be as well to liberate and make soldiers at once of the blacks themselves as to make them instruments for enlisting white Soldiers? It would certainly be more consonant to the principles of liberty which ought never to be lost sight of in a contest for liberty, and with white officers and a majority of white soldiers no imaginable danger could be feared from themselves, as there certainly could be none from the effect of the example on those who should remain in bondage: experience having shown that a freedman immediately loses all attachment and sympathy with his former slaves.

—JAMES MADISON (1751–1836)
To Joseph Jones,
November 28, 1780

Deep-roosted prejudices entertained by the whites; ten thousand recollections, by the blacks, of the injuries they have sustained; new provocations; the real distinctions which nature has made; and many other circumstances, will divide us into parties, and produce convulsions, which will probably never end but in the extermination of the one or the other race.

—THOMAS JEFFERSON
Notes on the State of Virginia, 1782

There must doubtless be an unhappy influence on the manners of our people produced by the existence of slavery among us. The whole commerce between master and slave is a perpetual exercise of the most boisterous passions, the most unremitting despotism on the one part, and degrading submissions on the other.

—THOMAS JEFFERSON
Notes on the State of Virginia, 1782

We have slaves likewise in our northern provinces; I hope the time draws near when they will be all emancipated; but how different their lot, how different their situation, in every possible respect!

—MICHEL GUILLAUME JEAN DE
CRÈVECOEUR (1735–1813)
Letters From an American Farmer
1782

A clergyman settled a few years ago at George-Town, and feeling as I do now, warmly recommended to the planters, from the pulpit, a relaxation of severity; he introduced the benignity of Christianity, and pathetically made use of the admerable precepts of that system to melt the hearts of his congregation into a greatear degree of compassion toward their slaves than had been hitherto customary; "Sir," (said one of his hearers), "we pay you a genteel salary to read to us the prayers of the liturgy, and to explain to us such parts of

the Gospel as the rule of the church directs; but we do not want you to teach us what we are to do with our blacks."

—MICHEL GUILLAUME JEAN DE
CRÈVECOEUR
Letters From an American Farmer
1782

The chosen race eat, drink, and live happy, while the unfortunate one grubs up the ground, raises indigo, or husks the rice; exposed to a sun full as scorching as their native one; without the support of good food, without the cordials of any cheering liquor.

—MICHEL GUILLAUME JEAN DE
CRÈVECOEUR
Letters From an American Farmer
1782

Thus planters get rich; so raw, so unexperienced am I in this mode of life, that were I to be possessed of a plantation, and my slaves treated as in general they are here, never could I rest in peace; my sleep would be perpetually disturbed by a retrospect of the frauds committed in Africa, in order to entrap them; frauds surpassing in enormity every thing which a common mind can possibly conceive. I should be thinking of the barbarous treatment they meet with on ship-board; of their anguish, of the despair necessarily inspired by their situation, when torn from their friends and relations; when delivered into the hands of a people differently coloured, whom they cannot understand; carried in a strange machine over an ever agitated element, which they had never seen before; and finally delivered over to the severities of the whippers, and the excessive labours of the field. Can it be possible that the force of custom should ever make me deaf to all these reflections, and as insensible to the injustice of that trade, and to their miseries, as the rich inhabitants of this town [Charlestown] seem to be? What then is man; this being who boasts so much of the excellence and dignity of his nature, among that variety of unscrutable mysteries, of unsolvable problems, with which he is surrounded?

—*MICHEL GUILLAUME JEAN DE CRÈVECOEUR*
Letters From an American Farmer
1782

What can be expected from wretches in such circumstances? Forced from their native country, cruelly treated when on board, and not less so on the plantations to which they are driven; is there any thing in this treatment but what must kindle all the passions, sow the seeds of inveterate resentment, and nourish a wish of perpetual revenge?

—*MICHEL GUILLAUME JEAN DE CRÈVECOEUR*
Letters From an American Farmer
1782

While all is joy, festivity, and happiness in Charles-Town, would you imagine that scenes of misery overspread in the country? Their ears by habit become deaf, their hearts are hardened; they neither see, hear, nor feel for the woes of their poor slaves, from whose painful labours all their wealth proceeds. Here the horrors of slavery, the hardship of incessant toils, are unseen; and no one thinks with compassion of those showers of sweat and tears which from the bodies of Africans, daily drop, and moisten the ground they till.

—*MICHEL GUILLAUME JEAN DE CRÈVECOEUR*
Letters From an American Farmer
1782

Another of my wishes is to depend as little as possible on the labour of slaves.

—*JAMES MADISON*
To Edmund Randolph,
July 26, 1785

It is much to be wished that slavery may be abolished. The honour of the States, as well as justice and humanity, in my opinion, loudly call upon them to emancipate these unhappy people. To contend for our own liberty, and to deny that blessing to others, involves an inconsistency not to be excused.

—*JOHN JAY* (1745–1829)
To R. Lushington,
March 15, 1786

There is not a man living who wishes more sincerely than I do to see a plan adopted for the abolition of slavery. But there is only one proper way and effectual mode by which it can be accomplished, and that is by legislative authority.

—*GEORGE WASHINGTON* (1732–1799)
Letter to Robert Morris,
April 12, 1786

To set the slaves afloat at once would I believe be productive of much inconvenience and mischief; but, by degrees, it certainly might and assuredly ought to be effected, and that, too, by legislative authority.

—*GEORGE WASHINGTON*
Letter to Robert Morris,
April 12, 1786

I never mean, unless some particular circumstance should compel me to it, to possess another slave by purchase, it being among my first wishes to see some plan adopted by which slavery in this country may be abolished by law.

—GEORGE WASHINGTON
To John Francis Mercer,
September 9, 1786

O come the time, and haste the day,
When man shall man no longer crush,
When Reason shall enforce her sway,
Nor these fair regions raise our blush,
Where still the African complains,
And mourns his yet unbroken chains.

—PHILIP FRENEAU (1752–1832)
"On the Emigration to America and Peopling the Western Country"
1786

[T]he glorious and ever memorable Revolution can be Justified on no other Principles but what doth plead with great Force for the emancipation of our Slaves ... as the oppression exercised over them exceeds the oppression formerly exercised by Great Britain over these States.

—ANONYMOUS
Antislavery petition presented to the Virginia legislature,
1786

We have seen the mere distinction of colour made in the most enlightened period of time, a ground of the most oppressive dominion ever exercised by man over man.

—JAMES MADISON
Speech at the Constitutional Convention,
June 6, 1787

There shall be neither Slavery nor involuntary Servitude in the said territory otherwise than in the punishment of crimes, whereof the party shall have been duly convicted; provided always that any person escaping into the same, from whom labor or service is lawfully claimed in any one of the original States, such fugitive may be lawfully reclaimed and conveyed to the person claiming his or her labor or service as aforesaid.

—ANONYMOUS
Northwest Ordinance, art. 6,
July 13, 1787

This abomination must have an end. And there is a superior bench reserved in Heaven for those who hasten it.

—THOMAS JEFFERSON
Letter to Edward Rutledge,
July 14, 1787

I apprehend that it is not in our power to do any thing for, or against, those who are in slavery in the southern States. No gentleman within these walls detests every idea of slavery more than I do: It is generally detested by the people of this Commonwealth,—and I ardently hope that the time will soon come, when our brethren in the southern States will view it as we do, and put a stop to it, but to this we have no right to compel them. Two questions naturally arise if we ratify the Constitution, shall we do any thing by our act to hold the blacks in slavery—or shall we become partakers of other men's sins. I think neither of them: Each State is sovereign and independent to a certain degree, and they have a right, and will regulate their own internal affairs, as to themselves appears proper; and shall we

297

refuse to eat, or to drink, or to be un-tied, with those who do not think, or act, just as we do, surely not. We are not in this case partakers of other men's sins, for in nothing do we voluntarily encourage the slavery of our fellow men, a restriction is laid on the federal government, which could not be avoided and a union take place: The federal Convention went as far as they could, the migration or importation, &c. is confined to the States now *existing only*, new States cannot claim it. Congress by their ordinance for erecting new States, some time sine, declared that the new States shall be republican, and that there shall be no slavery in them. But whether those in slavery in the southern States will be emancipated after the year 1808, I do not pretend to determine, I rather doubt it.

—WILLIAM HEATH (1737–1814)
Speech at Massachusetts Ratifying
Convention,
January 30, 1788

It is to be hoped that by expressing a national disapprobation of this trade we may destroy it, and make ourselves free from reproaches, and our posterity from the imbecility ever attendant on a country filled with slaves.

—JAMES MADISON
Speech to the House of Representatives,
May 13, 1789

Soon after this the blacks who brought me on board went off, and left me abandoned to despair. I now saw myself deprived of all chance of returning to my native country, or even the least glimpse of gaining the shore, which I now considered as friendly; and I even wished for my former slavery, in pref-erence to my present situation, which was filled with horrors of every kind, still heightened by my ignorance of what I was to undergo. I was not long suffered to indulge my grief. I was soon put down under the decks, and there I received such a salutation in my nos-trils as I had never experienced in my life: so that, with the loathsomeness of the stench, and with my crying to-gether, I became so sick and low that I was not able to eat, nor had I the least desire to taste anything. I now wished for the last friend, death, to relieve me; but soon, to my grief, two of the white men offered me eatables; and, on my refusing to eat, one of them held me fast by the hands, and laid me across, I think, the windlass, and tied my feet, while the other flogged me severely. ... In a little time after, amongst the poor chained men, I found some of my own nation, which in a small degree gave ease to my mind. I inquired of these what was to be done with us. They gave me to understand we were to be carried to these white people's country to work for them. ... We were landed up a river a good way from the sea, about Vir-ginia county. ... I was a few weeks weeding grass and gathering stones in a plantation. ... While I was in this plantation the gentleman to whom I sup-posed the estate belonged being unwell, I was one day sent for to his dwell-ing-house to fan him. When I came into the room where he was, I was much affrighted at some things I saw, and the more so, as I had seen a black woman slave as I came through the house, who was cooking the dinner, and the poor creature was cruelly loaded with various kinds of iron machines; she had one particularly on her head, which locked her mouth so fast that she could scarcely speak, and could not eat nor drink. I [was] much astonished and shocked at this contrivance, which I afterwards learned was called the iron muzzle.

—OLAUDAH EQUIANO (1745–1797)
The Interesting Narrative of the Life of Olaudah Equiano or Gustavus Vassa the African
1789

The unhappy man who has long been treated as a brute Animal too frequently sinks beneath the common standard of the human species; the galling chains that bind his body, do also fetter his intellectual faculties, and impair the social affections of his heart; accustomed to move like a meer Machine by the will of a master, Reflection is suspended; he has not the power of Choice, and Reason and Conscience have but little influence over his conduct, because he is chiefly governed by the passion of Fear. He is poor & friendless, perhaps worn out by extreme Labour, Age and Disease. Under such circumstances Freedom may often prove a misfortune to himself and prejudicial to Society.

—PENNSYLVANIA ABOLITION SOCIETY
1789

I wish most anxiously to see my much loved America—it is the Country from whence all reformations must originally spring—I despair of seeing an Abolition of the infernal traffic in Negroes— we must push that matter further on your side the water—I wish that a few well instructed Negroes could be sent among their Brethren in Bondage, for until they are enabled to take their own part nothing will be done.

—THOMAS PAINE (1737–1809)
To Benjamin Rush,
March 16, 1790

Sir, suffer me to recall to your mind that time in which the arms and tyranny of the British crown were exerted with every powerful effort in order to reduce you to a state of servitude; look back, I entreat you, on the variety of dangers to which you were exposed; reflect on that time in which every human aid appeared unavailable, and in which even hope and fortitude wore the aspect of inability to the conflict, and you cannot but be led to a serious and grateful sense of your miraculous and providential preservation; you cannot but acknowledge, that the present freedom and tranquility which you enjoy, you have mercifully received, and that is the peculiar blessing of heaven.

That, sir, was a time in which you clearly saw into the injustice of a state of slavery, and in which you had just apprehension of the horrors of its condition, it was not, sir, that your abhorrence thereof was so excited, that you publicly held forth this true and invaluable doctrine, which is worthy to be recorded and remembered in all succeeding ages. "We hold these truths to be self-evident, that all men are created equal, and that they are endowed by their creator with certain inalienable rights, that among these are life, liberty and the pursuit of happiness."

Here, sir, was a time in which your tender feelings for yourselves had engaged you thus to declare, you were then impressed with proper ideas of the great valuation of liberty, and the free possession of those blessings to which you were entitled by nature; but, sir, how pitiable is it to reflect that although you were so fully convinced of the benevolence of the Father of mankind, and of his equal and impartial distribution of those rights and privileges which he had conferred upon them, that you should at the same time counteract his mercies, in detaining by fraud and violence so numerous a part of my brethren, under groaning captivity and cruel oppression, that you should at the same time be found guilty of that most criminal act, which you professedly detested in others with respect to yourselves.

—BENJAMIN BANNEKER (1731–1806)
To Thomas Jefferson,
August 19, 1791

I thank you sincerely for your letter of the 19th instant and for the Almanac it contained. No body wishes more than I do to see such proofs as you exhibit, that nature has given to our black brethren, talents equal to those of the other colors of men, and that the appearance of a want of them is owing merely to the degraded condition of their existence, both in Africa & America. I can add with truth, that no body wishes more ardently to see a good system commenced for raising the condition both of their body & mind to what it ought to be, as fast as the imbecility of their present existence, and other circumstances which cannot be neglected, will admit.

—THOMAS JEFFERSON
Response to Benjamin Banneker's
August 19, 1791 letter,
August 30, 1791

In proportion as slavery prevails in a

State, the Government, however democratic in name, must be aristocratic in fact. The power lies in a part instead of the whole; in the hands of property, not of numbers.

—JAMES MADISON
Notes for Essays,
December 19, 1791–March 3, 1792

Is there any need of arguments to prove, that it is in a high degree unjust and cruel, to reduce one human creature to such an abject wretched state as this, that he may minister to the ease, luxury, or avarice of another? Has not that other the same right to have him reduced to this state, that he may minister to his interest or pleasure? On what is this right founded? Whence was it derived? Did it come from heaven, from earth, or from hell? Has the great King of heaven, the absolute sovereign disposer of all men, given this extraordinary right to white men over black men? Where is the charter? In whose hands is it lodged? Let it be produced and read, that we may know our privilege.

—DAVID RICE (1733–1816)
Address to the Constitutional Convention that drew up the first Kentucky Constitution,
1792

This day I attended the funeral of Wm. Gray's wife, a black woman, with about 50 more white persons and two Episcopal clergymen. The white attendants were chiefly the neighbours of the deceased. The sight was a new one in Philadelphia, for hitherto (a few cases excepted) the negroes alone attended each other's funerals. By this event it is to be hoped the partition wall which divided the Blacks from the

Whites will be still further broken down and a way prepared for their union as brethren and members of one great family.

—BENJAMIN RUSH
"Commonplace Book"
1793

Attended a dinner a mile below the tower in 2nd Street to celebrate the raising of the roof of the African Church. About 100 white persons, chiefly carpenters, dined at one table, who were waited upon by Africans. Afterward about 50 black people sat down at the same table, who were waited upon by white people. Never did I see people more happy. Some of them shed tears of joy. A old black man took Mr. Nicholson by the hand and said to him, "May you live long, and when you die, may you not die eternally." I gave them two toasts, viz: "Peace on earth and good will to man," and, "May African Churches everywhere soon succeed African bondage." The last was received with three cheers.

—BENJAMIN RUSH
"Commonplace Book"
1793

With respect to the other species of property, concerning which you ask my opinion, I shall frankly declare to you that I do not like even to think, much less talk of it. However, as you have put the question, I shall, in a few words, give you *my ideas* of it. Were it not then, that I am principled against selling negroes, as you would do cattle at a market, I would not in twelve months from this date, be possessed of one, as a slave. I shall be happily mistaken, if they are not found to be very trouble-some species of property ere many years pass over our heads.

—GEORGE WASHINGTON
To Alexander Spotswood,
November 23, 1794

Within a few years past, the subject of slavery has been repeatedly discussed, in the legislature of this state, with great force of reasoning, and eloquence. The injustice of it has been generally, if not uniformly acknowledged; and the practice of it severely reprobated. But, when the question of total abolition has been seriously put, it has met with steady opposition, and has hitherto miscarried, on the ground of political expediency— That is, it is confessed to be *morally wrong*, to subject any class of our fellow-creatures to the evils of slavery; but asserted to be *politically right, to keep them in* such subjection.

—THEODORE DWIGHT (1764–1846)
An oration before the Connecticut
Society,
1794

The color of the skin is in no ways connected with strength of the mind or intellectual powers.

—BENJAMIN BANNEKER
Banneker's Almanac
1796

The Boy is a Freeman as much as any of the young Men, and merely because his Face is Black, is he to be denied instruction? ... I have not thought it any disgrace to my self to take him into my parlour and teach him both to read and write.

—ABIGAIL ADAMS (1744–1818)
Letter to John Adams,
February 13, 1797

Upon the decease [of] my wife, it is my Will and desire th[at] all the Slaves which I hold in [my] *own right*, shall receive their free[dom.]
—*GEORGE WASHINGTON*
Last Will and Testament,
1799

The abolition of slavery must be gradual, and accomplished with much caution and circumspection.
—*JOHN ADAMS* (1735–1826)
Letter to George Churchman and
Jacob Lindley,
January 24, 1801

The turpitude, the inhumanity, the cruelty, and the infamy of the African commerce in slaves have been so impressively represented to the public by the highest powers of eloquence that nothing that I can say would increase the just odium in which it is and ought to be held. Every measure of prudence, therefore, ought to be assumed for the eventual total extirpation of slavery from the United States.
—*JOHN ADAMS*
Letter to T. Robert J. Evans,
June 8, 1819

Our opinions agree as to the evil, moral, political, and economical, of slavery.
—*JAMES MADISON*
To Francis Corbin,
November 26, 1820

But this momentous question, like a fire bell in the night, awakened and filled me with terror.
—*THOMAS JEFFERSON*
Letter to John Holmes, referring to
the Missouri Compromise,
April 22, 1820

SOLITUDE

Remember the proverb, *Bene qui latuit, bene vixit*, they are happy that live retiredly. If this be true, princes and their grandees, of all men, are the unhappiest: for they live least alone: and they that must be enjoyed by everybody, can never enjoy themselves as they should.
—*WILLIAM PENN* (1644–1718)
Some Fruits of Solitude
1693

SPEECHES & ORATION

Here comes the orator! with his flood of words, and his drop of reason.
—*BENJAMIN FRANKLIN* (1706–1790)
Poor Richard's Almanack
1737

A word to the wise is enough, and many words won't fill a bushel.
—*BENJAMIN FRANKLIN*
Poor Richard's Almanack
1758

Speeches measured by the hour, die with the hour.
—*THOMAS JEFFERSON* (1743–1826)
To David Harding,
April 20, 1824

STATES' RIGHTS & FEDERALISM

No position appears to me more true than this; that the General Govt. can not effectually exist without reserving to the States the possession of their local rights. They are the instruments upon which the Union must frequently depend for the support and execution of their powers, however immediately

operating upon the people, and not upon the States.
—CHARLES PINCKNEY (1757–1824)
"Plan for a Government for America,"
Constitutional Convention,
June 25, 1787

I am astonished to hear the ill-founded doctrine, that the states alone ought to be represented in the federal government; these must possess sovereign authority, forsooth, and the people be forgot. No. Let us *reascend* to first principles. That expression is not strong enough to do my ideas justice. Let us *retain* first principles. The people of the United States are now in the possession and exercise of their original rights; and while this doctrine is known, and operates, we shall have a cure for every disease.
—JAMES WILSON (1742–1798)
Pennsylvania Ratification Convention,
November 26, 1787

The powers not delegated to the United States by the Constitution, nor prohibited by it to the states, are reserved to the states respectively, or to the people.
—CONSTITUTION OF THE UNITED STATES
Amendment 10, The Bill of Rights
1787

Gentlemen indulge too many unreasonable apprehensions of danger to the state governments; they seem to suppose that the moment you put men into a national council [federal government], they become corrupt and lose all their affection for their fellow citizens.
—ALEXANDER HAMILTON (1755–1804)
Speech to New York Constitutional
Convention,
1787

Human affections, like the solar heat, lose their intensity as they depart from the center. ... On these principles, the attachment of the individual will be first and forever secured by state governments.
—ALEXANDER HAMILTON
Speech to New York Constitutional
Convention,
1787

The State governments possess inherent advantages, which will ever give them an influence and ascendancy over the National Government, and will for ever preclude the possibility of federal encroachments. That their liberties, indeed, can be subverted by the federal head, is repugnant to every rule of political calculation.
—ALEXANDER HAMILTON
To the New York Ratifying Convention,
June 17, 1788

When you assemble from your several counties in the Legislature, were every member to be guided only by the apparent interest of his county, government would be impracticable. There must be a perpetual accomodation and sacrifice of local advantage to general expediency.
—ALEXANDER HAMILTON
To the New York Ratifying Convention,
June 17, 1788

While the constitution continues to be read, and its principles known, the states, must, by every, rational man, be considered as essential component parts of the union; and therefore the idea of sacrificing the former to the latter is totally inadmissible.
—ALEXANDER HAMILTON
To the New York Ratifying Convention,
June 17, 1788

It is most important, likewise, that the habits of thinking in a free Country should inspire caution in those entrusted with its administration, to confine themselves within their respective Constitutional Spheres; avoiding in the exercise of the Powers of one department to encroach upon another.

—*GEORGE WASHINGTON* (1732–1799)
Farewell Address,
September 17, 1796

The way to have good and safe government, is not to trust it all to one; but to divide it among the many, distributing to every one exactly the functions he is competent to. Let the National government be entrusted with the defence of the nation, and its foreign & federal relations; the State governments with the civil rights, laws, police & administration of what concerns the states generally; the Counties with the local concerns of the counties, and each Ward direct the interests within itself. It is by dividing and subdividing these republics from the great National one down thro' all its subordinates, until it ends in the administration of every man's farm and affairs by himself; by placing under every one what his own eye may superintend, that all will be done for the best.

—*THOMAS JEFFERSON* (1743–1826)
To Joseph C. Cabell,
February 2, 1816

No political dreamer was ever wild enough to think of breaking down the lines which separate the States, and of compounding the American people into one common mass.

—*JOHN MARSHALL* (1755–1835)
McCulloch v. Maryland
1819

TAXES

Taxation without representation is tyranny.

—*James Otis* (1725–1783)
Attributed by John Adams and others,
1763

I can see no reason to doubt but that the imposition of taxes, whether on trade, or on land, or houses, or ships, on real or personal, fixed or floating property, in the colonies is absolutely irreconcilable with the rights of the colonists as British subjects. ... The very act of taxing exercised over those who are not represented appears to me to be depriving them of one of their most essential rights as freemen, and if continued seems to be in effect an entire disfranchisement of every civil right.

—*James Otis*
"Rights of the British Colonies
Asserted and Proved"
1764

The sum of my argument is: ... His Majesty GEORGE III is rightful King and sovereign, and, with his Parliament, the supreme legislative of Great Britain, France, and Ireland, and the dominions thereto belonging; that this constitution is the most free one and by far the best now existing on earth; that by this constitution every man in the dominions is a free man; that no part of His Majesty's dominions can be taxed without their consent; that every part has a right to be represented in the supreme or some subordinate legislature; that the refusal of this would seem to be a contradiction in practice to the theory of the constitution; that the colonies are subordinate dominions and are now in such a state as to make it best for the good of the whole that they should not only be continued in the enjoyment of subordinate legislation but be also represented in some proportion to their number and estates in the grand legislature of the nation; that this would firmly unite all parts of the British empire in the greatest peace and prosperity, and render if invulnerable and perpetual.

—*James Otis*
"Rights of the British Colonies
Asserted and Proved"
1764

We are not insensible that when liberty is in danger, the liberty of complaining is dangerous; yet a man on a wreck was never denied the liberty of roaring as loud as he could, says Dean Swift. And we believe no good reason can be given why the colonies should not modestly and

soberly inquire what right the Parliament of Great Britain have to tax them.
—*STEPHEN HOPKINS* (1701–1785)
"The Rights of Colonies Examined"
1764

Let these *truths* be indelibly impressed on our minds—that we cannot be HAPPY, *without being* FREE—that we cannot be free, *without being secure in our property*—that *we* cannot be secure in our property [under a system of taxation without representation, permitting no safeguard against confiscatory taxes].
—*JOHN DICKINSON* (1732–1794)
Pennsylvania Provincial Convention,
1774

The genius of liberty reprobates everything arbitrary or discretionary in taxation.
—*ALEXANDER HAMILTON* (1755–1804)
The Continentalist, No. 6.
N.Y. Packet,
July 4, 1782

Taxes on consumption are always least burdensome, because they are least felt, and are borne too by those who are both willing and able to pay them; that of all taxes on consumption, those on foreign commerce are most compatible with the genius and policy of free States.
—*JAMES MADISON* (1751–1836)
Address to the States,
April 25, 1783

It is a signal advantage of taxes on articles of consumption, that they contain in their own nature a security against excess. They prescribe their own limit; which cannot be exceeded without defeating the end proposed—that is an extension of the revenue. ...

If duties are too high, they lessen the consumption; the collection is eluded; and the product to the treasury is not so great as when they are confined within proper and moderate bounds.
—*ALEXANDER HAMILTON*
The Federalist Papers
1787

As to poll taxes, I, without scruple, confess my disapprobation of them; and though they have prevailed from an early period in those states which have uniformly been the most tenacious of their rights, I should lament to see them introduced into practice under the national government.
—*ALEXANDER HAMILTON*
The Federalist Papers
1787

Excisemen may come in multitudes; for the limitation of their numbers no man knows. They may, unless the general government be restrained by a bill of rights, or some similar restriction, go into your cellars and rooms, and search, ransack, and measure, every thing you eat, drink, and wear.
—*PATRICK HENRY* (1736–1799)
Debates in the Virginia Convention on the adoption of the Federal Constitution,
June 14, 1788

Direct taxation can go but little way towards raising a revenue. To raise money in this way, people must be provident; they must be constantly laying up money to answer the demands of the collector. But you cannot make people thus provident; if you would do anything to purpose you must come in when they are spending, and take a part

with them. This does not take away the tools of a man's business, or the necessary utensils of his family: It only comes in when he is taking his pleasure, and feels generous.
—OLIVER ELLSWORTH (1745–1807)
Connecticut Ratifying Convention,
1788

It is a general maxim, that all governments find a use for as much money as they can raise. Indeed they have commonly demands for more: Hence it is, that all, as far as we are acquainted, are in debt. I take this to be a settled truth, that they will spend as much as their revenue; that is, will live at least up to their income. Congress will ever exercise their powers, to levy as much money as the people can pay. They will not be restrained from direct taxes, by the consideration that necessity does not require them. If they forbear, it will be because the people cannot answer their demands.
—MELANCTON SMITH (1744–1798)
New York Ratifying Convention,
1788

[Mr. Madison] conceived taxes of all kinds to be evils in themselves, and that they were not otherwise admissible, than in order to avoid still greater evils. But of all the various kinds of taxes, he admitted the excise to be the most disagreeable; yet at the same time, he must say, that of the excise, that particular branch which related to ardent spirit was in itself the most proper; most likely to be productive, and least inconsistent with the spirit and disposition of the people of America.
—JAMES MADISON
Speech in Congress,
January 6, 1791

If, from the more wretched parts of the old world, we look at those which are in an advanced stage of improvement, we still find the greedy hand of government thrusting itself into every corner and crevice of industry, and grasping the spoil of the multitude. Invention is continually exercised, to furnish new pretenses for revenues and taxation. It watches prosperity as its prey and permits none to escape without tribute.
—THOMAS PAINE (1737–1809)
Rights of Man
1791

A just security to property is not afforded by that government under which unequal taxes oppress one species of property and reward another species; where arbitrary taxes invade the domestic sanctuaries of the rich, and excessive taxes grind the faces of the poor.
—JAMES MADISON
Essay in the *National Gazette*,
March 29, 1792

In New York the [Stamp A]ct was printed and cried about the streets under the title "*The folly of England, and the ruin of America.*"
—MERCY OTIS WARREN (1728–1814)
History of the Rise, Progress and Termination of the American Revolution
1805

However extensive the constitutional power of a government to impose taxes may be, I think it should not be so exercised as to impede or discourage the lawful and useful industry and exertions of individuals. Hence, the prudence of taxing the products of beneficial labor, either mental or manual, appears to be at least questionable. ... Whether taxation should extend only to property, or only to income, are points on which opinions have not been uniform. I am inclined to think that both should not be taxed.

—*JOHN JAY* (1745–1829)
Source unknown,
1812

To impose taxes when the public exigencies require them is an obligation of the most sacred character. ... To dispense with taxes when it may be done with perfect safety is equally the duty of their representatives.

—*JAMES MONROE* (1758–1831)
First annual message to Congress,
December 21, 1817

An *unlimited* right to tax, implies a right to destroy.

—*DANIEL WEBSTER* (1782–1852)
Argument in *McCulloch v. Maryland*,
February 22, 1819

That the power to tax involves the power to destroy; that the power to destroy may defeat and render useless the power to create; that there is a plain repugnance, in conferring on one government a power to control the constitutional measures of another, which other, with respect to those very measures, is declared to be supreme over that which exerts the control, are propositions not to be denied.

—*JOHN MARSHALL* (1755–1835)
McCulloch v. Maryland
1819

To constrain the brute force of the people, the European governments deem it necessary to keep them down by hard labor, poverty, and ignorance, and to take from them, as from bees, so much of their earnings, as that unremitting labor shall be necessary to obtain a sufficient surplus barely to sustain a scanty and miserable life. And these earnings they apply to maintain their privileged orders in splendor and idleness, to fascinate the eyes of the people, and excite in them an humble adoration and submission, as to an order of superior beings.

—*THOMAS JEFFERSON* (1743–1826)
To William Johnson,
1823

THEORY & PRACTICE

The moment a person forms a theory, his imagination sees in every object only the traits that favor that theory.

—*THOMAS JEFFERSON* (1743–1826)
Letter to Charles Thompson,
September 20, 1787

Yet experience & frequent disappointment have taught me not to be overconfident in theories or calculations, until actual trial of the whole combination has stamped it with approbation.

—*THOMAS JEFFERSON*
To George Fleming,
December 29, 1815

TIME

Dost thou love life, then do not squander time, for that's the stuff life is made of.

—*BENJAMIN FRANKLIN* (1706–1790)
Poor Richard's Almanack
1746

Lost time is never found again.
—*BENJAMIN FRANKLIN*
Poor Richard's Almanack
1748

Remember that time is money.
—*BENJAMIN FRANKLIN*
Advice to a Young Tradesman,
1748

Time makes more converts than reason.
—*THOMAS PAINE* (1737–1809)
Common Sense
1776

Determine never to be idle. No person will have occasion to complain of the want of time, who never loses any.
—*THOMAS JEFFERSON* (1743–1826)
To Martha Jefferson,
May 5, 1787

All grief, like all things else, will yield to the obliterating power of time.
—*THOMAS PAINE*
Forgetfulness
1794

Reason, religion, and philosophy teach us to do this [submit to Providence]; but 'tis time alone, that can ameliorate the pangs of humanity and soften its woes.
—*GEORGE WASHINGTON* (1732–1799)
To Henry Knox,
March 2, 1797

The man who does not estimate time as money will forever miscalculate.
—*GEORGE WASHINGTON*
To James Anderson,
December 21, 1797

TOBACCO

I remember with shame how formerly, when I had taken two or three pipes, I was presently ready for another, such a bewitching thing it is; but I thank God he has now given me power over it; sure there are many who may be better employed than sucking a stinking tobacco-pipe.
—*MARY ROWLANDSON* (c. 1636–1711)
A True History of the Captivity and Restoration of Mrs. Mary Rowlandson
1682

I have received your favor of the 9th, with a copy of your Lecture on Tobacco and ardent spirits. It is a powerful dissuasion from the pernicious use of such stimulants. ... Its foreign translations and its reaching a fifth Edition are encouraging evidences of its usefulness; however much it be feared that the listlessness of non-labourers, and the fatigues of hard labourers, will continue to plead for the relief of intoxicating liquors, or exhilarating plants; one or other of which seem to have been in use in every age and country.
—*JAMES MADISON* (1751–1836)
To Benjamin Waterhouse,
June 22, 1822

TREASON

If this be treason, make the most of it.
—*PATRICK HENRY* (1736–1799)
Speech to the Virginia House of Burgesses in opposition to the Stamp Act,
May 29, 1765

No punishment, in my opinion, is too

great for the man who can build his greatness upon his country's ruin.
—GEORGE WASHINGTON (1732–1799)
To Joseph Reed,
December 12, 1778

I have accepted the command at W[est]. P[oint]. As a Post in which I can render the most essential Services, and which will be in my disposal. The mass of the People are heartily tired of the War, and wish to be on their former footing—They are promised great events from this year's exertion—If—disappointed— you have only to persevere and the contest will soon be at an end. The present Struggles are like the pangs of a dying man, violent but of a short duration.
—BENEDICT ARNOLD (1741–1801)
To John Andre, in a letter which also provided useful information on American troop movements,
July 12, 1780

Treason against the United States, shall consist only in levying war against them, or in adhering to their enemies, giving them aid and comfort. No person shall be convicted of treason unless on the testimony of two witnesses to the same overt act, or on confession in open court.
—CONSTITUTION OF THE UNITED STATES
Article III, section 3,
1787

TRUTH

Inquiry is human, blind obedience, brutal. Truth never loses by the one, but often suffers by the other.
—WILLIAM PENN (1644–1718)
Some Fruits of Solitude
1693

Truth often suffers more by the heat of its defenders than from the arguments of its opposers.
—WILLIAM PENN
Some Fruits of Solitude
1693

Truth never lost ground by enquiry, because she is most of all reasonable.
—WILLIAM PENN
More Fruits of Solitude
1702

Half the truth is often a great lie.
—BENJAMIN FRANKLIN (1706–1790)
Poor Richard's Almanack
1758

It is much safer to follow truth alone, than to have all the world for company in the road of error.
—NATHANAEL GREENE (1742–1786)
To Samuel Ward, Jr.,
1771

I hate deception, even where the imagination only is concerned.
—GEORGE WASHINGTON (1732–1799)
To John Cochran,
August 16, 1779

We ought not to deceive ourselves.
—GEORGE WASHINGTON
To Joseph Reed,
May 28, 1780

So deeply rooted were all the governments of the old world, and so effectually had the tyranny and the antiquity of habit established itself over the mind, that no beginning could be made in Asia, Africa, or Europe, to reform the political condition of man. Freedom had been hunted round the globe; reason was considered as rebellion; and the slavery of fear had made men afraid to think. But such is the irresistible nature of truth, that all it asks, and all it wants, is the liberty of appearing. The sun needs no inscription to distinguish him from darkness; and no sooner [had] the American governments display[ed] themselves to the world, then despotism felt a shock, and man began to contemplate redress.

—THOMAS PAINE (1737–1809)
The Rights of Man, II
1792

Mystery is the antagonist of truth. It is a fog of human invention that obscures truth and represents it in distortion.

—THOMAS PAINE
The Age of Reason
1794

There is but one straight course, and that is to seek truth and pursue it steadily.

—GEORGE WASHINGTON
To Edmund Randolph,
July 31, 1795

Candor is not a more conspicuous trait in the character of governments than it is of individuals.

—GEORGE WASHINGTON
To Timothy Pickering,
August 29, 1797

We are not afraid to follow truth wherever it may lead, not to tolerate any error so long as reason is left free to combat it.

—THOMAS JEFFERSON (1743–1826)
To William Roscoe,
December 27, 1820

All should be laid open to you without reserve, for there is not a truth existing which I fear, or would wish unknown to the whole world.

—THOMAS JEFFERSON
To Henry Lee,
May 15, 1826

TYRANNY

Rebellion to tyrants is obedience to God.

—THOMAS JEFFERSON (1743–1826)
Personal motto, written on his seal,
Date unknown

Rex & Tyrannus are very differing characters: one rules his people by laws, to which they consent; the other by his absolute will and power. This is called freedom, this tyranny.

—WILLIAM PENN (1644–1718)
Some Fruits of Solitude
1693

The king is as much bound by his oath, not to infringe the legal rights of the people, as the people are bound to yield subjection to him. From whence it follows, that as soon as the prince sets himself up above law, he loses the king in the tyrant: he does to all intents and purposes, unking himself, by acting out of, and beyond, that sphere which the constitution allows him to move in. And in such cases, he has no more right to be obeyed, than any inferior officer who acts beyond his commission. The subject's obligation to allegiance then ceases of course; and to resist him, is no more *rebellion*, than to resist any foreign invader.

—JONATHAN MAYHEW (1720–1776)
"Unlimited Submission and Non-Resistance to the Higher Powers"
1750

God forbid, my lords, that there should be a power in this country of measuring the civil rights of the subject by his moral character, or by any other rule but the fixed laws of the land! ... Unlimited power is apt to corrupt the minds of those who possess it; and this I know, my lords, that where law ends, tyranny begins!

—*WILLIAM PITT, EARL OF CHATHAM*
(1708–1778)
"The English Constitution," speech delivered in the House of Lords, January 9, 1770

When rulers become tyrants, they cease to be kings, they can no longer be respected as God's vice regents, who violate the laws they were sworn to protect. The preacher may tell us of passive obedience, that tyrants are scourges in the hands of a righteous GOD to chastise a sinful nation, and are to be submitted to like plagues, famine and such like judgments:—such doctrine may serve to mislead ill-judging princes into a false security: but men are not to be harangued out of their senses; human nature and self-preservation will eternally arm the brave and vigilant, against slavery and oppression. ... To enjoy life as becomes rational creatures, to possess our souls with pleasure and satisfaction, we must be careful to maintain that blessing, liberty. By liberty I would be understood, the happiness of living under laws of our own making, by our personal consent, or that of our representatives.

—*BENJAMIN CHURCH* (1734–1778)
Boston Massacre Oration,
March 5, 1773

I am a friend to righteous government, to a government founded upon the principles of reason and justice; but I glory in publicly avowing my eternal enmity to tyranny. Is the present system, which the British administration have adopted for the government of the Colonies, a righteous government—or is it tyranny?

—*JOHN HANCOCK* (1737–1793)
Boston Massacre Oration,
March 5, 1774

Tyranny, like hell, is not easily conquered.

—*THOMAS PAINE* (1737–1809)
The Crisis
1776

[T]yranny and arbitrary power are utterly inconsistent with, and subversive of the very end and design of civil government, and directly contrary to natural law, which is the true foundation of civil government and all politick law: Consequently the authority of a tyrant is of itself null and void.

—*SAMUEL WEST* (1730–1807)
Election sermon,
1776

There is a natural and necessary progression from the extreme of anarchy to the extreme of tyranny.

—*GEORGE WASHINGTON* (1732–1799)
Circular to the States,
June 8, 1783

But there is a Degree of Watchfulness over all Men possessed of Power or Influence upon which the Liberties of Mankind much depend. It is necessary to guard against the Infirmities of the best as well as the Wickedness of the worst of Men. Such is the Weakness of

human Nature that Tyranny has oftener sprang from that than any other Source. It is this that unravels the Mystery of Millions being enslaved by a few.
> —SAMUEL ADAMS (1722–1803)
> To Elbridge Gerry,
> 1784

Let us not establish a tyranny. Energy is a very different thing from violence.
> —ALEXANDER HAMILTON (1755–1804)
> To Oliver Wolcott,
> June 29, 1798

I have sworn upon the altar of God, eternal hostility against every form of tyranny over the mind of men.
> —THOMAS JEFFERSON (1743–1826)
> Letter to Benjamin Rush,
> September 23, 1800

U

UNITY

Then join hand in hand, brave Americans all!
By uniting we stand, by dividing we fall.
—*JOHN DICKINSON* (1732–1794)
"The Liberty Song"
1768

If any should say, it is in vain for them as individuals to be vigilant, zealous and firm in pursuing any measures for the security of our rights, unless all would unite: I would reply:

Ages are composed of seconds, the earth of sands, and the sea of drops, too small to be seen by the naked eye. The smallest particles have their influence. Such is our state, that each individual has a proportion of influence on some neighbour at least; he, on another, and so on; as in a river, the following drop urges that which is before, and every one through the whole length of the stream has the like influence. We know not, what individuals may do. We are not at liberty to lie dormant until we can, at once, influence the whole. We must begin with the weight we have. Should the little springs neglect to flow till a general agreement should take place, the torrent that now bears down all before it, would never be formed. These mighty floods have their rise in single drops from the rocks, which, uniting, creep along till they meet with another combination so small that it might be absorbed by the travellers [sic] foot. These unite, proceed, enlarge, till mountains tremble at their sound. Let us receive instruction from the streams, and, without discouragement [sic], pursue a laudable plan.
—*NATHANIEL NILES* (1741–1828)
Two discourses on liberty; delivered at the North Church, in Newbury-port, June 5, 1774

I am under more apprehensions on account of our own dissensions than of the efforts of the enemy.
—*GEORGE WASHINGTON* (1732–1799)
To Benedict Arnold, December 13, 1778

[T]he general sentiment of the citizens of America, is expressed in the motto which some of them have chosen, UNITE OR DIE; and while we consider the extent of the country, so intersected and almost surrounded with navigable rivers, so separated and detached from the rest of the world, it is natural to presume that Providence has designed us for an united people, under one great political compact.
—*JAMES WILSON* (1742–1798)
Pennsylvania Ratifying Convention, November 24, 1787

It has often given me pleasure to observe, that independent America was not composed of detached and distant territories, but that one connected, fertile, wide-spreading country was the portion of our western sons of liberty. Providence has in a particular manner blessed it with a variety of soils and productions, and watered it with innumerable streams, for the delight and accommodation of its inhabitants. A succession of navigable waters forms a kind of chain round its borders, as if to bind it together; while the most noble rivers in the world, running at convenient distances, present them with highways for the easy communication of friendly aids, and the mutual transportation and exchange of their various commodities.

With equal pleasure I have as often taken notice, that Providence has been pleased to give this one connected country to one united people—a people descended from the same ancestors, speaking the same language, professing the same religion, attached to the same principles of government, very similar in their manners and customs and who, by their joint counsels, arms, and efforts, fighting side by side throughout a long and bloody war, have nobly established general liberty and independence.

—*JOHN JAY*(1745–1829)
The Federalist Papers
1787

This country and this people seem to have been made for each other, and it appears as if it was the design of Providence, that an inheritance so proper and convenient for a band of brethren, united to each other by the strongest ties, should never be split into a number of unsocial, jealous, and alien sovereignties.

—*JOHN JAY*
The Federalist Papers
1787

A firm Union will be of the utmost moment to the peace and liberty of the States, as a barrier against domestic faction and insurrection.

—*ALEXANDER HAMILTON*(1755–1804)
The Federalist Papers
1787

The Union of these States cannot in truth be too highly valued or too watchfully cherished. It is our best barrier against danger from without, and the only one against those armies and taxes, those wars and usurpations, which so readily grow out of the jealousies and ambition of neighbouring and independent States.

—*JAMES MADISON*(1751–1836)
To the Chairman of the Republican
Society of Hancock County,
Massachusetts,
March 15, 1809

In a government founded on the principles, and organized in the form, which distinguish that of the United States, discord alone, on points of vital importance, can reader the nation weak in itself, or deprive it of that respect which guarantees its peace and security. With a union of its citizens, a government thus identified with the nation, may be considered as the strongest in the world; the participation of every individual in the rights and welfare of the whole, adding the greatest moral, to the greatest physical strength of which political society is susceptible.

—*JAMES MADISON*
To the Republican Meeting of Cecil
County, Maryland,
March 5, 1810

Our Union is not held together by standing armies, or by any ties, other than the positive interests and powerful attractions of its parts toward each other.

—*JAMES MONROE* (1758–1831)
Message to Congress,
May 4, 1822

VALUE

When the well's dry, we know the worth of water.
——*BENJAMIN FRANKLIN* (1706–1790)
Poor Richard's Almanack
1746

A long life may not be good enough, but a good life is long enough.
——*BENJAMIN FRANKLIN*
Poor Richard's Almanack
1755

When I was a child of seven years old, my friends, on a holiday, filled my pocket with coppers. I went directly to a shop where they sold toys for children; and, being charmed with the sound of a whistle, that I met by the way in the hands of another boy, I voluntarily offered and gave all my money for one. I then came home, and went whistling all over the house, much pleased with my whistle, but disturbing all the family. My brothers, and sister, and cousins, understanding the bargain I had made, told me I had given four times as much for it as it was worth; put me in mind what good things I might have bought with the rest of the money; and laughed at me so much for my folly, that I cried with vexation; and the reflection gave me more cha-grin than the whistle gave me pleasure. This however was afterwards of use to me, the impression continuing on my mind; so that, often, when I was tempted to buy some unnecessary thing, I said to myself, Don't give too much for the whistle, and I saved my money.
——*BENJAMIN FRANKLIN*
Letter to Madame Brillon,
November 10, 1779

In short, I conceive that a great part of the miseries of mankind are brought upon them by the false estimates they have made of the value of things, and by their giving too much for their whistles.
——*BENJAMIN FRANKLIN*
Letter to Madame Brillon,
November 10, 1779

It is not the lowest priced goods that are always the cheapest—the quality is, or ought to be, as much an object with the purchaser as the price.
——*GEORGE WASHINGTON* (1732–1799)
To Philip Marsteller,
December 15, 1786

VENGENCE & REVENGE

But let us not forget the distressing occasion of this anniversary: the sullen ghosts of murdered fellow-citizens haunt my imagination "and harrow up my soul"; methinks the tainted air is hung with the dews of death, while Ate, hot from hell, cries havoc, and lets slip the dogs of war. Hark! the wan tenants of the grave still shriek for vengeance on their remorseless butchers: forgive us, Heaven! should we mingle involuntary execrations, while hovering in idea over the guiltless dead.

—BENJAMIN CHURCH (1734–1778)
Boston Massacre Oration,
March 5, 1773

It is incumbent on man as a moralist that he does not revenge an injury; and it is equally as good in a political sense; for there is no end to retaliation; each retaliates on the other, and calls it justice.

—THOMAS PAINE (1737–1809)
Age of Reason, II
1795

VICE PRESIDENCY

But my country has in its wisdom contrived for me the most insignificant office that ever the invention of man contrived or his imagination conceived. And as I can do neither good nor evil, I must be borne away by others, and meet the common fate.

—JOHN ADAMS (1735–1826)
To Thomas Jefferson,
December 6, 1787

The second office of the land is honorable and easy, the first is but a splendid misery.

—THOMAS JEFFERSON (1743–1826)
Letter to Elbridge Gerry,
May 13, 1797

VIRGINIA & VIRGINIANS

Heaven & earth never agreed better to frame a place for man's habitation; were it fully manured and inhabited by industrious people. Here are mountaines, hil[l]s, plaines, valleyes, rivers, and brookes, all running most pleasantly into a faire Bay, compassed but for the mouth, with fruitfull and delightsome land.

—CAPTAIN JOHN SMITH (1580–1631)
The Generall Historie of Virginia, New England & The Summer Isles,
referring to the countryside around
Chesapeake Bay
1606

The country is not mountainous nor yet low, but such pleasant plain hills and fertile valleys, one prettily crossing another, and watered so conveniently with their sweet brooks and crystal springs, as if art itself had devised them.

—CAPTAIN JOHN SMITH
The Description of Virginia
1607

The Virginians have little money and great pride, contempt of Northern men, and great fondness for a dissipated life. They do not understand grammar.

—NOAH WEBSTER (1758–1843)
Letter from Williamsburg, Virginia,
c. 1785

On the whole, I find nothing anywhere else, in point of climate, which Virginia need envy to any part of the world.

—THOMAS JEFFERSON (1743–1826)
Letter to Martha Jefferson Randolph,
May 31, 1791

The higher Virginians seem to venerate themselves as men.
—*JOHN DAVIS* (1775–1854)
Travels of Four Years and a Half in the United States of America
1803

Our society is neither scientific nor splendid, but independent, hospitable, correct, and neighborly.
—*THOMAS JEFFERSON*
Letter to Nathaniel Bowditch,
October 26, 1818

The good Old Dominion, the blessed mother of us all.
—*THOMAS JEFFERSON*
Thoughts on Lotteries
1826

VIRTUE & VICE

Search others for their virtues, thyself for thy vices.
—*BENJAMIN FRANKLIN* (1706–1790)
Poor Richard's Almanack
1738

With the old almanac and the old year, / Leave thy old vices though ne'er so dear.
—*BENJAMIN FRANKLIN*
Poor Richard's Almanack
1742

What is serving God? 'Tis doing good to man.
—*BENJAMIN FRANKLIN*
Poor Richard's Almanack
1747

Truth, honor, and religion are the only foundation to build human happiness upon. They never fail to yield a mind

solid satisfaction; For conscious virtue gives pleasure to the soul.
—*NATHANAEL GREENE* (1742–1786)
To Catharine Ward Greene,
1776

The happiness of man as well as his dignity consists in virtue.
—*JOHN ADAMS* (1735–1826)
Thoughts on Government
1776

Virtue is not always amiable.
—*JOHN ADAMS*
Diary entry,
February 9, 1779

Few men have virtue to withstand the highest bidder.
—*GEORGE WASHINGTON* (1732–1799)
Letter to Robert Howe,
August 17, 1779

Is there no virtue among us? If there be not, we are in a wretched situation. No theoretical checks—no form of government can render us secure. To suppose that any form of government will secure liberty or happiness without any virtue in the people, is a chimerical idea. If there be sufficient virtue and intelligence in the community, it will be exercised in the selection of these men. So that we do not depend on their virtue, or put confidence in our rulers, but in the people who are to choose them.
—*JAMES MADISON* (1751–1836)
Speech to the Virginia Ratifying Convention,
June 20, 1788

As there is a degree of depravity in mankind which requires a certain degree of circumspection and distrust: So there are other qualities in human nature, which justify a certain portion of esteem and confidence. Republican government presupposes the existence of these qualities in a higher degree than any other form. Were the pictures which have been drawn by the political jealousy of some among us, faithful likenesses of the human character, the inference would be that there is not sufficient virtue among men for self-government; and that nothing less than the chains of despotism can restrain them from destroying and devouring one another.

—*JAMES MADISON*
The Federalist Papers
1788

The virtues of men are of more consequence to society than their abilities; and for this reason, the heart should be cultivated with more assiduity than the head.

—*NOAH WEBSTER* (1758–1843)
On the Education of Youth in America
1788

Illustrious examples are displayed to our view that we may imitate as well as admire. Before we can be distinguished by the same honors, we must be distinguished by the same virtues. What are those virtues? They are chiefly the same virtues, which we have already seen to be descriptive of the American character—the love of liberty, and the love of law.

—*JAMES WILSON* (1742–1798)
Of the Study of the Law in the United States
c. 1790

It requires time to conquer bad habits, and hardly anything short of necessity is able to accomplish it.

—*GEORGE WASHINGTON*
To Arthur Young,
1791

When public virtue is gone, when the national spirit is fled ... the republic is lost in essence, though it may still exist in form.

—*JOHN ADAMS*
To Benjamin Rush,
1808

I agree with you that there is a natural aristocracy among men. The grounds of this are virtue and talents. Formerly, bodily powers gave place among the aristocracy. But since the invention of gunpowder has armed the weak as well as the strong with missile death, bodily strength, like beauty, good humor, politeness and other accomplishments, has become but an auxiliary ground for distinction.

—*THOMAS JEFFERSON* (1743–1826)
To John Adams,
October 28, 1813

W

WAR

But it is only defensive war that can be justified in the sight of God. When no injury is offered us, we have no right to molest others. And Christian meekness, patience and forbearance, are duties that ought to be practised both by kingdoms and individuals. Small injuries, that are not likely to be attended with any very pernicious consequences, are rather to be submitted to, than resisted by the sword. Both religion and humanity strongly forbid the bloody deeds of war, unless they are necessary. Even when the injury offered is great in itself, or big with fatal consequences, we should if there be opportunity, endeavour to prevent it by remonstrance, or by offering to leave that matter in dispute to indifferent judges, if they can be had. If these endeavours are unsuccessful, it then becomes proper, to use more forceable means of resistance.

—*Simeon Howard* (?–c. 1804)
Sermon to the Ancient and Honorable Artillery Company, in Boston,
June 7, 1773

A people may err by too long neglecting such means, and shamefully suffer the sword to rust in its scabberd, when it ought to be employed in defending their liberty. The most grasping and oppressive power will commonly let its neighbours remain in peace, if they will submit to its unjust demands. And an incautious people may submit to these demands, one after another, till its liberty is irrecoverably gone, before they saw the danger. Injuries small in themselves, may in their consequences be fatal to those who submit to them; especially if they are persisted in. And, with respect to such injuries, we should ever act upon that ancient maxim of prudence; obsta principiis. The first unjust demands of an encroaching power should be firmly withstood, when there appears a disposition to repeat and increase such demands. And oftentimes it may be both the right and duty of a people to engage in war, rather than give up to the demands of such a power, what they could, without any inconveniency, spare in the way of charity. War, though a great evil, is ever preferable to such concessions, as are likely to be fatal to public liberty.

—*Simeon Howard*
Sermon to the Ancient and Honorable Artillery Company, in Boston,
June 7, 1773

There are some who pretend that it is against their consciences to take up arms in defence of their country; but

321

can any rational being suppose that the Deity can require us to contradict the law of nature which he has written in our hearts, a part of which I am sure is the principle of self-defence, which strongly prompts us all to oppose any power that would take away our lives, or the lives of our friends?
—SAMUEL WEST (1730–1807)
"On the Right to Rebel Against Governors"
May 29, 1776

If this war be just and necessary on our part, as past all doubt it is, then we are engaged in the work of the Lord, which obliges us (under GOD mighty in battle) to use our "swords as instruments of righteousness, and calls us to the shocking, but necessary, important duty of shedding human blood"; not only in defence of our property, life and religion, but in obedience to him who hath said, "Cursed be he that keepeth back his sword from blood."
—JACOB CUSHING (1730–1809)
Sermon preached at Lexington, Massachusetts, April 20, 1778

GEORGE WASHINGTON

George Washington, Commander of the American armies, who, like Joshua of old, commanded the sun and the moon to stand still, and they obeyed him.
—BENJAMIN FRANKLIN (1706–1790)
Toast at the state dinner in France, c. 1784

Instead of adoring a Washington, mankind should applaud the nation which educated him ... I glory in the character of a Washington, because I know

him to be only an exemplification of the American character.
—JOHN ADAMS (1735–1826)
In George Washington, Man and Monument by Marcus Cunliffe, (1785)

He has not the imposing pomp of a Marechal de France who gives the order. A hero in a republic, he excites another sort of respect which seems to spring from the sole idea that the safety of each individual is attached to his person. ... The goodness and benevolence which characterize him are evident in all that surrounds him, but the confidence that he calls forth never occasions improper familiarity.
—FRANCOIS JEAN CHASTELLUX (1734–1788)
Travels in North America 1786

But it must be a bold adventurer in the paths of literature, who dreams of fame, in any degree commensurate with the duration of laurels reaped by an hero, who has led the armies of America to glory, victory and independence.
—MERCY OTIS WARREN (1728–1814)
Dedication to George Washington, President of the United States of America, Poems Dramatic and Miscellaneous 1790

Stand with Washington.
—ANONYMOUS
Slogan of the Federalist Party, c. 1790s

The character and services of this gentleman are sufficient to put all those men called kings to shame. ... He accepted no pay as commander-in-chief; he accepts none as President of the United States.

—THOMAS PAINE (1737–1809)
The Rights of Man
1791–1792

[Washington] errs as other men do, but errs with integrity.

—THOMAS JEFFERSON (1743–1826)
Letter to William B. Giles,
December 31, 1795

To the memory of the Man, first in war, first in peace, and first in the hearts of his countrymen.

—HENRY "LIGHT HORSE HARRY" LEE
(1756–1818)
Eulogy on the death of Washington,
December 1799

Death has robbed our country of its most distinguished ornament, and the world of one of its greatest benefactors. George Washington, the Hero of Liberty, the father of his Country, and the friend of man is no more. The General Assembly of his native state were ever the first to render him, living, the honors due to his virtues. They will not be the second, to pay to his memory the tribute of their tears.

—JAMES MADISON (1751–1836)
Speech in the Virginia General
Assembly,
December 18, 1799

The father of his country.

—FRANCES BAILEY (1735–1815)
Caption for portrait of Washington,
Nordamericanische Kalendar
1799

I can't tell a lie, Pa; you know I can't tell a lie. I did cut it with my hatchet.

—MASON LOCK "PARSON" WEEMS
(1759–1825)
The Life and Memorable Actions of George Washington, 5th edition
c. 1800

His mind was great and powerful, without being of the very first order; his penetration strong ... and, as far as he saw, no judgment was ever sounder. It was slow in operation, being little aided by invention or imagination, but sure in conclusion. ... Perhaps the strongest feature in his character was prudence, never acting until every circumstance, every consideration was maturely weighed ... but once decided, going through with his purpose, whatever obstacles opposed. His integrity was most pure, his justice the most inflexible I have ever known. ... He was, indeed, in every sense of the words, a wise, a good and a great man.

—THOMAS JEFFERSON
Letter to Doctor Walter Jones,
January 2, 1814

WITCHCRAFT

I would fain know of these Salem Gentlemen, but as yet could never know, how it comes about, that if these apprehended persons are witches, and, by a look of the eye, do cast the afflicted into their fitts by poisoning them, how it comes about, I say, that, by a look of their eye, they do not cast others into fitts, and poison others by their looks; and in particular, tender, fearfull women, who often are beheld by them, and as likely as any in the whole world to receive an ill impression from them. This Salem philosophy, some men may call the new philosophy; but I think it rather deserves the name of Salem superstition and sorcery, and it is not fit to be named in a land of such light as New England is.

> —*THOMAS BRATTLE* (1658–1713)
> Letter of Thomas Brattle,
> October 8, 1692

What will be the issue of these troubles, God only knows; I am afraid that ages will not wear off that reproach and those stains which these things will leave behind them upon our land. I pray God pity us, Humble us, Forgive us, and appear mercifully for us in this our mount of distress.

> —*THOMAS BRATTLE*
> Letter of Thomas Brattle,
> October 8, 1692

Do you think that a less clear Evidence is sufficient for Conviction in the Case of Witchcraft, than is necessary in other Capital Cases, suppose Murder. ... This is a dangerous Principle, and contrary to the mind of God, who hath appointed that there shall be good and clear proof against the Criminal: else he is not Providentially delivered into the hands of Justice, to be taken off from the earth. Nor hath God exempted this Case of Witchcraft from the General Rule. Besides, reason tells us, that the more horrid the Crime is, the more Cautious we ought to be in making any guilty of it.

> —*SAMUEL WILLARD* (1640–1707)
> "Some Miscellany Observations on
> our present Debates respecting
> Witchcrafts"
> 1692

Taking it for granted that there are Witches in NEW ENGLAND, which no rational man will dare to deny; I ask whether Innocent Persons may not be falsely accused of Witchcraft?

> —*SAMUEL WILLARD*
> "Some Miscellany Observations on
> our present Debates respecting
> Witchcrafts"
> 1692

For Explanation of the Law against Witchcraft and more particular direction therein the Execution thereof and for the better restraining the said Offences, and more severe punishing the same, Be it enacted by the Govern'r Council and Representatives in General Court Assembled and by the Authority of the same, That if any person or persons [after] shall use, practice or Exercise any Invocation or Conjuration of any evil and wicked Spirit, Or shall consult, covenant with, Entertain, Employ, feed or reward any evil and wicked Spirit to or for any intent or purpose; Or take up any dead man, woman or Child, out of his, her, or their grave, or any other place where the dead body resteth, or the Skin, bone or any other part of any dead person to be Employed or used in any manner of Witchcraft, Sorcery, Charm or Inchantment, Or shall use, practice or Exercise any Witchcraft, Inchantment, Charm or Sorcery, whereby any person shall be killed, destroyed, wasted, consumed, pined or lamed in his or her body, or any part thereof, That then every such Offender or Offenders, their Aiders, Abetters, and Counsellors being of any the said Offences duly and lawfully convicted and attainted, shall suffer pains of death as a Felon or Felons. And further to the intent that all manner of practice, use or exercise of witchcraft, Inchantment, charm or Sorcery, should be henceforth utterly avoided, abolished and taken away, Be it Enacted by the Authority afores'd That if any person or persons shall take upon him or them by Witchcraft, Inoffending, and being thereof lawfully convicted, shall for the said offence suffer Imprisonment by the space of one whole year without bail or mainprise and once in every Quarter of the s'd year shall in some Shire Town stand openly upon the pillory by the space of Six houres, and there shall openly confess his or her Error and offence, which said offence shall be written in Capitall Letters & placed upon the breast of said offender And if any person or persons being once convicted of the same Offence, and shall again commit the like Offence and being of any of the said Offences the second time lawfully & duely convicted and attainted as is aforesaid shall Suffer pains of death as a felon or felons.

—ANONYMOUS
"A Bill Against Conjurations, Witchcraft, and Dealing with Evil and Wicked Spirits"
1692

WOMEN

Now say have women worth? or have they none?
Or had they some, but with our queen is't gone?
Nay Masculines, you have thus taxt us long,
But she, though dead, will vindicate our wrong.
Let such as say our Sex is void of Reason,

Know 'tis a Slander now, but once a Treason.

—ANNE BRADSTREET (c. 1612–1672)
"In Honour of that High and Mighty Princess, Queen Elizabeth"
1678

Who was so good, so just, so learn'd, so wise,
From all the Kings on earth she won the prize.
Nor say I more than duly is her due,
Millions will testify that this is true.
She hath wip'd off th'aspersion of her Sex,
That women wisdome lack to play the Rex.

—ANNE BRADSTREET
"In Honour of that High and Mighty Princess, Queen Elizabeth"
1678

I long to hear that you have declared an independency. And in the new code of laws which I suppose it will be necessary for you to make, I desire you would remember the ladies, and be more generous and favorable to them than your ancestors.

—ABIGAIL ADAMS (1744–1818)
To John Adams,
1774

Do not put such unlimited power into the hands of husbands. Remember all men would be tyrants if they could. ... If particular care and attention is not paid to the Ladies we are determined to foment a Rebellion, and will not hold ourselves bound by any Laws in which we have no voice, or Representation.

—ABIGAIL ADAMS
Letter to John Adams,
March 31, 1776

If we mean to have heroes, statesmen and philosophers, we should have learned women. ... If much depends as is allowed upon the early education of youth and the first principles which are instilled take the deepest root, great benefit must arise from literary accomplishments in women.

—*ABIGAIL ADAMS*
Letter to John Adams,
August 14, 1776

I will never consent to have our sex considered an inferior point of light. Let each planet shine in their own orbit. God and nature designed it so—if man is Lord, woman is Lordess—that is what I contend for.

—*ABIGAIL ADAMS*
Letter to Eliza Peabody, her sister,
July 19, 1779

Nor would I rob the fairer sex of their share in the glory of a revolution so honorable to human nature, for, indeed, I think you ladies are in the number of the best patriots America can boast.

—*GEORGE WASHINGTON*
To Annie Boudinot Stockton,
August 31, 1788

Are we deficient in reason? We can only reason from what we know, and if an opportunity of acquiring knowledge hath been denied us, the inferiority of our sex cannot fairly be deduced from thence.

—*JUDITH SARGENT MURRAY* (1751–1820)
"On the Equality of the Sexes," in
Massachusetts Magazine
March and April 1790

Is the needle and kitchen sufficient to employ the operations of a soul? ... I should conceive not. Nay, it is a truth

that those very departments leave the intelligent principle vacant, and at liberty for speculation.

—*JUDITH SARGENT MURRAY*
"On the Equality of the Sexes," in
Massachusetts Magazine
March and April 1790

Will it be said that the judgment of a male two years old, is more sage that that of a female's of the same age? I believe the reverse is generally observed to be true. But from that period what partiality! how is the one exalted and the other depressed, by the contrary modes of education which are adopted! the one is taught to aspire, and the other is early confined and limited.

—*JUDITH SARGENT MURRAY*
"On the Equality of the Sexes," in
Massachusetts Magazine
March and April 1790

The capacity of the female mind for studies of the highest order can not be doubted; having been sufficiently illustrated by its works of genius, of erudition and of Science. That it merits an improved system of education, comprizing a due reference to the condition and duties of female life, as distinguished from those of the other sex, must be as readily admitted. How far a collection of female Students into a public Seminary would be the best of plans for educating them, is a point on which different opinions may be expected to arise. ... as experiment alone can fully decide the interesting problem, it is a justifiable wish that it may be made.

—*JAMES MADISON* (1751–1836)
To Albert Picket,
September 1821

The prejudices still to be found in Europe ... which would confine ... female conversation to the last new publication, new bonnet, and pas seul [nothing else] are entirely unknown here. The women are assuming their place as thinking beings.

—FRANCIS WRIGHT (1795–1852)
Views of Society & Manners in America
1821

y

YOUTH

My silliness did only take delight
In that which riper age did scorn and
slight.
>—*ANNE BRADSTREET* (c. 1612–1672)
>*Several Poems Compiled with Great*
>*Variety of Wit and Learning*
>1678

Distrust thy youth, experienced age
implore, / And borrow all the wisdom
of three score.
>—*BENJAMIN FRANKLIN* (1706–1790)
>*Poor Richard's Almanack*
>1749

Youth is most certainly a time of innocence when we have horror for vice;
which we never commit at first without doing violence to our nature. How
our soul startles when we attempt to
perpetrate a crime prohibited by laws
both human and divine!
>—*NATHANAEL GREENE* (1742–1786)
>To Samuel War, Jr.,
>1772

Youth is the seed time of good habits,
as well in nations as in individuals.
>—*THOMAS PAINE* (1737–1809)
>*Common Sense*
>1776

It is while we are young that the habit
of industry is formed. If not then, it
never is afterwards. The fortune of our
lives therefore depends on employing
well the short period of youth.
>—*THOMAS JEFFERSON* (1743–1826)
>To Martha Jefferson,
>March 28, 1787

Names Index

pain, 221
Paine, 211
parenting, 32, 33
patriotism, 215
peace, 191, 219
perseverance, 220
pessimism and
optimism, 220
pleasure, 221
politics and political
parties, 74, 222
posterity, 224
power, 230
presidency, 232, 233
pride, 234
property, 235
providence, 110
public office, 237, 239
punishment, 49
reason, 243–244
rebellion, 277
religion, 248, 252, 259,
260–261
republicanism, 60, 223
revolution, 279
rights of the people,
282, 283, 284
Rush on, 2
self-discipline, 287
silence, 287
slavery, 294–295, 297,
300, 302
South America, 96
speaking, 158
speeches, 302
states' rights, 304
taxes, 308
theory, 308
time, 309
truth, 311
tyranny, 311, 313
vice presidency, 318
Virginia, 318, 319
virtue, 320
war, 185, 189, 193, 195
Washington, 323
wealth, 226
writing, 158
youth, 328
Johnson, Samuel, 12, 293

Johnson, William, 160
Jones, John Paul, 133, 146–
147, 187, 188, 189

K

Kant, Immanuel, 221
Kent, James, 151–152, 166
Key, Francis Scott, 89, 260

L

Lafayette, Marquis de, 13,
59, 96–97
Langhorne, John, 184
Lawrence, James, 194
Lee, Arthur, 11
Lee, Charles, 188
Lee, Henry "Light Horse
Harry," 323
Lee, Richard Henry, 102,
115, 140, 163, 253, 283
Locke, John, x, xi, xiii, 80,
83, 161, 207, 248
Logan, James, 202

M

Madison, James
Adams, 1
adversity, 64
advisors, 3
agriculture, 6, 8
alcohol, 9
ambition, 10, 289
America, 15–16, 18
argument, 20
arts, 21
banks, 23
Bill of Rights, xii, 24–25
books, 25
business, 28–29
cities, 33
Clay on, 179
Congress, 34, 35
conscience, 37
consistency, 37
Constitution, 39–40, 42,
43, 45, 48, 164, 261
debt, national, 124
defamation, 56
democracy, 59
education, 69, 70–71, 72

elections, 73
expansion, 81
experience, 82
factions, 221–222
farming, 7
force, 91
foreign relations, 95, 96
freedom, 99, 102, 103
friendship, 105
God, 109–110
government, 117–119,
121, 124, 144, 156, 221,
287
Hamilton, 128
history, 132
immigration, 136–137
Jefferson, 146
justice, 153
knowledge, 143, 144
language, 159, 160
laws and lawyers, 162–
163, 164–165, 166
liberty, 174, 175, 176
majority, 179–180
medicine, 131
military, 190, 194, 196
money, 197
natural law, 206
opinion, 241
opinions, 83
patronage, 217
peace, 195, 196, 218–219
politics and political
parties, 72, 73, 221–
222, 223
poverty, 224, 226
power, 229–230, 231
property, 236
public office, 238, 239
religion, 247, 248, 249,
251, 253, 254, 261–263
republicanism, 60–61
revolution, 278, 279
rights of the people, 34,
80, 283, 284
Rush on, 179
separation of powers,
288, 289
slavery, 296, 297, 298,
300, 302

Subject Index

judgment, 4, 20
judiciary, 147–152, 161–
162, 229–230, 290
juries, 148, 152, 283
justice
Crèvecoeur on, 228
Defoe on, 155
Denham on, 48–49
Franklin on, 147, 152
Hancock on, 312
Henry on, 292
Jay on, 153
Jefferson on, 153
Langhorne on, 184
Madison on, 119, 153
Paine on, 152, 184, 185
Penn on, 152, 154
Rush on, 120
Washington on, 152–
153

K
Kentucky, 154
kings, 154–156
knowledge, 142–144

L
labor, 157–158, 308
See also slavery
language, 158–160
law(s)
Adams, Abigail, on, 228,
325
Adams, John, on, 162
Bacon on, 147
Barnard on, 227
Church on, 227
Ellsworth on, 253
Franklin on, 161
Hamilton on, 116, 148,
163
Jackson on, 226
Jefferson on, 162, 163,
165, 304
Madison on, 118, 162–
163, 164–165, 279
Marshall on, 122, 149–
150, 151, 290
Otis on, 161
Paine on, 141, 155, 164,

Penn on, 160, 311
Pitt on, 312
Rush on, 163, 292
Warren on, 270, 271
Washington on, 164
Webster on, 165
Wilson on, 163, 164, 320
See also natural law
lawyers, 165–168
laziness, 168, 202, 209
legislators, legislatures
Hamilton on, 303
Jefferson on, 206, 259
Madison on, 192, 193,
229–230, 279, 294
Marshall on, 289, 290
Story on, 151
Washington on, 296
Webster on, 288–289
liberty, ix, 115, 168–176,
188, 203
Adams, John, on, 68, 79,
169, 173, 175, 176, 205,
214, 227, 247, 250, 273
Adams, Samuel, on, 22,
186, 205, 268
Ames on, 59, 62, 230
Baldwin on, 88–89
Banneker on, 299–300
Barre on, 264–265
Burr on, 27
Church on, 312
Clay on, 261
Constitution on, 38
Dickinson on, 169–170,
172, 272
Downer on, 266
Franklin on, 169, 174, 175
Greene on, 69
Hamilton, Alexander on,
59, 73, 172, 174, 175,
190, 206, 303, 306, 315
Hamilton, Andrew on,
227
Hancock on, 213, 270
Hart on, 293
Henry, John Joseph on,
215
Henry, Patrick on, 172–
173, 174, 273, 292

Howard on, 90–91, 186,
269, 321
Jay on, 214, 296, 315
Jefferson on, 15, 54, 63,
117, 139, 175–176,
259, 277, 279, 282, 293
Madison on, 16, 24, 72,
118, 119, 174, 175, 176,
189, 192, 194, 222, 262,
284, 294, 319
Marshall on, 122
Mason on, 79
Mayhew on, 263
Monroe on, 71, 123, 251
Otis on, 168, 280, 281,
285, 291
Paine on, 12, 45, 49, 174,
175, 230, 248, 284
Penn on, 246
Pinckney on, 59
Pitt on, 139, 266
Rush on, 69, 70, 259, 292
Sewall on, 290
Smith on, 119–120
Warren on, 11, 268, 269
Washington on, 16, 17,
61, 174, 192, 213, 278
Webster, Daniel, on, 18,
165, 176
Webster, Noah, on, 70
West on, 273
Wilson on, 163, 282, 320
Wise on, 79
See also freedom
lies, 176–177, 310
liquor. See alcohol,
alcoholism
literacy, xi
literature, 22
Louisiana, 81
love, 4
luck, 178

M
majorities, 179–180, 223,
231
malice, 78
manifest destiny, 81–82
manners, 180–181, 192, 202
marriage, 181–183